The Vietnamese City in Transition

Cooperation Centre for Urban Development, Hanoi (Institut des Métiers de la Ville (IMV)) was created in 2001 by the People's Committee of Hanoi and the Ile-de-France Region (France) within their general cooperation agreement. It has for first vocation to improve the competences of the municipal staff in the field of urban planning and management of urban services. The concerned technical departments are the department of urban planning and architecture, the department of transport and civil engineering, the authority for public transports planning, the construction department... IMV organizes seminars to support decision-makers and technicians, finances studies, implements consultancies, contributes to knowledge dissemination by the translation of scientific and technical books, and maintains a library on urban planning.

Ho Chi Minh City Urban Development Management Support Centre (Centre de Prospective et d'Études Urbaines (PADDI)) was created in 2004 in cooperation between the People's Committee of Ho Chi Minh City and the Rhone-Alpes Region (France). Its office is located inside the Ho Chi Minh City Institute for Development Studies (HIDS). Competences of PADDI are training, consultancies and research. The PADDI organizes regularly training workshops to complete the training of civil servants of the city by making them aware about concepts, techniques and new methods in urban management. The answers to the urban planning problems given in France are compared with the situation in Vietnam to inspire new practices and new policies. The publication of the results of these workshops enables to associate a widened public.

The **Institute of Southeast Asian Studies (ISEAS)** was established as an autonomous organization in 1968. It is a regional centre dedicated to the study of socio-political, security and economic trends and developments in Southeast Asia and its wider geostrategic and economic environment. The Institute's research programmes are the Regional Economic Studies (RES, including ASEAN and APEC), Regional Strategic and Political Studies (RSPS), and Regional Social and Cultural Studies (RSCS).

ISEAS Publishing, an established academic press, has issued more than 2,000 books and journals. It is the largest scholarly publisher of research about Southeast Asia from within the region. ISEAS Publishing works with many other academic and trade publishers and distributors to disseminate important research and analyses from and about Southeast Asia to the rest of the world.

The Vietnamese City in Transition

Edited by
Patrick Gubry, Franck Castiglioni,
Jean-Michel Cusset,
Nguyen Thi Thieng, and Pham Thuy Huong

ISEAS
Institute of Southeast Asian Studies
Singapore

Hanoi
Île-de-France
IMV
Institute for Urban Training (Institut des Métiers de la Ville(IMV))
Hanoi, Vietnam

PADDI
Ho Chi Minh City Urban Development Management Support Centre
(Centre de Prospective et d'Études Urbaines (PADDI))
Ho Chi Minh City, Vietnam

First published in Singapore in 2010 by
Institute of Southeast Asian Studies (ISEAS)
30 Heng Mui Keng Terrace, Pasir Panjang
Singapore 119614
E-mail: publish@iseas.edu.sg *Website*: <http://bookshop.iseas.edu.sg>

jointly with

Institut des Métiers de la Ville (IMV)
[Cooperation Centre for Urban Development]
79 Ba Trieu, District Hai Ba Trung
Hanoi, Vietnam
Website: <www.imv-hanoi.com>

and

Centre de Prospective et d'Études Urbaines (PADDI)
[Ho Chi Minh City Urban Development Management Support Centre]
216 Nguyen Dinh Chieu, District 3
Ho Chi Minh City, Vietnam
Website: <www.paddi.vn>

This book is a revised translation from the book entitled *La Ville Vietnamienne en Transition*, published in 2006, in French by Éditions Karthala, Paris, and in Vietnamese by The Gioi Publishers, Hanoi.

ISEAS Library Cataloguing-in-Publication Data

The Vietnamese city in transition / edited by Patrick Gubry … [et al.].
1. Cities and towns—Vietnam.
2. Urbanization—Vietnam.
I. Gubry, Patrick.
HT384 V5V711 2010

ISBN 978-981-230-825-2 (soft cover)
ISBN 978-981-230-826-9 (E-book PDF)

Cover photo:
Eastern area of Hoan Kiem District in Hanoi, on the right bank of the Red River. This area was built beyond the dyke (seen here surmounted by the wide Tran Quang Khai Street) and is easily inundated during the flood season. "Compartment" houses mix with collective housing buildings. Both of Hanoi's central bridges are visible: Chuong Duong Bridge, which is used by motorized vehicles and Long Bien Bridge in the background (formerly Doumer Bridge). The latter was built between 1898 and 1902 by the company Dayde & Pille from Creil, and by Vietnamese workers, according to plans by Gustave Eiffel; it is 1,682 m long and its metallic armature contains nineteen spans. The bridge was considered a technical and architectural feat at the time. It suffered severe damage from American bombing between 1967 and 1971. Today, a railway track still crosses the bridge, which is also used by cyclists and pedestrians. Restoration work is planned. On the other side of the river, on the left bank, is Long Bien District (formerly Gia Lam) (*Photo: Patrick Gubry, November 2005*).

Typeset by International Typesetters Pte Ltd
Printed in Singapore by Photoplates Pte Ltd

Table of Contents

List of Tables

Hai Phong: Sunday stroll in a cyclo. *Photo: Myriam de Loenzien, July 2005*

List of Figures

Hanoi: Nguyen Trai Street. *Photo: Myriam de Loenzien, August 2003*

List of Colour Plates

Photo: Truong Quoc Toan, IMV, 2003

Hanoi: Panoramic view from a tower block in Nhan Chinh Development, Cau Giay District.

Foreword

The present work was undertaken as part of two cooperation programmes between French and Vietnamese local governments: one involving the Ile-de-France Region and Hanoi People's Committee, the other the Rhone-Alpes Region and Ho Chi Minh City People's Committee. It was published with financial support from the Cooperation and Cultural Action Office (SCAC) of the French Embassy in Vietnam. Gathered here are the main results obtained by the Franco-Vietnamese research teams involved in the Urban Research Programme for Development (PRUD) funded by the French Ministry of Foreign Affairs. As the outcome of joint concertation, it illustrates the coherence between the various French cooperation programmes in Vietnam.

The research presented here attempts to define the issues at stake in urban development in Vietnam under the economic and demographic push induced by the transition from a centralized planned economy to a globalized market economy, and by strong urban population growth. Processes at work such as international integration and fast-growing metropolisation, speeded up economic development, devolution/decentralization of urban management authorities, modernization of housing patterns, poorly controlled peri-urban urbanization, mutations in the management of urban services, etc., all require strengthening of skills for urban project management and local government.

To respond to this need, IMV (Cooperation Centre for Urban Development) was created by Hanoi People's Committee and the Ile-de-France Region in 2001. PADDI (Ho Chi Minh City Urban Development Management Support Centre) was founded in 2004 by Ho Chi Minh City People's Committee and Rhone-Alpes Regional Council. Both organizations are jointly headed *in situ* by representatives from each collectivity and are responsible for developing programmes in such areas as continuing education aimed at government cadres specialized in urban management, consultancy and technical expertise, investment in pilot operations and pilot infrastructures projects, assistance to consultancy firms and BPW companies, and for promoting Vietnamese and French research in the field of urbanism. *The Vietnamese City in Transition* is the first joint scientific work to be published by our two institutions.

Laurent Pandolfi
Co-director of IMV
Tran Van Luu
Co-director of IMV from 2004 till 2008

Ludovic Dewaele
Co-director of PADDI until 31 March 2006
David Margonstern
Co-director of PADDI since 1 April 2006 until 31 March 2009
Fanny Quertamp Nguyen
Co-director of PADDI since 1 April 2009
Nguyen Hong Van
Co-director of PADDI
Ho Chi Minh City

Acknowledgements

We would like to thank those who made this publication possible:

The French Ministry of Foreign Affairs, which funded the Urban Research Programme for Development (PRUD).

Annik Osmont and Charles Goldblum, who coordinated the PRUD programme through GEMDEV and ISTED.

Laurent Pandolfi, co-director of IMV (Cooperation Centre for Urban Development) in Hanoi, as well as Ludovic Dewaele, David Margonstern, and Fanny Quertamp Nguyen, the successive co-directors of PADDI (Ho Chi Minh City Urban Development Management Support Centre), who steadily supported the idea of publishing the results of the eight projects carried out in Vietnam within the scope of the PRUD in order to make them available to decision-makers and to the wider public.

The Ile-de-France Region, the Rhone-Alpes Region and the French Embassy in Vietnam, who financed the completion and publication of this book through IMV and PADDI.

Karthala Publishing House in Paris, The Gioi Publishers in Hanoi and the Institute of Southeast Asian Studies in Singapore, who respectively agreed to publish the French, Vietnamese and English versions of this book.

Valerie Mary, who assumed responsibility for the thankless task of formatting the French version and Annick Aing, photographer for IRD in Bondy, who kindly agreed to process the photographs despite an already heavy workload.

Stephane Jaggers and David Rorke, who translated most of the book into English.

The list of those who have helped and shown goodwill towards this project is much too long to be included here. We apologize in advance to all those not mentioned by name.

The Editorial Team

List of Acronyms

ADB: Asian Development Bank

ADEME: Agence de l'Environnement et de la Maîtrise de l'Énergie [*French Agency for Environment and Energy Management*]

ADETEF: Assistance au Développement des Échanges en Technologies Économiques et Financières [*Assistance for the Development of Exchanges in Economic and Financial Technologies*]

AFD: Agence Française de Développement [*French Development Agency, Paris*]

AFIMA: Association pour la Formation Intellectuelle et Morale des Annamites [*Association for the Intellectual and Moral Training of the Annamese*]

ASEAN: Association of Southeast Asian Nations

BCEOM: Bureau Central d'Études pour les Équipements d'Outre-Mer [*Central Office for the Study of Overseas Infrastructure, Paris*]

BCO: Basic Community Organisation

BOT: Build, Operate and Transfer

BPW: Buildings and Public Works

CEETIA: Centre of Environmental Engineering of Towns and Industrial Areas

CEFURDS: Centre for Urban and Development Studies, Ho Chi Minh City

CERTU: Centre d'Études sur les Réseaux de Transport et l'Urbanisme [*Research Centre on Public Networks, Transport, Urban Planning and Construction*]

CETE: Centre d'Études Techniques de l'Équipement [*Centre for Engineering Studies*]

CIDA: Canadian International Development Agency

CNEE: Centre National de formation aux métiers de l'Eau et de l'Environnement [*National Vocational Training Centre for Water and Environment*]
CNRS: Centre National de la Recherche Scientifique [*National Centre for Scientific Research, Paris*]
COMECON: Council for Mutual Economic Assistance
CSD: Centre d'études en Sociologie et Développement [*Centre for Sociology and Development Studies*]
DANIDA: Danish International Development Agency
DGCID: Direction Générale de la Coopération Internationale et du Développement [*General Directorate for International Cooperation and Development, Paris*]
DWS: Drinking Water Supply
EBAI: École des Beaux-Arts de l'Indochine [*Indochina School of Fine Arts*]
EPFL: École Polytechnique Fédérale de Lausanne [*Lausanne Federal Polytechnic School*]
ESCG: Environmental Services Community Group
FAO: United Nations Food and Agriculture Organisation
GEMDEV: Groupement d'intérêt scientifique pour l'Étude de la Mondialisation et du Développement [*Scientific Network for the Study of Globalisation and Development, Paris*]
GSO: General Statistics Office
HCMC: Ho Chi Minh City
HIDS: Ho Chi Minh City Institute for Development Studies
HOUTRANS: Ho Chi Minh City Urban Transport Master Plan and Feasibility Study
IER: Institute for Economic Research of Ho Chi Minh City
IMV: Institut des Métiers de la Ville [*Cooperation Centre for Urban Development, Hanoi*]
IPRAUS: Institut Parisien de Recherche: Architecture, Urbanistique, Société [*Parisian Research Institute: Architecture, Urbanism & Society*]
IRD: Institut de Recherche pour le Développement [*Institute of Research for Development, Paris*]
ISO: International Solidarity Organisation
ISTED: Institut des Sciences et des Techniques de l'Équipement et de l'Environnement pour le Développement [*Scientific and Technical Institute of Infrastructure and Environment for Development, Paris*]

JBIC: Japan Bank for International Cooperation
JICA: Japan International Cooperation Agency
KDT: *Khu Do Thi*
KTT: *Khu Tap The*
MARD: Ministry of Agriculture and Rural Development
MOC: Ministry of Construction
MOET: Ministry of Education and Training
MOF: Ministry of Finance
MOH: Ministry of Health
MOSTE: Ministry of Science, Technology and Environment
MPI: Ministry of Planning and Investment
NEA: National Environmental Agency (1993), affiliated with the MOSTE
NGO: Non-Governmental Organisation
NRWSS: National Rural Water Supply and Sanitation
ODA: Official Development Assistance
ODAP: Overseas Development Assistance
OTV: Subsidiary of Veolia Water
PACCOM: People's Aid Coordinating Committee (Vietnamese organisation that issues permits for interventions to foreign ISOs)
PADDI: Ho Chi Minh City Urban Development Management Support Centre
PMU: Project Management Unit
PPP: Public Private Partnership
PRUD: Programme de Recherche Urbaine pour le Développement [*Urban Research Programme for Development*]
RWP: Rural Water Programme
RATP: Régie Autonome des Transports Parisiens [*Autonomous Parisians Transport Administration*]
SADE: Subsidiary of Veolia Water
SAFEGE: Société Anonyme Française d'Études et de Gestion [*Limited Company for the Study of Management and Business*]
SAUR: Société d'Aménagement Urbain et Rural [*Company for Urban and Rural Planning*]
SCAC: Service de Coopération et d'Action Culturelle [*Cooperation and Cultural Action Office*]
SEDIF: Syndicat des Eaux d'Île-de-France [*Ile-de-France Water Authority*]
TDSI: Transport Development Strategy Institute

TPWS:	Transport and Public Works Service (under the authority of the Vietnamese municipality)
TRAMOC:	Transport Management and Operation Centre, Hanoi
TUPWS:	Transport and Urban Public Works (construction of water supply and drainage infrastructures)
UNDP:	United Nations Development Programme
URENCO:	Urban Environment Company
VCP:	Vietnamese Communist Party
VeT:	Villes en Transition [Association Cities in Transition]
VINACONEX:	Viet Nam Construction and Import Export Corporation
VND:	Vietnamese Dong
VWSA:	Viet Nam Water Supply and Sewerage Association

The Editors

Patrick Gubry, Demographer, Research Director at IRD, University Paris 1, Joint Research Unit "Development and Societies", is a specialist on migration, urbanization and population-environment relations. His work over the past fifteen years has focused on Vietnam.

Franck Castiglioni, Sociologist and Urban Planner, Programme Coordinator for the association *Villes en Transition* (Cities in Transition), has supervised the follow-up and implementation of urban social development projects in several countries in transition, especially Vietnam, since 1998. He has also contributed to various study and research projects in this capacity.

Jean-Michel Cusset, Research Director Emeritus at CNRS (National Centre for Scientific Research), Transport Economics Research Centre, is a specialist on urban transport in developing countries. He has initiated and participated in several research projects concerning this issue in Hanoi and Ho Chi Minh City.

Nguyen Thi Thieng, Demographer, Institute for Population and Social Studies (IPSS), Hanoi National Economics University, has been responsible for numerous training activities in the population field and has led research projects on reproductive health, mobility and environment.

Pham Thuy Huong, Deputy Head of the Centre for Human Resources Development, Hanoi National Economics University, works on issues of human resource management, migration and population–environment relations.

The Contributors

Eric Baye
Les Florentines
27 avenue Lacassagne
69003 Lyon
France
eric.baye@asconit.com

Franck Castiglioni
1F rue Phelypeaux, 5e etage
69100 Villeurbanne
France
stronzito@yahoo.fr

Emmanuel Cerise
14 rue des Panoyaux
75020 Paris
France
manu_ce@hotmail.com

Jean-Michel Cusset
93 rue Voltaire
69310 Pierre-Benite
France
michel.jean39@yahoo.fr

Ludovic Dewaele
chez Legrand Urtizberea
99 Chemin du Petit Poujeau
33290 Le Pian Medoc
France
luwae@yahoo.com

Charles Goldblum
14 rue des Tournelles
75004 Paris
France
charles.goldblum@wanadoo.fr

Patrick Gubry
Institut de Recherche pour le Developpement (IRD)
32 avenue Varagnat
93143 Bondy Cedex
France
gubry@ird.fr

Le Thi Huong
Ho Chi Minh City Institute for Development Studies (HIDS)
28 Le Quy Don, District 3
Ho Chi Minh City
Vietnam
lehuongloc@hotmail.com

David Margonstern
ADB, 6 ADB avenue
Mandaluyong City
1550 Metro Manila
Philippines
davidmargonstern@yahoo.com

Rene de Maximy
17 rue Piver
91260 Juvisy-Sur-Orge
France
rene.demaximy@neuf.fr

Claude de Miras
Institut de Recherche pour le Developpement (IRD)/
Université de Provence
LPED UMR151
3 place Victor Hugo, Case 10
13331 Marseille Cedex 3
France
demiras@up.univ-mrs.fr

Nguyen Duc Nhuan
Appartement B 306
79 quai Panhard et Levassor
75013 Paris
France
josenhuan@yahoo.fr

Nguyen Hong Van
Ho Chi Minh City Urban Development Management Support Centre (PADDI)
216 Nguyen Dinh Chieu, District 3
Ho Chi Minh City
Vietnam
vanngh@tphcm.gov.vn

Laurence Nguyen
Immeuble les bleuets
29 rue des Boulets
75011 Paris
France
laurence.nguyen.rosenthal@libertysurf.fr

Nguyen Quang Vinh
400/7 Le Van Sy, District 3,
Ho Chi Minh City
Vietnam
nqvi@hotmail.com

Nguyen Quoc Thong
Tong Bien Tap
Tap Chi Xay Dung
Ministry of Construction
37 rue Le Dai Hanh
Hanoi
Vietnam
tcxd.bxd@hn.vnn.vn

Nguyen Thi Thieng
National Economics University (NEU)
Institute for Population and Social Studies (IPSS)
207 Giai Phong, District Hai Ba Trung
Hanoi
Vietnam
thiengnt@yahoo.com

Nguyen Thien Phu
311 Chung Cu Tran Van Kieu
Ly Thuong Kiet Str.
Phuong 14, Quan 10
Ho Chi Minh City
Vietnam
nguyenthienphu@yahoo.com

Nguyen Trong Nam Tran
18, rue Mozart
94400 Vitry-Sur-Seine
France
namtran_ng@yahoo.fr

Laurent Pandolfi
Cooperation Centre for Urban Development (IMV)
79 Ba Trieu, District Hai Ba Trung
Hanoi
Vietnam
laurent.pandolfi@imv-hanoi.com

Rene Parenteau
Universite de Montreal
Institut d'Urbanisme
C.P. 6128 Succursale Centre-Ville
Montreal H3C 3J7
Canada
rene.parenteau@umontreal.ca

Christian Pedelahore de Loddis
33 rue de Poissy
75005 Paris
France
christian.pedelahore@free.fr

Pham Thuy Huong
National Economics University (NEU)
207 Giai Phong,
District Hai Ba Trung
Hanoi
Vietnam
pham.huong@neufie.edu.vn

Fanny Quertamp Nguyen
Ho Chi Minh City Urban Development Management Support Centre (PADDI)
216 Nguyen Dinh Chieu, District 3
Ho Chi Minh City
Vietnam
fannyquertamp@hotmail.com

Tran Thi Thanh Thuy
Ho Chi Minh City Institute for Development Studies (HIDS)
28, Le Quy Don, District 3
Ho Chi Minh City
Vietnam
thuytr47@yahoo.com

Tran Van Luu
Cooperation Centre for Urban Development (IMV)
79, Ba Trieu, District Hai Ba Trung
Hanoi
Vietnam
songoaivuhn@hn.vnn.vn

Vu Hoang Ngan
National Economics University (NEU)
207 Giai Phong, District Hai Ba Trung
Hanoi
Vietnam
vuhoang_ngan@yahoo.com

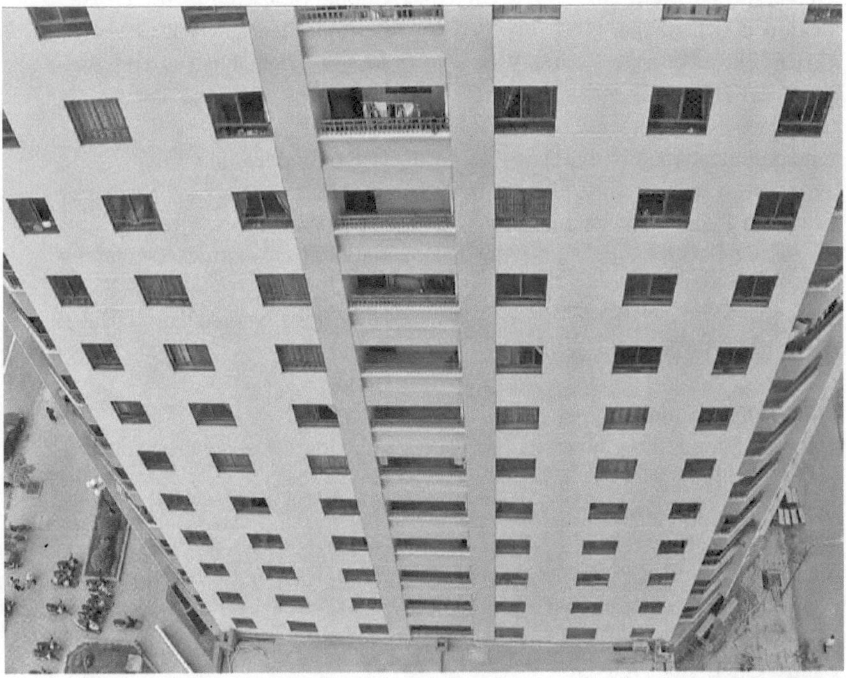

Photo: Truong Quoc Toan, IMV, 2003

Hanoi: Looking down from a tower block in Nhan Chinh Development, Cau Giay District

INTRODUCTION

Urban Research in Action: Context, Aims, Directions

Charles Goldblum

Vietnam was long absent or weakly represented in development approaches focusing on countries of the South, partly because of difficulties in accessing the field and to some extent due to geopolitical restrictions or doctrinal considerations. Now it is making a striking comeback as an 'emerging country' of Southeast Asia.

This general observation is also true of the field of urban studies wherein, up to the 1990's, Francophone scientific literature dealing with contemporary urbanization in Vietnam amounted to only a handful of early studies such as those authored by Lilian Halls-French, Nguyen Duc Nhuan, Langlet-Quach Thanh Tam and Christian Pedelahore (see comprehensive bibliography at the end of the book). On the other hand, subsequent to opening up under the *Doi Moi* economic reform, a lot of catching up has been done since the 1990s, thanks to studies carried out by doctorate-level academic scholars and leading public research agencies. Some of the latter include specialized research teams from the *Centre National de la Recherche Scientifique* (CNRS) [National Centre for Scientific Research] and the *Institut de Recherche pour le Développement* (IRD) [Institute of Research for Development, formerly ORSTOM], as well as schools of architecture that have had an impact in their own way, particularly through the architectural research network.

This book is published at the initiative of the *Institut des Métiers de la Ville* (IMV) [Cooperation Centre for Urban Development] and the Ho Chi Minh City Urban Development Management Support Centre (PADDI), under the scientific coordination of a team led by Patrick Gubry and including Franck Castiglioni, Jean-Michel Cusset, Nguyen Thi Thieng and Pham Thuy Huong, is a compendium of studies on this activity starting with the research results compiled between 2001 and 2004 by the *Programme de Recherche Urbaine pour le Développement* (PRUD) [Urban Research Programme for Development]. This collaborative work that got the ball rolling, with support from the Priority Solidarity Fund (French Ministry of Foreign Affairs), coordinated jointly by the *Institut des Sciences et Techniques de l'Équipement et de l'Environnement pour le Développement* (ISTED) [Institute of Science and Technology for Infrastructure and Environment for Development] and by the *Groupement d'intérêt scientifique pour l'Étude de la Mondialisation et du Développement* (GEMDEV) [Scientific Interest Group for the Study of Globalization and Development], is a groundbreaking contribution to urban research on Vietnam.

Indeed, this programme fits into the "priority solidarity zone" designation, a complex zone that now gives more space to countries targeted under France's development assistance policy, going beyond the former "countries in the field" of cooperation and reaching out notably to the three countries of old French Indochina — Cambodia, Laos, and Vietnam. In various ways it has promoted Vietnam's reinsertion into the field of urban studies relating to the theme of development.

With regard to scientific outputs, this reinsertion has brought together a number of heretofore unlinked studies conducted in rather challenging circumstances by Francophone researchers hailing from France, as well as from Switzerland, Belgium, and Canada. This has stimulated research on common themes carried out by mixed teams that always included Vietnamese researchers. Noteworthily, this book is evidence of the outstanding interest in the field, for out of a total of some thirty teams selected through the PRUD's call for proposals, eight of them were studying cities in Vietnam. This has yielded the eight chapters that make up this book and that include a number of the pioneer authors referred to earlier: Christian Pedelahore, with his outstanding interpretation of *"Hanoi: le cycle des metamorphoses"* [Hanoi: Cycle of Metamorphoses], and Nguyen Duc Nhuan. They were joined by other "pioneers" in Francophone research circles studying contemporary cities in Vietnam, such as Rene Parenteau, who is remembered for his early, successful initiatives on the themes of urban heritage and habitat that he conducted as part of a Canadian cooperation programme.

Other contributions, noteworthy because of their seminal nature, are those of Laurence Nguyen, in particular her thesis *Esquisse d'une politique de modernisation et de développement urbain à Hanoi et à Hô Chi Minh Ville (1986–1996)* [Outline of a Modernization and Urban Development Policy in Hanoi and Ho Chi Minh City]. This was the first thesis on Vietnam to be directed by the French Institute of Urban Planning (University of Paris 8) in 1999. As far as we know, it is also the first thesis to focus on what was being done and who was doing it in the realm of urban management in both of Vietnam's metropolises.

Furthermore, the theme put forward by PRUD was deliberately directed at analysing urban interventions in cities of the South, as well as stakeholder approaches and the strategies behind them or induced by them. It also highlighted the reinsertion taking place — in sync with the regional integration process at work in the Association of Southeast Asian Nations (ASEAN) — and the comparative opening and putting into perspective of research on Vietnam. Of course, only by reading this book between the lines does one discern the comparisons developed in the research that prompted them, first relating to the "Indochinese" context: Cambodia, Laos (Chapters 2 and 8), as well as to a country of the Mediterranean South, Morocco to be precise (Chapter 5). On the other hand, this desire to associate the quest for common trends in cities in the developing world and identification of special features of the urban context in Vietnam comes across clearly in the chapters that compare the contexts of Hanoi and Ho Chi Minh City, such as "Assessment of Projects Supported by Official Development Assistance Based on Partnership Formats" (Chapter 7) and the approach to "Intra-urban Mobility" (Chapter 3). The research programme on this theme thus enabled the team coached by Patrick Gubry to use a comparison approach to develop demographic research conducted earlier on Ho Chi Minh City and thereby highlight a number of features of the bipolar metropolising of Vietnam, which gives the reader an interesting bonus.

More broadly, the transition theme pervades all the research material herein, more specifically the links between the two figures of transition — economic transition and urban transition — in the approach to urban dynamics in Vietnam as in other countries of the South. Claude de Miras' team made this theme a specific focus. His research programme furthermore embraces a comparative introduction on the same theme. Taking the diverse facets of transition into account in this way highlights not only the distinctive features as described in Chapter 1, "Urban Transition in Vietnam: Its Processes and Stakeholders", but similarities as well, both the former and latter tending to refine, indeed renew the said approaches.

Likewise with the issues of metropolising and internationalizing urban production and functions and their links in a context wherein the realities of growth clash with lingering poverty, notably around issues of land and habitat, as shown in Chapter 4, "Resettlement Issues of Informal Areas in Ho Chi Minh City" and Chapter 6, "The Role of Civil Society in Urban Environmental Management". This underscores the shaky context in which the transition — economic and urban — is taking place, in which Vietnam's urban development policies are operating, attempting to develop principles of action that put the institutional stakeholders as well as the older grassroots organisations in new positions and confront them with new realities. These fresh approaches also illustrate how challenging it is to use notions such as *sustainable development* or *civil society* that have become internationalized in contexts where transition goes hand in hand with destabilization, as shown by the accelerated change in land patterns and, for many, have become synonymous with insecurity, notwithstanding the general — but not yet generalized — process of economic growth. The very notion of transition, in particular as it refers to stakeholder approaches in a context of transition, as debated by the researchers at an in-house workshop at the Hanoi IMV in November 2002, is revealed here in all its complexity.

Confronted with the received idea of standardization affecting urban morphologies as well as public and private intervention approaches, likewise with the stereotype of resistance to change, grasping urban transition requires a reading of the physical or institutional as well as mental traces, not only to comprehend what societies are tending to discard or trying to get away from, but also to comprehend the basic materials that generate urban transformation. Physically speaking, we will therefore not be surprised to see how far this research goes as it delves into water and traffic infrastructure issues, these sectors under regal authority upon which, as the authors see it, have devolved the role of vectors of urban transition and, through forms of delegation, the very substance that is bringing about the internationalization of the urban production.

By using the first chapter to draw the link between the long-term *processes* of urbanization and urban concepts as conceived by the *stakeholders,* the book shows clearly that the research prompted by PRUD's programme has broken new ground. The book's contents thereafter hinge upon these two dimensions. The early chapters introduce us to the *urban dynamics* evident at two distinct levels, that of morphological re-composition resulting from arterial system development and that of intra-urban mobility — telltale signs of urban mutation. The following chapters develop the *issues* that these dynamics engender from the standpoint of strategies: issues of rehousing when squatter settlements are slated for urban requalification; issues relating to the choices of how one particular urban utility will be managed, namely water. Finally, *stakeholder* approaches are highlighted in the three concluding chapters — stakeholders that are emblematic of the new urban scene given the contrasting positions they occupy and the interests or contrasting rationalities that they represent, because we have on the one hand the embryo of urban civil society as it is emerging from grassroots organizations, on the other international stakeholders broken down into two aspects that are frequently connected: the financial aspect through the donors providing official development assistance (Chapter 7) and the technical expertise aspect through the work done by international consultants and engineering offices (Chapter 8). We could not find a better account of the two extremes present in the nascent urban stakeholder system. Nevertheless, these chapters highlight common points of satisfaction and frustration encountered in urban infrastructure development and the related environmental issues.

Despite their diversity of aims — from sectoral actions to holistic planning, and scale of observation — from the urban scale to national policies, the research contained in this book makes no claim to be an exhaustive study — multi-faceted by nature — of urban research on post-*Doi Moi* Vietnam. On the other hand, the research led by PRUD has obviously benefited from the fruitage of research conducted earlier or in parallel for other reasons. Besides indispensable reference works such as the *Atlas du Vietnam* by Vu Tu Lap and Christian Taillard and the major studies on urban history that help fit the recent urban changes into the broader picture (the signal contribution of Philippe Papin), it is right and proper to mention the urban geography studies of Hanoi's peripheral growth directed by Professor Georges Rossi (in the *Atlas infographique de Hanoi* and thesis papers directed by the University of Bordeaux 3 that are original spin-offs of it). In a similar vein we have the noteworthy contributions of urban sociology research on metropolising and environment issues in Ho Chi Minh City conducted under the banner of Swiss cooperation under the leadership of Professor Michel Bassand. These publications and research articles have also found their way into thesis papers directed by the Federal Polytechnical School of Lausanne (EPFL). The active presence on PRUD teams of authors of thesis papers directed in each of the aforementioned contexts, namely Fanny Quertamp Nguyen for Bordeaux 3 and Sebastien Wust for EPFL, are evidence of this dissemination of knowledge about the cities of Vietnam and the scientifically beneficial character of its cumulative effects. Also noteworthy is the thesis on urban transit in Vietnam recently directed by the University Lumiere Lyon 2 by Nguyen Thien Phu, a member of the research team on expertise headed by Eric Baye and Jean-Michel Cusset. This paper is in fact a first on a theme of which the importance is seen because of the many references made to it in this book.

Tuning in to research conducted elsewhere in its field, the Urban Research for Development Programme also held to the principle of getting input from experts and NGO's, as seen by the presence of researchers from *Villes en Transition* (Cities in Transition) on PRUD teams, in an attempt to compare the research material with the actual sphere concerned by urban interventions — decision-makers and operational stakeholders on the one hand, citizens and users of urban services on the other. In this spirit, mid-term regional workshops were organized in part for internal exchanges between the researchers and programme supervisors and in part for these external exchanges. The first of a series of four, the workshop held in Hanoi on the theme "*Regards croisés sur Hanoi: Transition, spécificité urbaine et choix de développement*" [Swapping Views on Hanoi: Transition, Urban Specificities and Development Choices] in November 2002, from this standpoint provides special insight owing to a teaming up of PRUD (scientific coordinator), IMV and the Hanoi People's Committee in a decentralized cooperation project led by the Ile-de-France region and supported by the French Embassy. The role of the IMV and its two successive directors, including Laurent Pandolfi, a researcher on one of the PRUD teams and author of a remarkable thesis directed by the French Institute of Urban Planning in 2001, entitled "*Une terre sans prix. Réforme foncière et urbanisation au Vietnam. Hanoi 1986–2000*" [Priceless Land. Land Reform and Urbanisation in Vietnam. Hanoi 1986–2000], is especially noteworthy in this regard.

Thus, by showcasing urban development research in Vietnam developed at the incentive of PRUD, the publication herewith, as an outreach of this programme, entrenches the efforts put forth by Francophone countries through national or decentralized cooperation arrangements, offers fresh insight on urban development in Vietnam through scientific partnerships and thus provides enlightenment for government action in the relevant fields of urban development and international cooperation.

1

Urban Transition in Vietnam: Its Processes and Stakeholders

Christian Pedelahore de Loddis

The Mutating City: Getting to the Roots

Our research team[1] focused its efforts on analysing a number of key factors behind the urban explosion in Vietnam. Based on multi-disciplinary approaches, we sought to identify and reconstruct the key names, events and development processes associated with it.

A study of local urban phenomena was therefore framed in order to gain insight into the dialectic relationships between cultural continuities and economic developments. This, we felt, would enable us to interpret social transformations in the physical and symbolical forms evident in the spatial mutations.

Against this backdrop, our mission concentrated on a relatively unexplored field in Vietnam — the analysis of spatial cultures, operational modes and thinking patterns of the people involved in local urban development.

Using field observations as our primary tool, we looked for ways to explain the reference points and operations of two specific categories of persons. On the one hand, architects and urban planners who have an academic knowledge of and relationship with the city. On the other hand, the citizens, investors and builders who are a repository of customary know-how and intuitive, pragmatic, down-to-earth modes of invention.

Cities in Vietnam Today

"No transparency"; "can't make head or tail of it"; "nothing certain, always changing"; "inconsistencies everywhere"; "a hodge-podge of ad-hockery and tacky formalisms"; "orders and counter-orders". Those are a few of the expressions routinely used to describe the urban development scene in Vietnam.

Since our aim was to conduct collaborative research in this area, we took as the starting point for our study of spatial production and the interplay of urban affairs stakeholders, what outsiders had to say on the subject, including foreign investors, international experts and representatives of bilateral or multilateral cooperation arrangements.

Their appraisals highlighted the existence of complex, hard-to-penetrate situations wherein urban spaces are both the obvious venue and means of promoting internationalization processes as well as the brewing pot for the identity reactions that oppose them.

Moreover, since Vietnam opened its economy to the world (under the *Doi Moi* or Renovation policy), the construction and real estate activity stream has become a mainspring in the country. As such it is proving unequalled as a vector in the areas of improving living conditions, social differentiation and acquisition of wealth.

Even so, the culture of urban affairs in this country has historically defined and structured territories wherein specific contexts and local practices are holding their own and in fact, prospering. Such approaches continue to dominate and steer most[2] of what is being produced in new urban zones today which, in many respects, is still a far cry from the standard, unilateral practices of city planning at the international level.

In view of these features, we used a crossover of two complementary approaches, working first from actual physical transformations from the field standpoint (synchronic level) and then seeking to determine what might have been their cultural origins and their forms of continuity (diachronic level).

Our study develops in parallel a critical analysis of the urban objects and mechanisms produced as well as the identities and practices of the people behind them. It thereby highlights certain characteristics typical of cities in Vietnam in both their specific identity as well as in their evolution.

Urbanization: An Affair of Society

Since the 1990s, suburban zones of cities in Vietnam have been experiencing a non-stop movement of deals and building programmes, mainly at the family and individual level. In this country, the smallest piece of land is coveted and acquired after fierce rounds of transactions that invariably conclude with building or rebuilding at fever pitch that is contained only by the plot boundaries and principles of alignment with the main streets.

All levels of society have been caught up in this frantic rush to develop urban land or for that matter any land that can be urbanized. This is resulting in a palpable jostling among individuals, private contractors as well as a great number of institutions of every sort. It is a major affair, so much so that hardly a day goes by without each member of contemporary urban society thinking about how to develop city or suburban land.

As distant heirs of rural communalism under central and local management along with the autonomy and pragmatism that developed during the French and American wars, most government echelons and state-owned or quasi-state-owned enterprises, regardless of their principal activity or function, have a real estate department.[3]

Moreover, since 1975 and during the fifteen years that followed, governmental and municipal interventions, though modest in scale, could only be carried out marginally, essentially because of a crying lack of own-source funds.

In the last five years, municipal authorities in the major cities of Vietnam have, following a phase of capital build-up, launched a great number of infrastructure projects, including major primary networks (boulevards and avenues) that are increasingly sophisticated. In the wake of this, vast primary and recreational facilities are now being developed, accompanied by a resurgence of government-sponsored collective housing operations, allowing people to become homeowners.

This recent institutional take-over of urban and peri-urban development, while helping to a provide more orderly structure to the urban explosion, has by no means succeeded in marginalizing individual initiatives that quantitatively outnumber other approaches that weave together the fabric of the country's cities.

A Cross-over Approach to the City

The multi-year research program that we conducted in the framework of PRUD[4] focused on the consistency of both the physical and mental manifestations of urban development, as seen in the superposition and interaction of planned operations and individual initiatives.

To achieve our goal, we gave considerable attention to identifying and analysing the importation and dissemination of spatial production models in the broad sense of the term — architectural strategies, forms and postures — as well as symbolic and economic considerations.

Practices were examined from the inside in order to highlight the processes by which benchmarks, operational devices and ways of doing things were gradually built up and expanded upon by urban affairs professionals and private operators alike.

An orderly study of significant cases was then used as a basis to identify the patterns of thinking and representation of the people involved. Such patterns are especially difficult to grasp, given their unofficial and largely subconscious nature.

In fact, cities in Vietnam have been affected since the 1990s by the urban explosion taking place in tandem with internationalization of the stakeholders. They have had to come to grips with many sets of problems, some being common to Asia's urban centres, others the lot of developing metropolises, as well as cities in general opening up to the market economy.

Fifteen years of accelerated mutations now make it possible to analyse things with hindsight and put into perspective these transformations, as well as the development of common and cross-cutting themes concerning urban forms and cultural identities.

Meanwhile, these transformations call for the strengthening of forward-looking and innovative approaches in order to contribute to the revival of processes and working methods that are more in tune with the new scales of urban development in Asian cities.

A combination of resources and methods was used to study the city of Hanoi from three different angles: urbanistic, architectural and cultural (Christian Pedelahore and Shoichi Ota), sociological (Heinz Schutte), economic and historical (Dang Phong).

In our attempt to come to a common understanding of the symbolic references and physical processes behind the transformation of metropolises in Vietnam, we gathered and researched resources using three overlapping approaches: conducting and collating individual interviews; digging up, accumulating and studying archival and journalistic documents; *in situ* architectural and urban analysis of physical and tangible spatial productions.

Our effort was guided by the desire to create concrete opportunities to work among and compare two scientific communities, one made up of architects and urban planners, and the other, experts in the field of social science.[5]

The approach we used in this area involved putting to the researchers various subjects and objects (urban forms, buildings and housing) that are traditionally the purview of those in the first group. Then, by way of cross analysis, we tried to facilitate things so that the architects could assimilate the concepts and methods of the second group.[6]

Three assumptions were tested in order to structure the conceptual framework of this approach. We feel that these possibilities correspond to as many unofficial schemes that underlie the features specific to Vietnam's urban areas.

Firstly, the stakeholders themselves and city development are governed extensively by anthropological and cultural continuities on which an ideological framework is superimposed, covering them over, obscuring them, but not cancelling them out.

These continuities involve such things as a deeply rooted irredentism that is largely the product of the historical vicissitudes of Vietnamese civilization. So it is that the cities, and Hanoi in particular, were fashioned by an age-old culture of resistance and the desire to be different.

The modern-day spin-offs are illustrated and embodied in the abundance of urban transformations, all of which originate, however, from the unflinching and stubborn preservation of a small number of upgradable, unofficial models, patiently built up over time.

These forms of continuity are also found, in some instances knowingly but usually unknowingly, in the thinking patterns of the urban decision-makers and operators themselves.

Secondly, Hanoi's urbanity was historically built up and is in a continuing process of being rebuilt through an interactive relationship between external influences and endogenous models and representations.

This explains the relative ease, creativity and alacrity with which the economic and intellectual elite were able to grasp operationally and instrumentally the concepts and ways of doing things common to Western modernity, which ability they still have at this time.

Indeed, this living and dynamic culture is an extension of and rests upon an age-old experience of picking up on, transforming and digesting exogenous influences and models.

Thirdly, a particular historical context — at the intersecting steps of the Chinese and Western worlds — has spawned the development of a know-how that works, based on the control and subtle management of balances between powers and counter-powers, as well as a subtle strategic mastery of the weak-to-strong relationship.

This has enabled and developed in parallel a keen sense of collegial negotiation tied in with the acceptance, early on, of strongly individualized courses of action and choices.

It also explains why the boundaries between the formal and informal are so challenging to identify, as the stakeholders in urban affairs can relate alternately or even simultaneously with both of these worlds that seem opposing and irreconcilable.

The concept of the dialectical conciliation of opposites developed by Paul Mus comes to mind here, applying it to the relationships that are maintained and managed by the local urban development stakeholders.

Accessing the City through Its Movers and Shakers

Our research connects three complementary fields of investigation that are mutually enlightening and that focus on three target communities or specific groups:

- Urban affairs professionals (architects and urban planners);
- Private operators (individual and family);
- Decision-makers, administrators and government officials.

The case studies and interviews conducted in our research process began to reveal a certain qualitative resemblance between the current period and the initial wave of modernization in the 1930s in terms of postures, practices of blending and adapting know-how, methods and techniques originating from abroad.

These observations enabled us to anticipate the value of developing comparative approaches on these themes, although taking care to establish the quantitative and social differences, temporal contexts and relationships of scale and complexity that are found within them.

From this body of studies emerged a core issue, that being the relationship of the urban development stakeholders to modernity and to the external features of their spaces and thinking patterns — the field of exogenous references, practices and operational modes.

Thus, in this period of fast-track transition, urban affairs is enhanced by a further dimension, that of the spatial projection of socio-cultural space. Indeed, the city has returned to being the hinge node at the nationwide scale. It constitutes and institutes a dual location. It is both a surface of economic interchange between the customary network and the globalized network and a figure of contact and cultural mediation between traditions and modernities. This is strongly evident in architectural and spatial productions in Hanoi, from the mid-1980s up to the present time.

Using this combination of disciplines, we probed to some extent into the problematical and critical questionings that we feel have a measure of practical and operational value in these times of frenzied urban expansion.

It furthermore occurred to us that from the standpoint of analytical thinking, we were finding ourselves in parallel with the very development of these processes. Indeed, as a cultural if not anthropological constant, there seems to be an omnipresent extension of these tensions and oppositions that Vietnamese civilization is still eagerly seeking to reconcile as well as to become reconciled to itself.

Cultural Archaeology

As for the fields of architecture and urbanism, we focused our study on documentary material from the 1930s and 1950s in an attempt to identify pivotal times and subsequently at what point the Vietnamese intelligentsia began doing its own thinking and updating.

This gradual construction, in the face of the challenges of the time, of a renewed identity posture, came into being through a local approach to modernity and technical and social modernization conceived as unavoidable evolutions.

This position can be summarized in the following way, using the very terms of those who were behind it:[7]

1. Creation of *endogenous works* in contrast to the transfer or simple translation of foreign works.
2. Intellectual production of a *social* nature contributing to modernization and development of society.
3. These productions are both intended for, and have as their subject, the Vietnamese people. They are concerned with popular practices, manifestations of the *common person* as well as the simplicity of daily life.
4. They make an express claim to belong to modernity, to youth, to struggle as well as to belief in progress.
5. They place respect for *personal freedom* at the heart of their practice, thereby rejecting Confucian tradition.
6. They demand that the national production — physical and intellectual — benefit from bringing in and applying Western scientific methods.

In the area of physical forms, we located and exhumed the seminal activity of the AFIMA,[8] an institution that was the articulating link between purely French undertakings and the gradual emergence of Vietnamese stakeholders.

In 1926, this institution launched the first local architecture competition. Highlighting subjects that translated the will to deal realistically with the issue of "indigenous" housing, it had three sections: a modern residence in traditional Annamese style for a rich family, a three-metre-wide shop house in an indigenous quarter (a long narrow semi-detached house) and a six-metre-wide shop house for a craftsman in a market district.

The study of this event enabled us to understand how a small group of Vietnamese professionals, most of who worked for departments of the Indochina Ministry of Public Works, came into being and what factors led to its emergence. These professionals took advantage of the opportunity to initiate local thinking on ways of *associating* Western technical know-how with the forms, values and spirit of traditional architecture.

The second decisive time with regard to national architecture is seen in the *Anh Sang* [Light] Association founded in 1937 by writer Nhat Linh (Nguyen Tuong Tam), the purpose of which was to coordinate the concrete interventions of intellectuals in the social field, notably in the direction of rural areas. Symptomatically, this association's first project was the creation of a model rural dwelling, modernizing traditional types with the incorporation of ideas from the Western school.[9]

However, the most emblematic achievement of Anh Sang was in the urban area, through a large-scale project, that of the engineering study and completion of the Sand Bank Quarter, located directly north of Doumer Bridge.[10]

This predominantly working-class neighbourhood with 670 lots and 25,000 inhabitants, marks a dual landmark in the assertion of a scholarly Vietnamese architectural culture.

Firstly, in the emergence at that time of the first generation of Vietnamese architects on the Hanoi scene, trained at the *École des Beaux-Arts de l'Indochine* (Indochina School of Fine Arts [EBAI]) that would gradually supersede the generation of draughtsmen and associates of the time.

Secondly, in the development of a local way of thinking in architectural circles that gained strength both in terms of scale by tackling the urban dimension and in terms of social engagement by focussing attention on the living and residential conditions of the working class.

A third milestone is seen in the World War II period during which the government led by Admiral Decoux, gave attention locally to the themes of national character, autarky, local materials, modern development of cities and working-class housing. This took place in the framework of French-Vietnamese cooperation arrangements that claimed to be taking a fresh approach.

This period illustrates the spreading of the emblematic role devolving upon architecture and major infrastructure work in the physical manifestation of the vigour and hegemonic character of a power that held sway over the development and modernization of the country, as well as the forward-looking vision of the future and improved urban living conditions.

In this context we analysed how these tangible ideological transformations were received locally and the operational use that was later made of them — invariably through incorporation and adaptation — in the symbolic and material construction of a country regaining its independence.

Along similar lines, we also studied the evolution of urban master plans, the physical witnesses of the building up and gradual affirmation of a national policy that would shape plans and prospects for all urban territories. More specifically, we attempted to make a critical analysis of a set of operations contained in the first Hanoi Master Plan, framed by Vietnamese architects from 1957 to 1959.[11] As a founding element of contemporary Vietnamese urbanism, this set of drawings and scale models — for which the precise history still remains to be clarified in detail — supplies valuable insight regarding the conceptual environment, ways of doing things and constraints of a significant segment of architecture professionals active in North Vietnam immediately after independence. The study of this corpus enabled us to decrypt ways of doing things and benchmarks, both of which are obscure and unofficial, and to highlight their heterodox and composite character that often ran contrary to the much more unequivocal official policy of the time.

We also provide evidence that beyond the historical desire to break away and the use of concepts from the Socialist city, unofficial forms of continuity were nevertheless maintained due to knowledge transfer with practices of design inherited mainly from the Indochina School of Fine Arts (EBAI), as well as due to the seminal work done by Ernest Hebrard and Louis-Georges Pineau (Pédelahore de Loddis, 1995 and 2001).

Vietnam's archives — historical, institutional, corporate and private — covering the field of construction economics from the 1940s to the 1980s were also explored.

Therein we again identified forms of historical continuities for both state-owned companies as well as the private sector. Pragmatically, the latter had been maintained up until the late 1950s, then marginalized and mothballed, rendered transparent and informal, but it succeeded in surviving discreetly to be reborn and flourish, cross-fertilizing both official and parallel forms of economic activities during the *Doi Moi* period.

So what has often been presented as a miraculous, spontaneous, generation of opening to the market, is in actual fact deeply rooted in a century of memory and endogenous experiences.

Situations

We first of all drew up an inventory of the contemporary processes and stakeholders in urban transformation.

This highlighted four cross-cutting features, including the essentially individual incentive behind these transformations, the vitality and budding inventiveness that they denote, the experimental and cumulative pragmatism that is characteristic thereof (the area of institutional interventions being no exception), as well as the overriding interconnection of interactions between the private sphere and public domain in terms of spaces, operators and ways of doing things.

In the physical reality, identification of the spatial transformation processes of KTTs (*Khu Tap The*, collective housing) enabled us to show how the new expertise that the residents themselves have developed *in situ* is leading the make-over of the "Socialist complexes" found in Hanoi's first rim. These refined and inventive practices of densification, partitioning and individualization are found simultaneously in the make-over of colonial villas in the downtown core and constitute a vernacular model of spatial and social intervention.

These processes were the forerunner and foundation for the benchmarks and hands-on savvy put to use by individual builders in the 1990s. The semi-detached buildings they put up yielded linear urbanization patterns, followed by blocks that have increased the density of the suburban spaces and organically colonized, in a ripple effect, Hanoi's agricultural hinterland.

Beginning in the 2000s the first signs of a stronger will of intentional marginalization of individualized interventions and practices became evident. To achieve this, the regulatory authorities took advantage of the particularly symbolic opportunity when Hanoi was host to the SEA Games in December 2003, to undertake some face-lifting operations, as well as to standardize and strengthen the codes governing the occupation and use of public urban space.

These actions are contributing to imprint and disseminate the municipal policy and clarify its underlying doctrine in the physical structures of the city. The urban image that it throws back is a framed, unilateral, conformist and internationalized vision of the forms, modes of production and management of urban spaces.

Observed from the standpoint of urban realities, this vision appears abstract, voluntaristic and somewhat futuristic. It fails to deal with what civil society has done and aspires to do. It also sidelines the central and strategic issues of national identity[12] and of urban heritage that have very consequential economic, if not cultural weight. Yet, this direction is the stated objective that institutional policies are seeking to achieve and it signals that standardization and control will increase in the next few years.

The emergence of an urban civil society was studied in parallel, on the basis of the wide coverage given in the Vietnamese media to the stormy debates sparked by projects to construct the first high-rise buildings in the Hanoi downtown core.

Indeed, it has almost always been in the realm of urban controversy that is fired up whenever there an attempt was made to undertake some major real estate venture under foreign capital and management that the voice of this emergent civil society was able to be heard.

The latter very soon learned how to make strategic use of the role of go-between that the Vietnamese Government claims to play and indeed does play, since it was able, in this case alone, to spread around the demands of the residents with regard to heritage, identity and land (compensation).

The recurrent reminder of the cultural and national character of historic cities is a second example of the operational use of and picking up on institutional policy, in order to wedge the voice of the citizenry into the controlled field of information and media.

This component of the study also looked at the forms and meanings of contemporary architectural syncretism. This is primarily the fruitage of a work of transcription and declension of the spatial and stylistic elements of colonial architecture, and only in a secondary way, of those originating with traditional Vietnamese architecture, given the persistent strong attraction and socially enhancing function of the urban villa model and its neo-classical or neo-regionalist stylistic universe.

However, there were rather infrequent limited or isolated quotations. What we preferred to look for was the more or less successful attempt to create, for an individual building, a unitarian statement (often baroque and flashy to the observer), but possessing a character of consistency and originality in the mind of both its designer and owner.

So what we are seeing is recreation and recomposition, attempts at new combinations and the rapid refinement thereof in time (in a matter of years only), that are characterizing these processes, rather than direct copy in the sense of transfer or reproduction.

At the same time there is a remarkable attempt to express a strong creative autonomy — individual, differentiated and homespun — insisting consciously or unconsciously that it be unique and non-reproducible.[13] In this sense, the shop house and town house, spaces of Hanoi urbanity, still constitute identity locations, whether they are commonplace or high-end productions, not by any means generic, interchangeable products that are characteristic of consumer society.

As indicated in previous studies, the façades of these buildings are symbolically overdone (Pédelahore de Loddis 2000). Their primary function is to project out to the community an image of the personality and success of the homeowner who is invariably also the designer. Dwellings thus feature interiors that are functional and domestic and exteriors that make a statement of social standing.

At this point we can use the parallel illustration of food in which a distinction is made between foods of foreign influence and foods that are strictly endogenous (*an com tay va an com ta*) — and another one which goes even deeper because the institution is older, the distinction between *close relative* and *distant relative* (see Nguyên Van Huyên 1944).

Nevertheless, this separation into two differentiated scales enables us to ensure at the same time an internal continuity of practices and a swift adaptation to symbolic and stylistic influences from abroad.

These operational modes are by no means specific to the contemporary period, because traces of them are found in the façades of shop houses along the "36 Streets",[14] dating back to the early years of the twentieth century (Pédelahore de Loddis 1983).

These individualized ways of doing things remain largely dominant today, as the developer-builder echelon is as yet only weakly represented. In the rare instances of repetitive buildings,[15] purchasers do not hesitate for a moment to modify and personalize their dwelling.

These examples can also be interpreted as acts of resistance to the penetration of purely exogenous models, and have also been studied on the basis of one particular operation that is emblematic and decisive for more than one reason, that of the *Japanese Village*.[16] The case study enabled us to identify concretely the weight — unofficial, of course, but no less meaningful — of the networks of belonging that enabled only one of many earlier inhabitants to hold on to, against the logic of the project, against the foreign investor and the city, the permanency of a private enclave. This shows that the phenomena — very conspicuous of course — tending to internationalize metropolises, are rarely unequivocal and are not without generating powerful backlashes and reactions on the part of local social groups.

Trajectories

This section combines thirteen descriptive studies and four analyses dealing with real estate, land tenure and spatial patterns.

Most of these were individual case studies to which were added — using the same methodological research principle — a number of trajectories noted regarding plots, buildings and institutional actors.

We looked at individual activities that, although differentiated, nevertheless bring together a consequential relationship to *exteriority*, whether it is seen in the area of architectural references, construction methods or financing, but frequently all three of them.

The case studies of the involvement of academics, businessmen, architects and working class people in real estate development show that business — and often times cultural — travel abroad is a very significant factor.

The detour or passage through a distant world that these people have made and its effects are seen to result in innovative tools and procedures by setting these persons up socially as key movers and *passeurs* (that is, intercultural intermediaries) behind the urban transformations taking place.

We are thus able to identify and question the dual function of this intermediary role, that is, the cultural and financial aspects.

The study led to the characterization of specific paths that, by articulating with real estate and financial strategies, constitute powerful vectors for both urban intervention and social ascension.

Here, the functions of cultural and economic intermediation were identified. They are often separate, but in the case of Hanoi, they have been developed in an astonishingly syncretic fashion by unique stakeholders.

Along with these local forms of incorporating and adapting foreign know-how, a study was also made of domestic spatial forms of breaking way and resistance seen in an updating of traditional models in what we have put together under the heading of the "Nha San Movement".[17] This trend that has been developing steadily since the 1990s, corresponds to a reinterpretation, largely mythicized, of historical rural cultures and expresses a will to oppose, or at least rebalance, the market values promoted by globalization with the endogenous historical values of civilization.

Because it seeks both value enhancement and cultural modernization, this movement has some similarities with the intellectual and artistic movement of the 1930s, notably with the approach developed by Nguyen Cao Luyen throughout his life (Pédelahore de Loddis 1992, pp. 383–97) and extended in part today, on another scale, by organicist Vietnamese architects.

The City in Perspective: A Cultural Typology of the Urban Transition

The Quantitative Preponderance of the Family Home

The changes taking place today in the urbanity of Hanoi always go back to the family dwelling as the leading, preferred form of materializing urban development.

In this sense, as has been shown for several years now by numerous related international studies, the home is at the centre of strategies that Vietnamese households use to invest money, hoard money or make gainful use of savings.

Firstly, this plays the dual function of privately securing assets and secondly securing a space for one's own self or one's family. Both functions are particularly strategic in a situation of scarcity and high density, as well as of the exponential hike in land prices.

The pivotal role of the individual home is thus reinforced, in the sense of being a corollary to owning land, which is the main area in which most Vietnamese invest their savings, or even — for a small number of them — a sudden windfall.

Deeply Meaningful Family and Customary Structures

Historically, the cities of Vietnam, notably those on the Red River Delta, were built over a hinterland comprising a very dense network of villages. This is still the case today.

These powerful circular relationships between hamlets, regional towns and main cities are being maintained in a revitalized mode today.

Although in a process of destabilization due to the spatial, economic and demographic urban explosion, family and village tropism is holding on — albeit symbolically — at the level of social practices and it is continuing to be the organizing factor of an unofficial system of networks of interwoven obligations that directly structure urban project framing processes and investments, although behind the scenes and largely upstream.

Even in the case of government operations, this system is an important link in the decision-making and operational chain, often contributing to alter, correct and adapt institutional designs in a localized way.

Thus, even in the suburban extensions of Hanoi and Ho Chi Minh City (Saigon), metropolises that have been around for a thousand years, there is a continuation and renewal of community insularity and groupings that are a continuation and extension of historical sociability modes, in an updated way.

Duality and Wavering in Urban Society in Vietnam

Recognizing the function of the central authorities in major decisions of national scope and implication, but having at all times practiced day-to-day management at the local proximity level, the grass-roots producers of urban space have a relevant role in this dialectic operating rule,[18] without however demanding to do so openly. Even today it remains something tacit, something unofficial.

The administrations themselves reserve the right to modify and adjust master plans and urban zoning and development plans, even though they have received very official approval.

Architects that spend their day designing new districts made up of high-rises and lines strongly influenced by trivialized international models, upon leaving their offices in the evening, moonlight as private players devoted to the domestic forms of the shop house and townhouse, or for the wealthier, the villa of colonial inspiration.

Similarly, the separation between the sectors referred to as formal and informal in the West is in a state of flux and very difficult to make out due to the co-existence and superimposition of differentiated and sometimes contradictory statutes depending on the level one is dealing with: municipal, ward or street.

This actual state of urban mechanisms that emerges from an analysis of actual operations is also blocked out for the most part by the central and municipal authorities who feel that it is regressive and too loaded with pragmatics. However, if it were to be recognized, it could just as well be developed, and beneficially so, as an advanced form of decentralization and collective responsibility-building for urban affairs stakeholders.

A Historical Framework of Permanencies

Recent arrivals to a metropolitan network that is increasingly universal and globalized, the cities of Vietnam in this early twenty-first century concurrently and forcefully show the decisive power of temporal and identity continuities, provided that the development movers and shakers are given the means to renew and update them in an inventive and flexible fashion.

The impression of anarchy that one gets when first looking at the activity of the many agents in the urban stream and the physical development of the cities only appears that way on the surface. When one delves deeper, forms of order come to light that govern social relationships. These are the relationships of the extended family, their networks and agreements, which are significant and provide a factor of organization. They cut through and superimpose themselves on the power of the state and institutions.

In doing this, these local contemporary practices stem from deep forms of cultural continuities that appear on a time line and of which the historical points of change are found, for the twentieth century, in the 1930s, 1950s and 1980s.

Upon these permanencies are superimposed manifestations of internationalization that, in the case of Vietnam, are only *second* to them. The latter cover them over, hide them, without yet having succeeded in supplanting them or making them inoperative. Rather than being a direct effect of today's globalization, these manifestations correspond to a quantitative intensification and acceleration of a historical process fostered by a long experience of colonization. Digested rapidly and effectively, the many breakaways are reabsorbed here in the form of mutations in space and society. As is true of the vicissitudes of high-rise buildings and shopping centres as far as physical manifestations are concerned, so it is likewise with ways of life, subject to gradual interbreeding. These evolutions, the force of which is restrained and softened, are to the credit of the scholarly expertise of a culture forged in response to outside influences and interferences, a culture having the effect of mixing, adapting and protecting. It is indeed this science of intercultural relations, of hybridizing processes, of refined incorporations, of control of backlashes and chain reactions, that are becoming the reality in this new context.

This singular culture, marked by resistance, setting oneself apart and the merging of opposing currents, pursues and perpetuates an operational and creative response to ten centuries of Chinese rule, nearly a century of French rule, thirteen years of North-American intervention and soon two decades of internationalization.

Blending the Exogenous and Modernity: A Structuring Relationship

Our study highlights the key position occupied by a dynamic relationship to *exteriority* — that of international modernity — that is thought out and instrumented here as a borrowing, an adaptation and contextualization of exogenous models and ways of doing things.

Such models give a strategic and leading position to stakeholders who have had and continue to have the ability to appropriate them and generate endogenous counter-reactions that take the form of resistance from civil society and dominated groups and feed the expression and development of alternative counter-models that are the mainstay of other privileged intermediaries, notably intellectuals and artists.

A further specificity resides in the fact that this two-pronged, always intricate phenomenon, is being led by single stakeholders who, while belonging to State or municipal institutions, are also frequently involved in personal, private real estate activities.

Thus, the relationship to the exogenous blends in and superimposes itself broadly upon the relationship to modernity, both notions being perceived as equivalents in Vietnam.

A Social Intermediation Figure: The "*Passeur*"

The case studies of individuals and groups enabled us to ferret out the essential behind the existential and thus delve into the historical sedimentations of structuring collective schemes.

The identification and analysis on a few of these operational figures enables us to start with an initial understanding of the deployment and diversity of endogenous blending practices. They make up and provide a foundation for the essential of contemporary transformations of the urban space in Vietnam.

The most dynamic and inventive stakeholders of urban fabrication, while having strongly differentiated paths, are found in the transversal figure of the "carrier". What these people actually have in common is that they occupy a position that straddles several worlds, literally and figuratively.

These carriers owe their leading role to the close association of two parameters. The first is economic (an individual or family accumulation of capital), while the second is cultural and intellectual (they import, transform and adapt practices and models that, for the most part, are still Western at the present time).

To this first characteristic is added a second one, constituted due to the fact that the majority of people in this group associate a scholarly, intellectual openness to the exogenous (generally outside of the construction and development work sites) with the enriching experience of travel abroad that prompted or confirmed this openness to the international.[19]

The carrier is also seen to be the very embodiment of the values of openness advocated by *Doi Moi*. He is the materialization and reflection thereof, at this basic echelon of society, the individual.

This means that his actions become representative of all in his group and make it, first individually then collectively, into a referent and model, even a paradigm, for the rest of the social system.

The carrier also represents a key intermediation figure in the sense that due to his social status and what he does, he acts as a bridge and establishes links between traditions and modernities, between local ways of doing things and exogenous knowledge.

Furthermore, the carrier is a vector of application over a long period of time, in that he makes himself an agent of dissemination of a body of updated knowledge and practices spanning the distant past and the most recent past.

The carrier is an inventor and creator, a recycler and mixer of operational know-how. He takes advantage of and updates the close historical interactions of Vietnamese culture with exogenous cultures as well as with international modernity.

He is a producer of adaptive models and ways of doing things which, when gradually disseminated throughout the community, provide inspiration for the practices and strategies of local urban affairs stakeholders.

Lastly, the carrier plays an interface role within his professional and family group similar to that played by the metropolises and cities of the country at the territorial and national level.

Dualisms and Dialectics of Conciliation

Unlike the more linear mechanisms operating in developed countries where institutional echelons predominate, urban planning operations in Vietnam are always discussed at length and revised at each decision-making level (national, city-province, ward, block, street). Moreover, the customary family networks, very active in the civil service, weigh in upstream in these multiple opportunities and ponder, transversally, over their elaboration and implementation.

This inescapable fact thrusts itself on all operations, regardless of whether they are funded through the national budget or through bilateral or multilateral aid. Even in the case of grants and 100 per cent foreign investments, project contents and programmes are bitterly negotiated and often altered.

This *de facto* obligation — not officially acknowledged in policy — that makes it binding upon any operator to negotiate, adjust and amend his project, is also found in the relationships between institutions and investors, (small or large, private or public), municipalities and residents.

Going through the formal procedures rarely dispenses a person of having to conduct parallel negotiations with the block and ward officials as well as with his immediate neighbours. This is also true of temporary or permanent encroachments on public space by a business or residential operation, which always have to be negotiated locally. And it also applies to larger projects such as when a large facility requires expansion[20] and when the institutions themselves find that they have to negotiate with long-term occupants on their own land. But unlike cities in Latin America for instance, in Vietnam there is no eviction, rarely any demolition; negotiation takes place and compensation — even symbolics — is made.[21]

The field of urban affairs is therefore seen to be traversed in fact by a dialectical organization of practices that enables the coexistence and development of bilateral relations on a day-to-day basis.

There is an inter-reaction and association — over and above their origins — of policies, forms of organization and implementation that, in other contexts, would conflict with each other. In this country there is a coexistence of institutional planning actions expected to be unitary and applying to everyone, as well as of individual strategies and practices[22] that are strongly contextual and differentiated. All of them are traversed by logics of networks, clans, agreements, extended families and personal objectives. Although at times contradictory and opposing, they are always carefully sifted through and reconciled.

These complex production mechanisms of the city illustrate very deep historical continuities and reflect, as we see it, an Asian tradition — enriched extensively and specifically in Vietnam under its current form since the early twentieth century — ensuring, through multiple refined forms of negotiation and conciliation of opposing sides, the functioning of society in general and that of urban development in particular.

Thus there exist two interrelated worlds, two levels of references, strategies and actions. Despite the appearance of irreconcilable differences, these two spheres continue to be intimately linked at this time, but perhaps for a short while. They refer to what could be likened to a dual register of language and structure, in a dual heterotype,[23] the urban universe of Vietnam.

These concrete ways of doing things demonstrate — with stepped-up vitality in the present period of transition — their effectiveness and capability of ensuring, in depth and from day to day, the flexible and dynamic management (albeit not free of inconsistencies and fragmentation) of a structure with a dual orientation that, elsewhere, would be synonymous with irreconcilable contradictions, multiple clashes and blockage situations.

These forms of articulation are seen here as playing a core and organizing role by symbolically bringing together the private and institutional fields of urban practices. They manage to combine ideological and technical references that are strongly unifying and reductionist on the one hand, and operational situations marked by a permanent, inventive and binding contextual pragmatism on the other.

Future-oriented Ways to a Revitalized Urbanity

The City: Melting Pot of Vietnamese Identity Today

It appears obvious to us that "The City" must be perceived and understood as a physical place giving substance, as the reflection and projection on the soil of actual, concrete socio-economic relationships that are both symbolic and cultural. Although influenced by globalization, the urban space extends the crystallized expression of the civilization that fashioned it in its material forms. In Vietnam, the march of standardization is still struggling — fortunately, perhaps — to penetrate deeper than the surface layer.

The historical and sedimentary city is fundamentally impure in the sense that it constitutes the point of convergence and expression of multiple superimposed relationships, which are only very rarely unequivocal. Rather, dualities, dialectical oppositions, permeate it through and through.

The urban space is also complex in that it can be analysed as a physical reality as well as a mental and symbolic construction.

As is true of other metropolises that have strong specificities, Vietnam's big cities are both a frontier and a relay. They are an advanced frontier of dissemination — indeed of interference — from the world outside to the heart of the national community, but also, in a bottom-up return, a relay of expression and reaction of historical continuities and identity structures.

Urban Dialogics

On this breeding ground, what insight can urban research possibly bring to the field of practices and institutional action, as well as to international cooperation?

We will not go into the exhaustive range of operational methods, mechanisms and strategies of intervention that seemingly could be developed with benefit as this would necessitate the implementation of a specific programme.

We will limit ourselves to outlining some directions that we feel are promising, as they are founded on the conditions prevailing in the urban reality of Vietnam's cities.

The first point suggested by our study is the importance of strengthening the contribution of the context as a medium and tool for new urban projects. Today this is quite neglected in its morphological and cultural dimensions, but it would be a way to try to reduce internally the gap between official policy and the way things are actually done, between the theory and local practices of urbanism.

Indeed, common sense and the quest for efficiency seem to argue in favour of acceptance and an institutional and professional factor of interventions by the people, of what could be described as contemporary vernacular and historical architectural and urban types. These could beneficially constitute the building blocks of an active, reasoned policy for the city.

In this area, a critical atlas of urban forms of cities in Vietnam would be an indispensable tool of familiarization with the actual state of things with regard to urban morphology. It would enable the balanced development, the scholarly and institutionalized updating, of popular evolutions and of the current dynamism of construction and habitat modes.

Secondly, this picking up on the long historical and anthropological time line of cities in Vietnam, as highlighted by our research, is a powerful means of enlarging the concepts that we feel should be brought together upstream to develop the various tools of operational urbanism, still too often dominated by quantitative, functional studies alone. It would put things in perspective, enabling both an identification and extension of endogenous historical continuities as well as experimentation with the most contextual paths of a vision of the city having qualitative objectives and identity designs over and above its technical and quantitative dimensions.

It would also have the advantage of bridging the heritage urban zones and extension zones, integrating them into one territorial conglomerate. In this decompartmentalized operational practice, a tight link to contemporary experimentations would be established with a tangible, symbolic, socially shared heritage. This would be an active medium and source of fresh inspiration for the new scales of Vietnamese urbanity.

The third constituent element that our research has brought to the surface of the Vietnamese identity is that of composite and dually linked negotiation and experimental pragmatism. As an integral part of daily relationships and actions, it remains alive and active, both at the political and social levels.[24]

This specific cultural attribute is a tremendous counterpoint to current technocratic standardizing trends. If sought for and enhanced as the foundation of a negotiated urbanism, it could be a powerful tool of balance and conciliation of the contradictory forces and powers at work on urban territories. Moreover, this approach involving the coordination of several spatial scales would make it possible to respond more effectively and suitably to the challenges stemming from a metropolitan gigantism that is increasingly uncontrollable using the classic tools of institutional planning and supervision alone.

Even though quite poorly handled today, the pragmatism and taste for unconventional experimentation and inventiveness are nevertheless a dynamic counterpoint to this tradition of reconciling opposing sides. They are a unique opportunity to pursue the development of a specific urbanism and architecture as well as to take a position unfettered by the powerful international models dominated by the merchandizing of the city and the spectacularity of architectural forms.

It therefore seems that the reality of the cities of Vietnam is inviting us to change the institutional urbanism paradigm, that being complexity. It has become inescapable due to the simultaneous metropolising and globalising of regional and international networks, as well as due to the stratification and interconnection of interventions, requiring a parallel enlargement of urban planning tools.

Systematic, open-ended procedures could then be developed based on the study and implementation of actual projects. This is an urbanism of complex situations, one that takes into account and at the same time weaves in the opening to the market and to local practices, as a pragmatic, contextualized, iterated and sustainable design is developed for the form and content of cities.

Thus, through operational, concrete means of implementing *City Projects* on a revitalized "Living Together" theme — that are yet to be identified and defined — intervention methods can be put in place in the field. This would reinforce the locally adapted procedures of a dialogic urbanism open to the demands of civil society, open to endogenous practices and know-how. Furthermore, these approaches would be sustained by input from both foreign operators and the rich historical and cultural, tangible and intangible, heritage of Vietnam's cities.

Notes

1 Dang Phong, Heinz Schutte, Shoichi Ota and Christian Pedelahore (scientific director).

2 This accounted for 80 per cent of built-up surfaces in the early 2000s. It is now tapering off with the increased power being wielded by development companies that are strongly supported by the municipalities.

3 This is true of state-owned agriculture companies (industrial crops), mining companies and of the ministries themselves.

4 *Programme de Recherche Urbaine pour le Développement* [Urban Research Programme for Development]. "Changes in Spatial Cultures and Dynamics of Urban Development Stakeholders in Vietnam" Programme (PRUD 79).

5 Sociology, economy, geography, anthropology, history, philosophy and archaeology.

6 Transition from a purely descriptive history to speculative analyses, formulations of hypotheses and use of survey protocols in order to establish a scientific foundation to deal with issues that are no longer over-arching or general, but localized and in-depth.

7 In harmony with the profession of faith of the *Free Literary Group* [*Tu Luc Van Doan*], published in the *Phong Hoa* magazine of 2 March 1934. It expressed not only the position of this group of writers and poets, but more broadly that of avant-garde painters and architects who went along with it.

8 *Association pour la Formation Intellectuelle et Morale des Annamites* (Association for the Intellectual and Moral Training of the Annamese), a reformist institution established in 1919 by Albert Sarraut, Louis Marty and scholar Pham Quynh.

9 Hygiene, functionality and new materials.

10 The kingpin and main originator of this project was architect Nguyen Cao Luyen, founder of the first architecture agency in Vietnam. He was an active member of the cultural and artistic avant-garde and principal player in a scholarly rapprochement between working-class spatial cultures and the universalistic values of the modern architecture movement.

11 This corpus, as yet unpublished, was painstakingly compiled with the assistance of Professor Ngo Huy Quynh.

12 This is a fundamental pillar in the legitimating policies of the government and Communist Party of Vietnam.

13 In the meaning given by Walter Benjamin in his analysis of the work of art in the age of its mechanized reproduction.

14 Hanoi's historic business district, located between the citadel and the Red River.

15 For instance in Linh Dam, site of the third municipal row housing project.

16 Construction of an exclusive residential district located south of West Lake [*Ho Tay*], the first in Hanoi.

17 Literally, houses on stilts. By extension, it can refer to any traditional house of wood construction. Such houses are purchased from Montagnard minority peoples or from peasants in Central Vietnam and reassembled in the city, sometimes as the top floor of masonry buildings.

18 Thus, even the signature of a minister only very rarely means that there is no need to convince decision-makers and operators at the intermediary levels on a one-to-one basis.

19 What we are referring to here is the massive circular migration to countries of the East (in the 1980s, then in other forms in the 1990s), which relates to the same process — expanding it to the intellectual middle classes (civil servants) and specialized workers — as to that of the intellectual elite from the 1920s to 1940s in France. This migration system, put in place in COMECON [Council for Mutual Economic Assistance], was widely used locally. It acted as a central mechanism for trade and debt settlement, as Vietnam was considered to be the poorest of the Socialist countries. After *Doi Moi,* it has grown almost to the point of becoming an industry. So it is that today a number of labour companies are placing thousands of Vietnamese workers abroad, for the most part in Asia, the Middle East and Africa at the present time. Thus, it has become quite commonplace in the social system for individuals to spend a period of time abroad, and this is increasing since the occupations involved have been extended to non-specialized workers, unskilled labourers, and in some cases even to craftsmen and farmers.

20 Case of the University of Construction (DHXD), located south of Hanoi.

21 The setting up of an international complex on West Lake required no less than eight phases of negotiation and over two million dollars in compensation.

22 Private for the most part but also sometimes public.

23 According to the meaning given by Michel Foucault, 1994, pp. 752–62.

24 A symptomatic confirmation of this is found in the slogan coined at the outset of *Doi Moi: "The Government and people work together".*

References

Foucault, Michel. *Dits et écrits, 1954–1988. Tome IV*. Paris: Gallimard, 1994.

Nguyên, Van Huyên. *La civilisation annamite*. Hanoi, 1944.

Pédelahore de Loddis, Christian. *Les éléments constitutifs de Hanoi*. Paris: BRA/MULT, 1983, 150 pp.

———. "Constituent elements of Hanoi city, 19th–20th centuries" (1983), English version. In *Vietnamese Studies* no. 12 (no. 82), Foreign Publishing House, Hanoi, 1986; pp. 92–140, ill. n&b.

———. "Hanoi, Miroir de l'architecture indochinoise. Notices biographiques". In *Architectures françaises outre-mer*. Liège: Mardaga, 1992.

———. "Hanoi, Mirror of Indochinese Architecture", (1990). In *Architectures Françaises Outre Mer*, Mardaga Editeur, Liège, 1992, pp. 292–319, et Notices Biographiques pp. 383–97, Ill. Cl & nb., Bibliog., index.

English version in "Etudes Vietnamiennes", no. 1/1993 (no. 107), Foreign Publishing House, Hanoi, 1993, pp. 24–56.

———. "Tracés parisiens et Paris immatériels d'Asie". In *Paris s'exporte. Architecture modèle ou Modèles d'architecture*. Paris: Pavillon de l'Arsenal, Picard Editeur, 1995.

———. "Where East and West Meet, Hanoi". In *Sifting of French Architecture*. Vietnam Cultural Window, no. 3, June 1998, pp. 4–7, ill. nb.

———. "Hanoi. Figures et identités du patrimoine architectural". Colloque Patrimoine, Vientiane, 2000.

———. "Ernest Hébrard et l'Indochine. Une synthèse entre Orient et Occident". In *Ernest Hébrard, vie illustrée d'un architecte planétaire. De la Grèce à l'Indochine*, edited by Haris Yiakoumis and Christian Pedelahore De Loddis. Athènes: Editions Bastos-Plessas. Paris: Picard, 2001.

———. "Tribulations d'un modèle architectural dominé, le *Compartiment* vietnamien". *Espaces et Sociétés* numéro 113/114 (no. 2–3 /2003), l'Harmattan, Paris, 2003, pp. 89–108., ill. (English abstract p. 307).

———. "Pour un urbanisme syncrétique et identitaire" [Hà Nội: Vì một quá trình đô thị hoá hỗn hợp và giàu bản sắc]. In Regards croisés sur Hanoi: transition, spécificité urbaine et choix de développement, Actes du séminaire international, 12–14 November 2002, Hanoi, Vietnam, Institut des Métiers de la Ville Ed. [Dự án đào tạo chuyên ngành đô thị] Hanoi, December 2003, pp. 31–34 (35–38), ill.

———. "Continuités et métamorphoses d'un patrimoine partagé: Architectures urbaines des XIXe et XXe siècles au Vietnam". In Architecture Coloniale et Patrimoine; Institut National du Patrimoine — Somogy Éditions d'Art, Paris, 2005, pp. 148–57.

Hanoi: The Red River and its flotilla of fluvial transport at the beginning of the twentieth century. (*Postcard*)

Ho Chi Minh City: Notre Dame cathedral and the central post office, circa 1920. (*Postcard sent on 15 August 1920*)

2

Road System and Urban Recomposition in Hanoi

Emmanuel Cerise
Rene de Maximy

City and Projects: Trends

A City in Motion

The millennial city of Hanoi is a new city. This apparent paradox reflects the Vietnamese capital's drastic transformation, in the space of a few years, from a small town into a rapidly expanding metropolis. This is a brief and concise account of that evolution, as observed over a period of several years by an architect interested in its architecture and its neighbourhoods and a geographer-urbanist researcher who has undertaken several assignments in the city since the country opened to market economy in 1986. These observations are based on meticulous data collected *in situ* and supported by numerous interviews with urban property developers and users, investors, and urban planning decision-makers and professionals. The collected data are compared with existing archives and publications and complemented by available censual data which has been refined and revised through periodic visits in the field; sectoral research by architecture students has also been of great value. These are not the results of inconclusive hard data surveys, but analyses based on an in-depth knowledge of the city, which we have covered time and again on foot, by bicycle and on motorcycle — the most suitable means of transportation for the early twenty-first century Hanoian.

Besides the city's architectural and urban evolution, we will also deal with the motivations that drive both private and official players in the areas of conservation and transformation, the two chief aspects that will determine the growth of the city. Indeed, Hanoi is facing some major and highly topical issues: respect of its urban and architectural heritage, and in particular built heritage and patterns of urban composition; the recognition of vibrant traditional customs practised by both previously established and newly arrived city dwellers; the improvement of living conditions for the general public, housing and appropriation through use of public space; control of urban growth and appearance of extensions, which make Hanoi the hub of an amazingly dynamic urban area. Most significant is the manner in which Hanoians have adapted their culturally ingrained way of organizing their habitat and the use of public spaces near their place of life. Political authorities must take these deeply rooted habits into account. A highly pragmatic approach can thus be observed, whereby social, economic and political forces combine and harmonize through mutual concessions.

In a city where market economy co-exists alongside government policies based on an officially communist ideology and vibrant traditional values, we have chosen to look into the changes and transformation of a historical main road to fully grasp the practical mindset which makes it possible to adapt to such a contradictory context. This road is situated partly on the southern edge of the so-called Old Quarter and of the French-colonial district, and partly on the southern edge of the post-colonial city and the new and fast-expanding districts, which are either already built-up or undergoing urbanization. It offers for analysis a number of situations that bear witness to the confrontation of societal forces at work in Hanoi, where all-conquering urban planning is founded upon a vibrant dynamism.

Our purpose here is merely to introduce a significant sample of the questions facing modern Hanoi. The city currently lacks a clearly defined problematic and is having to re-adapt its land legislation and regulate motorized traffic, which is increasingly subjected to the dictum of individual initiative and of a poorly codified use of urbanized space. The need is being felt for an informed dialogue between the city's policymakers and the multitude of individual initiatives.

Hanoi, a Millennial City

Hanoi has been shaped by the past ten centuries, with the greatest transformations occurring in the past 120 years due to the French presence. The ancient imperial city contained within the walls of the citadel symbolizes power overthrown by the conquering French. It has given way to a military and administrative quarter, while the neighbouring merchant's quarter remains to this day. Indeed, contrary to many conquerors and revolutionaries, the Vietnamese have appreciated, absorbed and preserved the architectural heritage and patterns of urban composition brought by their invaders. Signs of this long history permeate what remains of the old quarter. Although they remain in evidence, they are not always found where one would expect. Naturally, a number of monuments still attest to this past through their architecture and particular history: they are the preserved witnesses of their own role in a bygone age. Very ancient foundations have also recently been found in the middle of the citadel demolished by the French at the end of the nineteenth century.

However, these relics are not the focus of our study. Throughout the last thousand years, an art of living has developed around work and everyday life. This way of life still endures to the present day, like constantly reshuffled sediment carrying within it the elements which intimately constitute it. Their cultural dimension is deeply rooted in the customs of Hanoians, to the point where they remain in use in the current extensions. Though this phenomenon is obviously not unique to Hanoi, understanding its place and significance helps to appreciate the capacity for appropriation of urban space, which reflects the population's undeniable integration. The street and the buildings alongside it are the first indicators of this phenomenon.

Several cities in Southeast Asia uphold a system whereby each trade and each craft is assigned a specific street. This system is a cornerstone of such cities, and expresses the way in which cultural permanence can link together contemporary urban dwellers with a deep acknowledgement of their past.

The street, however, reveals more than an organizational and socially structured dimension. More so in Hanoi than in Ho Chi Minh City, the first and most striking impression when walking in the streets — especially in densely populated areas — concerns the way they are being used. The majority of open public spaces, which extend into buildings and are characterized by the hodge-podge paving of roadways and — except in the case of alleys and *cul de sacs* — by pavements, are taken over by the activities of the inhabitants. Their use varies according to the time of day, from one hour after dawn until four hours after sunset. However, the permanent and integral presence of people is not limited to the areas equipped for the functioning of the city and the safety of pedestrians; indeed, be it on foot, on bicycle or on motorcycle, inhabitants and passers-by monopolize the roads and intersections. When in motion, this is a population of Centaurs,[1] which tolerates cars as long as they remain discreet. At the start of the twenty-first century, two-wheeled vehicles are like the legendary seven league boots. They act as an extension of the city dwellers, to the point where, during working hours, they are parked on the pavement of narrow streets, which are thus rendered impracticable for pedestrians. At night, they are kept in workshops, restaurants, shops and living rooms.

This description of the current state of things reflects ancient customs perpetuated — though less noisily — through the habits of residents. There is more to the street than can be seen at first glance: residents consider the street and pavement as legitimate extensions of their dwellings or workplace. The pedestrian constantly has to sidestep craftsmen at work, as in the tinsmith street of Hang Thiec — one of the "36 streets" — or avoid housewives washing dishes or cooking a meal. People eat lunch on the pavement in front of their doorstep, where small eateries are set up during mealtimes. Men in reclining chairs take naps or read the newspapers in a doorway wide open onto the street; seated in groups of two or three, they converse or smoke rustic water pipes. Women sit on low stools and busy themselves with commercial or domestic activities unless they are busy chatting. Such behaviour is commonplace and demonstrates that Hanoi's popular neighbourhoods maintain the same century-old customs. This way of life originates from an urban education passed down through the generations, which promotes a lifestyle based on the neighbourhood. The *dinh* is a prime example of this takeover of the streets and neighbourhoods. Originating from the countryside, the *dinh* has an identity-building role and functions as a communal house for the neighbourhood. It is collectively managed by and belongs to city dwellers who often hail from the same village or district and have settled in the same *phuong* — the city's basic unit where, traditionally and to this day, each street or street section hosts one specific commercial activity. The *phuong* are places for building and expressing identity and define the boundaries of a turf which has been symbolically as well as physically appropriated. The *dinh,* as well as pagodas, are still common, although they are not clearly visible to the casual passer-by.

Various accounts confirm the customs thus observed and contribute to justifying and explaining their endurance. According to inhabitants who invited us in their home — whether close friends or strangers we briefly sympathized with — and were kind enough to talk with us at length, certain village customs have been strongly upheld in Hanoi, though they have been subjected to *de facto* constraints. This constantly growing city has long absorbed a flow of newly arrived peasants. The twentieth century brought in such new migrants under the most dramatic circumstances, namely the fifty-year multiform war[2] which gave birth to modern Vietnam and whose repercussions still run deep — although in the past fifteen years economic reforms have gradually reduced their impact. These peasants consider the exterior access to their lodging to be part and parcel of the individual's and the family's living space, regardless of how much it may encroach on public space. Things have always been this way in their villages and will remain so in the big city they now inhabit. But while there is no lack of outdoor space in the rice paddies, vegetable plots and orchards of the deltas and low-lying fluvial and coastal plains, in Hanoi this much-needed space is, at best, reduced to a small garden or a tiny courtyard, and more often than not to a shared alleyway or *cul-de-sac*. The pavement more commonly serves this purpose. Each household must negotiate the quasi private use they make of it with law enforcement representatives who, fearing women's outspoken animosity towards them, prefer to settle matters quietly with their husbands to assure themselves of an undeclared income. Thus resume many rural traditions on the city pavements, and explains why they are always crowded with motorbikes during the day.

Motorcycles are a social phenomenon with vast consequences on urban life and on the spatial spread of the capital. No family is without a motorcycle or, if they are too poor, a bicycle. It has become a basic essential item allowing greater freedom of movement: one can ride it to work, use it as a work tool or to carry all kinds of supplies, for entertainment, or to settle in the outskirts where housing is cheaper. As a result, it becomes possible to sell an obsolete and cramped city centre property — usually shared by one or more mixed-generation families — and use the available capital to buy modern housing two to three times more spacious, better equipped, and lower maintenance.[3] The flipside is its location several kilometres away or even beyond urban limits. This intra-urban migration contributes to the decongestion of old neighbourhoods, which facilitates their — at times merciless — renovation, and enables a more lucrative use of space where restored and renovated old dwellings are put to a new use.

The purpose of some streets and alleys in Hanoi is limited to transit and access to the innermost parts of a system of structures, which distributes and compartmentalizes the most humble of houses, and their most ordinary immediate surroundings. These passageways are narrow corridors often dozens of metres in length. They travel through low buildings leading to the entrance of a multitude of dwellings and across narrow courtyards. Inconspicuous and protected, these pathways form gradually as the lot densifies. Such linear and concealed distribution can also be identified in the ancient quarters of other cities in Vietnam. These structures are completed by a great number of blind alleys and transverse, labyrinthine passages only accessible to pedestrians, cyclists, and the occasional motorcycle. When they are situated outside, these spaces — semi-private in practice — complete the aforementioned spaces in the street and are deliberately laid out. Where they are situated in areas self-established by Hanoians in search of habitat location and compelled to settle without formal municipal authorization, they are usually the result of a negotiation process.

It is thus fair to say that a great number of city dwellers living modestly in the densely populated areas of a city where habitat is traditionally low-rise — seldom over two storeys — share common spaces which are not necessarily communal. Hanoi is their home. Should urbanism fail to take into account and disrupt such urban expressions of their sociability, spontaneous arrangements would probably arise, which municipal popular authorities would then have to subscribe to. This will be made all the easier if urban planners and their backers are previously aware of the issue.

The area known as the "36 streets" in old Hanoi — as well as numerous houses, streets and alleys built in colonial times which, for half a century after the French departure, continued to colonize farmland in response to unstoppable urban growth — display the above-described characteristics, which we qualify as moral and cultural. This is one of the main aspects of the twentieth-century city's societal role, together with the more lavishly spread areas created by the French presence. This role will be measured against a new one currently taking shape with the construction of the city.

For a more rigorous analytical perspective, the above observations must be completed by taking into account urban attitudes recently emerging amongst city dwellers in tune with transnational modernity. Such attitudes relate to the new possibilities for housing localization and siting and the uses they entail. New types of city dwellers are appearing. Several factors can influence their behaviour in relation to urban insertion: an above average level of income may favour openness to new and different ways of inhabiting; the possibility for land or real estate speculation may encourage taking advantage of opportunities left open by gaps in urban regulation — supposing such regulations were universally respected; a low income might push the most destitute to overstep traditional taboos such as squatting on former cemeteries or places considered as cursed.

The first group have generally acquired a different lifestyle through circumstances ranging from a long stay abroad, during which they would have experienced a habitat they now feel better corresponds to their personal taste, to a desire to comply with a conception of modern life as popularized by a so-called "Western culture". One must be able to afford such lifestyle choices, and especially the financial means needed to acquire a habitat providing adequate domestic space. The new architectural forms currently being built influence and strongly reinforce such choices. One keeps a different kind of company but chooses friends and peers to reflect the new image, while the overriding importance of the family wanes.

The second group seeks to match a quest for social prestige with a lodging that testifies to their openness to the outside world, connoted as Western. This goes alongside lucrative societal or commercial aspirations or possibilities — one does not necessarily exclude the other. Their homes are often characterized by a garishness common to *nouveau riche* social climbers throughout the world.

The last group are merely after better accommodation than they previously had or would have nearer the city centre. Their decision entails selling their previous lodging and owning a motorcycle, which enables access to any location for purchases, work or services previously available locally, whatever their distance from one's dwellings. This approach has in common with the previous group the desire to leave behind the precariousness of outdated or peasant dwellings and the abundant dust of the central working-class neighbourhoods for access to solid, better equipped, cleaner and glossier housing — in short, to enjoy a "hygienic and high quality" housing, as our informants put it. The current policy of building new developments on the outskirts encourages this trend towards delocalization sustained by the sale with a high capital gain of one's former centrally located — and thus commercially attractive — lodging, and goes alongside the introduction on the market of high quality and affordable collective housing. Such a housing complex policy has already been tested with the *Khu Tap The* (KTT), as this study will later show.

For the time being, the societal importance of the first two types of behaviour is greater than the number of people they actually represent. They function as referents for a trend which is begging to expand. The third type of behaviour, however, justifies the options of a housing policy which soon enough should trigger a redistribution of population densities in the various districts of Hanoi.

The Old City: Altered and Remodelled, Maintained and Expanded

Before 1954

In 1954, before the French departure, the population of Hanoi numbered 380,000 inhabitants over a surface area of 1,300 hectares. It comprised three different types of districts:

The most ancient was originally divided into thirty-six streets: "*at the end of the 15th century, Hanoi was redistributed into 36 streets and corporations which to this day still form the heart of the capital*".[4] It is shaped like a triangle whose northern apex is situated to the north of Long Bien Bridge. Its eastern edge is bordered by the dyke which runs alongside and contains the Red River [Song Hong]; to the west, it is edged by the railway line and, more precisely, by the limits of the ancient citadel; to the south, by Hang Bong which turns into Hang Gai then Cau Go. This commercial and residential district is well integrated in urban life and hosts a socially diverse Vietnamese population. It still thrives with a multitude of workshops, stalls, shops and services. Its inhabitants have intimately appropriated its use, including public spaces, which they occupy freely and with a strong presence.

To the west, on the grounds of the ancient citadel, lies the administrative and military district built by the French. Further west, it gives way to a large city park. Its space is very open, and is divided between a self-contained, closed military quarter and adjoining large public edifices built to house general interest administrations. The presidential palace, the Communist Party headquarters, ministries, the National Assembly and numerous buildings housing central administrations can be found there. Handsome art deco or modernist colonial villas are also the seat of several embassies. This district is identical to the French quarter. The Vietnamese have maintained it for two apparent reasons: firstly because, having just reconquered their assets, they had an immediate need for those facilities, and secondly because they decided, controversially, to appropriate the colonial city, which they consider today as the urban jewel of their heritage. This is undoubtedly a more intelligent approach than the destruction of a large part of the remaining ramparts and gates of old Beijing triggered by Mao during the Cultural Revolution. This part of the French quarter stands as a national avatar of the imperial city and the destroyed citadel.

The French quarter where "colonial might was wrought into stone" (Papin 2001) continues to the south on the same mode of spatial composition. A few ministries and central administrations occupy the official buildings built by the French. Some of the handsome colonial residences with gardens have become the seat of foreign embassies. Similarities to the district described above continue: the functions assigned by the old regime have been maintained: the main Post Office, the Town Hall turned into the People's Committee and schools can be found in the first administrative district created by the French between Hoan Kiem Lake and the river. The district extends to the other side and to the south of the lake, with wide avenues and notably few craftsmen's workshops or merchants' shops. French colonization intended to leave its imprint through the alignment and construction of wide perpendicular avenues lined with opulent villas and imposing public buildings of high quality architectural workmanship. Social housing did not feature in this policy of grandeur.

This typical urban unit based around Hoan Kiem Lake densifies up to the Red River dyke on one side and up to the railway line on the other. It extends to the south along the same strict pattern of orthogonal streets. There are, in addition, a few housing developments initially built as accommodation for colonial public servants. This is the representation of an idea of a tropical city which, although — or is it because? — it draws its inspiration from a republican and French empire, remains a reference of harmony and good taste for the intelligentsia and municipal authorities of Hanoi.[5]

The southern edge of the city as it was then is delineated by what is now Dai Co Viet Road and Tran Khat Chan Road, at the end of a thoroughfare built on a dyke at the entrance to the city and which links Son Tay to the capital. Already in colonial days, Hanoi's entrance and exit ways were populated by a great number of houses where a throng of Vietnamese inhabitants working in the capital lived.

Between 1954 and 1986[6]

During these years, Vietnam underwent a long period of isolation which caused it to steer its economy towards the Soviet Union. Exchanges with this parental figure were constant but also meant that Vietnam had to base its supplies — and especially its food supplies — on a largely self-sufficient socialist economy. After independence, as soon as it was liberated from yet another intolerable foreign presence in its history, Hanoi strove to build the capital of a new country. Besides reclaiming heritage built under the French, the government also had to deal with severe housing shortage. Circumstances led it to take inspiration from the Soviet model, which led to the construction of KTT: collective housing sub-divisions built in rows, usually three to four storeys high and aggregated into large estates. This type of housing is widespread in Hanoi.[7] Its implementation offered an opportunity to relinquish the use of traditional materials in favour of reinforced concrete prefabricated materials. KTTs are usually low-rise and built around basic collective facilities sited in their centre, and almost always situated near a village in the surrounding outskirts. Their scale is reasonably human and city dwellers housed or rehoused there experienced a considerable improvement in living conditions.

Deliberate juxtaposition of a village with a KTT sited along a carriageway — asphalted during site development if not previously — has created urban sprawl in peri-urban space. This situation — which existed previously but was less visible — has reinforced the city's tendency to extend through annexation — either illegal or at least uncontrolled — of the unbuilt spaces between such planned site developments and the pre-1954 city. Progressively and inescapably, through such intense pressure, the density of built space and the tightening of urban fabric have joined the former city without interruption to what initially appeared to be semi-rural surrounding suburbs. But uncontrolled housing does not necessarily equate low-quality housing. This can frequently be seen along main streets where plush-looking compartments, usually recessed from the avenue, can be found next to the low-rise houses lining the streets, alleys and *cul-de-sacs*, and replicate a way of inhabiting and organize the phuong modelled on the "36 streets".

Their appearance and layout, as well as the houses' distribution and the siting of their access, would lead to think that such constructions are the outcome of a concerted strategy. However, production owing to informal economy is clearly visible as confirmed by the localization of unbuilt markets.

KTT only differ from the pre-colonial "36 streets" in terms of density — otherwise their rhythm and customs are comparable. The 1986 city — whose customs and built space are strongly appropriated — already reached To Lich River to the west and, to the south of Truong Chinh Boulevard, Minh Khai Avenue, which prolongs the large carriageway running parallel to To Lich River then turns east towards the Red River; a bridge is being planned there according to the latest urban planning master plan.

The Extension of Hanoi after 1986

Independent of urban policy, social forces constantly shape the city's working-class areas and preserve the more ancient ways of occupying space. Their influence is obvious in the abovementioned areas. They are also highly visible through the deep changes which have taken place in the space of one generation in the appearance and organization of some KTT, whose building facades have been thoroughly altered by successive additions — whether they were DIY or structurally grafted. The impact of such alterations is not merely technical, but also sociocultural: when walking along streets that run parallel or across these housing projects, the different ways of living, of making use of the street at the foot of the buildings, and of carrying out one's craft or trade by occupying part of the collectively used public space, one could easily forget that this is a housing estate.

This also comes across through the localization of Hanoi's permanent markets. Covered markets were built by the municipality whilst outdoor markets usually occupy a street or an intersection and block access to anything but two-wheeled vehicles, which are merely tolerated and can proceed no faster than pedestrians. The representation of markets as a whole offers a telling picture of the entanglement of various types of occupation of urbanized space. The first type is characterized by planned housing policy; the second is either a heritage from residual or more or less maintained village structures, or they are an element of response from rural-to-urban migrants compelled to carve out their own habitat due to demographic or conjunctural pressures. In the latter case, they duplicate housing patterns according to techniques already known to them. The use they make of them — whether they concern the structure of the dwelling or the composition of nearby public space — replicates and adapts to their needs patterns described earlier in relation to the "36 streets", with similar use being made of the house and street. We have already indicated the strength of this permanence. Though similar in style to the ancient city, the overall impression is not as intense since these urbanized spaces are more spread out. These site developments were imposed under pressure from users subjected to urban economic necessity.

Markets also indicate the different stages of urban growth. They reveal the scattering of collective housing projects — markets were a basic facility in KTT plans and remain so in *Khu Do Thi (KDT)* — as well as the presence of main roads conveying the spread of controlled urbanization; they also testify to the apparent "filling in" of spaces occupied in a less regulated way, which translates into ways of using public land replicating those of the ancient districts. KTT and built markets underline the tendency of planned urbanization to create radial roads spread out in a fan-shaped layout. Outdoor markets give a more muddled impression: on the one hand, they reinforce the representation of the role of major roads; on the other hand, they make it easier to locate areas of very high population density. This also makes the southern edge of the colonial district more visible and probably maps out a peripheral urbanisation front line which would have been poorly controlled prior to 1954: at that time, itinerant markets formed part of the traditional facilities of nearby villages where rural-to-urban migrants could find low-cost accommodation outside the city perimeter. These villages were later swallowed up by the city. In order to respond to the needs of an expanding — often tenfold — population, they were either altered or partially transformed, or destroyed and recomposed, or else their habitat was densified and reconstructed according to other models. Their markets, however, remained and prospered by diversifying the products on offer.

Although markets are usually fixed points acting as urban markers, more spectacular landmarks have begun to appear across the city in the shape of towers and major building sites, which offer a glimpse of a new dimension in Hanoi's urban planning. Although there has been no clean break with the previous era, the market has been boosted by the country's opening to the outside world and by the State's official endorsement of market economy. Independently managed state enterprises have developed. Trade and private enterprise have been legalized. These days, their dynamism has a deep impact on the landscape and on the management of new extensions, which are characterised by their scope and diversity, large investments and the swift activation of construction: there has been a radical change of scale in the work undertaken in the past few years. There is a huge hunger for construction. In particular, the "new urban housing areas" — *Khu Do Thi* (KDT) in Vietnamese — are currently under construction. However, the newly developed housing estates give a significant place to planned construction of individual houses, which nowadays tend to be paired with collective housing blocks. This low-cost housing is reputed to be better quality than the run-down houses which tens of thousands of people still inhabit. They also grant occupancy status to households who would otherwise be vulnerable to expropriation with no guarantee of compensation. Due to the spread of individual motorized transport, distance from KDT to the city centre is no longer an obstacle to delocalization, which provides better living conditions for individuals and families. The capacity of different neighbourhoods to satisfy the needs of their inhabitants is evolving, such that facilities now combine with integration.

Most innovative is the policy on road infrastructure and other urban networks launched by the state. Its objectives are as follows: a network of radial and transverse roads; two bridges across the Red River in the near future (their construction is part of the new urban planning projects); new luxury residential developments, including "Hanoi New Town" on the road to the airport, which has received extensive media coverage. These new subdivisions implicitly refer to Hong Kong models favouring vertical sprawl, which is not part of Hanoi's culture. One thing is certain: the Vietnamese capital is discovering its outer suburbs and increasingly tends to become a megapolis whose urbanization movement includes its entire region — and even beyond its administrative boundaries. Since less than five years, new residential areas have appeared on the eastern side of the Red River, where a large industrial zone is also being built. This is the first link in a long, discontinuous chain of factories and industrial cities forming a straight line from Hanoi to Haiphong. Could a new linear conurbation appear as in Germany's Ruhr Valley or Manchuria's Laoyang?

The promotional and speculative aspects of this new situation mean that Hanoi's municipality will have to rethink its public road network rationally, signpost it strictly, enforce the highway code, speed up the implementation of its public transport policy, and change the convivial but undisciplined use of public space, especially of the street. The impact of such unprecedented changes urgently needs to be analysed, and the change in the habits of appropriation of urbanized space, which city dwellers will be subjected to as inhabitants, shopkeepers, craftsmen or service suppliers — and mostly as motorcycle users — will need to be examined. There is no doubt that both urban planners and property developers will need to be open-minded about such issues. A thorough understanding of sociocultural issues is required if we are to avoid spontaneous re-appropriation by Hanoians of the seemingly available space left open by these future housing projects, within the loose mesh associated with the establishment of large-scale new developments. A new land regulation, whose implementation decree is not as yet operational, has recently been drawn up to address the issue. However, a code of urban planning is imperative and should not be based solely on pre-existing models used elsewhere, however remarkable they may be. Hanoi's past way of functioning requires awareness-raising from a multiplicity of perspectives; which should be undertaken with a clear understanding of the issues as well as a solid dose of humility and stringency, not through rigid ideology.

The urban policy currently underway aims to turn Hanoi into a modern, well-functioning capital in tune with the requirements of international trade.

The Urban Context of a Mutating City

Urban transformations in Hanoi today are all more or less linked to the new public road network projected by the master plan to be completed in 2020. Long deprived of means and resources, Hanoi is now carrying out works on a previously unparalleled scale, thus propelling itself into a new phase of its history. The diversity of works undertaken reflects a proactive and determined modernization policy: industrial zones, a new road system, dredging and development of the lakes, organization of an urban public transport network, new residential areas, major installations, etc., as well as new land regulation. Vietnam's economic situation since its integration in the world market has triggered a change in the scale of financing, implementation and management of new urban projects. The Vietnamese habit whereby individual sectors work in isolation is being altered: these projects are more integrated and bring together new multi-disciplinary teams.

A New Master Plan for the Public Road Network

Analysis of the public road network is based on available maps. Maps of Hanoi for a study on the scale of the conurbation are relatively rare. In addition to the master plan for 2020, only three maps show with reasonable clarity the current public road network or projects currently underway.[8] The first, dated 1992 and 1:10000 in scale, is published by the Vietnam Department of Geography. It offers a reference overview of the network on the scale of the area urbanized at the beginning of *Doi Moi*. On the second map, published by TRAMOC and IMV[9] within the framework of the Asiatrans 2002 project, the public road system is represented on the same scale and in its most up-to-date state. But despite its precision, the fact that certain areas of the city are not represented undermines its usefulness. The last map used is the latest tourist map for sale in Hanoi, titled "Where Hanoi" and published by the House of Cartography on a scale of 1:25,000. It includes the city's ambitious road system projects. This particularly meticulous edition was the image map of Hanoi displayed for the 22nd "*Seagames*" (*Southeast Asian Games*) which took place in the Vietnamese capital in late 2003. As it is first and foremost a tourist map, road proportions are not accurate; however, it does convey the real or desired importance of each street. As for the master plan, it offers an image of the desired city; this 1:25,000 map is primarily a zoning of projected extensions and land use based on the future public road network, whose structure, however, is not easily discernible.

Combined analysis of these maps and of our observations in the field reveals a type of organisation of road network in the conurbation of Hanoi built around a system of ring roads and radial main roads or urban motorways. This pattern outlines a "half spiderweb" centred around the historic city[10] and attached to the Red River. Its circular roads are captioned as "Ring Roads" and other roads directed away from the city centre are captioned as "Main Road". They are presented as urban or suburban boulevards about fifty metres wide. The trend thus seems to be towards progressive introduction of this type of very wide roads without questioning their traffic efficiency or their alignment.

Flyovers also form part of the works carried out to fulfil the 2020 master plan. So far three of them are operational: the first crosses the Red River dyke and provides access to Chuong Duong Bridge, Gia Lam District and the road to Haiphong; the second, on Highway One, crosses over a street which is due to become Hanoi's second ring road; the third is on the road to the airport and crosses over Cau Giay Boulevard, a major urban motorway at the western entrance of the city.

The construction of these flyovers and the type of new urban boulevards being built essentially takes into account the traffic function of the street; their outward aim is to unblock major congestion in the city centre and improve circulation between the centre and the outskirts.

Due to very high population density in urbanised areas, to city dwellers' high mobility and to an inadequate public road network, traffic problems are making urban and suburban travel increasingly difficult. Traffic congestion at rush hour lasts longer and occurs more frequently, which paralyses circulation.

Observations on traffic trends in Hanoi[11]

Leaders of the Hanoi People's Committee Management Unit for large-scale urban development projects are concerned about the uncontrolled motor traffic situation on the streets of Hanoi. In order to deal with the issue, they have established a list of priority actions whose cost they estimate at US$1,333,333 (VND200,000 million in 2003) and requested partial financing from the Japanese bank JIBIC. The execution of these projects will result in 20,000 displaced persons needing to be rehoused. The municipality uses compensation grids, but these are different for public road works, which offer better financial or material compensation as they are considered to be in the public interest. Compensation of dispossessed households is a sensitive issue. There have been instances when its importance was underestimated and became the main reason for axing certain projects. The fact that the authorities are now regulating this issue and including its costs in the financing of projects shows their determination to carry out and complete public road works planned for 2020.

Works on the Water Network

Three of the city's major lakes, Thien Quang, Giang Vo and Thanh Cong which collect wastewater, are currently being cleaned up. Thien Quang is located south of the colonial district. Since the 1940s, the lakeside has been developed into a public promenade integrated within the city. The two other lakes are located within KTT collective housing neighbourhoods in Hanoi's inner-ring suburbs. With these large-scale projects came infrastructure installations: water supply stations and renovation of the lakes in order to provide adequate capacity for drainage of nearby neighbourhoods. However, lack of separation in these sewerage systems has turned the lakes into repositories of wastewater which they are unable to absorb.

The current situation of the water system has resulted in the progressive disappearance of several lakes of various sizes, both in the centre and in the outskirts. Some lakes have nevertheless acquired urban status, thus ensuring their durability. In such instances, the lakeside has been developed and houses along the lake have increased in value.

Moreover, a large-scale project is under consideration for a 200-hectare park to be established in a low-lying area south of the city currently occupied by large lakes. Again, the major part of their expanse would be filled but a few lakes in the centre would be developed.

Some rivers, such as To Lich and Kim Nguu, are having their banks canalized and cemented in concrete and their bed cleaned up. The municipality might consider cleaning up Hoan Kiem Lake. Its symbolic value as the heart of Hanoi encourages the city's inhabitants to pay attention to its environment.

Khu Do Thi: The New Housing Areas

Active production of collective housing began in Hanoi straight after independence. The first reason for this was the influx of new city dwellers come to work for the administration and State enterprises that had to find accommodation in the capital of the new Socialist Republic of Vietnam. Demand was so high that construction of these housing complexes was not even interrupted during American bombing. Following the downfall of communism in the USSR and in Eastern Europe at the end of the 1980s, the economic crisis provoked by the disintegration of COMECON (or MEAC — Mutual Economic Assistance Council) reverberated in Asian brethren countries. The Vietnamese government rapidly withdrew its collective housing programme. Previously built housing was sold as property to the inhabitants under the condition that they should take responsibility for its maintenance.

Only recently has the Vietnamese government rekindled its construction activities through a complete overhaul of its housing policy.

Khu Do Thi were thus created, together with independently managed state enterprises responsible for the new housing programmes. The latter manage their assets so as to make profitable investments in the very short term, as would a private company. As a result, the new residential area programmes differ widely from their KTT predecessors. Flats available in the new high-rise *Khu Do Thi* buildings offer a much larger inhabitable surface than ratios in effect in KTT or in the cramped lodgings of the city's overpopulated central districts. However, the spatial and architectural quality of these flats remains largely questionable.

Most KTT were built for a very specific population — usually government employees, workers or members of the military. Some buildings were reserved for postal or ministry employees, or for the workers of a nearby factory. Such flats were part of the benefits weighed against low wages. Nowadays, priority allocation of housing in KDT is not as efficient and has no ideological or social basis, despite the claims of the companies that build them. Flats are not rented but sold before construction work has even started on the buildings. Although these constructions belong to the public sector, they enter the realm of private speculation as soon as they are first sold. Current demand for housing is such that speculation is taking place around the sale and resale of these flats. As a result, their price quickly increases two- or threefold.

Moreover, despite being devised and implemented by the KDT management company, social equipment and services linked to housing are built after the residential buildings and sometimes even after the inhabitants have moved in. Public enterprises often request inhabitants' financial participation in order to speed up construction, which is usually held back by slowness of payments from the municipality.

These new neighbourhoods are organized around facilities such as parks, nurseries, schools, administrative offices, etc. This is similar to Soviet planning methods, which Vietnamese urban planners acquired when KTT were first conceived. There is nevertheless one non-negligible difference: no markets have so far been planned in the KDT, whereas they were often central to the KTT.

As with social equipment and services, infrastructure installations are conceived by public enterprises after agreement and approval from supervising authorities (Ministry of Construction, Ministry of Finance and municipality). Investment for public road works within the boundaries of the new urbanization area will not be paid for by the municipality as had initially been planned. As with the KTT, these developments are sited on former farmland declared "new urbanization area" by the municipality, and in districts having recently acquired urban status (*quan* and no longer *huyen*). They are planned near an existing road, which is sometimes widened, or near a newly built road which they are connected to. They form part of the urban sprawl of Hanoi's suburbs, composed of KTT, former villages, major installations, residual farmland, industry and now KDT.

Some buildings in the earliest such projects (especially in the Dinh Cong *Khu Do Thi*) suffer from numerous faults and defects. Demand is very high, and the additional surface afforded by these flats is enough to convince their future inhabitants, who seem to consider such deficiencies to be minor issues. For instance, inhabitants have to install their own air conditioning. Water management is not collective. The maintenance of collective buildings should be taken care of through inhabitants' financial participation. Such arrangements remain theoretical, and lack of sufficient management might well result in severe dysfunction in the very short term.

Methods of production are also regulated in theory, but vary widely according to the clients' requirements.

A municipal decree exists which bans construction of compartments in these new districts.[12] They nevertheless remain the housing model of choice for a large part of the urban population. The decree therefore seems to remain a dead letter considering the number of compartments planned and built in *Khu Do Thi*, not to mention the individual urban dynamism which uses and abuses this type of highly popular construction.

Restructuration of KTT

Certain methods apply the same process as the phased community rehousing programmes commonly used in France in the 1960s and 1970s, when similar issues arose regarding the renovation of low-cost collective housing which had become obsolete. Some viewed these methods as brutal, and they are indeed expeditious. In any case, they testify to the authorities' intention to renovate, improve and expand working-class housing without displacing the inhabitants. One such project is currently underway in Kiem Lien: the inhabitants of four-storey blocks remain in their current lodgings while two new twelve-storey buildings are being erected; once the latter are completed, the inhabitants of the smaller buildings will be rehoused on the lower floors, in lodgings strictly equivalent in surface to the former. The four-storey buildings will then be destroyed, which will free up new equipped space for the construction of four eighteen-storey and twenty-two-storey towers.

Other Projects

The master plan shows the city extending far beyond the Red River. Although few projects have been implemented so far compared to the provisions of this plan, some of them include:

- the project for "Hanoi New Town" currently under consideration in cooperation with a Japanese investor. This new town is located on the other side of the river, on the road to the international airport, and aims to be pluri-functional, grouping together housing, facilities and services, industries and businesses; different types of housing will be available in each neighbourhood: collective buildings of various heights as well as villas. Existing villages will be integrated into new low-density planned housing areas;
- Gia Lam industrial zone on the road to Haiphong and Thanh Long industrial zone on the road to the international airport both house domestic and international companies;
- The international airport was already expanded in 1999. Work continues as part of a wider development project financed by the Japanese, and will eventually integrate this installation within the nearby industrial and technological zone.

Alterations to De La Thanh Road

After having briefly summed up the stages, conditions, and socio-political and urban characteristics of Hanoi's urbanization, it would be useful to delve into the history of this dyke rampart. De La Thanh became a city boundary, then an east-west transverse frontage road joining a highly structured city to its more uncertain extensions, before turning, through necessity, into the alignment of a semicircular road, which — besides its function as a link between neighbourhoods — is the dividing line between the twentieth century city, with its culturally internalized architecture and patterns of urban composition, and the decisively oversize twenty-first century city. Construction work on this road — due to become a large boulevard sited in an already highly urbanized environment — will require solving a number of sociocultural and technical issues characteristic of the difficulties raised by the construction of a network of primary roads in Hanoi.

Yet the transformation of this small capital into a large vibrant metropolis rests on the creation of infrastructure for attendant roads and other urban networks. The history of De La Thanh is an example of the urbanistic shock and its social and architecural repercussions which Hanoi must deal with in order to achieve successful integration into market economy and globalization.

Establishment of a Circular Road on the Former Dyke Road, De La Thanh

Current Situation

De La Thanh Road links the Red River dyke — southeast of the historical centre[13] — to Cau Giay, the "Paper Bridge" on To Lich River. It then continues as Cau Giay Boulevard, then as the road leading to the international airport. It goes through the urban districts of Hai Ba Trung, Dong Da and Ba Dinh, and leads to Cau Giay, which became an urban district in 1999. Its total length is 7.7 kilometres. Depending on it condition, its width varies between 2.7 metres and 50 metres, as we will see.

Etymology

De La Thanh Road is a road on a dyke (*De* means dyke in Vietnamese, but the word is also used to describe a street or road functioning as a dyke, as the two are often combined in this country of rice paddies). The Red River plain, where Hanoi is located, is organised around this type of infrastructure enabling the irrigation of large polders: control and distribution of water is of prime importance for any agricultural or human facilities in this deltaic landscape.

La Thanh means "outer wall". The character *La* is used to designate an enclosed or circular space; the character *Thanh* means "fortification" (the same root is found in the Vietnamese word for city: *Thanh Pho*). This terminology is used to describe the early fortifications built on the site of Hanoi, before the capital was settled there in 1010. In 767, Chinese governor Zhang Boyi erected a new citadel north of To Lich River and named it La Thanh. During the Vietnamese Hung kings' uprising, the Chinese had to rebuild the citadel several times. In 806, another Chinese governor, Zhang Zhou, named the citadel he had just built south of To Lich River — on the final site for the city — An Nam La Thanh (Papin 2001). The term *La Thanh* was then used for the outermost wall. It was presumably called "dyke of the outer wall", De La Thanh, because it was contiguous with Kim Nguu [golden buffalo] River dyke and thus became an outer wall.

Through part of its alignment, this road forms a point of contact between the colonial city's southernmost edge and the inner-ring suburb urbanized after independence. Throughout the rest of its alignment, it goes through the inner-ring suburb. As a result, it runs through and serves a diversified urban fabric composed of:

- former villages swallowed up by the city (Kim Lien, Trung Tu, Giang Vo, Thanh Cong, Tran Khat Chan);
- extensions of the colonial city between the civil servant district, and Bach Mai university and hospital (former René Robin hospital);
- large KTT collective housing developments: Kim Lien, Trung Tu, Thanh Cong;
- facilities complexes: universities (transport, polytechnic, industrial arts, culture), national television, Russian diplomatic quarter.

There are two reasons for choosing to study this road rather than any other urban road: its transverse position connecting two centres of urban dynamism, and its ambivalent status as a road currently undergoing transformation.

The structure of the public road network, in Hanoi's master plan for 2020, presents De La Thanh Road as an urban boulevard and the first ring road in a system of four to circle the historical centre. As it stands today, the entire road has not yet been turned into this projected circular road. Each stage of its evolution can be observed along its various sections. Because of its length — over seven kilometres — and the methods used to turn it into a boulevard, work cannot be carried out simultaneously over its entire length. Consequently, the successive stages of the road's alteration coexist. Urban recompositions incidental to the road system project are thus easily identifiable.

As it is located near the ancient centre and runs through the inner-ring suburbs, this main road will act as a privileged connection between the southern part of the colonial district and the western part of the inner-ring suburbs. These two areas have been hubs of intense urban dynamism in the past few years. Indeed, in the past four years (1999–2003), four primary network roads have been engineered or widened around the former southern colonial boundary formed by De La Thanh Road; eight towers over fifteen storeys high are under construction and entire districts are being restructured (the areas around Bach Hoa university and Bach Mai hospital; a new park is being developed…) and renovation of two large KTT is being planned. In the second area, west of the inner-ring suburb, new construction also testifies to the scale of changes underway: five major road construction projects have been completed between 1999 and 2003 (the extension of Lieu

Giai Street opened in November 2003); more than ten towers over fifteen storeys high are under construction and six more already exist, as well as ten others between ten and fifteen storeys high built between 1997 and 2000. At present, traffic between the two areas is problematic. One of the issues at stake in the engineering of this ring road will consist in balancing the bipolarity created by those two hubs, with De La Thanh Road acting as the future axis for development.

A Dyke Turned Boulevard

Very early on, despite not being located in the historical centre, De La Thanh Road played a structuring role within the urban system. It is commonly agreed that the city was founded in 1010 under the Ly Dynasty (1009–1225). After a premonitory dream, Emperor Ly Thai To transferred the capital to Hanoi's current site. At the time, the city was composed of the imperial citadel, which included the palaces, and the civilian city, itself composed of quarters dedicated to crafts, trades or agriculture. The new capital's boundaries were set by three rivers: the Red River to the east, To Lich to the north and to the west, and Kim Nguu to the south. The dykes containing these rivers thus became fortifications and were erected alongside trenches filled with water. De La Thanh Road formed the southern edge, part wall and part dyke protecting the city against the waters of Kim Nguu River.

Throughout its history, De La Thanh Road has gone from being a path on a dyke to a colonial road, still within a rural landscape, then progressively became urban and aquired a commercial function as it ran through increasingly structured areas. Today, it is being turned into a boulevard, one section at a time. It may have lost its function as a dyke, but its alignment has remained unchanged throughout its slow evolution.

The Dyke Road Seen through Cartograph

The dyke road has been in existence ever since the city was first founded. In order to understand its historical development, we have analysed its representation in the cartography of Hanoi. We restricted ourselved to historical maps contemporary with the major stages of Hanoi's growth.[14]

The dyke appears on the reconstituted map of 1470, on which feature the successive city walls: the first walls surround the citadel — the seat of political, military and administrative power; the second walls are much wider and encircle the citadel, villages and their *finage*,[15] as well as significant elements in the landscape such as pagodas and mounds. De La Thanh Road appears as a dyke whose western-most section constitutes part of the second wall. There are several theories regarding the city's progressive shift to the east. On this map, the outer wall does not yet include the area between the river and the citadel (today's "36 streets"), nor the Temple of Literature, nor other temples and pagodas of prime importance. De La Thanh Road, however, remains a dyke throughout its entire alignment, and thus protects this *extra muros* area. On this map, the entire outer wall is called De La Thanh.

When the French settled in Hanoi in 1873, the dyke connected the "Paper Bridge" [Cau Giay] on To Lich River to the Red River. It features on Pham Dinh Bach's map[16] and is named after the outer wall on which the southern part of its alignment is juxtaposed. This second wall has shifted several times, always according to the dyke's alignment. The centre of Hanoi is particularly detailed on this map, which remains precise for the part that interests us: around De La Thanh Road. The legend shows three gates along this wall: Cho Dua gate (coconut market); Kim Lien gate on the Mandarin Road, with the mention "swamp"; and Cau Ren gate. Kim Nguu River features in the legend Song To Lich as follows: the Mandarin To Lich, sent by the Chinese emperor to be governor of Annam under the Duong, dug a canal around the dyke of the Ly and named it after himself.

As the first master plans of the colonial period were either improvement or development plans, the roads and highways department played an essential part in their elaboration. In 1890, the development plan was mapped out by staff from the roads and highways department under Leclanger's leadership.[17] It has two main points of interest: first, it determines with precision, both physically and administratively, the southern edge of the city on De La Thanh Road, while showing its state in 1890. Secondly, it documents the first developments carried out by the French, and the colonial grid project south of Hoan Kiem Lake, following the direction of Paul Bert Street (current Trang Tien street), the main artery connecting the French concession on the bank of the river to the citadel (turned into the French military quarter). This plan represents De La Thanh Road as the boundary between the city and the countryside. Districts facing the city (Thanh Tri and Thanh Hoai) are designated as *huyen*, the name used for rural districts: four gates located on this border are clearly indicated. Only the villages situated inside the city wall are represented. None of those holding an ambiguous position in relation to the dyke is featured. For instance, the *extra muros* grouping of houses of Trung Tu village, which is represented on the 1873 map, does not appear on this plan. Moreover, there is no indication that circulation might be possible on the dyke. Its representation near the gates make it look more like a fortification, but at the western end of the city wall, a path (currently Giang Vo) connects to it as it would to a traffic lane.

The 1924 development plan drawn up by Ernest Hébrard[18] does not seem to include any particular strategy for De La Thanh Road. However, the planned network of public roads connecting the centre to peripheral spaces comprises a series of urban motorways crossing De La Thanh Road. This new network project covers a large part of an area which has not yet been urbanized.

According to this dynamics, during the colonial period, the urbanized area extended progressively towards the south of the Vietnamese city (originally composed of the citadel and the "36 streets") and reached increasingly close to La Thanh dyke. In the 1940s, the city crossed over the limit formalized by La Thanh dyke. This was the era during which major installations, including the university campus and René Robin Hospital (nowadays Bach Mai Hospital), were built on either side of the Mandarin Road leading to the southern provinces. On this particular site, urban extensions tended to consist more in setting up facilities and equipment which would become anchor points for the new agglomeration centres — and which to this day still mark the landscape — rather than in the development of "suburbs" or in the annexation of village space. The development plan drawn up by Pineau in 1943 fully integrates La Thanh dyke within the city.[19] Since some of its segments are already considered as boulevards, he projected to widen it throughout its entire alignment. But yet again, projected alterations are not specific to this road; they are part of the setting up of a network, together with numerous other roads on the outskirts close to the city centre. Projected alterations to La Thanh dyke are the consequence of its integration and connection into the network of roads as suggested by the architect.

From the end of the Indochina War, the brand new government's fledgling institutions started drawing up development plans with the declared intention of turning Hanoi into a socialist and modern city.

The development plan drawn up with the assistance of Soviet urban planners, "*Hanoi General Plan of City up to Year 2000*", and published in the 1984 atlas of Hanoi, envisaged building a series of ring roads around the historical centre[20] according to a concentric logic. La Thanh Road would be widened and its alignment altered in places (running north rather than south of Thu Le park, which would be turned into a zoological park) so as to form the first of these ring roads. This plan was not implemented, and the direction of following master plans corresponds to the existing alignment.

The 1986 plan, mapped out by the Vietnamese department of cartography, is, to our knowledge, the last representation of the city before economic opening, *Doi Moi*, and before the Vietnamese capital entered the realm of world metropolises. It offers an account of the situation before ulterior architectural and urban reconfigurations started taking place. It is thus a reference document for the study of Hanoi's contemporary transformations. It includes in particular the numerous lakes and canals along the dyke road: they can be found near Cau Giay Bridge, in front of Thanh Cong village, near Cho Dua market, between Kim Lien village and the collective housing area of the same name, and partly along Dai Co Viet Boulevard. They are the last remnants of Kim Nguu River, which ran parallel to the dyke. In those days, although urbanisation had largely crossed over to the other side of La Thanh dyke, the latter weaved its way through a heterogenous and low-density urban fabric (alternating between villages, farmland, floodplains, housing projects…). The section between Lenin Park and Tran Khat Chan Street is the only one serving more densely populated spaces, in the exact place where the first peri-urban colonial installations had been developed, near the old Mandarin Road.

De La Thanh Road through the Master Plan

Although successive master plans followed different and sometimes conflicting directions, the development and widening of De La Thanh Road were never questioned. It is one of the recurrent elements in these projects.

In the latest master plan, which maps out the city for 2020, De La Thanh Road is presented as a wide urban boulevard connecting the "Paper Bridge" on To Lich River to the Red River dyke, going from Cau Giay District through the districts of Ba Dinh, Dong Da and Hai Ba Trung. This new circular road is supposed to improve linkage between areas in the centre and the suburban districts, where issues concerning the contemporary city are being played out. As an added benefit, this new road provides a direct connection to the road to the international airport.

The office of Hanoi's chief architect has produced a representation of the 2020 master plan on the scale of each district. It is far more precise than the 1:25,000 map on the scale of the city; however, it is merely a zoning showing functional allocation of land similar to a plan of intention. It offers guidelines and directions regarding the district's future development but no precise information on projects: it displays an image of the future city.

The boulevard's development will take place in stages. The Ministry of Construction is responsible for the project. Work is being carried out by large state or international enterprises through complex financing packages involving local government, the state and foreign capital. The Japanese are actively investing in expensive infrastructure work and — via banks such as JIBIC — financing the construction of bridges, streets, and neighbourhoods for rehousing displaced populations.

Resistance from local government has been a powerful obstacle on certain sections of De La Thanh Road, where work was either slowed down or efficiently opposed. This is still the case for the section where the dyke runs alongside Kim Lien and Trung Tu. Disposessions and compensations, which are often subject to negotiation with the concerned parties, increase the financial cost of such works. As a result, planning of the circular road's execution must remain adaptable so as to avoid creating too many tensions with the inhabitants. Flexible planning is needed in addition to flexible finances.

Conclusion

Hanoi is a city with a long history, whose population has always displayed a strong attachment to its customs and traditions, as well as an enterprising and undisciplined spirit. Such personality traits are deeply rooted in city dwellers' behaviour and were perpetuated under colonial rule and through half a century of anti-colonial, civil and international war. They live on in the lifestyle of today's city.

Attachment to tradition and the ability to integrate outside influence have enabled the preservation of the commercial part of the ancient imperial city, even though it has been much altered and densified through the decades. Its way of life endures and its heritage is now listed. The patterns of urban composition, the conception of housing, and a particular way of inhabiting remain sturdy referents in many of the neighbourhoods scattered on the outskirts of the colonial city; they infiltrate villages swallowed by urban expansion, penetrate collective housing projects — the oldest of which are half a century old — and are sometimes reproduced in the recent extensions. Attachment to traditions has also engulfed the French urban legacy, which today is well integrated and claimed as national heritage.

Demographic pressure has resulted in the extension of the city's urban perimeter from the first days of the country's independence in 1954 and even under American bombing. The driving force of this new phase of urbanization, which took place under emergency conditions and with very limited means, was the development of KTT, large collective housing projects built around facilities essential to their functioning and to the need of their inhabitants. The public road network was rationally extended to serve the KTT. This also enabled access to a multitude of villages on the outskirts which had already begun to accommodate a migrant working population before 1954. The Vietnamese enterprising spirit was thus put into practice through a very empirical type of urbanism, on which models imported from the USSR also exerted a strong influence.

Doi Moi has given free rein to the entrepreneurial spirit of a population who has been quick to adapt to the rules of capitalism as implemented in the officially socialist republic. State enterprises managed with relative freedom have started up a new urbanism of networks, covered by an all-conquering road system and signalled by buildings of varied workmanship coming out of the ground along the options of a master plan which, for the time being, looks like its objective is to create intensive urban sprawl in the spaces opened to concentric urbanization. Widespread construction fever is erecting a new generation of compartments borne of the private initiative of a multitude of small property developers. They exist alongside and compete with *Khu Do Thi*, the new generation of low-cost housing areas. Finally, separate suburbs seem to be in the making through massive intervention from a few big companies. And let us not forget the projected bridges and motorways reaching beyond the city of Hanoi, forerunners of the Red River Delta's forthcoming urban organization.

We have kept to describing the current situation: the importance of the urban transformation underway, the resistance of populations inconvenienced by these changes, the Hanoian population's ability to maintain its customs, as well as the trends of an affluent generation which is taking shape and opening up to the rest of the world. Our approach has been very down-to-earth. It is obvious to us that the streets and dwellings they serve or sustain have made, and will continue to make, Hanoi. It is also obvious that intimate appropriation of the use of urbanized space by city dwellers — both as individuals and as a whole — acting to maintain the usage of a firmly cultural everyday life, is the *sine qua non* condition which will allow the project-based urban planning currently at work in Hanoi to result in an actual improvement of living conditions. The new city currently emerging is not guaranteed to keep the promise of social and economic development under control.

Notes

1 Mythical being, part human and part horse, which according to legend lived in Thessalia in ancient Greece. The Centaur symbolizes the strength of the warrior and the horse's velocity. The motorcycle seems similarly grafted onto the modern-day Hanoian, who cannot go further than a few steps without riding his rickety mount.

2 From 1940: Japanese Occupation; 1946–54, Indochina War; 1964–75, Vietnam War; 1978–79, conflict with Cambodia; 1979, armed conflict with China; 1991, peace agreement with Cambodia and normalization of relations with China.

3 This is especially the case in the working-class but commercially attractive neighbourhoods of old Hanoi.

4 This is a quote from Le Ba Thao (1997, p. 300). For data regarding the ancient part of Hanoi, we mostly refer to the edition of *Docteur Hocquard* (1999) with an introduction and notes by Philippe Papin of the Ecole Française d'Extreme-Orient [French School of Asian Studies]. We have also used various maps published in a special issue of the *Cahiers de l'IPRAUS* (Clément et al. 2001).

5 We came to this conclusion through our discussions with several senior officials and Vietnamese university professors during informal, non-protocolar meetings. This is also corroborated by the *Cahiers de l'IPRAUS* on Hanoi published in 2001 during the French Architecture Institute exhibition.

6 The Renovation, *Doi Moi*, was proclaimed in 1986, but only started being implemented at the beginning of the 1990s.

7 Incidentally, this type of housing is not specific to socialist countries.

8 Because of Hanoi's extraordinary vitality, maps and plans are constantly being altered.

9 TRAMOC is Hanoi's public transport company and IMV is the Cooperation Centre for Urban Development (Institut des Métiers de la Ville), the outcome of a cooperation between Hanoi People's Committee and the Ile-de-France region.

10 Composed of the "36 streets", the citadel and the old colonial quarter.

11 These observations are based on a November 2003 interview with Duong Thi Vuong, acting chief of the Department of Category 1 Projects, Hanoi management unit for large-scale urban development projects, Hanoi People's Committee.

12 Decree no. 123/2001/OD-UB, signed 6 December 2001. Section 7 states that new neighbourhoods (*Khu Do Thi)* should comprise 60 per cent collective buildings over nine storeys, and 40 per cent villas with garden. The second paragraph of this section stipulates that there should not be any construction of compartments in these new neighbourhoods. ("Compartments" are typical penetrating contiguous houses widespread in Hanoi and Ho Chi Minh City).

13 Historical centre: see note 10.

14 We have used the inventory of maps of cities of Asia Pacific established by Nathalie Lancret at IPRAUS; and in particular, the 2001 CD-ROM "Hanoi, The City In Maps, 1873–1943", in collaboration with the French Centre of Overseas

Archives [Centre des archives d'Outre-Mer] and the archive centre of the French Architecture Institute.

15 *Finage*: this French geographical term describes the area within the boundaries of a jurisdiction or parish territory.

16 This map represents the city in 1873. It was published by the Indochina Geographical Department in 1916. Original document, 1:25,000 (no graphic scale), on paper, colour representation, northwest orientation, note "approximate scale 1:25,000", the legend includes four categories: Gates (1-16), monuments (17-74), concessions (a-g) and citadel (A-R), two sheets (map and legend), dimensions: 68 x 65 cm.

17 Plan of the city, 9 April 1890, mapped out by Leclanger, head of the municipal roads and highways department, republished in November 1924 by l'*Éveil économique de l'Indochine*. Original document, 1:10,000 (graphic scale included), on paper, colour representation, north-east orientation, note: "in conformity with the general alignment plan approved on 9 April 1890". The legend includes information on constructions pertaining to the colonial order (1-50), brick constructions and thatched huts, public and religious buildings, road and water networks, as well as the site's geographical characteristics. Dimensions: 77 × 63 cm.

18 Ernest Hébrard was chief architect of Civilian Buildings and National Palaces and the first chief architect of the French Central Department of Architecture and Urbanism in Indochina in 1923.

19 Louis Georges Pineau was a first class architect of Indochina's Public Works Department from 1930 to 1945 and assistant director of the French Central Department of Architecture and Urbanism in Hanoi in 1941 and 1942.

20 According to this layout, the historical centre spread far to the north and included Tay Lake.

References

Cerise, Emmanuel. *Hanoi: Ville et habitats*. Mémoire de TPFE à l'École d'architecture de Nancy sous la direction de Marie-Josée Canonica, 1999, 220 pp.

Chardonneau, François and Do Hau (dir.) *Hanoi, enjeux modernes d'une ville millénaire*. Montréal: Éditions Trames, Faculté de l'aménagement, Université de Montréal, 2002, 270 pp.

Clement, Pierre and Nathalie Lancret (dir.) Cerise, Emmanuel, Dominique Delaunay, Ines Gaulis and Lisa Ros (collab.) *Hanoi. Le cycle des métamorphoses. Formes architecturales et urbaines*. Paris: Éditions Recherches, IPRAUS, 2001, 351 pp. (Les Cahiers de l'IPRAUS, architecture, urbanistique, société).

Culot, Maurice and Jean-Marie Thiveraud (dir.) *Architectures françaises outre-mer*. Liège: Éditions Mardaga, 1992, 407 pp. (Collection villes).

Decoster, François and Djamel Klouche. Hanoi, dynamiques urbaines, fragments de mutation. Rapport de mission, 1995, 333 pp.

Études vietnamiennes, no. 48 Hanoi (1), *Des origines au 19e siècle*. Hanoi, 1977, 190 pp.

Hocquard, Docteur. *Une campagne au Tonkin* (présenté par Philippe Papin). Paris: Éditions Arléa, 1999, 683 pp.

Le, Ba Thao. *Vietnam, the Country and Its Geographical Regions*. Hanoi: The Gioi, 1997, 617 pp.

Logan, William Stewart. Hanoi — *Biography of a City*. Seattle WA: University of Washington Press, 2000, xvi–304 pp.

Papin, Philippe. *Histoire de Hanoi*. Paris: Fayard, 2001, 404 pp. (Histoire des grandes villes du monde).

3

Intra-Urban Mobility in Ho Chi Minh City and Hanoi

Patrick Gubry
Le Thi Huong
Tran Thi Thanh Thuy
Nguyen Thi Thieng
Pham Thuy Huong
Vu Hoang Ngan

Ho Chi Minh City and Hanoi are the two largest urban centres in Vietnam as far as population and economic potential are concerned. In recent years, population growth has been a major factor in the economic growth of these centres. However, in both Ho Chi Minh City and Hanoi, the hike in population is causing critical problems in the urban development process. As these cities grow, so does the movement of people in them.

Intra-urban Movement

There has been a tremendous increase in population movement in Vietnam since 1986, when an economic liberalization policy (*Doi Moi* or Renovation) began to be implemented. Although considerable research has already been done on the migration aspect, there is still not a clear understanding of mobility within the major centres, with a particular focus on the two largest ones, Ho Chi Minh City (overall population of 5 million with 3.7 million in the urban area in 1999[1]) and Hanoi (overall population of 2.7 million with 1.5 million in the urban area). A positive migration balance from the city centres to the suburbs has been observed, based on the two most recent censuses, one conducted in 1989 and the other in 1999. There is a considerable increase in intra-urban mobility in the wake of fast-track urbanization, and this is becoming a key urban planning consideration. This evolution and the policies implemented are impacting the living space of citizens in terms of environment (suggesting improvement) and are tending to increase routine travel distances (suggesting deterioration).

Such intra-urban mobility (that taking place within the administrative limits of the two cities) includes on the one hand intra-urban migration or residential mobility (changing one's residence within the administrative limits), and on the other hand temporary mobility, including commuting movements.[2] This is tending to accentuate the inadequacy of urban infrastructure and transit because of increasing the density of suburban zones, which are the least affluent. Indeed, urban infrastructure work in Ho Chi Minh City and Hanoi is not only obsolete to a considerable extent, which has been pointed out many times previously, but also unequally distributed geographically and by force of circumstances, often non-existent in recently urbanized suburban zones.

The patterns of such internal mobility, the evolution of the daily needs of the people as a function of the modification of their living space, in a foreseeable context of strong urban growth and increased metropolising, are therefore major problems to be studied and taken into consideration in the urban planning process.

A targeted research based on a household survey

The research project on "intra-urban mobility in Ho Chi Minh City and Hanoi", carried out in the framework of the Urban Research Programme for Development [*Programme de Recherche Urbaine pour le Développement* (PRUD)] was a cooperative project linking the Institute for Economic Research of Ho Chi Minh City, the Population Centre of the Hanoi National Economics University (PC) and the Paris *Institut de Recherche pour le Développement* (IRD), working as a team with a comparative intent (Gubry et al. 2002, 2004 and 2008).

An original methodology using a household survey in the two metropolises of Vietnam was used in order to significantly reduce the cluster effect that was largely ignored in the past.[3] Indeed, a two-tier survey approach, with a random sample including a systematic drawing, was used for the first time to deal with the very tight "division into blocks" phenomenon in the urban milieu. Tier 1 of the survey thus enabled us to take directly into consideration the blocks (*to dan pho*), much smaller in size than the wards (*phuong*) or communes (*xa*), the units immediately below the district, urban and rural respectively, which had generally been used up to the present. The list of households was then established in the field in selected blocks.[4] The survey covered 2,000 households (8,623 people) in Ho Chi Minh City and 1,500 households (5,971 persons) in Hanoi, selected by draw at tier 2. The survey was conducted in March-April 2003.

The household survey aimed at the commuting movements and temporary comings and goings of the population, as well as migration history. It enabled information to be gathered on the characteristics of the household and the population, non-migrant and migrant households, the migration history of recent migrants, short-term travel patterns, opinions on routine travelling and future migration plans. The questionnaire associates quantitative and qualitative data. These movements are increasing in size with the very strong urban growth that is foreseeable in the two large metropolises in Vietnam in the years to come.

An additional analysis of the 1999 census results focused on migration shifts (changes of residence within the administrative limits of the two centres).

1999 Census Findings: A Population Shift to the Suburbs

The census is an irreplaceable tool for the study of migrations (changes of residence), including the smallest geographical areas, since by nature it is exhaustive, save for mistakes made in data collection. A census makes it easier to study immigration into a given zone (wherein the immigrants are concentrated) than emigration out of the same zone (which process disperses the emigrants among all the administrative units of the country, or all countries of the world for that matter).

In Ho Chi Minh City (HCMC), if we take the population aged five or older in 1999, 83.7 per cent were already living in the same district in 1994, five years earlier, 6.7 per cent were living in another district of HCMC, 9.3 per cent lived in another province and 0.2 per cent abroad.

In Hanoi, the corresponding figures are as follows: 87.7 per cent of the inhabitants lived in the same district of Hanoi in 1999 as in 1994, 4.0 per cent lived in another district of Hanoi, 8.0 per cent lived in another province and 0.3 per cent abroad. Overall, the population is seen to be a little more "stable" in Hanoi, which has had a growth rate slightly lower than that of Ho Chi Minh City.

In various other countries, according to local conditions and specificities of the cities, as a rule people moving into major centres select either the downtown core or the suburbs. In Vietnam, there is a very clear trend for immigrants to prefer the districts immediately around the downtown core, both in Ho Chi Minh City and Hanoi. In HCMC, 62.3 per cent of the immigrants between 1994 and 1999 were living in the following seven districts (in descending order, including districts that took in at least 5 per cent of the migrants): Tan Binh, Go Vap, Thu Duc, Binh Chanh, Binh Thanh, 12 and 9. Three of the five new "urban" districts (*quan*) are on this list (Thu Duc, 12 and 9). In Hanoi during the same period, 70.7 per cent of immigrants lived in the following five districts: Dong Da, Cau Giay, Hai Ba Trung, Thanh Xuan and Tu Liem. This includes two of the three new districts (Cau Giay and Thanh Xuan).

The population census is also a tool for the study of intra-urban migrations within the broad administrative boundaries of Ho Chi Minh City and Hanoi.

In both of these cities, movements are only significant in the central districts and the immediate surrounding districts. There was very little change in the rural zones between 1994 and 1999 with regard to movement of people aged five or older in Cu Chi, Nha Be and Can Gio Districts (in Ho Chi Minh City) or Soc Son District (in Hanoi). We are therefore going to focus on the movement taking place in the core area (Figures 3.1 and 3.2).

The existence of a positive migration balance from the centre to the suburbs in both cities is confirmed, leading to a "dispersal" of the population. This shift is mainly due to the increase of the cost of land in the downtown core caused by increased marketing; it is reinforced locally by the "dispersal" or "deconcentration" policies of the municipalities aiming to improve sanitary conditions in certain central zones that are very densely populated and unhealthy.

In Ho Chi Minh City, the zones that have been urbanized for the longest time have become the source zones for intra-urban migration. These are mainly Districts 1, 3, 10 (Sai Gon zone), 5, 6, 11 (Cho Lon zone), Binh Thanh and Phu Nhuan (Gia Dinh zone).

FIGURE 3.1
Ho Chi Minh City: Main Intra-urban Migratory Movements between Districts from 1994 to 1999 (Population Aged Five or Older in 1999; Net Movements Greater than 1,000 Persons)

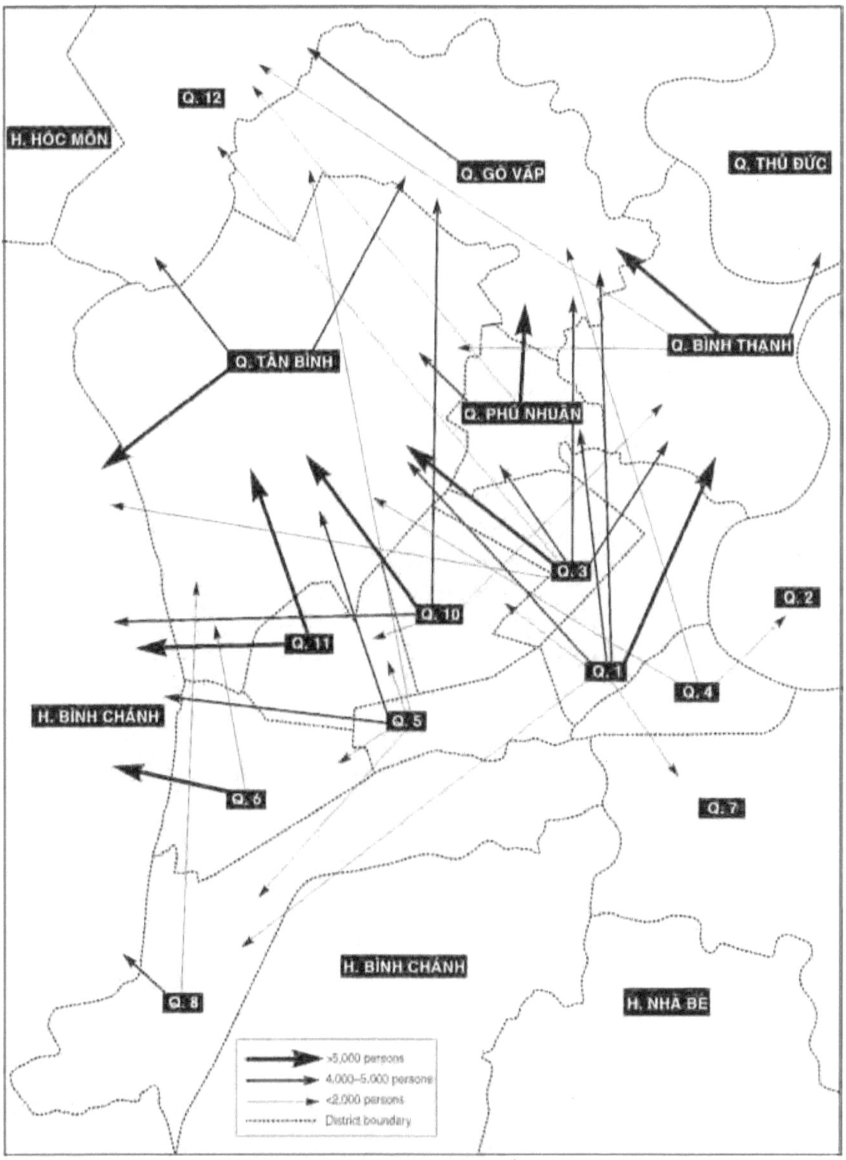

Source: 1999 Census of Vietnam

FIGURE 3.2
Hanoi: Main Intra-urban Migratory Movements between Districts from 1994 to 1999 (Population Aged Five or Older in 1999; Net Movements Greater than 500 Persons)

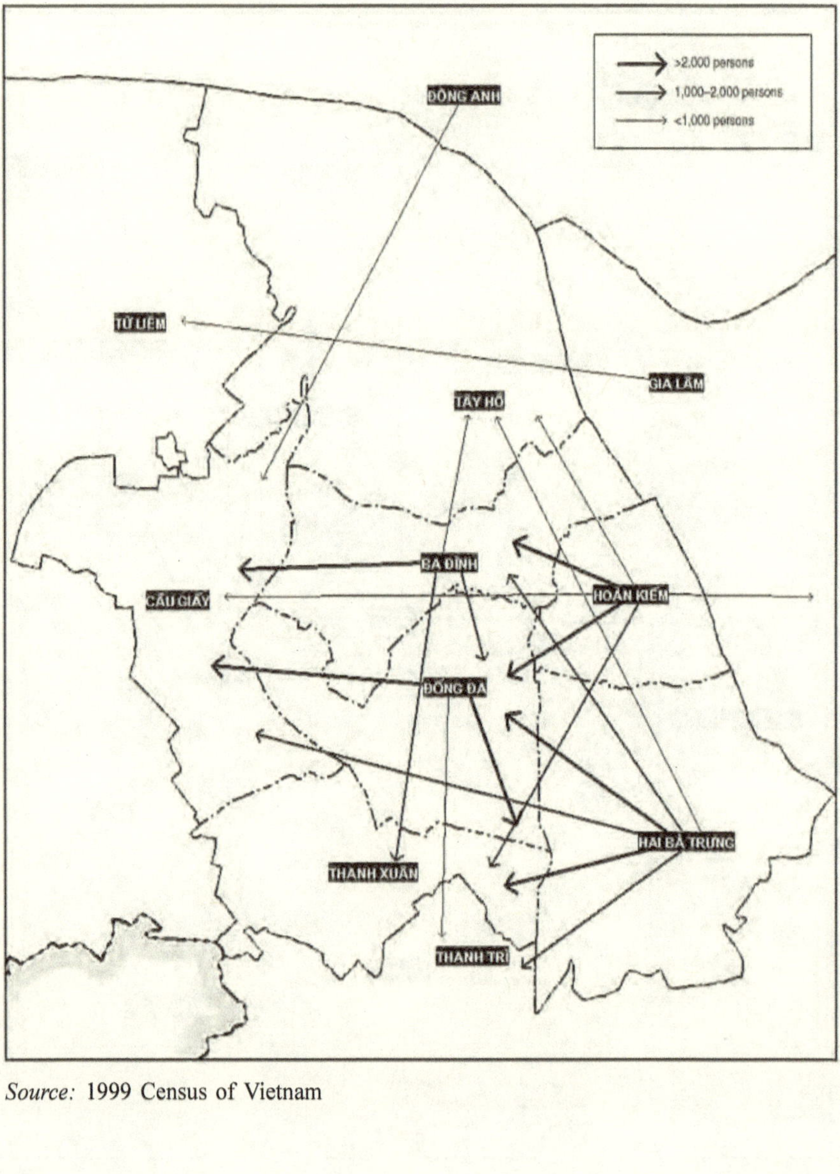

Source: 1999 Census of Vietnam

The districts to which these people are moving are located in the very close periphery of these central districts, be they "urban" such as Tan Binh (agricultural and military land that has recently been subdivided or collective housing) or "semi-urban" such as District 12 (individual houses), or "rural", such as Binh Chanh (new industrial zones and collective sub-divisions that are being urbanized very quickly). The attractiveness of "new" zones observed is due to many job opportunities being available in industry, such as Thu Duc District and District 7 or District 2, with its residential vocation including the Thu Thiem project, for example. However, the impact of the "Saigon South" project development in District 7 and Nha Be and Binh Chanh Districts had not yet become visible at the time of the survey.

District 8 and Binh Thanh District are zones of both immigration and emigration. The reason for this would require a study at the ward (*phuong*) level, for people are moving out of some of them and moving into others. These districts are also transit zones toward districts further removed from the centre, such as Go Vap (for Binh Thanh) and Binh Chanh (for District 8) as the price of land continues to skyrocket.

Interestingly, District 4 appears to have been "repulsive" from 1994 to 1999, with no inward migration due to the major environmental problems encountered between the port zone and the many industrial establishments.

In Hanoi, the phenomenon of population dispersal was also seen in the oldest central districts (Hoan Kiem and Ba Dinh), in which land prices have become prohibitive. The evolution is differentiated in the other central districts. Hai Ba Trung District is experiencing a certain loss of interest in favour of Dong Da District, which is reputed to be more up-scale and closer to the centre, while prices have not gone as sky-high as in the older quarters. This would indicate that people have been "selected" due to an increased income differentiation. Dong Da is seen to be a transit zone, receiving migrants from the central districts and Hai Ba Trung while sending people who are less affluent to the suburban districts of Cau Giay and Thanh Tri.

Generally speaking, districts located close to the centre are in-migration zones: Thanh Tri, Thanh Xuan, Cau Giay and Tay Ho. Among them are found the three new "urban" districts.[5]

A look at a number of key geographical indicators for the greater urban communities of Ho Chi Minh City and Hanoi reveals very strong convergences, which may appear surprising at first glance for two cities that are differentiated by many socioeconomic and geographical features, not to mention the history of each one that was radically "separate" for a long time. But they also show some remarkable specificities.

The main common feature seen here in both centres is the recent "dispersal" of the population from the downtown areas out to the close suburbs.

To a considerable extent, intra-urban mobilities are seen to be a new phenomena in as much as they are most certainly linked to the recent economic liberalization and the social differentiation gradually resulting therefrom.

Both of these phenomena are consistent with an urban recomposition process, the consequences of which in terms of infrastructure and urban transit, for instance, particularly in the peri-urban zone, have yet to be grasped in their entirety.

Characteristics of the Population and Households Surveyed

Social changes invariably influence the nature, characteristics and functions of the family. Since 1975, Vietnamese society has undergone profound changes. Vietnam moved from being a society in a time of war with a planned, centralized economy to a market economy (in rural areas, the family returned to being a unit of production and consumption). The obsolete agricultural economy is being restructured in the direction of mechanization and modernization, accompanied by a net improvement in the living standards, as well as by a rural exodus subsequent to a reallotment of land and consolidation of farms. Changes in activity and income are affecting relationships among household members. The country has left its isolation to rapidly integrate regional and international social and economic affairs. This evolution is causing conflicts among the generations regarding values such as the way of looking at life, how to conduct business, love, marriage, family, and so on. During the last quarter of the twentieth century, especially since the "Renovation" policy began taking effect in 1986, in an indirect way this evolution has radically transformed Vietnamese society. It can therefore be assumed that the Vietnamese family in general and the family in the major urban areas of Ho Chi Minh City and Hanoi in particular, have undergone a profound change: drastic drop in fertility, greater empowerment of women and the beginning of nuclear families with younger generations going off to live on their own.

Demographic and Socioeconomic Characteristics of the Population

An analysis of the population structure by sex in Ho Chi Minh City and Hanoi highlights the following points: in Ho Chi Minh City, females outnumber males (51 per cent), while in Hanoi the two sexes are basically equal in number. Concomitantly, there is a preponderance of females noted among migrants, which is one of the distinctive features of some Southeast Asian cities.

The age structure of the population in Ho Chi Minh City and Hanoi shows similarities: a relatively low proportion of children due to the recent widespread acceptance of family planning, a swelling of the pyramids at working ages owing to rural-urban migration and a relatively high proportion of elderly persons. In both cities, the population is not very young and it can be said that it has started to age (Figure 3.3).[6] In the 0–14 age group, the sex ratio (number of boys for 100 girls) is very high, that is, 111 in Ho Chi Minh City and 119 in Hanoi. This is possibly an indirect consequence of having fewer children, with a selective interruption of pregnancy by couples systematically wanting a boy, as has been noted in many Asian countries (China, India, South Korea, Taiwan, etc.). An in-depth study of the reasons for selective abortions would be necessary to substantiate any affirmation.

The proportion of inhabitants whose place of birth and current place of residence are the same is higher in Hanoi than in Ho Chi Minh City. Only 67.8 per cent of the people in Ho Chi Minh City were born there, whereas the proportion of people in Hanoi that were born in Hanoi is 76.3 per cent. The proportion of married persons is higher in Hanoi than in Ho Chi Minh City, 71.3 per cent compared to 63.1 per cent. Migrants to Hanoi originate from the northern provinces, mostly from the Red River Delta (14.9 per cent). On the other hand, migrants to Ho Chi Minh City originate from all regions of the country, with those from the Mekong Delta making up the majority (9.8 per cent). Next are migrants from the Red River Delta (6.2 per cent), then from the southeastern provinces (4.2 per cent) (Figure 3.4). The appeal of Ho Chi Minh City and Hanoi is due to their better socioeconomic and geographical conditions, for instance, the large seaport in Ho Chi Minh City, the level of investment and size of their labour market.

The law in Vietnam requires that each person be registered as a permanent resident. However, not having this status is no longer an impediment to migration. A person without permanent residential status runs into some minor complications in daily life or is penalized with regard to land or vehicle ownership. The proportion of persons registered at their place of residence is lower in Ho Chi Minh City than in Hanoi (80.7 per cent and 89.9 per cent respectively), which may be due to the fact that this civil

FIGURE 3.3
Age Pyramids in Ho Chi Minh City and Hanoi

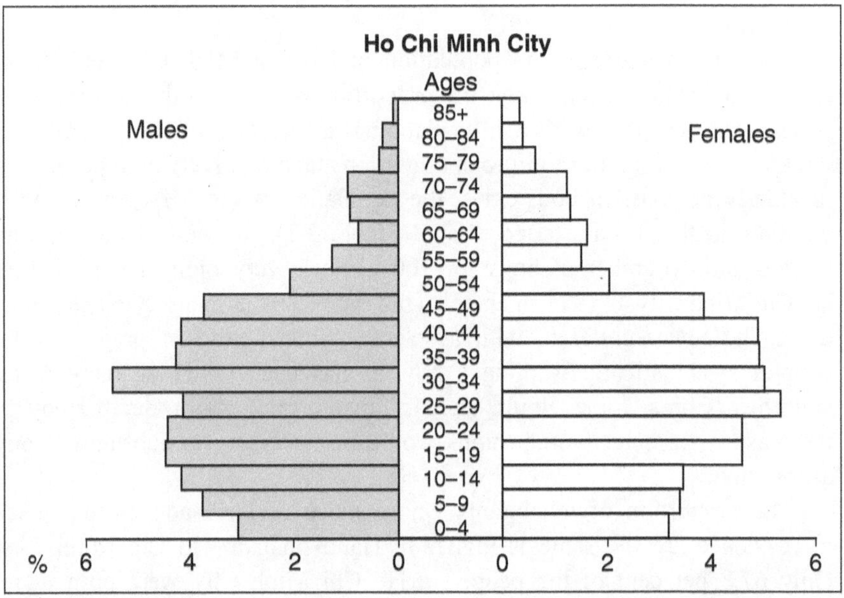

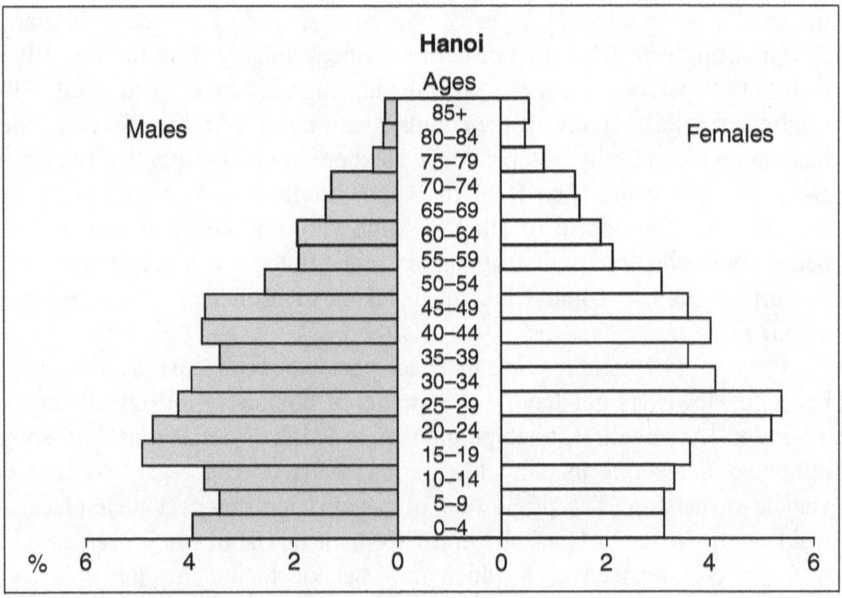

Source: PRUD Project, IER, PC, IRD, 2003

FIGURE 3.4
Distribution of Population Born outside of Ho Chi Minh City or Hanoi by Province of Birth
(% – octagons = abroad)

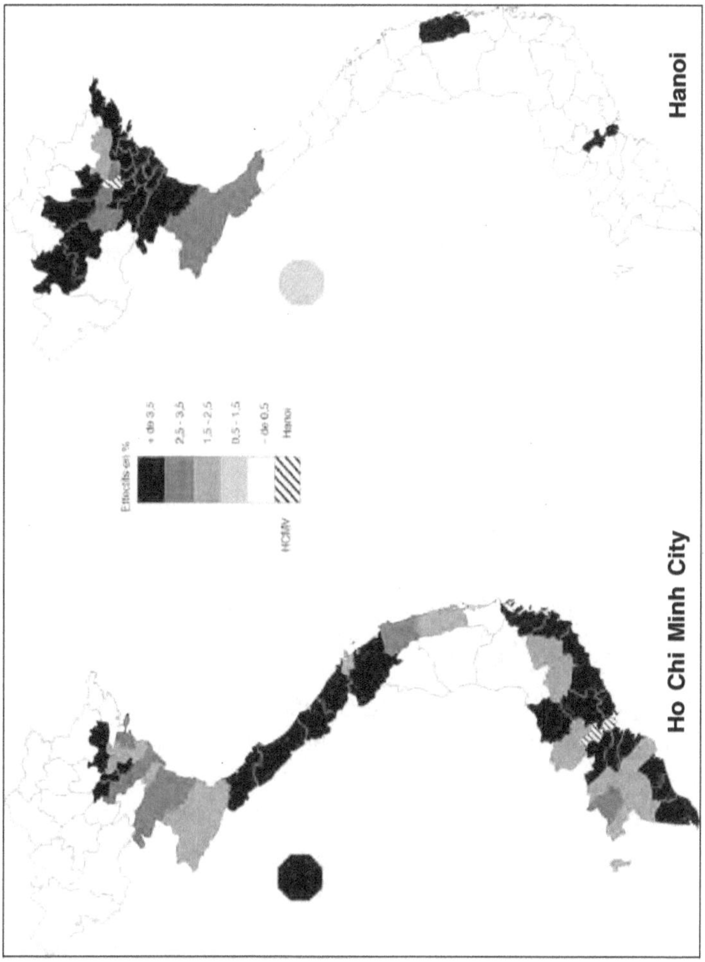

Source: PRUD Project, IER, PC, IRD, 2003 (Map by Yves Blanca, IRD)

formality existed in Hanoi long before it was enforced in Ho Chi Minh City, as well as to the preponderance of the informal sector in the latter city. Nevertheless, there are some characteristics common to both cities: the fast-paced rate of urbanization, the appeal they have for the migrant population and the concern to stem the migration rate.

The average number of years of education is lower in Ho Chi Minh City than in Hanoi (7.1 and 8.5 respectively). The difference in level of education between the two cities is only a matter of concern for individuals aged fifteen or over. The proportion of persons who have gone through higher education is 8.8 per cent in Ho Chi Minh City compared to 19.5 per cent in Hanoi. The average number of years of education drops progressively as one moves out into the suburbs. Generally, the level of education is higher for men than for women and the difference grows wider with age, which highlights the recent progress made in the south in the field of education and the brain drain to the political capital.

The proportion of persons who have no occupational training is 80.0 per cent in Ho Chi Minh City compared to 60.3 per cent in Hanoi. Although the majority of migrants go to Ho Chi Minh City in search of work, the reason most frequently given by migrants to Hanoi is their desire to further their education.

There is virtually no gap between Ho Chi Minh City and Hanoi with regard to the proportion of persons aged thirteen years or over that are working (56.1 per cent and 55.8 per cent respectively). But the proportion of homemakers is much higher in Ho Chi Minh City than in Hanoi (13.3 per cent compared to 3.9 per cent), where a higher number of women have entered the labour force.

In Ho Chi Minh City, industry and handicraft (27.6 per cent), services (20.8 per cent) and business (19.0 per cent) are the sectors that are drawing the most workers. In Hanoi, however, agriculture remains the sector that absorbs most of the labour (24.8 per cent), even though Soc Son District, almost entirely agricultural, was not included in the survey. The public sector (23.5 per cent) comes in second place.

Nearly half of the population 13 years of age or older in Ho Chi Minh City works in family businesses (43.8 per cent), private companies or corporations (27.7 per cent). In Hanoi, on the other hand, the public sector and corporate sector are the two economic sectors that are absorbing most of the workers (58.5 per cent combined). In both cities, workers are mostly salaried employees on fixed-term or open-ended contracts, 58.7 per cent in Ho Chi Minh City and 61.8 per cent in Hanoi.

Household Characteristics: Size and Living Standards

Borne along by social transformations, households are gradually becoming better adjusted to the new social context without completely leaving behind traditional Vietnamese family values. It used to be common for a household to have many children, whereas currently in both cities, the average household size is tending to grow smaller. In Ho Chi Minh City, households with three children or more account for about 28 per cent compared to only 15.1 per cent in Hanoi.

The average number of persons per household is higher in Ho Chi Minh City (4.3 persons) than in Hanoi (4.0 persons). Most heads of households are men, but due to recent historical conditions the proportion of households headed by women remains very high compared to that of other countries. At the same time, the number of nuclear households is high: 55 per cent in Ho Chi Minh City and 62.3 per cent in Hanoi.

In a one-off survey as was this one, specific data on income could not be collected using direct questions. We therefore opted to make an assessment of the living standards by gathering data on the qualitative characteristics of the dwelling and household equipment. Using this as a basis for critical evaluation, we classified the households interviewed into three groups based on their standard of living: low, average and high. The standard of living is seen to be higher in Ho Chi Minh City than in Hanoi: the proportion of households with a high standard of living in that city is 14.7 per cent compared to only 11.4 per cent in Hanoi. On the other hand, households with a low standard of living in Ho Chi Minh City and Hanoi are rated at 37.3 per cent and 39.6 per cent respectively. In both cities, the further out one goes into the suburbs, the greater is the proportion of households that have a low standard of living. There is a noteworthy difference between the two cities: in Ho Chi Minh City, the proportion of households with a low standard of living is much greater among households of persons who migrated in the last five years than among non-migrants. In Hanoi, the opposite situation exists because migrant households have a better standard of living. In both cities, the proportion of households enjoying a good standard of living is higher for migrants than for non-migrants.

While wanting to avoid stereotyping, several characteristics often reported regarding the way of living and thinking of the inhabitants of Ho Chi Minh City and Hanoi are nevertheless found between the lines, notably the industrious aspect of the economic capital and the intellectual role of the political capital. Other differences surface when the migrations are studied.

Residential Migrations: What Prompts Them, How They are Carried out and Their Consequences

Nuances between the Two Cities Regarding the Motives and Manner of Migration

A difference is observed between Ho Chi Minh City and Hanoi with regard to the motives for migration. In Ho Chi Minh City, starting up a new household is the reason most frequently given for migrating. In Hanoi, people move in order to have a bigger house (27.4 per cent); these households have increased their living area considerably. The most remarkable increase is noted for households that, prior to migration, lived in the central districts. In both cities, the desire to live close to one's place of work is the second-most frequent reason for moving, 13.2 per cent in Ho Chi Minh City compared to 14.5 per cent in Hanoi. The advantages are many, including a saving of time and money and less fatigue. In Ho Chi Minh City, the third-most frequent reason for migrating is the desire to own one's own home. In this city, many households wish to become homeowners and consider land and a home as very valuable assets.

In Ho Chi Minh City as in Hanoi, intra-urban migration takes place essentially between the central districts. This is explained by the advantage that these districts offer as far as social, economic and cultural infrastructures are concerned in relation to suburban and rural districts. Intra-urban migration is also taking place from the central districts to suburban districts, 8.1 per cent in Ho Chi Minh City compared to 11.0 per cent in Hanoi. Migration between suburban districts is higher in Hanoi where 12.2 per cent of households have made this choice. In Ho Chi Minh City, 10.0 per cent of migrant households have chosen a rural district as a place to move to compared to 2.2 per cent in Hanoi.

Improved Living Conditions for Migrants after Migration

Many questions were asked regarding the nature and quality of the housing, as well as regarding comfort considerations. In both instances some changes were experienced subsequent to intra-urban migration.

Housing

The great majority of housing is in the form of townhouses or rows of attached dwellings, often referred to as "shop houses" (84.7 per cent in Ho Chi Minh City and 52.0 per cent in Hanoi). In Hanoi, the proportion of independent houses is higher than in Ho Chi Minh City. The difference in the level of housing between non-migrant and migrant households is only sensed in Hanoi, but as a general rule more migrants live in apartment buildings than non-migrants. In Hanoi, 22.9 per cent of migrant households live in apartment buildings, which is 2.8 times higher than in Ho Chi Minh City. In Hanoi, compared to the situation prior to migration, it is observed that migrant households have frequently left an apartment, such as in a KTT (*Khu Tap The*, public housing unit), for a townhouse. Such things as expropriation, property inheritance and the desire to own a home explain this change.

Most houses in both cities are located in lanes that are less than 4 metres wide (house on a narrow lane). In Hanoi, the proportion of houses on narrow lanes is higher than in Ho Chi Minh City. There is no difference with regard to the location of the dwelling between migrant households and non-migrant households in Ho Chi Minh City. In Hanoi, the proportion of migrant households with a house on the street and those of migrant households owning a house on a narrow lane is dropping, whereas that of households with a house on a wide lane is increasing. The desire to enjoy more comfort or to live in a dwelling that is more in harmony with what one's aspirations, are also reasons for migration.

The proportion of dwellings owned outright is 92.0 per cent in Ho Chi Minh City and 88.6 per cent in Hanoi. It is lower for migrant households, although the percentage of ownership increases significantly when they move. In Ho Chi Minh City, the proportion of migrant households that rent a house from a private person is higher than in Hanoi. In Hanoi, the living space has clearly increased after migration, from an average of 56.5 square metres per household to 89.4 square metres. On the other hand, there is no big difference in living space before and after migration in Ho Chi Minh City. The increased living space is linked to the increase in the number of rooms. For migrant households, the proportion of one- or two-room homes is dropping, while that of homes with three or more rooms is increasing.

Regarding housing quality, there is a big difference in the materials used in the two cities. In Ho Chi Minh City, most roofs are made of sheet metal, walls with brick or more basic materials such as bamboo or wood. In Hanoi, roofs are most often of concrete construction (usually in the form of a roof terrace), with the walls of brick.

Dwellings have an independent kitchen in 71.0 per cent of cases in Ho Chi Minh City compared to only 43.9 per cent of cases in Hanoi. Furthermore, in Hanoi 30 per cent of households have a kitchen separate from the living area. There is a preponderance of combined toilet-washroom facilities inside the dwelling. In Ho Chi Minh City, the proportion of separate toilets in the dwelling is greater than in Hanoi. As far as kitchen and toilet facilities are concerned, migrant households report a higher level of comfort compared to their previous situation.

Streets and Public Utility Hook-ups

Street quality is not as good in Ho Chi Minh City as in Hanoi. In the latter, streets are better in the new places of residence. In Ho Chi Minh City, migration is not necessarily synonymous with better infrastructure. At the present time, infrastructure is still poor in rural districts. Yet, given the fast pace of urbanization, migrant households anticipate that the streets will be improved in the near future.

As many as 18.5 per cent of households in Ho Chi Minh City compared to 13.5 per cent in Hanoi live in zones subject to flooding due to rainwater or river overflow. It is sometimes difficult to distinguish the respective role of rainwater or river overflow: in Ho Chi Minh City, rainwater causes major flooding at the time of high tide, which reverses the flow of the river. Migrant households have often chosen a site less subject to flooding due to rainfall. With regard to flooding caused by river overflow, the proportion of households affected does not go down, but rather increases slightly after migration. In addition to the weakness and deficiency of the water drainage system, the topography of both cites is rather flat, which is not conducive to good drainage.

Virtually all households in both cities are connected to the national electricity grid, be it formally or informally, but scarcely half of them have a water tap inside their dwelling. The situation of migrant households differs between the two cities. In Ho Chi Minh City, the use of piped-in water in migrant households is less than that of well-water due to the ongoing deficiency of the water supply facility in suburban and rural districts. In Hanoi, the proportion of migrant households having a water meter is higher than that of non-migrant households and overall, a greater number of households use piped-in water after relocating. This is to be seen in the light of the fact that a lower proportion of households settle in suburban areas.

There is home refuse collection in 87.0 per cent of cases in Ho Chi Minh City compared to only 56.6 per cent of cases in Hanoi, where a high proportion of households have to take their refuse out to a disposal point. The proportion of migrant households making use of collection networks increases after relocation, particularly in Hanoi.

Household Appliances and Power

The acquisition rate of household appliances (iron, telephone, fan, etc.) is similar in both cities. As for means of transportation, motorcycles and bicycles are strongly predominant in both cities (Figure 3.5, following page): in Ho Chi Minh City, more people own motorcycles than bicycles (58.8 per cent compared to 38.8 per cent); in Hanoi, the figures are almost identical for both methods of transport (48.7 per cent compared to 49.5 per cent). The proportion of households owning a motorcycle or a car increases after migration.

Migrants have a rather Positive Opinion Regarding Intra-urban Migration

The very great majority of households surveyed feel that their overall situation improved after migrating in the city. But these feelings need to be qualified.

Education and Training

In both cities, most migrant households feel that they enjoy more advantages as far as education is concerned since their migration, to the extent that the distance between home and school has been lessened, and the quality of instruction in the new place of residence is better. Moreover, having a quieter, roomier place to study is another advantage for migrant households in Hanoi. Among households that state that migration did not bring about any change in the study conditions of their members, most are currently living in the central districts of the two cities.

On the other hand, with regard to healthcare, leisure, quality of the streets and traffic conditions, there is a contrasting situation between the two cities.

Health

Migrants in Ho Chi Minh City point out that they encounter more problems in the area of healthcare, as some of them want to continue getting treatment from the same establishment as before, which means that they have to travel longer distances. In Hanoi, the situation in this regard has improved after migration.

Leisure Activities and Entertainment

Migrants in Hanoi have easier access to parks, cultural and arts centres and libraries than those in Ho Chi Minh City. Places of leisure such as cultural

FIGURE 3.5
Means of Transportation Available in Households in Ho Chi Minh City and Hanoi (%)

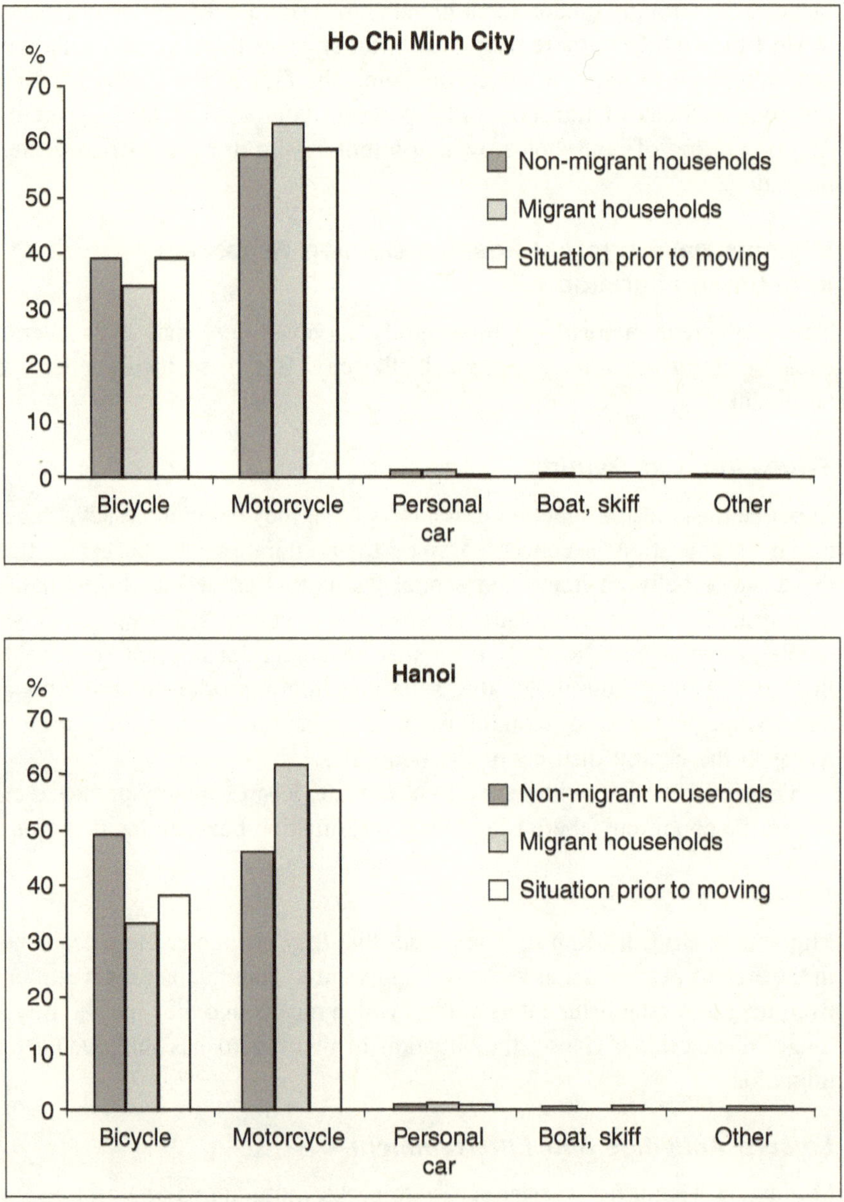

Source: PRUD Project, IER, PC, IRD, 2003

centres and parks are often located in the central districts. Households living in the suburban and rural districts therefore find it more challenging to take advantage of these services.

Street Infrastructure and Traffic

In the area of infrastructure and traffic, migrant households in Ho Chi Minh City report that conditions are worse, while those in Hanoi report an improvement. This reflects the situation in the preferred target districts.

Changes in Employment and Place of Work

In Ho Chi Minh City, the proportion of persons who changed their place of work after migration is higher than in Hanoi. Persons who changed their place of work have a lower level of education and vocational skills than those who did not change. Fewer people working in the tertiary sector changed place of work compared to other sectors. In the informal sector, people working for sole proprietorship or family-owned private companies changed their place of work more frequently.

A change in place of work proved to be advantageous for workers in many ways. In addition to higher pay (an advantage that was mentioned frequently), they enjoy other benefits such as a shorter distance between their place of work and place of residence and now their work is more interesting.

Short-term Comings and Goings

An analysis of daily travel patterns is a priority matter for the different activity sectors as well as governmental authorities at all echelons, all the more so because traffic congestion, pollution and sound nuisance are worsening in Vietnam's major cities. At the same time, an increase in distances has an undeniably negative impact on living conditions.

Reasons for Leaving One's Home

During the survey, a preliminary question was asked to isolate the types of travelling done throughout the week: "For what reason did you leave your home yesterday?"

The reasons for leaving one's home were put into nine categories, with a tenth category for persons who did not leave their home (Table 3.1).

TABLE 3.1
Reasons for Leaving One's Home during the Day Preceding visit of the Interviewer by Sex and City (%)

Reasons for leaving one's home	Ho Chi Minh City			Hanoi Raw data			Hanoi Weighted data*		
	Aggregate	M	F	Aggregate	M	F	Aggregate	M	F
0. Did not go out	16.4	16.0	16.9	17.4	19.3	15.5	18.7	20.6	16.8
1. Work	46.1	57.1	36.1	44.3	47.9	40.9	43.7	47.2	40.2
2. School/training	13.0	13.5	12.6	14.4	16.3	12.5	14.1	16.1	12.1
3. Take children to school	6.5	5.6	7.3	3.1	2.6	3.7	4.4	3.9	5.0
4. Shopping	21.8	4.9	37.1	21.7	4.6	38.3	22.0	4.7	38.8
5. Visit relatives	3.5	3.7	3.3	4.2	4.2	4.2	4.4	4.2	4.6
6. Visit friends	4.9	6.6	3.4	6.2	7.9	4.5	6.4	8.1	4.7
7. Trip to the clinic/hospital	0.9	0.5	1.2	0.5	0.4	0.6	1.9	1.8	1.9
8. Entertainment	5.1	6.3	4.0	5.2	6.9	3.5	6.5	8.2	4.8
9. Miscellaneous	0.8	1.1	0.5	0.5	0.6	0.5	1.9	2.0	1.7

Classification of reasons for going away from one's home:

0. Did not go out
1. Work (other comments made: business, wholesaling, looking for work partners, looking for work, military training, "I went to work to ask for permission to take time off")
2. School/training (other comment: looking for a place to take training) [this heading included the regular school attended by children and teenagers, refresher education or private tutoring, as well as continuing education in the evening]
3. Take children to/from school/training
4. Shopping
5. Visit relatives [in the city or in the country]
6. Visit friends
7. Trip to the clinic/hospital (other comment: trip to the drugstore/getting medication)
8. Entertainment (comments: bar, "go out for a drink", "go out for breakfast", casual drive, stroll, go out with friends, sports activities, exercises, football, roller skating, tennis, chess, social activities, cultural centre, tourism)
9. Miscellaneous (comments: pagoda, church, funeral, veterans' meeting, ward meeting, "I had to go out to deliver food").

12,009 persons aged 13 or over; several possible responses.
* *Interview schedule identical to that of HCMC*
Source: PRUD Project, IER, PC, IRD, 2003

With the exception of Sunday, over 80 per cent of those surveyed left their homes daily in both cities. The structure of the reasons for leaving is similar in both cities, with a few small differences. The main reason for leaving is to go to work. Interestingly, people go to work practically every day of the week, with only a small decrease on the weekend. Additional reasons included shopping trips, travel to school or to a training course, which includes students and persons enrolled in evening classes. Other reasons for going out such as to visit friends or neighbours, relax, etc., are cited less often. Taking children to school seems to be more common in Ho Chi Minh City, no doubt because the distances in that city are greater, but also because the parents have more means of transportation available. On the other hand, it is observed that a larger proportion of children walk to school in Hanoi. Leisure activities were more common in Ho Chi Minh City, due to the fact that the standard of living is higher, because a person has to have the wherewithal to engage in such activities.

The most interesting findings with regard to reasons for going out highlight the following:

- The fact that the reason for leaving one's home is to go to work every day of the week, including the weekend, shows that there is no let-up in economic activity. This is more so in Ho Chi Minh City than in Hanoi.
- Reasons for going out vary according to sex. Men more frequently say they go out to go to work, while women are more frequently saddled with the traditional chores, like shopping and taking the children to school. Men, moreover, enjoy a considerably higher range of recreational activities such as visiting friends and entertainment.
- Each of the two cities has its own specificities: more women in Hanoi have entered the labour force than in Ho Chi Minh City.

Time, Distance and Distribution of Trips during the Day

Travel times to go to work average 20.3 minutes (min) in Ho Chi Minh City compared to 16.3 minutes in Hanoi (Table 3.2). These travel times are overall quite reasonable considering the sprawl of these cities and traffic problems. Logically, the bigger the city, the longer the travel times will be. The same is true of distances as assessed by the people interviewed.

It is noteworthy that the longest distances are reported for suburban districts, wherein employment opportunities are yet few in relation to the population increase, which means people have to look for work in the downtown area or keep the jobs they had there prior to moving out to

TABLE 3.2
Average Shortest Distance and Average Time Spent Going to Work by Residential Zone and City

Residential zone	Ho Chi Minh City		Hanoi	
	Distance (km)	Time (min)	Distance (km)	Time (min)
Central districts	4.91	20.0	4.24	16.2
Suburban districts	5.10	20.3	5.08	19.1
Rural districts	4.50	20.2	3.29	15.4
Aggregate	4.88	20.6	3.97	16.3

Source: PRUD Project, IER, PC, IRD, 2003

the suburbs. Distances are shortest in the rural districts, where a farming population still prevails and where fields are located close to the homes of the people.

The average time spent going to school is 14.7 minutes in Ho Chi Minh City compared to 15.2 minutes in Hanoi. These times are logically less than that of travelling to work because the density of schools is higher than that of businesses or government offices. Travel time increases consistently from the downtown area to the suburbs because of the decrease in density of school facilities. Obviously, this analysis could be made as a function of the type of school the pupil or student is attending.

Distances travelled to attend supplementary courses are seen to be shorter. Logically, a person will select such a course near one's home or place of work. There is often no choice regarding the location of one's place of work and citizens must comply with the school-zone map. Neither of these constraints applies to personal development courses. In both cities, this type of course is more often chosen not far from one's place of work because it is convenient to attend after work at the end of the day. Rural districts are penalized because of the poorer offer in this area.

The analysis furthermore shows that women generally work closer to their homes than men. However, the differences by sex in distances travelled to attend a training session, whether it is a school or personal development course, are not clear.

Figure 3.6 combines the times for the three types of travel that were analysed — going to work, attending school or taking supplementary training. The trips include going both to and from the concerned activity.

FIGURE 3.6
Aggregate Times for Travel to Work, School or Supplementary Courses by City (%)

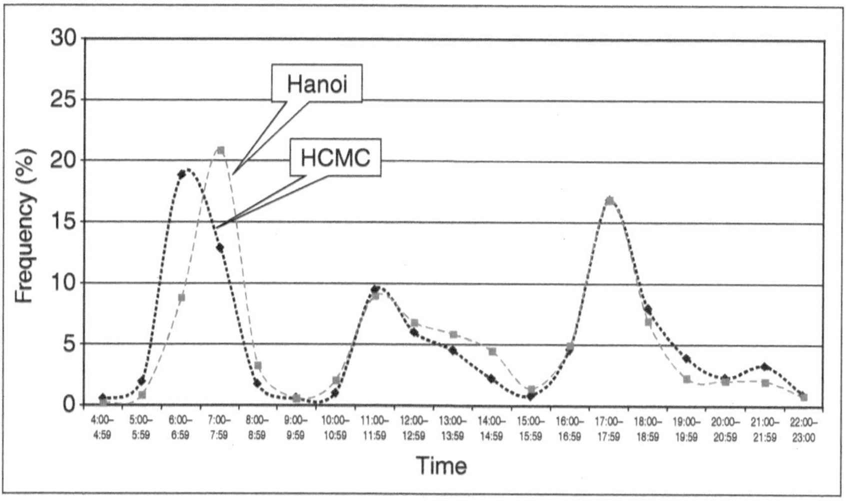

Source: PRUD Project, IER, PC, IRD, 2003

In this way, we obtain a good picture of the rush hours when traffic congestion is likely to be encountered. Three peak traffic times are noted: morning, mid-day and late afternoon. Experience shows that few traffic jams occur in either city at mid-day, which indicates that many people have lunch near their place of work. A ceiling of 10 per cent of people on the streets out of those who travel during the day can be viewed as the minimum limit for the risk of traffic congestion. Under these conditions, it is observed that there is a major risk of traffic jams at the following times: from 6:00 a.m. to 8:00 a.m. and 5:00 p.m. to 6:20 p.m. in Ho Chi Minh City; from 6:45 a.m. to 8:15 a.m. and likewise 5:00 p.m. to 6:20 p.m. in Hanoi. People start travelling earlier in Ho Chi Minh City and traffic continues later. It is observed that there is heavier traffic in the afternoon in Hanoi. The earlier rush hour in the southern metropolis is largely due to the fact that later "winter hours" were in place in Hanoi at the time of the survey. In the late afternoon, peak traffic occurs in both cities at 5 p.m., which is the official closing time of government offices.

Means of Transportation Used

Modes of travel are dominated by personal transportation, mostly motorcycle (75.1 per cent in Ho Chi Minh City, 57.9 per cent in Hanoi). A greater number of people walk or bicycle in Hanoi. The passenger bus has recently come on the scene, with only a 1.0 per cent use in Ho Chi Minh City and 2.3 per cent in Hanoi.

Shopping

Six types of shopping venues were identified: proximity street markets, *ad hoc* sidewalk markets, small neighbourhood markets, larger centrally located markets, small food supermarkets or shops and superstores. The concepts are no doubt not all totally alike between the two cities, because retail superstores did not exist as such in Hanoi in 2003, which at the time had few supermarkets larger than the neighbourhood food store. This question was put to the population aged thirteen or older. The proportion of inhabitants of Ho Chi Minh City that go to proximity street markets is lower than that of people in Hanoi (16.8 per cent compared to 27.0 per cent). Small markets are the daily routine choice in both cities (17.6 per cent in Ho Chi Minh City and 19.6 per cent in Hanoi). The frequency of daily travel to big markets and small food supermarkets is very low. A proportion of 57.4 per cent of people in Ho Chi Minh City and 74.4 per cent of those in Hanoi has never gone to a superstore (supermarket in the case of Hanoi). Women outnumber men in shopping at the smaller markets and are more likely to go to them. This gap narrows considerably for superstores; men willingly go shopping there with their wives and the two of them bring purchases home together, especially because the items are generally heavier. It is thus seen that the higher the standard of living, the greater the measure of equality between the sexes.

Entertainment: Visiting and Leisure

Visiting neighbours or friends is a common practice of the Vietnamese people in both Ho Chi Minh City and Hanoi. It is the most popular activity as approximately 90 per cent of the inhabitants practise it.

Going to the cinema is the most popular form of entertainment, followed by theatre. Yet, no less that 88.1 per cent of the inhabitants of Ho Chi Minh City and 74.3 per cent of people in Hanoi say they never go to the cinema.

Concerts remain low on the entertainment list. The rate of frequenting cultural or youth centres, discotheques and nightclubs is low in both cities. This is also the case for figures relating to neighbourhood activities, going to the pagoda or to church, picnicking and pleasure trips or travel, but these activities have no doubt not always been viewed as leisure.

Frequenting a karaoke parlour is clearly more popular in Ho Chi Minh City than in Hanoi. The same is true for cafes and bars. People in Hanoi prefer going out for a stroll due to the favourable climate that prevails for a greater part of the year, to the urban environment and extension of sidewalks, but also no doubt because it is free. In Hanoi 30.6 per cent of people compared to 18.6 per cent of inhabitants of Ho Chi Minh City practise this activity.

Opinions on Current Travel Conditions

The growth of population and more travel in the urban area are increasingly overburdening the infrastructure and having an alarming effect on traffic and road safety. As for infrastructure, Ho Chi Minh City currently has 0.81 kilometres of streets per square kilometre while the minimum need is between 4 and 6 kilometres per square kilometre.[7] It is noteworthy that in Ho Chi Minh City and Hanoi, the number of individual trips made for the most part on motorcycle, is very high. Added to that, the public transit system in both Ho Chi Minh City and Hanoi only covers 3.7 per cent and 9 per cent respectively of the transportation needs,[8] which are rates much below those of metropolises of similar size in the world.

The survey sample included 12,010 persons aged thirteen years or over (7,111 in Ho Chi Minh City and 4,899 in Hanoi). Among these, only 5,753 were actually at home and could give their opinions (3,423 in Ho Chi Minh City and 2,330 in Hanoi). Based on their residential zone, they can be divided into three groups: downtown, suburban and rural.

In concrete terms, the survey focused on:

- Difficulties encountered in course of travel and the cost of travel;
- Quality of the road network;
- Traffic policing;
- Public transit system, more specifically quality of service provided by these methods of transport.

Difficulties Encountered in the Course of Travel

Surprisingly, the number of persons stating that they do not encounter any problem in course of travel makes up the highest proportion, 44.7 per cent in Ho Chi Minh City and 53.9 per cent in Hanoi. The explanation seems to be that they do not have a great need to travel, they rarely leave home or they use means of locomotion driven by other persons, which means they do not have to deal with the difficulties.

In both cities, the difficulties reported with travelling essentially involve traffic jams and risks of traffic accidents, which account for 34.6 per cent and 20.6 per cent respectively of the opinions expressed in Ho Chi Minh City, and 29.9 per cent and 14.0 per cent in Hanoi. The rapid pace of urbanization, while infrastructure remains inadequate and poorly designed both in Ho Chi Minh City and in Hanoi, explains why traffic jams are the leading cause of concern.

These rather positive findings are due in part to the recent efforts of the two municipalities to modernise and upgrade the quality of infrastructure such as the street network, create new districts, eliminate bottlenecks and distribute traffic streams to promote freer flow.

Generally speaking, people feel that because of congestion and accident risk, travel is more challenging in downtown areas rather than in the other districts. In Ho Chi Minh City, 42.9 per cent of downtown inhabitants complained about traffic jams, compared to only 17.6 per cent and 19.4 per cent of people living in suburban or rural zones. In Hanoi, there is not much of a spread between those living in the downtown core and those in the periphery districts, although it is great between city core dwellers and people in the rural zone (41.6 per cent, 33.7 per cent and 9.5 per cent). People living in rural districts expressed themselves more positively about traffic jams since the population density is the lowest in those districts. But other problems in these districts are viewed as more serious, such as the lack of a bus service.

The cost of travel is not viewed as a real difficulty since only 1.6 per cent of the people surveyed in Ho Chi Minh City and Hanoi commented on it. The 30.4 per cent of persons in Ho Chi Minh City and 33.2 per cent in Hanoi who stated they did not have any travel expenses would mostly be persons working at home, elderly persons or young people whose parents take them to school. In Ho Chi Minh City, the persons interviewed spend an average of 105,500 dong a month on their travel compared to only 72,000 dong in Hanoi. The majority of people stating that they have to pay for their travel (72.3 per cent in Ho Chi Minh City and 84 per cent in Hanoi) spend less than 100,000 VND a month.

Opinions on Street Quality

In Ho Chi Minh City and Hanoi, 36.9 per cent and 36.3 per cent of the population respectively consider the quality of streets as 'good' or 'very good', 16.2 per cent and 16.7 per cent feel they are in 'bad' or even 'very bad' condition, while 46.9 per cent and 44.5 per cent reckon it to be 'average'. In reality, it is difficult to make an assessment of roads that were very recently upgraded, and it is not known to what precise period the opinions expressed applies.

Those who rate the quality of the street network as 'good' or 'very good' reside mainly in the central districts of Ho Chi Minh City (40.9 per cent), while only 29.9 per cent and 28.4 per cent of those living in suburban districts or rural districts share this opinion. In Hanoi, the gap is less prominent. Generally, the quality of roads is not the same everywhere, with investments in infrastructure favouring the downtown area over the suburban area.

Opinions on Traffic Policing

The responses given on this count are rather positive. Respectively 36.5 per cent and 52.0 per cent of persons surveyed in Ho Chi Minh City and Hanoi rate traffic policing as 'good' or 'very good'. Only 5.7 per cent and 6.4 per cent respectively consider it to be 'bad' or 'very bad'.

Those interviewed support their positive assessment with the following reasons: continuous presence and adequate number of officers on duty; effective intervention in the event of traffic jams or accidents; very positive view of behaviour and conduct such as helpfulness and frequent reminders of traffic rules.

Negative assessments highlight problems of partiality and corruption (bribes) on the part of officers, inadequate staffing and therefore a low police presence, and lack of effective intervention in the event of traffic jams or infractions. Affairs involving police corruption are rated to be more serious in Hanoi (25.3 per cent) than in Ho Chi Minh City (9.0 per cent).

Opinions on the Quality of Public Transit

For over a year, in the major centres and in Ho Chi Minh City and in Hanoi in particular, there is a greater routine presence of buses. When asked to express themselves on the quality of public transportation, the majority of citizens find it to be average (58.1 per cent in Ho Chi Minh City and 30.4 per cent in Hanoi). However, 31.4 per cent of those interviewed in Ho Chi Minh City and 55.7 per cent in Hanoi rate it as good or very good. Only 8.9 per cent and 4.1 per cent respectively of the inhabitants of the two cities find it 'bad' or 'very bad'. This is a rather positive appraisal, and the service seems to be more appreciated in Hanoi.

The favourable remarks highlight the number of vehicles (sufficient, meets travel needs), their quality (comfortable, clean), quality of the service (keeping schedule times, good service) and reasonable fares. Among these reasons, bus quality and comfort are most frequently mentioned (45.9 per cent in Ho Chi Minh City and 40.1 per cent in Hanoi), followed by reasonable fares (33.8 per cent and 20.6 per cent), keeping to scheduled times and service quality. These opinions can be explained by the bus improvement strategy undertaken since early 2002 in Hanoi and Ho Chi Minh City. In Ho Chi Minh City, new models that are more powerful and equipped with air conditioning are replacing all of the old buses.[9]

In order to overcome the prejudice of citizens toward buses and improve service quality, the organization of the workload and salaries of drivers and ticket sellers were reformed. The fixed charge system was eliminated so that drivers are no longer obliged to take on the greatest possible number of passengers.[10] In addition to their basic wages, drivers are entitled to bonuses, overtime pay, etc. An allowance for service quality has been put in place. To monitor and assess precisely the performance of drivers and ticket sellers, the Public Transit Company has established a department whose job is to ensure service quality and bus maintenance. The results are used to determine the level of bonuses. That is one of the reasons why users are left with a good impression.

FIGURE 3.7
Opinions on the Quality of Public Transit in Ho Chi Minh City and Hanoi (%)

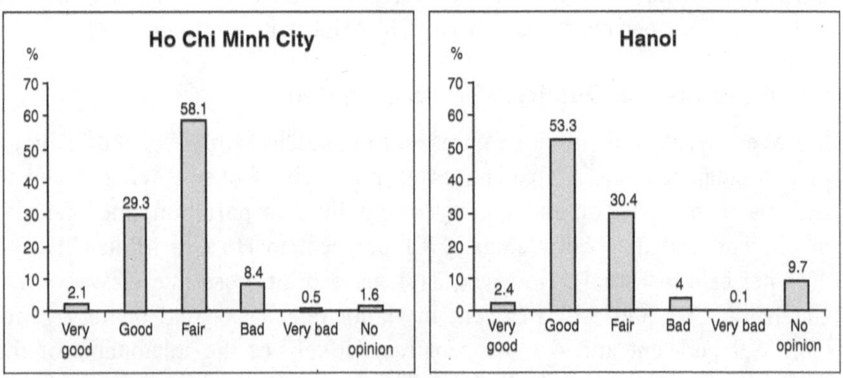

Source: PRUD Project, IER, PC, IRD, 2003

Fares are based on a flat rate (2,000 dong in Ho Chi Minh City and 3,000 dong in Hanoi) and are valid on all lines regardless of the distance.[11] We are left wondering how relevant the single tariff can be for faraway destinations.

As for the negative comments about public transit, in Ho Chi Minh City the highest proportion of opinions (40.9 per cent), were critical of the poor quality of the buses (too risky) and were expressed mainly by people living in suburban districts (46.5 per cent), Recent accidents due to technical problems and age of the vehicles that resulted in personal injury and property damage, were advanced in support of this. The insufficient number of bus lines comes in second place with 18.9 per cent of votes, mainly expressed in rural areas (19.6 per cent). The reality is that there are not yet enough buses to meet the need, which explains the gaps in service.

Downtown residents criticise the poor service (14.8 per cent), irregularity (10.5 per cent) and overcrowding on the buses (6.4 per cent). Also, 8.2 per cent of users complain that the buses are too big for the width of the thoroughfares. There are currently many vehicles with over fifty seats that are hard to manoeuvre in the downtown areas, and this makes it difficult for them to keep on schedule, especially during the rush hours.

Proposals to Improve the Public Transit System

The majority of persons surveyed (39.3 per cent in Ho Chi Minh City and 61.1 per cent in Hanoi) propose an increase in the number of buses, as well as opening up new lines and increasing the frequency of runs to cut down on waiting time and avoid overcrowding the vehicles.

Other points raised involved having bus stops close to residential areas as well as diversifying the modes of public transit. Streetcars and subways would round out the bus network and thus contribute to improving public transit in the two cities.

After comments on various quantitative factors, strong support was voiced for infrastructure modernisation (17.9 per cent and 16.1 per cent of people living in Ho Chi Minh City and Hanoi). Upgrading the quality of the routes would promote the use of buses, currently many of which are considered too cumbersome and harshly criticized whenever traffic congestion occurs.

The quality of service needs particular attention. This was pointed out by 6 per cent of persons interviewed in Ho Chi Minh City and 6.9 per cent of those living in Hanoi. For consistent, quality service, awareness is needed on the part drivers and ticket sales personnel and management must be streamlined.

Respectively 2.7 per cent and 3.8 per cent of people interviewed in Ho Chi Minh City and Hanoi feel that it is necessary to subsidize public transit. The current fare structure indicates that there is already a high level of subsidization, but there is no other choice in order to win users and get people to adopt new travelling habits. Without aiming at full cost recovery, there would be a need to increase fares substantially in the long run, making them more "realistic".

A number of citizens (3.2 per cent in HCMC and 2.2 per cent in Hanoi) underscore the important role of communication between transport companies and the public. The advantages of public transit must be highlighted, and awareness must be raised regarding the traffic code and compliance with it, but using attractive communication techniques. The awareness-raising and information campaign must take an encouraging and informative form and resolutely avoid propaganda. The various media need to be associated in this undertaking.

Future Projects for Residential Mobility

A study of the future mobility plans of people living in Ho Chi Minh City and Hanoi is important for researchers and decision-makers. It will enable them to ascertain the foreseeable evolution of population distribution in both of the two major centres of the country in order to give direction so that appropriate urban planning policies are framed that are in keeping with the way society is evolving.

Given the strong urban growth in both centres, how many people intend to migrate? What reasons are motivating them to migrate? Will those who migrated in the last five years migrate again? What are the differences in the profiles of persons who plan to move compared to those who have no such plan? The analysis of issues relating to the aspirations of the people regarding their future place of residence will enable us to draw some conclusions.

A Limited Number of People Want to Migrate

When asked about their future residence plans, 78.8 per cent of people in Ho Chi Minh City and 80.2 per cent in Hanoi said they had no intention of moving. That is perfectly logical. Moving upsets people's lives. People do not like change, especially as they get older. It also causes problems for children going to school. So if one's current dwelling is not too bad, people generally prefer to stay where they have settled.

The percentage of people who do intend to move in both cities is very low: 9.6 per cent in Ho Chi Minh City and 4.6 per cent in Hanoi, which is half as many. Those currently living in the central districts show a greater desire to migrate than those in suburban districts and rural districts. This can be understood in the light of the tremendous density and overcrowding in a number of central districts in both cities, which prompts people to want more spacious accommodation.

Despite the low proportion of those who express the wish to move, it is noted that those who moved during the last five years ("migrants") are more inclined to think about changing their residence than those who did not migrate ("non-migrants"). This trend is seen in both Ho Chi Minh City and Hanoi. In Hanoi, the percentage is 7.1 per cent for migrants, but only 4.1 per cent for non-migrants. Undoubtedly some of those who have already experienced a move are not fully satisfied with their current accommodation; and if one has successfully moved once, migrating again is not such a frightening thing.

Most People Who Intend to Move are Undecided as to Where to Move

The proportion of citizens who intend to migrate is not only low in both cities, but those who are thinking about it have not yet necessarily chosen their destination (Figure 3.8).

FIGURE 3.8
Destination Contemplated by Those with the Intention of Migrating in Ho Chi Minh City and Hanoi

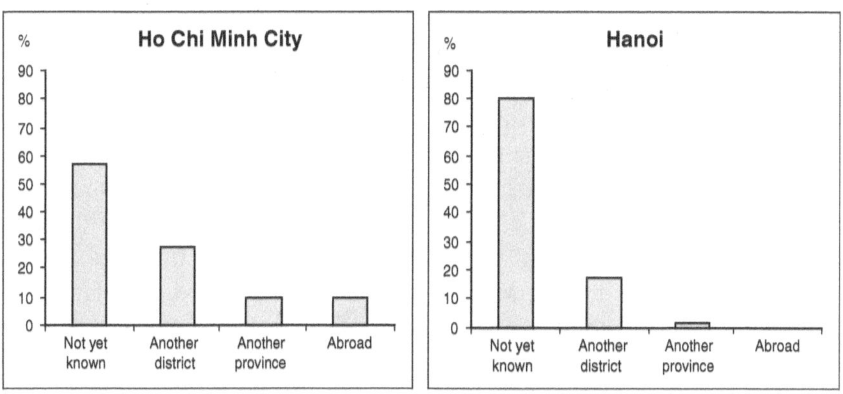

Source: PRUD Project, IER, PC, IRD, 2003

Those who do not yet know where they would move amount to 57.8 per cent in Ho Chi Minh City, but the number is even greater in Hanoi (80.2 per cent). A comparison of those who have already migrated with those who have not yet done so underscores a difference between the two cities. In Ho Chi Minh City the percentage of persons who did not have any idea about their future place of residence is higher for migrants (53.8 per cent for non-migrants compared to 63.8 per cent for migrants). In Hanoi, the inverse is true: 83.3 per cent of non- migrants do not have a clear idea of their future destination compared to only 57.4 per cent for those who have previously moved.

Having the intention to move without yet knowing where can be explained by the fact that the person is not happy with his or her present accommodation, but because of a lack of information or funds, it has not yet been possible to pick a specific location. Suitable accommodation may be too expensive, while accommodation that suits one's available budget is found in districts where the infrastructure needs to be improved.

Central Districts are the Planned Destination for nearly Half of Those Who have Decided where They Want to Move

Among those who have chosen their future destination, many are looking at the central districts. This percentage is 48.6 per cent and 42.7 per cent for Ho Chi Minh City and Hanoi respectively.

In Ho Chi Minh City, 52.2 per cent of people currently residing in the central districts, 19 per cent living in suburban districts and 68.5 per cent living in rural districts expressed the intention to settle in a central district. In Hanoi, these figures are respectively 59 per cent, 8.5 per cent and 36.4 per cent. The central districts are a drawing card because of practical considerations: travel is minimized and the environment is more conducive to business. Services such as markets, hospitals and leisure activities are more developed. Schools in such locations are also highly rated. The trend to migrate into the central districts therefore appears to be logical.

In Ho Chi Minh City, the rural districts do not appear among the choices of those who want to migrate. The reason is that the density of some central districts such as Tan Binh and Go Vap is still low and they are therefore the preferred destinations of those who wish to migrate. In Hanoi, besides the central districts, the suburban districts are also attractive destinations for migrants. Nearly a third (29.8 per cent) of citizens who wish to migrate, would like to settle in a rural district. The urbanization policies for the suburban districts of Hanoi — still often classified as rural in 2003 — are the reason for it. The high urban growth of Hanoi in recent years is drawing people into the suburban districts and rural districts because the cost of land is lower and infrastructure is progressively being upgraded.[12]

Reasons Why People Wish to Change Their Place of Residence

The very diverse reasons for changing one's residence can be put into the following four categories (Figure 3.9):

- Unsatisfactory natural environment
- Family reunification and marriage
- Desire to own one's own home
- Other.

The highest number is for those who intend to migrate for family reunification or marriage: 45.7 per cent in Ho Chi Minh City and 44.5 per cent in Hanoi. The proportion of people wanting to migrate is higher for non-migrants than migrants in both cities: 48.1 per cent for non-migrants compared to 38.9 per cent for migrants in Ho Chi Minh City. The respective figures for Hanoi are 39.9 per cent compared to 43.2 per cent. This is probably due to the fact that when the migrants moved on an earlier occasion, it was for reasons of family reunification or marriage.

FIGURE 3.9
Reasons for Moving in Ho Chi Minh City and Hanoi

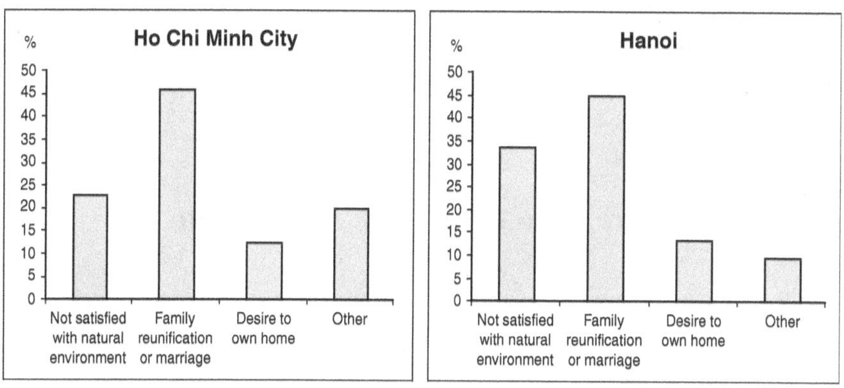

Source: PRUD Project, IER, PC, IRD, 2003

Dissatisfaction with the natural environment (pollution) or social conditions ("social evils", insecurity) is also a major consideration: 22.5 per cent in Ho Chi Minh City and 33.4 per cent in Hanoi. Environment is a very important factor for people today. People in the work force all want to live in a good environment and where people have a high level of education. Security is also essential. Non-migrants and migrants also show differences with regard to the reasons for which they want to migrate. Environment is the reason given by 20.5 per cent of non-migrants compared to 27.1 per cent of migrants in Ho Chi Minh City. In Hanoi, the corresponding figures are 34.5 per cent and 26.5 per cent.

The desire to own their own home is the third reason people give for migrating, 12 per cent in Ho Chi Minh City and 13 per cent in Hanoi. Traditionally, after getting married, the young couple lives with the husband's family for a time. And because of difficulties in the area of housing, many young couples are unable to live on their own. So, many such persons will migrate in the future if and when conditions allow it so as to live away from their parents. There is a difference in the trend between non-migrants and migrants in Ho Chi Minh City and Hanoi. In Ho Chi Minh City, migrants most often give this reason (10.5 per cent for non-migrants compared to 16.2 per cent for migrants). In Hanoi, migrants who want to change their dwelling for this reason are only slightly more numerous.

Other reasons such as a change in one's place of work, choice of a good school for one's children, inheritance, means of communication, etc., are advanced by a low proportion of persons.

Profile of Persons Wishing to Change their Place of Residence

The determination seen in the profile of persons wishing to move enables the government to put deconcentration policies in place. These have to be implemented, while at the same time developing infrastructure to meet the needs of the people.

Young People are more Desirous of Moving than Older Persons

In Ho Chi Minh City and in Hanoi, the group between twenty and twenty-nine years of age is the most desirous of a change of residence (Figure 3.10).

A rather large segment of the group aged twenty to twenty-nine expressed the desire to move (33.2 per cent in Ho Chi Minh City and 42.6 per cent in Hanoi). These are single persons or newly married persons, who are fully

FIGURE 3.10
Distribution of Persons Intending to Migrate in Ho Chi Minh City and Hanoi by Age

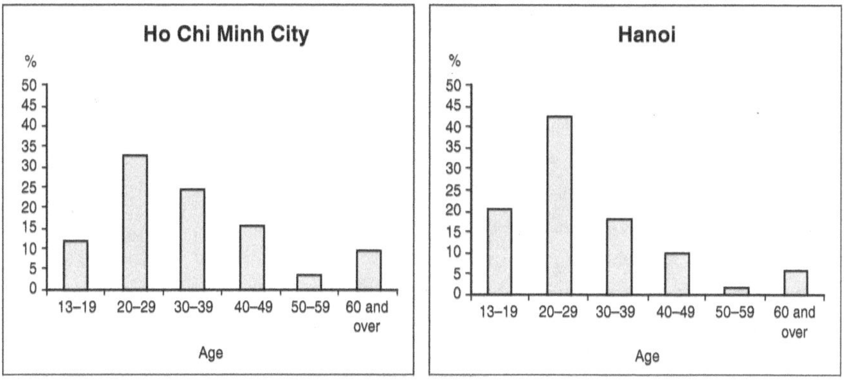

Source: PRUD Project, IER, PC, IRD, 2003

in tune with their family evolution and career path. They are in the greatest need of a new dwelling because they would like to live on their own, and they would like a new dwelling that is more comfortable because they are better off financially. Those under twenty years of age tend to follow their parents. For persons older than fifty, the number of those wanting to migrate is small (3.9 per cent in Ho Chi Minh City and 2.1 per cent in Hanoi). But this proportion grows after the age of sixty, notably in Ho Chi Minh City. This is explained by the fact that after reaching that age, problems arise involving the dependency of elderly parents on their children due to diminished financial means and declining health.

Persons desirous of migrating often have a high skills level, have jobs and work in business, services or handicrafts

In Ho Chi Minh City, the desire to migrate on the average is higher for persons who have a high skills level, work in the public sector or have their own company in the business or services sector. Indeed, 14.6 per cent of those having an academic education are desirous of migrating. These are also people who are better off financially and can afford to look for a better place to live. In reality, migration will not have any impact on their work, as they will stick with the same job after moving.

Conclusion

Urban growth in Ho Chi Minh City and Hanoi these last few years is prompting more people to move. The proportion of intra-urban migrants is also tending to increase. The migration flow from central districts to suburbia is very pronounced in Ho Chi Minh City. A similar trend is observed in Hanoi, although the final destination is more diversified. This trend is explained by the lower cost of land as well as by the gradual improvement of infrastructure in the suburban districts, making them more attractive. Nevertheless, difficulties are encountered due to means of transportation and inadequate infrastructure in these zones.

Migration generally enables those involved to enjoy better residential conditions because of improved housing quality and more amenities. Many households are thus able to own their own homes, and a home is considered to be a valuable asset, both economically and socially. Although improvement of one's living environment as well as increasing one's living space are patent, this evolution is also to be related to a selectivity of migrants in relation to the rest of the population, because migration demands certain means. Migrants are far from being a group of people who are simply escaping the downtown core.

With regard to short-term to-and-from travel, it is noted that the inhabitants of Ho Chi Minh City and Hanoi leave their homes every day, with a drop on Sunday. Obviously there are many reasons for going out of one's home: work, shopping, school or evening courses, visiting friends and neighbours, leisure activities, etc. However, the work factor remains important even on Sunday, showing that economic activity is unrelenting.

The inhabitants generally express themselves positively with regard to the quality of streets, traffic policing and quality of the transit service. To improve public transit, they suggest that quantitative measures and measures involving the putting in of new stops near residences be accompanied with a diversification of means (such as streetcar and subway).

The desire to move is not very widespread. Furthermore, a high proportion of potential migrants have not yet chosen their destination. Most people intending to migrate in the years to come are eying the central districts as their destination because of the proximity of key infrastructures. This conclusion should draw the attention of urban planning decision-makers to infrastructure development so as to meet the needs of the people and make the suburban and rural districts a destination of choice. This will help reduce the population overload in the central districts and enable incoming migrants to settle there in better conditions.

Notes

This research work is the result of a cooperation arrangement between the Paris Institute of Research for Development (IRD), the Institute for Economic Research of Ho Chi Minh City (IER) and the Population Centre of the Hanoi National Economics University (now, Institute for Population and Social Studies (IPSS)). We thank the following researchers for their contributions to this research project and assistance in the preparation of this chapter: Du Phuoc Tan, Gilles Greneche, Patrick Gubry, Le Thi Huong, Le Van Thanh, Nguyen Quoc Huy, Nguyen The Chinh, Nguyen Thi Thieng, Nguyen Thi Tuong Van, Pham Thi Thanh Hien, Pham Thuy Huong, Pham Van Khiet, Tran Thi Thanh Thuy and Vu Hoang Ngan.

1 The urban population based on the administrative definitions of the census is 4.2 million inhabitants.

2 Repetitive daily travel.

3 Statistical bias caused by the presence in a sample of too large clusters of individuals, similar to one another, within the cluster and thereby throwing off the representativeness of the sample.

4 Cu Chi and Can Gio Districts in Ho Chi Minh City and Soc Son District in Hanoi, which are still mostly rural, were excluded from the survey. It focused on twenty districts in Ho Chi Minh City and eleven districts in Hanoi. In November 2003, a redistricting measure lead to the creation of two new districts in each of the cities. We are using here the administrative distribution that prevailed prior to this date.

5 Thanh Xuan District is a special case in that it was created as the result of a split of the 'urban' district of Dong Da and the annexing of a number of rural communes (*xa*) in the suburbs.

6 Some discrepancies in the pyramids are due to the limited size of the sample.

7 *Báo cáo của sở Giao thông Công chính Thành phố Hồ Chí Minh.* [Report of the Ministry of Transportation and Public Works, Ho Chi Minh City].

8 *Đề án quy hoạch phát triển giao thông vận tải Thành phố Hồ Chí Minh và Hà Nội đến năm 2020.* [Planning and Development Project for the Ho Chi Minh City and Hanoi Transportation Networks to 2020].

9 *Lao Dong* (Hanoi), 2 December 2003.

10 Previously, drivers had to pay a fixed amount to the company in order to have the right to drive the vehicle. If drivers collected more than that amount, they pocketed the difference. But they had to pay out of pocket if there was a shortfall in receipts. So drivers would try to pack in the largest possible number of passengers.

11 Fares in 2005. Ho Chi Minh City is considering a raise, but has not yet enforced it.

12 Two new urban districts were established in November 2003 in each of the two cities.

References

Gubry, Patrick, et al. "Hô Chi Minh Ville et Hanoi: Population et migrations intra-urbaines". Séminaire «Regards croisés sur Hanoi: Transition, spécificité urbaine et choix de développement», Hanoi (12–14 November 2002), 42 pp.

Gubry, Patrick, Lê Thi Huong, Nguyén Thi Thiêng and Trân Thi Thanh Thuy. "Les mobilités temporaires au sein des métropoles vietnamiennes: Hô Chi Minh Ville et Hano". In Goldblum, Charles, Annik Osmont and Isabel Diaz (coord.), Gouverner les villes du Sud. Défis pour la recherche et pour l'action. Actes du colloque international du PRUD (Paris, UNESCO, 5–7 May 2004). Paris: Ministère des Affaires étrangères (Direction Générale de la Coopération Internationale et du Développement, DGCID), GEMDEV, ISTED, 2004, 296 pp., pp. 92–97.

Gubry Patrick, Lê Thi Huong, Nguyên Thi Thiêng, Pham Thuy Huong, Trân Thi Thanh Thuy, Vu Hoang Ngân (Dir.)/Nguyễn Thị Thiềng, Lê Thị Hương, Phạm Thúy Hương, Vũ Hoàng Ngân, Trần Thị Thanh Thủy, Gubry Patrick (Chủ biên), Bouger pour vivre mieux. *Les mobilités intra-urbaines à Hô Chi Minh Ville et Hanoi (Viêt-nam)/Di chuyển để sống tốt hơn. Di dân nội thị tại Thành Phố Hồ Chí Minh và Hà Nội (Việt Nam)*. Hanoi: Université nationale d'économie/Hà Nội: Nhà Xuất Bản Trường Đại Học Kinh Tế Quốc Dân, 2008, 293 pp. + 278 tr.

Photo: Emmanuel Cerise, 2002

Hanoi: an urban boulevard, Cau Giay boulevard (Paper Bridge) on the La Thanh trunk road as it crosses To Lich River, Cau Giay District

4

Resettlement Issues of Informal Settlement Areas in Ho Chi Minh City: From Large-scale Programmes to Micro-projects

Franck Castiglioni
Ludovic Dewaele
Nguyen Quang Vinh

Research Presentation[1]

The present research is the outcome of multi-disciplinary teamwork between Lausanne Federal Polytechnic School–LaSUR Laboratory (Switzerland), the Centre of Sociology and Development (Vietnamese centre for sociology research based in Ho Chi Minh City) and the French NGO Villes en Transition or VeT (Cities in Transition), which managed a resettlement pilot project in Ho Chi Minh City in 2000. This project is the object of the present research.

The theoretical framework for this study consists in analysing the implementation and impact of large-scale resettlement operations in Ho Chi Minh City and of a resettlement micro-project carried out by VeT.

The methodology used for this research consists mainly of semi-directive interviews with the resettled people themselves, with social service providers from Vietnamese mass organizations, and with political and technical decision-makers involved in the resettlement operations studied.

This research has been an opportunity for exchanges as well as disagreements between stakeholders from diverging backgrounds as resettlement and its attendant issues are particularly sensitive in Vietnam.

The requirements of urbanization and the need to improve the environment and living conditions of disadvantaged populations have led to planned resettlement operations in Ho Chi Minh City. The large-scale programme for Nhieu Loc-Thi Nghe canal and the micro-project for the Binh Trung Dong ward (District 2) exemplify this.

Within this framework, we have focused on measuring the socioeconomic impact of resettlement operations: that is to say, the mechanisms which generate socioeconomic effects, whether they are socially beneficial or detrimental.

Our objective was not to establish a comparative analysis *stricto sensu* between large-scale programmes and a resettlement micro-project so as to determine which approach works best, since it is difficult to establish elements of comparison between an operation covering a population of about 20,000 households and a micro-project concerning a mere fifty-five households. Our point is not to promote one methodology over another, even though VeT originally developed its resettlement programme to try to avoid the pernicious effects observed during former large-scale planned resettlement operations, such as the exclusion of residents in illegal situations, socially and financially inadequate housing, debt, resale and replication of insalubrious housing.

Instead, one of the objectives of this research is to improve our understanding of the socioeconomic effects of such urban programmes and observe the way in which they can either reduce or reinforce precariousness in the living conditions and residential situation of displaced populations, and incite them to have recourse to defence mechanisms in order to secure their urban insertion.

We will also attempt to formulate recommendations aiming to avoid or mitigate the most harmful consequences of resettlement.

In fact, we will observe that the two studied methods of resettlement cannot simply be opposed to one another, but contribute to an array of possible solutions for resettlement and thus enable us to seek beyond a uniform, one-solution approach.

Before we launch into the actual results of the research, it would be useful to provide a few contextual elements.

Contextual Elements and Macroeconomic Data

Opening to Market Economy

Vietnam's opening to market economy and the political determination of its decision-makers to modernize have brought about the implementation of international standards for housing and contruction.

In parallel, the development of a market system induces particularly strong speculation in large urban centres and causes an increase in land and housing costs. This marginalizes disadvantaged populations whose financial means do not match market standards.

Strong Demographic Growth

Current population pressure is high and projections confirm this trend. The General Statistics Office (GSO) anticipates a population increase of approximately 23 million inhabitants between 1999 and 2024. The overall population would thus rise from 77 million to 100 million in 25 years. This is a higher population increase than occurred in France after World War II.

In Ho Chi Minh City, preliminary results of the census carried out in October 2004 by the Office of Regional Statistics under the aegis of the People's Committee show a total of 6,117,251 inhabitants in the entire administrative unit, including 5,140,412 inhabitants in urban districts (Gubry and Le Thi Huong 2005).[2]

If we merely apply the current mean annual growth rate in urban districts (2.2 per cent), the urban population in Ho Chi Minh City would reach 5.9 million by 2010 and 7.3 million by 2020. However, actual figures will no doubt be vastly superior as the growth rate is rising. Moreover, rural areas on the outskirts will be reclassified as urban areas (in particular the Bien Hoa conurbation, which will by then be integrated into the Ho Chi Minh City conurbation).

Increasing Rural Migration due to Growing Disparity between City and Countryside

A growing disparity between city and countryside increases rural migration. The current global distribution of the Vietnamese population is 23 per cent urban and 77 per cent rural. The GSO forecasts a 45 per cent urban and 55 per cent rural population by 2020. Ho Chi Minh City occupies a particular place in the national context as it is the country's conurbation which attracts the greatest number of migrants from northern and southern provinces.

According to the 2002 census, Ho Chi Minh City has a population of 5.5 million inhabitants, which is below real figures as this understates the numbers of undocumented populations. According to the latest half-term of the 2004 census, the population has reached 6.1 million inhabitants, 30.1 per cent of which are migrants. Between 1999 and 2004, the population increased by 160,000 inhabitants per year on average, with a natural growth rate of 1.27 per cent and a mechanical growth rate of 2.33 per cent. Demographic projections anticipate that the city's population will reach 7 million to 8 million in 2010 and will double by 2020.

Eighty Per Cent Informal Economy

This results in a high proportion of low incomes. In 2002, being poor in Ho Chi Minh City meant an income below or equal to US$16 per month per person. This represents 3 per cent of households (the poverty threshold for the country as a whole is fixed at US$10 per month per person).[3] In 2004, a new poverty threshold was fixed for the 2004–10 period at VND 6 million per person per year. Using this new threshold, the total figure for poor households in Ho Chi Minh City reaches 60,000, or 5.27 per cent of the city's households.[4]

Low income is exacerbated by chronic employment instability due to poorly qualified, seasonal and/or irregular work (motorbike taxi, informal vendors, caretakers, cascade subcontracting). Table 4.1 might help clarify the standards of living of the population of Ho Chi Minh City, particularly in groups with low living standards (this table was drawn up according to average consumption per person per month in VND).

Very low living standards combined with irregular income affect the ability of households to assume responsibility for the acquisition and maintenance

TABLE 4.1
Living Standards of the Population of Ho Chi Minh City (Average Consumption per Person per Month, in thousand VND)

Categories	2000		2001		2002	
Poor	<238	9.8%	<246	9.9%	<287	10.2%
Temporarily stable	239–396	16.0%	246–398	15.0%	288–452	15.8%
Middle	397–529	21.0%	399–579	21.5%	453–583	20.0%
Upper Middle	530–696	23.0%	580–769	24.7%	584–831	24.1%
Upper	>969	29.3%	>1,068	28.9%	>1,144	29.9%

Source: Ho Chi Minh City Annual Statistics Yearbook — 2002.

FIGURE 4.1
Income Distribution in Ho Chi Minh City in 2000

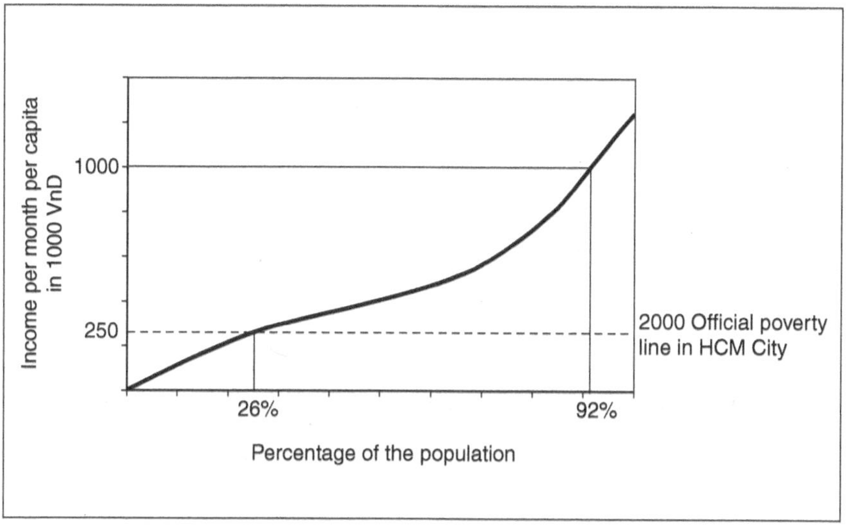

Source: Villes en Transition Vietnam (2003), on the basis of a survey conducted by the Ho Chi Minh City Poverty Reduction Centre.

costs of modern housing; moreover, they are incompatible with the repayment of a bank mortgage over several years (eight to twenty years).

Massive Housing Needs

The housing sector, and especially social housing, which has been the subject of recent work, is characteristic of the scale of efforts needed in this area:

- financing of social housing from 1996 to 2000 stands at around 0.2 to 0.3 per cent of Vietnamese GNP and has only addressed 15 per cent to 20 per cent of identified needs;
- covering costs for the estimated demand only in the 2000–2010 period would require an effort of around 2 per cent of GNP, or ten times more than the current figure.

Until now, a large part of the demand has been covered by informal practices within the private sector, which causes problems in the quantitative and qualitative control of housing production, as well as issues of land management, management of built infrastructure, taxation and transport.

FIGURE 4.2
Ho Chi Minh City: A Metropolis of Five Million Inhabitants

Photo: Sébastien Wust, 2000

The Vietnamese state has limited financial means at its disposal, due largely to flaws in its fiscal and taxation system. This does not mean that its efforts in this area are non-existent, but they are insufficient in the face of existing and future needs and will remain so if the state merely maintains its current production support policy.

Residential Law, Land Rights and Resettlement

Housing Vulnerability Determines Access to Services

Access to Urban Services

Residential status determines housing precariousness; each individual is registered in a residential book known as *Ho Khau*, which defines one's permanent residence in a given district. One's effective residence at any given time corresponds to a type of residential permit or "KT" ranging from level 1 to 4. KT level determines accessibility to basic urban services: water supply (access nevertheless remains possible for "illegal" residents, but only through middlemen who resell access to the service for their own benefit and charge top price compared to the official rate), electricity network (same system), sanitation, waste collection, postal services, healthcare and education. However, this situation is not rigid and discretional arrangements enable illegal residents to have access to urban services on a case-by-case basis, but more often than not at an added cost.

Access to Social Assistance

Residential status also has an impact on the ability to benefit from Vietnamese social policies: the Governmental Poverty Reduction and Growth Strategy (GPRS) does not consider KT4 permit holders as beneficiaries, and KT3 only partially so. This situation can be explained by the fact that populations with KT4 permits are considered to be persons in transit and therefore cannot benefit from a social assistance policy aimed at those registered as permanent residents.

Access to the Formal Banking Sector

Absence of legal registration is a cause for rejection from access to the formal banking sector before level of income and income stability are even considered. Should those in an illegal or temporary situation be in need of financing, they only have recourse to money-lenders in the informal sector charging interest rates as high as 20 per cent to 30 per cent per month.

Access to Formal and Stable Employment

The level of residential legality also comes into play in the area of access to employment in the civil service, which requires permanent residency status in the city of recruitment.

Access to Citizenship

Becoming a member of one of the five mass organizations (that is, Union of Women, Fatherland Front, Youth Federation, and Pensioners' Union) requires permanent residential status. Temporary residential status prevents access to the activities and solidarity network — and thus to a universally recognized social status — provided by membership in one such organization. It should be noted that this is problematic from the perspective of mass organizations themselves as they deploy much energy and resources trying to recruit new members.

Access to Real Estate Ownership

Access to land ownership is determined largely by proof of the household's residential status. We will, later in this article, go into further detail on the ins and outs of this situation, which is fundamental in the current context of urban development in Vietnam.

Households residing in the same place for a period of about five years are usually progressively legalized as their KT level gets upgraded. However, such legalization of residential status is not systematic and remains discretional;

TABLE 4.2
Residential Status and Access to Services

Permit	Type of residential status	Access to urban services (US)	Access to social assistance	Access to banking system
KT1	Status as permanent legal resident in the city; residence in the *phuong* of registration (administrative unit below district level)	Access to US	Social assistance	Formal banking sector
KT2	Status as permanent legal resident in the city; residence in a *phuong* other than the *phuong* of registration	Access to US	Social assistance	Formal banking sector
KT3	Long-term temporary resident status	Excluded from US (except for local exceptions, otherwise informal access through intermediaries)	Partial access to social assistance	No access to traditional banking sector
KT4	Short-term temporary resident status	Excluded from US (informal access through intermediaries)	No social assistance	No access to traditional banking sector

Source: Villes en Transition Vietnam, 2005

it also fails to provide a solution for land use status. Indeed, there are cases of residents who are legal as far as residential status is concerned, but not in terms of land ownership. This affects compensation amounts in case of resettlement.

Residential precariousness results from the official residential control system, which consists in registering with the local authorities when moving and the issuing of a residence permit or residence book.

This system is very constraining and many people, when they move, are unable to provide all the required documents. As a consequence, when arriving in an urban area, most migrants find themselves in an illegal residential situation for a more or less prolonged period. Members of KT1 households can also lose their residential status if they change residential district within the same city (intra-urban migration) — although the status downgrade is of lesser importance compared to migrants who change province of residence.

This complex situation is worthy of its own specific research so as to elucidate the ins and outs of this residential system and its many consequences and implications in the everyday life of populations. This phenomenon is all the more pronounced among poor populations who can show proof of neither stable and official employment in a large company or government agency, nor of land-use rights (equivalent to a title of land ownership).

Precariousness of Land Rights

Ownership of Land-use Rights is Decisive for Access to Compensation Measures

Poor migrants usually do not have the financial means to buy land legally (that is, the acquisition of land-use rights), hence their recourse to illegal methods like the informal acquisition and occupation of vacant land.

Illegal land occupation becomes a real problem during land-use planning operations requiring the displacement and resettlement of populations. Within the context of official operations, only households with a valid title of land ownership have access to land compensation measures (also amended according to residential status).

Illegal Land Use Means One is Entitled to Compensation for Loss of Housing Only, but not to any Land Rights

To all others (that is, those in situations of illegal land use), only resettlement compensation to the value of the built infrastructure is granted.

This compensation is calculated according to the estimated quality of the built infrastructure. In the case of precarious housing, the amount of this compensation, known in administrative terms as "resettlement compensation", is almost symbolic and is not sufficient to build another house nor to acquire land legally.

As an illustration, the current cost of a square metre in District 2, which is undergoing rapid urbanization, is US$800 (improved building land). The cost of construction is around US$60 per square metre (sq. m.) for good quality workmanship and US$25 for basic quality. The average amount of compensation for 20 square metre lodgings is around US$230, or US$11.5 per square metre.

Table 4.3 illustrates the impossibility for poor populations engaged in illegal land use to cope with resettlement with nothing but the resettlement compensation they are generally entitled to.

The average amount of compensation does not cover the acquisition cost of a square metre of improved land, nor even the purchase cost of a basic lodging excluding cost of land.

TABLE 4.3
Comparative Table: Compensations *vs.* Costs of Construction in Ho Chi Minh City District 2

Type of costs	Prices recorded in 2004	Construction costs for 20 metres	40 sq.m. lot (statutory minimum)
Cost per sq.m. of improved land (area of medium standards)	US$800[5]		US$32,000 vacant land
Good quality construction costs per sq.m.	US$60–150	US$1,200–3,000	
Basic quality construction costs per sq.m.	US$25	US$500	
Housing compensation average per sq.m.	US$11.5	US$230	

Source: Villes en Transition Vietnam, 2005

Summary of Main Results

Similarities and Divergences between the Large-scale Programme and the Micro-project

Binh Trung Dong Micro-project

- Resettlement operation on 1 hectare of improved land.
- Population concerned: fifty-five households.
- The objective is for the authorities of District 2 to reclaim 11 hectares for land-use planning.

Nhieu Loc-Thi Nghe Large-scale Project

- Large-scale state resettlement programme.
- Population concerned: 20,000 households living on the banks of the city's canals.
- Along *Nhieu Loc-Thi Nghe* canal.

FIGURE 4.3
Location Map

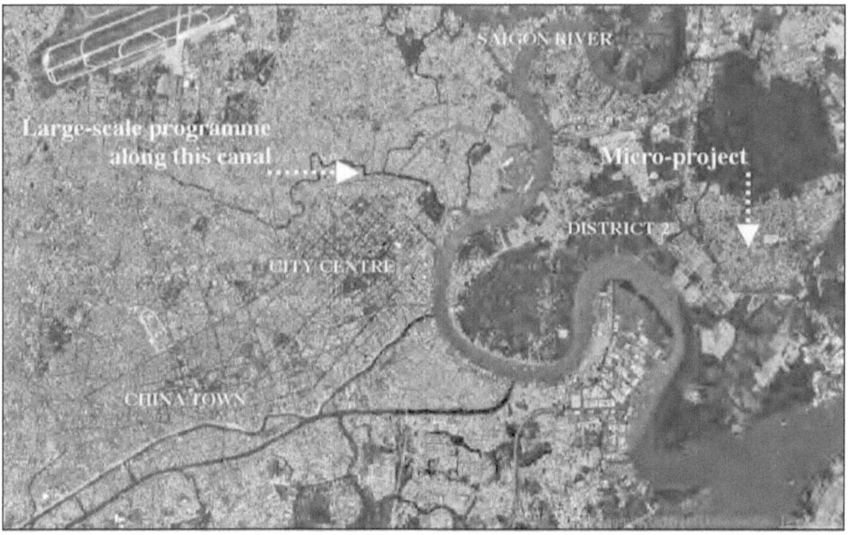

Source: Google Maps and Villes en Transition, 2005

FIGURE 4.4
Binh Trung Dong: Resettlement on an Improved Area of 1 hectare of Fifty-five Households Illegally Distributed over 11 hectares

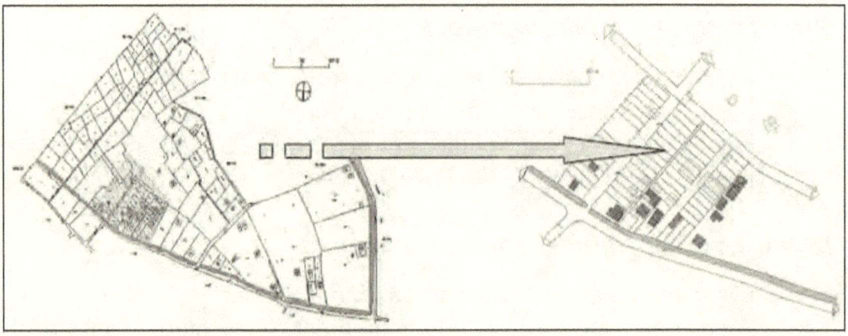

Source: Villes en Transition, 2002

TABLE 4.4
Project Modalities: Detailed Presentation

Modalities	NLTN large-scale programme	BTD micro-project
Eligibility criteria	Permanent resident status (KT1 and KT2). Other KT categories are excluded	Owning a lodging on the eviction area — residential status not considered
Type of compensation system	Direct application of Vietnamese law	Implementation of a local system
Functioning of the compensation system	No land use rights: compensation for the existing built infrastructure only, hence difficulties in financing the purchase of a flat (exclusion or money-lender debt)	Same, except that households are systematically integrated in the resettlement process
Type of habitat	Vertical collective housing (4 to 6 storeys)	Individual housing on lots

TABLE 4.4 *(cont'd)*

Modalities	NLTN large-scale programme	BTD micro-project
Cost of habitat	From US$3,600 to US$9,000	US$2,140
Loan	Ten-year interest-free loan for up to 70% of selling price	Ceiling price of US$1,070 (50% of total price); interest at 0.7% per month over eight years
Financing	Minimum 30% contribution	Minimum 40% contribution and possibility of contribution in labour
Follow-up	Support allowance (one ration of rice per person for six months) No socioeconomic rehabilitation measures	Dynamic community strengthening through credit-savings groups, actions to create replacement activities and construction of collective facilities.
Institutional structure	Complex: central municipality, five districts and corresponding wards: institutional compartmentalization and complex procedures	Simple: central municipality, district and ward
Land constraints	High: city centre localization	Low: peri-urban area
Legalization process	Procurement of title of ownership and title of land use — those in illegal situations are excluded (see above)	Procurement of title of ownership for built infrastructure; Procurement of two-year land lease with the promise of complete legalization thereafter (lack of legal clarity)

Source: Sebastien Wust and Villes en Transition.

The Impact of Resettlement in Nhieu Loc-Thi Nghe and Binh Trung Dong

As far as spatial, social and economic repercussions are concerned, research demonstrates that the Binh Trung Dong micro-project had a less severe impact on disadvantaged families than the large-scale planned resettlement programme of Nhieu Loc-Thi Nghe. Although the latter satisfies the public authorities' ambition to modernise the image of the city — a modernisation which they see as synonymous with improvement and rehabilitation — the same effects and consequences of the resettlement process can be found in both case figures.

The Case of the Nhieu Loc-Thi Nghe Programme

Restrictive Eligibility Criteria: 30 Per Cent are Excluded

Two eligibility criteria have been used in order to carry out a selection among households affected by eviction and resettlement. The first criterion excludes temporary residents entirely: that is to say, all households in possession of a KT3 or KT4 residential permit, tenants and unregistered households. This constitutes around 30 per cent of the total population in the area considered, tenants excluded. Although such households are entitled to compensation for loss of housing, these compensations remain symbolic with regards to real market prices, and enable neither access to acquisition of state housing, nor do they make it possible to build a house — even in precarious conditions — and even less to legally own land. For such households, resettlement results in loss of housing, loss of land and often loss of employment, as the latter tends to depend on localised social networks.

The second selection criterion consists in offering a choice to the remaining "permanent" KT1 and 2 households: they can either resettle themselves through their own means after having received a cash payment in compensation for the eviction, loss of housing and loss of land, or accept the project's offer of resettlement. If they chose the latter option, the cost of acquisition of the new lodging is reduced by an amount equivalent to that of the compensation.

However, the eligible population (KT1 and 2) is not exempted from the impact of resettlement and finds itself caught in a scissor effect resulting from increased expenses linked to the new lodging and a drop in income due to the move.

Increase in Housing-related Costs

Occupancy expenses (that is, water, electricity, waste collection, maintenance of communal areas) and debt (that is, repayments to the state and sometimes money-lender debt contracted to gather the initial financial contribution not covered by the amount of compensations) contribute to increasing the cost of housing. The share of a family's income devoted to housing costs thus rose from 4 per cent to 22 per cent after the planned resettlement.

Drop in Income (30 per cent of Households Concerned)

This is a direct consequence of housing that is ill-adapted to professional use (e.g., workshops, corner shops, etc.): verticality acts as an economic and social barrier. There is usually no garage to keep bicycles, motorcycles or hawker's stalls; the social networks crucial to essentially informal employment are lacking, as are the former solidarity networks; the need for travel increases. The drop in income is an additional source of debt on top of that generated by rehousing.

In 2005, across the entire city, the average rate of KT1 and KT2 households who had chosen to resettle themselves through their own means was superior or equal to 50 per cent of households affected by eviction. This gives an indication of the popularity of large-scale resettlement operations.

The Case of the Micro-project

The phenomenon of exclusion is *a priori* less pronounced here for the following reasons:

- The entire population of the eviction area is entitled to resettlement and its modalities are applied evenly.
- Resettlement is carried out in the vicinity of the eviction area. The distance of the move is limited; the community is not fragmented and thus retains the bonds that existed prior to resettlement.
- The "compartment" typology allows multi-functionality, which is reinforced by the possible use of the lot. Moreover, the housing unit provided, which is both basic and minimal, is upgradable and can be either lengthened or raised by adding extra storeys, according to the needs and financial capacity of each household.
- The morphology of the neighbourhood and the fact that households know each other prior to resettlement facilitate the maintenance of neighbourly social and family relations.

From an economical perspective, on-site resettlement as well as the chosen habitat typology (that is, multi-functional housing with direct access to the street level) also seem to facilitate the maintenance or rehabilitation of household members' economic activity; they either resume previous activities, with some possible adjustments (for example, switching from agriculture to market gardening or horticulture), or make use of the opportunities generated by resettlement: opening corner shops or small workshops supported both by existing and identified customers and by the site's new layout, which facilitates outside access (that is, road access).

It should be noted that the economic activities of the resettled populations remain in large part informal and therefore unstable and not very profitable.

As with large-scale resettlement operations, however, the resettled population of Binh Trung Dong are confronted with increased housing costs. Two major items have increased in family budgets following resettlement: the first item is rental expenses, which were previously almost non-existent. They divided up into the following sub-categories: rental of land-use rights for the lot, access to water through the official counter — although in most cases drawing water from the well remains a possible alternative

FIGURE 4.5
Typology and Morphology of Houses on Offer for the Binh Trung Dong Project

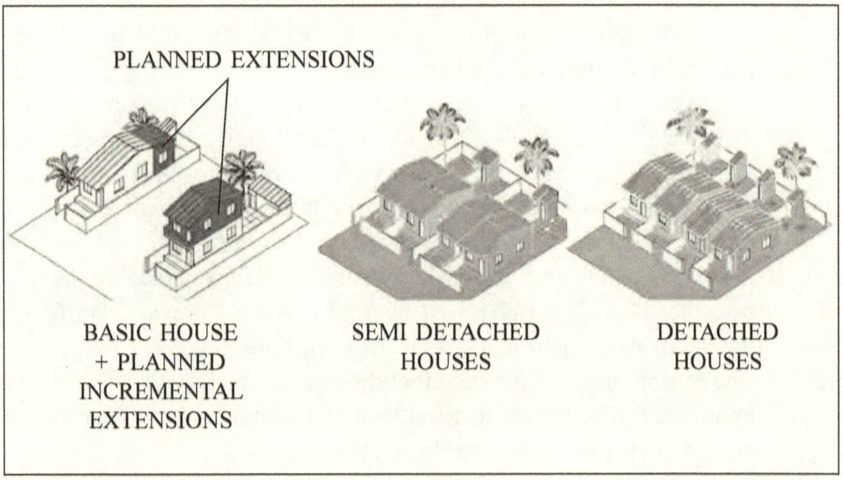

Source: Villes en Transition, 2002

FIGURE 4.6
Typical Housing Unit on Binh Trung Dong Resettlement Project

Photo: Villes en Transition Vietnam, 2002

FIGURE 4.7
General View of the Binh Trung Dong Resettlement Project

Source: Villes en Transition Vietnam, 2002

— and waste collection. Electricity is the only item which has become less expensive due to access to an official counter after resettling, as opposed to the previous situation whereby it was only available to such households informally, through an officially equipped middleman.

The second new expense item consists in debt contracted as a consequence of the resettlement operation: debt owed to the real estate loan fund, and 50 per cent informal credit with monthly interest rates bordering on 20 per cent to fulfil the requirement of a 40 per cent own contribution, and/or in order to invest an amount in excess of the loan ceiling in the construction of the new lodging.

For the poorest, housing costs can reach 50 per cent of the overall family income. This is amplified by the fact that their income is neither stable nor regular, as opposed to the debt itself. As a result, it can become impossible to fulfil the financial effort required during the off-season (for example, construction sector or sales activities during the rainy season).

Negative Effects Recorded in Both Case Studies

Indebtedness and Overindebtedness

The appeal of the new lodging leads households to withstand an untenable economic situation for as long as possible. Access to modern standard housing induces deep changes in the living conditions of resettled households, which are much easier than before despite the fact that such housing is often ill-adapted to their usual lifestyle. From this perspective, resettlement is perceived as a godsend and as the promise of a new and better life.

For all its constraints and disadvantages, most inhabitants choose to stay in their new habitat at all costs, to the point of ignoring its economic impact, if need be. This generally means contracting additional debt, on top of that already generated by resettlement, in order to keep up with new financial needs and make up for the loss of income caused by resettlement. Indebtedness is intensified by the fact that such debt is contracted with money-lenders who charge high rates of interest.

Resale of the property only takes place once households have run out of options, including recourse to money-lenders.

The Resale Phenomenon

Resale is the only possible way for households to solve their debt problem — especially money-lender debt — by using capital from the sale of their lodging to repay their loans.

However, prices tend to be slashed as resales take place in urgent and illegal conditions, which plays against the resellers (recorded prices are 40 per cent to 50 per cent below market value).

In most cases, resettlement operations impose conditions or at least provide terms and conditions for resale. In the case of the Nhieu Loc-Thi Nghe canal operation, resale of the flat is prohibited prior to repayment of the state loan, which carries a three-year safety period. Rules are slightly different for Binh Trung Dong. In this case, it was not possible to resell the lot, which was being rented from the district authorities; only the built infrastructure could be sold, but as this excluded land, this would *a priori* preclude any cession. As it turned out, informal resales took place by transferring the lodging's land lease and building permit to the buyer, who would speculate on the future likelihood of legalizing his land-use situation. Despite the constraints imposed, resales did occur in both case figures, but the very regulations established by the resettlement operation meant that they had to take place under informal circumstances. As a consequence, resellers lost a substantial share of profits in the transaction.

It should be noted that on the Binh Trung Dong site, resales were motivated both by the need to escape debt and by the potential for large capital gain due to land speculation following the area's urban development. Despite the fact that average recorded resale prices were below market prices, profit margins remained substantial.

Resales on the large-scale resettlement programme of Nhieu Loc-Thi Nghe canal reached over 70 per cent of total housing stock four years after the operation was over.

Resales were slightly below 50 per cent on the Binh Trung Dong micro-project three years after the end of the operation.

Resales end up benefiting households not initially targeted by these programmes. In both situations, the measures implemented by local authorities — whether through preferential loan rates or allocation of land — have been hijacked by populations not initially targeted by these transactions. In the case of Nhieu Loc-Thi Nghe, the average resale price of flats is one-third below market price. This is reinforced by the fact that an interest-free real estate loan system had been put in place for the resettled population.

In the case of Binh Trung Dong, preferential interest rates are associated with vastly underestimated land rental: US$2 per month for the rental of land-use rights, which would allow repayment of a loan approximating US$240 over ten years, whereas the estimated value of lots in this area wavered between US$6,700 and US$13,500 in 2001.

As for poor populations, they benefit on the margins of such operations at best (as in the case of Binh Trung Dong); at worst they find themselves destitute and in a more precarious situation than prior to resettlement.

In both cases, second-hand buyers are profiting indirectly from measures put in place for the benefit of the most disadvantaged populations. Public efforts in this area, which in this instance consist in low interest rates and/or generous land prices, do not reach the populations initially targeted.

Recurrence of Informal Settlements

Nhieu Loc-Thi Nghe: Resales, Return to Illegality and Economic Disruption and Vulnerability

One noticeable difference is that in the case of the Nhieu Loc-Thi Nghe programme, the proceeds of the resale are essentially used to soak up debt resulting from resettlement. Indebtedness results from the State loan contracted within the framework of the resettlement operation and from moneylender debt contracted privately to cover additional costs and/or make up for the loss of the previous source of income. Once heavily in debt, resellers do not have the necessary capital to consider buying land and/or housing, even on a more modest scale. They generally rebuild habitat that is both physically and legally precarious on the outskirts of the city, where land remains affordable. They then have to deal with the issue of finding work in these areas, which are less busy, or else with the need to travel in order to find work.

They thus find themselves thrown back to an illegal situation, both in terms of residential status and land rights. To a certain extent, this is a return to the situation prior to resettlement, made worse by distance from the city centre and the loss of social and interpersonal bonds which, amongst other things, enable access to gainful activities.

Binh Trung Dong: Return to an Illegal Situation, but without the Casualization Noted on the Large-scale Resettlement Operation

In Binh Trung Dong, proceeds from the resale have, in the majority of cases, enabled repayment of debt contracted due to resettlement, and have also generated sufficient profit for purchasing lots and reconstructing houses. Although these houses are reconstructed on illegally bought land, they are usually of higher quality than those prior to resettlement and on the resettlement site (profit margins can reach US$3,350). These reinstallations

FIGURE 4.8
Examples of Informal Settlements

Photo: Villes en Transition Vietnam, 2002

FIGURE 4.9
Group of Houses Self-built by Binh Trung Dong Resellers on Lots Bought near the Resettlement Site

Photo: Centre for Socialogy and Development

have taken place in the vicinity of the area of resettlement, which means that their new inhabitants do not find themselves isolated in a new and unfamiliar context where they would have to find their bearings all over again. Therefore, local relocation following resale does not have the negative consequences observed previously (that is, loss of networks, remoteness), and resellers lose neither job nor income.

Although, contrary to the canal resellers, they do not return to their initial economic precariousness or worse, Binh Trung Dong resellers do return to a totally illegal residential and land use situation. This constitutes a failure for local authorities, who are once again confronted with uncontrolled urbanisation that does not fit into their planification.

In both cases, for a large part of resettled people, the process ends with the return to a precarious situation following resale, although in the case of the micro-project the consequences of resettlement are more nuanced and include some positive aspects.

This process results in the replication of precarious or semi-precarious habitat zones — precisely the opposite of the objectives set by these operations: in the case of Nhieu Loc-Thi Nghe, the rehabilitation of the canal's bank; and in the case of Binh Trung Dong, reclaiming of land by local authorities.

FIGURE 4.10

Diagram Illustrating the Replication of Precarious Habitat after Resettlement

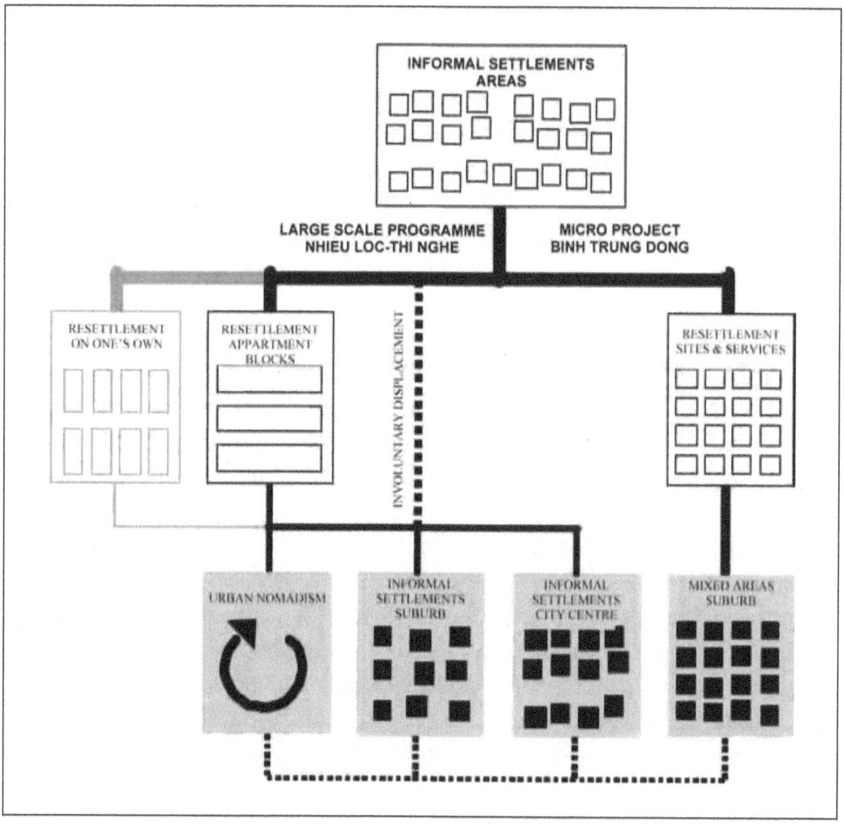

Notes:

1) In the case of large-scale resettlement programmes: replication of precarious habitat zones after resale
2) In the case of the micro-project: replication of semi-precarious habitat zones after resale.

Source: Sébastien Wust, 2004 (translated by Ludovic Dewaele).

In parallel, and in both cases, the families who leave once they have resold their house are replaced by new and more economically privileged inhabitants: in this way, resettlement areas undergo progressive gentrification.

This change in population could be considered as a diversion of state subsidies, which end up benefiting households not initially targeted by these measures.

Orientations

One Principle Should Apply: Narrow the Gap between Two Ways of Inhabiting and Two Lifestyles and Keep Distances — Whether Spatial, Economic or Social — to a Minimum

The remarks and proposals formulated below are an attempt at solving the following quandary: on the one hand, the need to take into account the real life conditions of households, including the most disadvantaged (that is, financial capacity, lifestyle, type of professional activity) and, on the other hand, the political determination to modernise. In such conditions, how can both — equally legitimate — requirements be reconciled through public policy without generating their share of exclusion?

Our aim is to go beyond the conflict between "small is beautiful" supporters and those of the all-inclusive, sweeping approach. Indeed, although modalities differ, some recurrent phenomena can be observed that go way beyond the framework of resettlement operations: insufficient overall housing supply, high speculation, largely informal lifestyles and wide income gap, limited capacity for financing social housing, and the issue of legality concerning residential status and land use.

International as well as Vietnamese experience has shown that there is no miracle formula to solve the issues of resettlement projects, and that it is difficult to reconcile all the contradictory needs that arise in each instance. However, it would be useful to state a number of principles to aim for, in the manner of an asymptote.

Globally speaking, resettlement operations should strive to restrain the gap between two ways of inhabiting and two lifestyles, and to keep distances — whether spatial, economic or social — to a minimum.

Housing should provide acceptable shelter against climate, health and social constraints, and should make it possible to carry out a wide range of activities.

It should enable its inhabitants access to the people, resources, institutions and public facilities which they depend on for their livelihood.

It should provide sufficient residential security for it to be worth settling in and maintaining.

Lastly, the cost of housing should neither threaten nor compromise the economic situation of the household and its members.

We emphasize that any approach to a resettlement operation should strive to take into account the aforementioned points: habitability, accessibility, residential security and financial capacity of the resettled population, and seek appropriate operational solutions.

Operational Recommendations

In terms of operational recommendations, the promotion of participative urban planning would ensure a better assessment of the aspirations, but mostly of the constraints — whether social, economic or spatial — that affect the most disadvantaged populations.

This perspective entails cutting resettlement operations down to a minimum, in favour of policies to rehabilitate precarious neighbourhoods through on-site improvement operations. Where resettlement cannot be avoided, it is essential that operations of more modest ambitions be promoted (that is, lowering the standards of social housing and conducting operations on a smaller scale).

Inevitably, the economic capacity of both households and the State will have to be taken into consideration, and equitable eligibility criteria will have to be applied. Compensations should not be restricted to those with legal residential permits and land rights. The use and targeting of subsidies should be optimized in order to reduce diversion and speculative resales to a minimum.

It is essential that public authorities should be able to offer several well-adapted and financially accessible alternatives for resettlement to the wide range of affected households. Such alternatives would go beyond the framework of the projects studied: rental system, emphyteutic land lease, parcels of improved land (sites and services), self-construction, etc.

In a context where expensive housing project operations are unilaterally and uniformly promoted, as is currently the case in Ho Chi Minh City, promoting micro-, small and medium-scale projects would mean that a greater diversity of appropriate solutions would be available in response to the wide range of requirements and profiles of resettled populations.

We should bear in mind that "micro-project" does not necessarily entail individual horizontal housing. Conversely, "large-scale project" is not exclusively collective vertical housing, and can also refer to individual housing operations.

Whatever the case may be, smaller-scale operations are conducive to the implementation of a participative process and to inhabitants' mobilization and involvement.

In order to reduce the exclusion mechanisms caused by planned resettlement to a minimum, the State should do its utmost to offer alternatives which preserve the community's cohesion within displaced populations. Individual resettlement breaks up the community and should be avoided as far as possible. This is one reason for favouring on-site resettlement or on-site improvement approaches.

Economic and social support measures need to be implemented in order for projects to succeed. Support of displaced households must be maintained not only before resettlement (preparing for a change in professional activity, accumulation of personal savings), but also throughout the entire transitional period after resettlement. This is a particularly critical period, during which households may be substantially affected by the negative impacts of resettlement (debt, loss of social and economic references, new constraints linked to housing).

As for administrative and institutional organization, planned resettlement should be carried out through lighter, more flexible and less hierarchised administrative structures. This would enable public authorities to control the operations more efficiently, mainly through a stronger presence in the field and increased responsiveness.

This would require greater emphasis on the planning, management and assessment of activities, as well as setting up an efficient organisational structure in order to limit the duration of the projects. An appropriate step in the implementation of such projects might be the creation at municipal level of an administrative unit specialising in planned resettlement operations.

Beyond Recommendations

Land and real estate prices remain an unresolved issue which hinders future resettlement operations.

A Compensation System that Fails to Replace the Value of Lost Assets

In addition to official compensation measures and with support from the real estate loan system, households must deploy their own financial efforts in order to cover housing costs. However, their efforts remain insufficient, especially as they fail to cover the cost of land. This observation holds especially true in the current context where the market value of land is on the rise, and where legal acquisition of land is increasingly prohibitive for poor and low income populations.

The rise in the price of land is amplified by the expansion of the country's large conurbations and by chronic shortage of housing construction regardless of standards.

Although Vietnam is currently experiencing a generalised increase in wealth, the income gap between rich and poor is also widening. This is particularly noticeable in urban centres. The type of housing being built, and the lifestyle and costs it implies, are better suited to a wage-earning population, or at least to those on a stable income, in particular due to the need to access traditional real estate loans. Yet it appears that the vast majority of the population still does not fit this description and will not for a long time.

Property Value Obtained through Resettlement as a Source of Resale

Resale is not only a way of escaping debt following resettlement, but can also be a source of profit due to increasing land value. In the case of the Binh Trung Dong operation, a system of lot rental was set up to address the problem of land value. In doing so, local authorities were granting an important concession, land being the stumbling block of resettlement programmes. The idea was also to cut down potential resales as resettled inhabitants could not make a profit from the land, which remained the property of local authorities.

Nevertheless, this system of land rental has not been able to prevent informal resales: these have consisted in the reseller transferring the land lease and building permit to the buyer.

Depending on the period, average recorded resale prices waver between VND70 million (US$4,100) and VND150 million (US$8,800) for an 80-square metre to 100-square metre lot. With a value of around VND32 million (US$2,140), the dwelling itself represents only a part and even a minority share of the overall stakes of the transaction. This brings us back to the problem of land management in Vietnam, an issue that reaches beyond the scope of resettlement operations. This will remain a chronic and crucial issue as long as a land administration system has not been rigorously established and as long as gaps in income and issues of legal status contribute to perpetuating the system of informal resale.

The Residential Permit System Penalizes the Poorest

Another thorny issue reaching beyond the mere question of resettlement and directly linked to the issue of land administration concerns the residential permit system. This system determines access to urban services and social assistance according to residential permit type and also contributes to an exclusion from official resettlement operations. This was the case in the Nhieu Loc-Thi Nghe canal operation where over 30 per cent of the population in the resettlement area was *a priori* not taken into account. Moreover, residential status has a direct impact on the level of compensation.

Beyond such aspects, the current residential system also contributes to urban impoverishment (health, education, hygiene) through penalisation of the most disadvantaged populations.

Social Policies of Redistribution Need to be Established

Based on the current situation as well as on previous experience of resettlement projects within which building up of savings and reinforcement of income-generating activities were implemented as a prerequisite and a preparation for resettlement, we have made the following observations:

- In the best of cases, households' potential savings would enable the acquisition of a lodging of basic workmanship over a period of twenty years of savings. This period can be shortened with specific real estate loans such as were granted in the operation studied here.
- Current land prices at market rates make it impossible for resettled inhabitants to bear the cost of land acquisition, not even for lots reduced to their minimum legal size (40 square metres in Ho Chi Minh City).

Prospective improvement of the compensation/indemnification system (no exclusion of illegal residents, recognition of land use rights even in the case of unlawful occupation) would not allow compensation of land costs at current market rates either.

The Vietnamese State would not be able to bear the financial cost of a compensation policy based on market prices.

This brings us back to reflect well on rental buildings and emphyteutic leases, which in any case require that authorities have a solid grasp of land management: the establishment of reserved areas for social housing and setting up of a system of social housing provision within the framework of resettlement and social housing operations.

Secondly, in order to meet those needs, the Vietnamese State will have to implement a more efficient fiscal and taxation system. This would ultimately enable the setting up of social policies of redistribution to compensate for the growing gap between rich and poor.

Finally, it would be worth exploring the angle of reorienting public policy so as to managing a demand-oriented approached of habitat production to the detriment of the current costly "supply-driven" support.

Notes

1 The research team was composed of Jean-Claude Bolay and Sebastien Wust (Laboratory of Urban Sociology, Polytechnic Institute, Lausanne, Switzerland); Franck Castiglioni, Ludovic Dewaele and Vuong Van Pho Danh (Cities in Transition, Lyon and Ho Chi Minh City); Van Thi Ngoc Lan, Nguyen Quang Vinh, Tran Dan Tam and Tran Thai Ngoc Thanh (Centre of Sociology and

Development, Ho Chi Minh City). The authors thank all those involved for their ideas, which have partly been used in this chapter.

2 The 2004 census of 100 per cent of HCMC population eventually availed 30 per cent of temporary residents (KT4 & KT3 residential status holders) over its total population.

3 From 1997 to 2003, the poverty threshold for Ho Chi Minh City was defined as follows: In the city centre, the threshold is VND3 million/person/year; in the outskirts, VND2.5 million/person/year. Using this threshold, poverty percentages were: 12.3% of households in 1997; 11.82% in 1998; 9.5% in 1999; 7.8% in 2000; 5.6% in 2001; 3% in 2002; 0.15% in 2003.

4 Source: Ho Chi Minh City Anti-poverty committee report — 2004.

5 2004 prices in areas subject to strong speculation.

References

Acres International Limited. "Vietnam National Resettlement Policy Project (NRPP)". Report no. 1 and no. 2. Hanoi: Acres International, 1997.

Bassand, Michel, et al., eds. Métropolisation, crise écologique et développement durable: l'eau et l'habitat précaire à Ho Chi Minh Ville, Vietnam. Lausanne: PPUR, 2000.

Belgian Administration Development Cooperation (BADC). "Tan Hoa-Lo Gom Analysis: Results for the Definition of PMU 415 Pilot Projects". Canal TH-LG Sanitation and Urban Upgrading Project (PMU 415). HCMC: BADC, 1998*a*.

———. Tan Hoa-Lo Gom Project. "Results of 400 Sample Socioeconomic Survey".

Canal TH-LG Sanitation and Urban Upgrading Project (PMU 415). HCMC: BADC, 1998*b*.

Bolay, Jean-Claude. "Hô Chi Minh Ville: chronique d'une métropolisation annoncée". In *Urbanisme*, no. 303 (1998): 14–19.

Bolay, Jean-Claude, et al. "Sustainable Development and Urban Growth: Precarious Habitat and Water Management in HCMC, Vietnam". In *Habitat International* 21, no. 2 (1997): 185–97.

Bolay, Jean-Claude and Thai Thi Ngoc Du. "Sustainable Development, Urbanization and Environmental Risks: The Priority of Local Actions in Ho Chi Minh City, Vietnam". In *Journal of Urban Technology* 6, no. 2 (1999): 65–85.

Cartoux, Sophie. "L'habitat spontané à Hô Chi Minh Ville: des quartiers en transition". DEA, Villes et Sociétés, Université Lyon Lumière, Institut d'Urbanisme de Lyon, 1997.

Cartoux, Sophie and H. De Reboul. Le «logement social» à Hô Chi Minh Ville, Vietnam. Hô Chi Minh-Ville: ENDA Vietnam, 1995.

Communauté urbaine de Lyon (Agence d'urbanisme). "L'urbanisme de HCMV: Perspectives et projets des services municipaux". Rapport de synthèse. Lyon-HCMV: Communauté urbaine de Lyon, 1995.

———. Étude préparatoire à la révision du schéma directeur du 1er arrondissement de HCMV. Lyon-HCMV: Communauté urbaine de Lyon, 1996.

Dewaele, Ludovic. Le logement social à Ho Chi Minh Ville — Les standards actuels sont-ils appropriés à la production massive de logements sociaux? Les Cahiers de la Coopération française au Vietnam, Ambassade de France dans la République socialiste du Vietnam, cahier no. 10 (2003): 46.

Do Thai Dong. "Économie de marché et transformations sociales au Vietnam". In *Alternatives Sud* 1, no. 2 (1994): 121–34.

Gaillard M.–N., Niebudek Jan. Hô Chi Minh Ville, le spontané et la ville planifiée. Mémoire de fin d'études. Versailles: École d'Architecture de Versailles, 1995.

Gubry, Patrick, Jerrold W. Huguet, Truong Si Anh and Vu Thi Hong. "Ho Chi Minh Ville, de la migration à l'emploi". Paris: CEPED, Les dossiers du CEPED, no. 40, 1996.

Gubry, Patrick, Jerrold W. Huguet, Doan Mau Diep and Trinh Khac Tham. "L'émergence des migrations spontanées au Vietnam: le cas de Vung Tau et de Dong Nai". Paris: CEPED, Les dossiers du CEPED, no. 45, 1996.

Gubry, Patrick (dir.). *Population et développement au Viêt-nam*. Paris: Karthala-CEPED, 2000.

Gubry, Patrick and Le Thi Huong. "Are the 'Left Behind' Really Left? Shared Advantages in Rural-urban Migration from Mekong Delta to Ho Chi Minh City". *Vietnam's Socio-Economic Development* (Hanoi), no. 44, (Winter 2005): 54–70.

Gunnewiek, H.K. and C. Mosselman. "Housing in Ho Chi Minh City: A Study of Slum Upgrading and Redevelopment". Amsterdam: DCA/SD, Vrije Universiteit, Urban Research Working Papers, no. 39, 1995.

Lindfield, M. and Du Phuoc Tan. "The Tau Hu Canal Rehabilitation Prefeasibility Study". National Project VIE/95/051. HCMV: AHURI-IER, 1997.

Metzger, R. "Sustainable Slum Upgrading, Architectural Analysis of a Slum in Ward 15". HCMC: EPFL, 2000.

Nguyen Phuong Chi. "Le secteur privé du bâtiment a-t-il un intérêt à investir dans les logements sociaux?" Le cas de HCMV. Mémoire de recherche. HCMV: Centre Franco-Vietnamien de Formation à la Gestion (CFVG), 1997.

Nguyen Vu Hop. *Enquête auprès des premières familles relogées à Binh Trung Dong*. HCMV: VeT, 2000.

Niebudek, Jan. *Quelques éléments de connaissance sur les familles de Binh Trung Dong devant être prochainement relogées*. HCMC: VeT, 1999.

Parenteau, René. *Habitat et environnement urbain au Viêt-nam. Hanoi et Hô Chi Minh-Ville*. Paris-Ottawa: Karthala-CRDI, 1997.

Peltenburg, M. and Du Phuoc Tan. "Relocation and Resettlement within the Context of Tau Hu Canal Rehabilitation Pilot Project". National Project VIE/95/051. HCMV: IHS-IER, 1997.

Phan Anh Quan To. "NGO Community Participation in Vietnam". In *ENDA-VeT, Hô Chi Minh Ville, développement tout azimut*. HCMV: ENDA-VeT, 1996.

Phan Thi Chu Truyen. "La construction du logement social à HCMV: Peut-on réduire les coûts?" Mémoire de recherche. HCMV: Centre Franco-Vietnamien de Formation à la Gestion (CFVG), 1977.

Quach-Langlet, T. "Saigon, capitale de la république du Sud Vietnam (1954–1975), ou une urbanisation sauvage". In *Péninsule indochinoise: Études urbaines*, edited by P.B. Lafont. Paris: L'Harmattan, 1991.

Thai Thi Ngoc Du. "Socioeconomic Characteristics and Preferences for Resettlement Options of Households to be Relocated in Ward 11, District 6". Preliminary results of survey. HCMC, PMU415, 2000.

Thai Thi Ngoc Du. "Métropolisation, gestion des villes et habitation à Ho Chi Minh Ville". In *Cahiers d'Outre-Mer*, no. 196 (1996*a*): 377–86.

———, "Le secteur informel à Ho Chi Minh-Ville". In *Cahiers d'Outre-Mer*, no. 196 (1996*b*): 387–96.

Villes en Transition (VeT). "Étude d'aménagement: projet pilote pour la réhabilitation du quartier Tan Dinh, Ho Chi Minh Ville". HCMV: VeT, 1998.

Wust, Sébastien. "Expertise in Relocation Policy for the Canal Tan Hoa-Lo Gom Sanitation and Urban Upgrading Project". Report no. 1. Lausanne: IREC-EPFL, 15 May 2000, 28 pp.

———, "Métropolisation, habitat précaire et relogement forcé: entre phénomènes d'exclusion et tactiques populaires d'intégration. Le cas du canal Nhieu Loc-Thi Nghe à Ho Chi Minh Ville, Vietnam". Thèse de doctorat. Lausanne: EPFL, 2001.

Wust, Sébastien, Jean-Claude, Bolay and Thai Thi Ngoc Du. "Metropolization and the Ecological Crisis: Precarious Settlements in Ho Chi Minh City, Vietnam". In *Environment & Urbanization* 14, no. 2 (2002): 211–24.

Ho Chi Minh City: New housing estate in District 2. *Photo: P. Gubry, November 2008*

5

Changes in Public Water Management: Transition, Compromise, and Innovation

Claude de Miras
Fanny Quertamp Nguyen

For nearly two decades now, the "decentralization, privatization and liberalization" triangle touted in adjustment policies has become the new paradigm for development in all parts of the world. Yet, effective implementation of institutional decentralization coupled with an appeal to the private sector to promote open competition and growth is failing to impact all countries uniformly. A case in point is Vietnam with its socialist-oriented market economy. Is it going through a gradual transition towards a liberal economy? Compromising between internal constraints and external demands? Or, rather, going the way of innovation, seeking a specific model that has not yet fully taken shape?

In Vietnam, the "transition/ compromise/ innovation" pathways are fraught with complexity and uncertainty, something we can confirm by taking a look at urban water distribution.[1]

To begin with, in the early 1990s transition was the buzzword in neoliberal strategies applied to contexts that were still recently collectivist. Transition was needed on two fronts — from collectivism to capitalism and from underdevelopment to development. But it is noteworthy that the transformations that took place in Vietnam (*Doi Moi*, 1986) predated generalization of the notion of transition. Chronologically, the notion of transition was not the force behind the remake that took place in the late 1980s. Rather, it sprung from new national public policy directions and gave them a meaning they did not previously have (the march to liberalism). The transition idea in a way came to the rescue in a story of radical upheavals, the like of which had not been planned or anticipated. But perhaps not wanting to lose out on any new history-making advancement and convinced that valuable lessons could be learned from the recent remake, it was thought that transition should be something predictable and applicable to social action in general.

From both the economic and political standpoint, the concept of transition came to mean both a liberal and democratic model that had become unavoidable and toward which economically collectivist countries were invited to turn. It was a convenient prenotion that was thought capable of announcing that the story was about to end (Fukuyama 1994), but it became obvious in practice that much more was involved in building an efficient market economy than the simple enjoinder of "less government!" That transition, affirming the end of collectivism and *ipso facto* the forward march towards a triumphant market economy, has dragged on and on. The anticipated model did not emerge from what took place in Russia or the more significant dynamics manifested by China.

Rather than a switchover, as might be inferred by the word transition, compromise appears to have the upper hand (with reference to a sluggish response in some areas or sectors, patching things over and attempting to run the old with the new). But looking at the future, there is no certainty that we have seen the last of the values of the past in Vietnam, where "public-private partnerships" (PPP) are, as we shall see, something of an innovation. The observable changes surely do not mean the end of the previous system. The clout wielded by external stakeholders and their catchphrases have indeed had no small impact in the transformations observed, but it must be kept in mind that these transformations had become necessary. The existing systems would perhaps not have been able to replicate them and ensure their political survival if meltdown initiatives had not been taken just in time. In other words, there was no doubt a timely coincidence between external warnings voiced from the outside and necessity felt on the inside, pushing the government to change in the face of the urban challenge and the need to restructure a moribund system.

Unless of course the changes taking place will see as yet unthought-of mechanisms come into being, resulting from a combination of policy adjustments and stakeholder feedback, while still clinging to deeply-rooted political ideology in some cases or to social or cultural practices in others. Rather than being a transition of straightforward design, the pathway is seen to be winding and uncertain. Often, beyond initial intentions, the principle of reality appears to prevail. Although international urging has indeed promoted some endogenous changes, it would be wrong to interpret the institutional and social transformations as mechanical projections of external enjoinders and patent evidence of transition on the march.

Thus, it is not so much the transition from "collectivism" to "liberalism" as it is the compromise between the "demand for urban public utilities" and "national resilience" that will be the main theme in our approach to urban Clean Water Supply (CWS) in the metropolised Red River region in northern Vietnam.

Although since *Doi Moi* in 1986, there has been a great deal of institutional revamping, and although it is certain that collectivist economics had been strongly challenged from the inside, prompting a vast restructuring movement, it is clear that the swing foretold in the free enterprise system, with the generalization of the invisible hand and disappearance of the welfare state, did not occur. In its stead a socialist-oriented market economy developed, so fluid that it seems more like a process than a state. The observable transformations over the last ten years in the urban CWS sector shows that flexibility, inventiveness and innovation have been displayed in urban water management in Vietnam. They also testify to the difficulty in defining the precise nature of this Vietnamese model, intangible in certain political aspects (supremacy of the Communist Party) while being totally deregulated and liberalized in other aspects (informal sector, low social coverage, growing inequities). But is it the collective ownership of means of production that now defines a socialist regime or rather, more prosaically, its capability of reducing or eliminating poverty by driving socially inclusive economic policies?

Structural Data: Urban Extension, Demand and Water Resources

With a population of nearly 80 million inhabitants in 1999, the urbanization rate in Vietnam stood at 23.5 per cent. This as yet limited level of urbanization was the result of a recent increase in internal migratory movement due to a loosening of control over migration. Positive urban growth, a still low but growing urbanization rate and an annual population growth rate of 2.1 per cent all combined to induce a substantial future demand for clean water.

Growing Urbanization Raises the Demand for Water

Water, an element of nature and of myth, plays a very concrete role in the urban structure of Vietnam. Cities are growing and the economy has been growing since *Doi Moi.* This is now having an impact on the water issue. The resource — groundwater — is being polluted directly by both domestic and industrial urban effluent, as well as by nitrates used in intensive peri-urban agriculture. City land is being covered over and sealed; the sewage system is antiquated; this multiplies the risk of surface water flooding and urban soil leaching. The crossover pollution between peri-urban rural zones and urbanized areas is aggravated as the urban stain spreads and engulfs villages in the suburbs. One of the theoretical consequences of these crossover nuisances is their inflationist effect on the cost of water treatment for the city.

Demographic and economic growth over the last ten years has caused the domestic and industrial demand in Hanoi to spiral. In 1997, according to the Japan International Cooperation Agency (JICA), the household demand for clean water was 180 litres per person per day (l/p/d), while the city's water companies could only supply about 100 l/p/d (JICA, 1997). The industrial demand (17 per cent) and that of miscellaneous users (15 per cent) must be added to this domestic demand that accounts for 68 per cent of the total.

Countrywide, it is anticipated that the need for water in urban areas will multiply five-fold between 1995 and 2025.

TABLE 5.1
Projection of the Water Demand in Vietnam between 1995 and 2025 (billions of m^3/year)

Type of need	1995	2000	2010	2020	2025
Urban	1.2	1.8	3.3	4.8	6
Industrial	2.8	3.6	5.9	9.6	12.3
Rural	0.6	0.7	0.9	1.1	1.2
Total	4.6	6.1	10.1	15.5	19.5

Source: World Bank, 1996.

Population growth, diversification of urban activities, improvement of the standard of living and changing lifestyles are driving up the demand for water in the main urban centres. Thus, for the city of Hanoi, between 1995 and 2010, average needs are expected to jump from 344,800 cubic metres per day (m^3/d) to 528,600 m^3/d,[2] an increase of 53 per cent in fifteen years.

Legacy of a Command Economy

Vietnam remains marked by the collectivist period despite taking many steps on the roadway to change since *Doi Moi*. According to socialist economics, current consumption goods (such as oil, petrol, sugar, rice and meat) and the great majority of marketed products (housing, electricity, water, etc.) were subject to subsidization and rationing. Today, trade in goods dominates all economic sectors directly or indirectly, including the land market and real estate. The reform of state-owned enterprises and the policy of partial privatization of public utilities, including education and health, are evidence of the end of an era governed by a command, subsidized economy. Nevertheless, a number of strategic, symbolic assets — one of them clean water — do not appear to have been included this commercialization process. Water remains cheap because it continues to be subsidized.

Water is certainly one of the token areas in which the collectivist approach is being perennialized or holding its own. Unlike electricity, telephone, individual means of transportation and housing, the price of clean water has been kept relatively low, with virtually no change. In contrast, the price of electricity increased non-stop throughout the 1990s. In four years, the average price per Kw/h, tax free, was multiplied by 1.6, that is, a linear annual increase of nearly 13 per cent in a low inflation context.

TABLE 5.2
Changes in the Price of Water in Hanoi between 1994 and 2004 (dongs per m^3)

Users	Before 1994	1994	1997	2001	2004
Domestic users	600	1,000	1,500	2,000	2,000
Government offices	1,600	2,000	3,000	3,500	3,500
Businesses, services		5,000		6,500	6,500
Foreigners		5,000		6,500	3,500
Average price in dongs		3,250			3,875
Average price in US$		0.3			0.2

Source: Water Distribution Company

The price of water has been stable since the last raise in 2001, while it had gone up an average of 4.2 per cent a year between 1997 and 2001. In the ten years from 1994 to 2004, the nominal price of water increased at an annual rate of less than 3 per cent. Considering the low inflation rate (sometimes even negative as in 1999 and 2000) during the same period, it is possible to infer that the real price of water (deflated) was stable or increased only slightly during the decade from 1994-2004. Expressed in US dollars (US$), the price of water even decreased.[3]

Data from the Water Company show that while 23 per cent of the connected population had a meter, 49 per cent of the total amount of water was charged on a lump-sum basis and only 30 per cent corresponded to the volume actually delivered and billed based on the meter reading. A 70-per cent loss rate was tallied, caused by such things as the poor condition of the mains (2.3 per cent), dilapidation of the distribution network and hook-up points (31.8 per cent) or no billing (35 per cent). In 1994, the city had 900 public street fountains and taps that were slated for gradual elimination.

The foregoing provides insight into the way the water companies are operating. Until only recently they were run according to a quantitative production approach based on a delivery volume target. This is commensurate with the socialist concept of material production: the delivery quantity is based on targets set by the government with no concern for managing quality, productivity and profitability. So it was that in 1994, the official deficit of the Hanoi Water Company was estimated at 10.112 billion dongs.

We feel that this fact is crucial to understanding the institutional practices and ideological presuppositions intrinsically linked to the social distribution of water (diversity of uses, waste, etc.). Symmetrically, this institutional and ideological legacy — felt particularly in urban clean water distribution — has weighed in on the pattern and pace of the CWS sector reform. Water remains a specific social issue. It is the last heavily subsidized production and also the last economic symbol of the collectivist period for some political spheres of the Vietnamese Communist Party as well as the fringe of population that grew up and lived under this Mother State image.

The culture of structural subsidization is alive and well both in the government apparatus and the domestic economics of Hanoi households. Water companies are riveted on subsidization regardless of the economic outcome. For most water company directors, it would seem that the first concern is to meet water production volume targets, not show that they are good managers. In economic terms, this approach is structurally inefficient, because the greater the loss of water, the higher the subsidies are. The firm's viability is still totally detached from its accounting results, which are not used as an incentive to improve economic performance. Moreover, this system of structural subsidization and its workings are often opaque. And people who see water as relatively cheap are using the resource as if it was inexhaustible. This in turn, is contributing to the growing problem of wasteful use. If nothing is done to change this way of thinking, it will become impossible to continue restructuring the water sector and public utilities in general.

The subsidies approach, added to the fact that water resources in Vietnam are particularly abundant, has a considerable influence on practices associated with water. Generally speaking, access to water can be broken down schematically into three main categories: clean water for large cities, where individual home hook-ups are becoming routine, well or drilled water and "natural" water sourced from bodies of water and rainwater (impluvium). Depending on how the water is accessed and its quality, it will be used in various ways (cooking, drinking, lavatory, washing, etc.). Two main billing systems for clean water exist side by side: the water meter and lump-sum charge. Continued use of the fixed billing system independent from actual consumption obviously does nothing to promote a realistic perception of the cost of clean water delivery.

Water sector reform started in the late 1980s and is one facet of the turnaround from a planned economy to a socialist-oriented market economy. During the 1980s, given the disastrous situation Vietnam was in, supplying a certain volume had to be a top priority. Starting in 1991, supplying water in both urban and rural areas became a government priority. Bilateral and multilateral international assistance was then used to renovate, strengthen and extend water conveyance and delivery systems. After that, gradual institutional reform of the water sector became a necessary condition for its development, but without necessarily forcing it to fall in line with the international enjoinders for privatisation or concession. Similarly, Vietnam's position in the area of cost recovery and water marketing remains specific in comparison with the global liberalization wave. Its CWS strategy is gradually evolving according to a scheme not necessarily immediately predictable because the meaning and scope of discernable facets of its evolution often remain difficult to grasp because of being composite, temperamental and innovative in character.

In our approach to policy reform in the area of the urban access to water, we considered the overall offer at the national level, using as a basis on legislation and national programmes for urban areas. Three case studies were developed in the PRUD study — Hanoi, Hai Phong and Ha Dong — that we will summarize briefly below.

In Hanoi, network deterioration, lump-sum billing (66 per cent), the high loss rate (57 per cent) and the current institutional setup make water sector reform particularly challenging. Hai Phong is a notable example of financial management that finds favour with funding agencies (World Bank) and of a unique situation from the point of view of both the physical conditions — brackish water — and the types of users, wherein the industrial demand accounts for a large share. We rounded out the picture by studying Ha Dong, a smaller city adjacent to Hanoi, as it allowed inclusion of the problem of network ramification on different administrative territories.

Evolution of the Urban Water Supply Strategy

Based on legislation and interviews with officials in charge of urban CWS, we will provide a synthesis of the national urban water supply strategy and its evolution in three stages since the 1990s.

From the Late 1980s to 1994: Abandonment of Planned Economy and Effort to Reduce Water Loss[4]

For water companies in Vietnam, the 1990s were marked by an effort to reduce their water loss rate and increase their revenues. These two objectives resulted from a government decision made in the late 1980s to eliminate the public sector subsidy system or at least do something about the recurrent and exclusive nature thereof. Given this new direction, water companies ceased to be considered as production units under a central, planned system. They were even called upon to improve their internal financing capacity. Public companies had to start changing their operational mode by optimizing water production. The installation of individual meters became generalized, along with the closure of public street fountains. Methods were devised for individualized billing and receipt collection; new accounting practices were applied; and network maintenance and repair programmes were introduced. Water companies also looked into establishing customer service departments as a means of boosting their image and improving their operations.

Although water supply had become a government priority back in 1991, one of the first water sector reform measures was taken in 1994 and focused on reducing water loss from both the physical and financial standpoints (see decision No. 06/BXD/DT of 18/04/1994). Nationally, the water loss rate stood at an average of 40 to 50 per cent, reaching 70 per cent in cities such as Hai Phong. These losses resulted from the decrepitude and poor maintenance of the networks (physical losses), as well as from unpaid bills (financial losses). This forced the issue of network quality and upkeep and challenged the commercial management of water companies. Thus, an initial programme of water loss reduction was put in place in 1994. It aimed firstly at diagnosing local situations in an effort to assess losses and what was causing them. The programme centred essentially on generalizing metre installation, eliminating the lump-sum arrangement and cutting down on unpaid bills. The programme also promoted service improvement — leak detection, reduction of main failures, etc. — and prevention of waste. That was an initial but crucial step in reforming the national water supply sector.

This initial phase was also marked by the multiplication of projects funded through bilateral aid, with the Finnish project for Hanoi no doubt being the most typical example thereof. In the late 1980s, foreign companies under bilateral aid initiatives started positioning themselves in this sector, in anticipation of making a profit. The French policy in this regard is representative. Through it, private companies were able to get established in Vietnam through the so-called "credit protocol" programme. In the mid-1990s, multilateral funding took over from this earlier form of financing. Thus, the Asian Development Bank, the World Bank and the *Agence française de développement* [French Development Agency (AFD)] gradually took over in order to concentrate increasingly larger funding packages and distribute projects more effectively countrywide.

1998–99: A Parent Law and Circular Setting the Tariff Scale, a Definite Boost to the Reform

The urban water supply strategy actually dates from 1998.[5] The main targets are quantitative in nature, essentially aimed at improving water production and delivery capacities throughout the country while aiming to ensure access to clean water for 80 per cent of the urban population by 2000 (that is, 80 to 100 l/p/d). The main cities of the country — Hanoi, Ho Chi Minh City and Hai Phong — were privileged, the objective for them being to hook up 100 per cent of the population and meet the norm of 120 to 150 l/p/d.[6]

The situation in urban areas in 1998 can be described as follows:

- 190 water pumping stations with a total production capacity of 2.6 million cubic metres per day.
- Network affected by severe deterioration. Out of 5,400 kilometres of network, 60 per cent was at least thirty-five years old. The network as is could only meet 40 per cent of the demand. Very high loss rate (>30 per cent).
- Low hook-up rate: 60 per cent of the people had network hook-up in large cities, 50 per cent in average sized cities and less than

30 per cent in other urban centres (towns and villages). Overall, less than half of the urban population had access to clean water.
- Supply standards were in the order of 50 to 60 l/p/d. Pumps had to be used to get water into houses and water supply tanks on floors higher up. Frequent periods of cut off or supply shortage.
- Quality of the water did not meet hygiene standards.
- Insufficient coordination of the various government levels intervening in water production and delivery. Various ministries were involved, firstly the Ministry of Construction, then the Ministry of Agriculture and Rural Development, Ministry of Planning and Investment, etc.
- System fraught with deficiencies in terms of management and marketing training, hence major losses of funds experienced (total physical and financial losses were estimated to be between 50 and 60 per cent of production).

Geographically, priorities centred on the three economic zones of Hanoi-Hai Phong-Quang Ninh, Hô Chi Minh City-Bien Hoa-Vung Tau and Da Nang-Hue-Dung Quat. The standards set for tier-1 cities was having 80 per cent of the population hooked up by 2000 (150 l/p/d), 100 per cent by 2010 (160 l/p/d) and 100 per cent by 2020 (180 l/p/d) in order to be in line with the major Asian metropolises of Bangkok, Kuala Lumpur, Jakarta, etc.

To meet these needs, a directive from the prime minister was issued in late 1998 with the following targets:

- Territory management based on priority projects;
- Reform of water companies aimed at building financial self-sufficiency and reducing the need for government subsidization (which implied internal financing, revamping the tariff structure and accounting system, computerizing the billing process, etc.);
- Preventing financial losses;
- Streamlining technology and producing the necessary equipment and machinery;
- Protection and efficient use of water resources;
- Capacity building in national engineering offices.

In 1999, the Ministry of Construction (Decision No. 2834/BXD/KTQH) rounded out Decision 63 by outlining a core programme of "development guidelines for urban water delivery in Vietnam to 2020". Emphasis was placed on protecting water resources, territory management, acceleration of ongoing projects funded through Official Development Assistance (ODA) and preventing water loss. Also in 1999, the Ministry of Construction and the

TABLE 5.3
Estimated Water Needs in 1998

Period	Urban pop. (millions)	Hook-up rate (per cent)	Standard (litres/ per/day)	Domestic water (millions m^3/ day)	Industrial water (millions m^3/day)	Total (millions m^3/day)	Investment required (millions of US$)
1998	14.7	47	—	—	—	2.5	—
By 2000	23.4	75	120	2.1	2.2	4.3	900
By 2010	30.4	95	150	4.5	4.5	8.8	2,165
By 2020	46.0	100	160	7.6	8.3	15.9	3,570

Source: Ministry of Construction, 1998, p. 14.

Government Price Commission jointly put out a circular on the water tariff structure (No. 03/1999 TTLT/BXD-BVGCP of 16/06/1999). This instruction set out the principles for setting the selling price of clean water, including operating costs resulting from the production, delivery and marketing phases. It made provision for customer feedback, customer affordability and reimbursement of loans, as well as the proper level of accounting balance (operation) and financial balance (investment) for water companies. This latter decision showed the nature of water company reform, although the price remained government administered,[7] wavering between the commercial balance of the firms and user/customer affordability.

The 2000s: Assessment, Blockages and Trends

In 2000, the urban water supply situation countrywide could be described as follows:

- 50 to 60 per cent of the urban population hooked up to the network;
- Growing demand: While consumption was then estimated to be 70 l/p/d, it was anticipated to reach 120 to 150 l/p/d in the next few years;
- Water loss (physical and financial) was estimated at an average of 30 to 40 per cent;
- Deterioration of water quality due to groundwater pollution was becoming flagrant;
- Price of water remaining low (an average of 3,000 dongs per m^3, or about 0.20 euro), while operating and investment costs required sizeable hikes — for balance sheet purposes only.

The many projects funded through multilateral and bilateral assistance helped measurably to improve the water supply situation in the majority of Vietnam's urban centres. The 61 cities with provincial status were equipped with water supply systems. Statistics showed 241 pumping stations with a total planned capacity of 2.96 million m^3/d. Among the 547 towns and smaller urban centres of the country, 140 had water supply systems of a capacity from 163,680 m^3/d, with 66 per cent of the stations using surface water and 34 per cent using groundwater. The main cities had large-scale increasingly modern water supply systems: Ho Chi Minh City (850,000 m^3/d), Hanoi (400,000 m^3/d) and Hai Phong (136,000 m^3/d).

The total amount of investment dedicated to CWS projects in Vietnamese cities during the 1996–2000 period reached over US$ one billion (US$200 million in the form of non-repayable loans, about US$400 million in official development assistance and US$350 million in loans from international organizations); to that is to be added nearly 2,000 billion dongs invested by the government of Vietnam both centrally and locally. These investments enabled an increase in water production capacity to a total of 600,000 m^3/d.

In 2001, the Fourth National Conference on Urban Water Supply provided an opportunity for an initial results assessment. Territorial coverage had been extended and routine service was being provided in the provinces. However, many and varied difficulties continued to be observed, including poor water quality, high water loss rates, retention of old ways of managing water companies, an inappropriate tariff structure, etc. Many factors explain this: the high pace of urbanization; unwieldy administrative and financing procedures; lack of coordination between treatment plants and the delivery network; and the financial management of the water companies. As a result, water loss rates in urban centres remained high, between 30 and 40 per cent. The lowest rates were in Da Lat (19.2 per cent) and Vung Tau (21.5 per cent), while the highest loss rates were in places like Hanoi with 57 per cent. In some cities, although the stations had recently been put in, loss rates continued to be high (>50 per cent) due to worn out water mains in provinces such as Tra Vinh, Nam Dinh, Can Tho and Ha Tinh.

In late 2001, the most recent report highlighted 170 projects implemented in Vietnam's urban water supply sector (11,500 billion dongs including 8,562 billion from foreign funding agencies). The water production capacity had reached 3.27 million cubic metres or 1.75 times what it was in 1991. Since 2001, the term of loans has been 10 years with an annual interest rate kept down to 5.4 per cent, while projects implemented earlier continued to bear interest at 7.2 per cent per annum.

The years 1998–2000 saw the introduction of two new dictates: "sustainable development" and "socialization" of the rural water supply. Infrastructure proved to be costly and required investments too heavy for Vietnam to assume alone. The country went looking for new forms of funding in addition to ODA that had begun to have more conditions attached. Although all the economic and social stakeholders were mobilized, their participation differed depending on whether the rural or urban sector was involved. In rural areas, the "socialization" policy took shape and was officially promoted in 2000. This policy "aims to mobilise all of the people to share in activities, diversify investment models, create favourable conditions for groups such as households, commercial groups, cooperatives, businesses, to share in the capital; and to share in the implementation, maintenance, management and marketing of clean water supply projects and services". In urban areas, the price of water was passed on to the more affluent social or economic classes in order to enable the poor in general to have access to water.

This report then had to come to grips with the paradoxes in tariff structure. Indeed, the current price of water was not consistent with the spirit of Instruction 40/1998/CT-TTg that encouraged better management balanced with development of the urban water supply. To achieve this, "the price of water must be set according to accounting principles commensurate with the payment capability of customers and reimbursement of the debt".

Two hindrances were thus identified in the report: on the one hand, the unprofitability of water companies and continued widespread subsidisation of the sector and, on the other, new conditional modes of funding in the face of a growing demand. The government started looking for new forms of investment and new ways of management that were not restricted to just one model. It appeared that forms of private-public partnership were thus going to be called upon to develop in the overall area of infrastructure and public utilities.

Partnership Strategies and Forms of Private-Public Partnership

Generally, in both the urban and rural contexts, the 1990s saw a national water supply strategy emerge that enabled long-term targets to be set and improvements to be made in the area of operational efficiency. Although good progress had been made, the situation remained unsatisfactory for more than one reason and the early 2000s saw many urban and peri-urban zones still deprived of clean water supply systems worthy of the name. Indeed, the national programme had not given much attention to urban growth, either demographically or spatially, and the substantial increase in the demand for water, limited local water resources and the growing volume of wastewater. This forced the issue of sustainable development. Moreover, the CWS institutional reform project had gained ground, but remained largely exploratory, leaving many questions unanswered, in particular that of the funding mechanisms and management forms to be adopted. This set of problems that came to the fore in the late 1990s in Vietnam is strategic for development of the CWS sector and is feeding current ideological, social and economic debates as it shapes Vietnam's relationship with international institutions and development agencies.

Institutional Assessment: Different Forms of Public-Private Partnership

Reform of the urban clean water supply sector took shape in the early 1990s with the gradual linking of institutional changes and investment packages in the corresponding infrastructure.

The first phase in water supply development resulted in an increase of water production capacity (treatment plants and network overhaul).

The second phase, in the late 1990s, enabled the extension of delivery networks and development of CWS projects countrywide while laying the basis for institutional reform. Since the early 2000s, this reform has become the central focus of the CWS portfolio and is also crucial to the sustainable development of the sector, therefore challenging the economic and financial "sustainability" of the reform underway. Indeed, the time had come for the first loans granted from 1985 to 1990 (for example, Hanoi) to be reimbursed. Given the insolvency of the water companies, funding agencies set new loan conditions by putting the public water companies in competition with each other and proposing new forms of public-private partnership.

Starting in 2001, international funding agencies (World Bank, ADB, AFD), provincial water companies — through the Vietnam Water and Sanitation Association (VWSA) and the concerned levels of government (Ministry of Construction and Ministry of Finance) — came to an agreement on the limits allowed as they revised their common strategy. The volume of investment necessary for CWS and sanitation implied that the government would have to gradually step back from being the sole player. However, for the Vietnamese authorities, privatization of urban CWS did not appear to be an acceptable alternative in the give-and-take formula.

The World Bank's Strategy

The World Bank is one of the main donors in the urban water supply sector in Vietnam's urban centres and therefore represents one of the major and most influential stakeholders in Vietnam's CWS sector reform. Between 1998 and 2003, the World Bank invested US$98.6 million in the water supply sector, to which is to be added over US$80 million for the sanitation programme in the country's three main cities. The World Bank's strategy in the CWS sector can be described as gradual. Early in the 1990s, its policy was based on the slogans of "privatization" and "profitability". Gradually, though, faced with reality,[8] the international institution found that it had to adopt a more flexible, open-ended approach.

Currently, the World Bank is seeking to develop a flexible partnership between "private" and "public", focusing on the performance of the mechanisms being promoted, regardless of the types of players, investors or businesses involved. Water companies had a hard time repaying the loans they received in the late 1980s because of the constantly recurring matter of public subsidizing. On the other hand, since 2000, loans given out have been conditional and encourage competition among the water companies to improve their performance. Through its new project *"Urban Supply Performance Benchmarking"* (2002), the World Bank puts public water companies in competition with one another when it agrees to make additional loans. The Bank makes more discreet reference to the private sector that, on this count, stays within the directions set by the government through the Ministry of Construction.

In this CWS reform process, the social dimension — a constant concern of the national authorities — is being given greater consideration in international financing policies. The public powers in Vietnam do not want to privatise CWS across the board, especially in the large cities, with its risk of marginalizing the poorest and possibly triggering a social and political crisis.

As far as the World Bank is concerned, private operators are already present in the water sector. It is encouraging the establishment of joint ventures between public works and construction entrepreneurs and provincial water companies. It wants such ventures to be independent from the People's Committees and to operate on the basis of a contract entered into between two business entities. The World Bank feels that the government is open to such new approaches but the workings will have to be tested first through a pilot project. The role of the Association of Water Companies needs to be strengthened and formalised. It would be advisable to establish a forum with a number of such companies on it. Hai Phong has been put forward as an example of this approach.

In the World Bank's view, if water companies are to become profitable, the tariff structure must be under the purview of these companies; otherwise, if the objective is political, it boils down to a social assistance system.

The Asian Development Bank's Strategy

The ADB has been involved in development activities in the water supply sector and sanitation infrastructure since 1993. The aid programme included technical assistance granted to the municipality of Ho Chi Minh City to prepare the water supply master plan, as well as three projects covering eighteen provinces for a total of US$195 million in loans. Recognizing the importance of the private sector's role in water supply infrastructure development, the ADB made a concessional loan in 2000 of US$35 million for a BOT (build-operate-transfer) project for the Thu Duc water treatment plant in Ho Chi Minh City. This was the largest privately contributed BOT project (totalling US$140 million) and it illustrates ADB's wish to promote new forms of public-private partnership. The ADB's presence in this type of project enables private companies to get long-term loans, propose efficient management forms and construction technologies and at the same time speed up project execution.[9]

Although the ADB's wish is clear and comes across strongly in favour of private sector development, the recent BOT projects did not prove to be successful. They reveal a pattern of firm resistance on the part of the Vietnamese authorities to these new methods of funding and managing CWS infrastructure.

The French Strategy — The French Development Agency's Economic Mission

Starting in 1989, France spent a decade assisting French corporations to get established in Vietnam through "protocols of agreement". The idea was to help them get into this emerging market and to expand in the long term. Today, however, the assessment report is mixed because some of these corporations are pulling out due to setbacks they suffered. In the final analysis, the CWS sector is viewed as unprofitable. Indeed, although BOT projects had been promoted from 1997 onward and seemed to be developing in several types of infrastructure such as roads, railway, etc., their transposition into the water sector was unsuccessful in a number of cases, which has led to putting this approach on the back burner. And although some donors still feel that this is a potential avenue for funding, the Vietnamese government seems very reticent to support its generalization.

At the conclusion of the first ten years of project funding in the water sector and assisting French businesses to get set up in Vietnam, the picture is rather dismal. Of almost a dozen firms established here at the end of the 1990s, only a minority are continuing to operate for various reasons.[10] So the water sector that looked like a promising inroad for French firms of international reputation has proven to be very narrow, if not a dead end.

Since the late 1990s, the AFD took over the Economic Expansion Post (EEP) in the CWS sector. This post has now begun targeting sanitation and waste treatment projects deemed to be more profitable. This change reveals

France's new position in the CWS sector. From now on, the AFD, as the other key donors, is advocating public-private partnership development in Vietnam.

Summary of Institutional Strategies

At the conclusion of this first decade of CWS reform, it is possible to see the sectors that stand out because of the successful transformations made in them and those for which greater change must yet be made.

Schematically, ten years of reform have seen a fundamental increase in the volume of water produced and technical improvements due to the overhauling of old systems or implementing new investment projects to cope with a growing demand. The main objectives were the reduction of physical and financial losses, increase in production capacity, network extension and widespread installation of meters in the homes of customers. Efforts ended up being focused on increasing production capacity to such an extent that some projects were overdone (Viêt Tri, Hai Duong, Yen Bai, Lao Cai and Gia Lam), with distribution networks often suffering neglect in terms of necessary overhauling and extension.

Currently, from the standpoint of demand, the growth of the main urban centres suggests that there will be a major demand increase and that water use will diversify (domestic, industrial, agricultural, tourism, etc.). Given the worrisome environmental situation in some cities with regard to sanitation, new costly technical water treatment procedures will become necessary. Meeting the needs everywhere and maintaining water quality therefore will require heavy investment in the future. The matter of funding these projects has not been resolved. Although in the recent past multilateral and bilateral assistance enabled needs to be met by helping production catch up, foreign loans will not suffice to finance future needs. Moreover, new multilateral funding will only be available if conditions are met that involve reform of the water companies and injection of a significant dose of private initiative. Regardless of the funding solution advocated, the issue of tariff structure has to be dealt with and is the keystone of the reform and its viability.

But beyond these financial and economic aspects, it appears that access to water and its tariff structure are strategic political issues. Will the People's Committees be willing to accept an increase in the price of water and yield to the financial and accounting arguments of the water companies? In order for international donors to support CWS reform, will they have to impose their model on Vietnam — by attaching more demanding conditions to their funding — as they appeal increasingly for private sector involvement?

Will demand take over for needs and become the new cornerstone for CWS "sustainability"? Will the commercialization of water governed by international dictates prevail over a regulated, social approach to water? This would be the likely scenario if the Vietnamese authorities do not extend the commercial approach to the CWS sector as it did for health and education that were "socialized", that is, in part privatized.

Vietnam is clearly at the crossroads with regard to the future of its water policy. But it must also be understood that what is involved is not simply a matter of two technical models of clean water management that previously existed and that have been competing with one another for a decade now, with neither of them gaining the upper hand. Such a comparison cannot be applied here. For the international levels, the panorama is clear, the slogans are well established and the tools running smoothly, but for the Vietnamese side, there is a very different problem. The authorities appear to know exactly what they don't want, in fact, what makes them shudder. On the other hand, the CWS reform pathway has not been out. Although the ideological foundations of the socialist-oriented market economy are immutable, the forms of management to be promoted, the pace of these reforms, the relinquishments to be accepted and innovations to be allowed are a matter under debate. A vast — and dual — field is open with regard to CWS as well as to institutional and political reform — in the literal sense — that is to direct and stimulate the former.

Since 1997, experiments have been conducted on these management models in both urban and rural contexts. In this area, the South seems to be a laboratory of choice because nearly all of the conceivable new options have been tried there, such as BOT projects in Hô Chi Minh City or sector privatization initiatives (construction). Although these experiments have been limited and not particularly diversified, they nevertheless represent a body of pilot projects that the authorities (MoC and government) are giving particular attention to their "cost recovery" and their "affordability" or "agree to pay" component on the part of users-consumers.

Key Facets of the Vietnamese Clean Water Management Model

Although the international debate can be broken down into two main lines of thought (firstly the liberal line as represented by the World Bank and large private consortiums and secondly the alter-globalists line),[11] in Vietnam the debate is hinging on several issues without taking a firm stand for one line of thinking or the other. Is there a specifically Vietnamese model? Even though Vietnam is obliged to reform its water companies and different forms of public-private partnership are being explored, it is not certain that Vietnam will eventually accept the principle. The privatization tests and the expectations that the BOT's might have aroused seem to be implicitly disavowed at the present time.

Forward and backward movements have punctuated the reform period. Regardless of the option chosen by the government, many questions remain, showing that beyond the economic issues, the matter of water remains politically and socially sensitive. The current blockages centre on several interdependent considerations: the status and degree of decentralization of the water companies, the tariff structure and the management models of the water companies.

Status of the Water Companies

Since 1995, the Law on Businesses has also purported to promote the reform of public sector enterprises. In 1998, water companies were classified as public utility economic units with the duty to relinquish subsidization while remaining under People's Committee control. The long-term objective was to "supply the people with water for production and routine requirements while remaining financially self-sufficient and fulfilling their public utility objective". The resolution of the Plenum of the Ninth Communist Party Congress (2001) on the subject of "pursuing the policy followed for overhauling, developing and improving the performance of State-owned enterprises", stipulated that water companies are no longer public utility but commercial companies.

The change in status from public utility enterprises to commercial enterprises is tending to become generalized and is being referred to with increasing clarity in legislation (see the Law on State-owned Enterprises). The water company monopoly was perceived as an obstacle to reform of the sector. Now, opening it up to other enterprises is still a sensitive matter, especially in the large cities. Water companies are in a monopoly situation and they are not to take unfair advantage of it. So the government needs to put in the necessary legislative framework to protect user interests. However, water companies can only be effectively reformed if they are granted a greater degree of independence in relation to People's Committees.

In 1990, Resolution 217 stated that the tariff structure of water is to be decentralized from the Governmental Price Commission to the Provincial People's Committees. At the same time, government subsidies have been cut back. Since then, each People's Committee approves, after deliberation by the People's Council, the tariffs set by the provincial water company. The relationship between the local authorities and water companies is tense, sometimes even antagonistic. The degree of dependency of the water companies towards the local authorities, however, is such that there can be no actual enforcement of the real prices. A clear split between the two entities is necessary. At the present time, price decision-making power resides with the People's Council, which is the legislative agency at the provincial level. Circular 03 of the MoC is currently the recommended tariff schedule. But for it to be enforced by the water companies, they have to submit their tariff schedule to the People's Committee who in turn has to have it approved by the People's Council.

This level of decentralization is a serious obstacle to development of the sector. While prices of electricity, petrol and labour are on the rise, the price of water remains unchanged. This decentralization process has meant a disparity in the prices charged in provinces that border on one another but in which natural conditions are the same, thus creating social imbalances. Studies conducted in several cities indeed reveal strong differences between the price of water and the average income of the population, with large cities such as Hanoi and Hô Chi Minh City benefiting from generously subsidized water while provinces in the north are paying the full price. These disparities are increasingly criticized in the disadvantaged provinces and creating new sources of conflict.

Water Tariff Structure

In most developed countries, water is considered to be an economic asset that has costs of production, delivery, collection and treatment. As for water distribution and access to it, one of the current benchmark principles affirms that "water pays for itself",[12] in other words the users cover the basic expenses entailed by the investment in and operation of water equipment through their water bill. In Vietnam, tariff setting is therefore a core issue and is the subject of strategic debates.

A seminar on the issue of pricing water was held in 2002 by the Vietnam Water and Sanitation Association (VWSA). The problems debated included the issue of water company self-financing and the price-setting process. Case studies showed that the Hanoi Water Company was now faced with repaying loans taken out from Finland although it did not have sufficient own-source income to cover all of its own expenses (electricity, wages, etc.). The water company therefore continues to be subsidized by the

Hanoi People's Committee. The proposal made by the Water and Sanitation Association was to advocate the self-financing of water companies, which meant doubling the price of water, in order to ensure the profitability of the firms. But the Hanoi People's Committee and more importantly the People's Council were opposed to the idea of increasing the price of water. Hanoi's situation is not unique and it characterises in fact a widespread and now recurrent problem in Vietnam.

The water problem is different from that of electricity for an institutional reason. In the latter sector, the Ministry of Industry decides the price in accord with the government, while the city People's Committee, under the authority of the People's Council, is the decision-maker for water supply and sanitation. The problem is therefore of a political nature, relating to the social policy concerning water. There is already a policy for war invalids and national heroes. For electoral reasons, the members of the People's Council do not want to give the green light to an increase in water prices. Water sector reform seems to be in a stalemate in Hanoi due to being tied in with ideological conflicts of interest on the backdrop of the collectivist legacy of the subsidization mechanism,[13] as much at the level of the poorest of the poor as with the subsidized water companies.

When the idea of a rate acceptable to the people is mentioned, it is not clear what this notion covers. And very often in debates on the issue of price setting, the people are not consulted. But surveys conducted in the cities of Hanoi and Hai Phong show that people are generally prepared to pay more in return for a regular, good quality water supply service. The price of water does not appear as a major expense for urban households, although it would be a different matter for rural communities. Overall, people are aware that water is subsidized and know that in the long run, the price of water is bound to increase as it has for other utilities. However, on the side of the demand, the requirements of the people will condition any announced price hike, that is, for a higher fee, the water company — or any other operator — will be obliged to offer quality service.

The Asian Development Bank is advocating a rate of less than 3 per cent of the household's monthly income. According to statistics from 2002, the average urban monthly income is 1.3 million dongs while the price of water is 2,100 dongs per cubic metre (m^3), or 0.65 per cent of the average monthly income, which would indicate in theory that households can afford to pay the price of water. Moreover, the share that the water bill takes from the average monthly income per capita is very disparate geographically: 0.8 per cent in Hanoi, 0.6 per cent in Hô Chi Minh City, 0.8 per cent in

Da Nang, 0.5 per cent in Vung Tau compared to 3.5 per cent in Ha Giang, 3.2 per cent in Cao Bang, 1.5 per cent in Hung Yen and 2.1 per cent in Tiên Giang. Decentralization of the water policy and in particular the price-setting system is leading to major socio-spatial inequities favouring big cities where the standard of living is the highest.

A further criticism is voiced by the water companies regarding the subsidization of water: the social policy regarding water is to help disadvantaged groups, considering a minimum volume consumed of 16 cubic metres per month (135 litres per day). However, based on World Bank reports, minimum consumption can be set at 8 cubic metres (50 to 60 litres per day), which means that a very large part of the population is being classified as poor, while the people actually can afford to pay for water. The standard of 16 m^3 is therefore misleading and is contributing to the water price subsidy.

In order to make up for losses due to the low price of domestic water, some provinces have increased the price of water for other tariff categories (such as industries and services) to an excessive degree (5,000 to 7,000 dongs per cubic metre), with the immediate consequence being the multiplication of private drillings. The high cost for industries means that firms are inclined to do their own drilling in order to access cheap water, which compounds management of the resource and the problem of verifying groundwater quality.

In addition to the issue of tariff fixing there is the problem that part of the income from water cannot be collected due to leaks and the poor performance of the management system. Indeed, the payment of a lump sum continues — sometimes even after a meter has been put in — and the lack of consistency between users and rates leads to major financial losses despite the notable improvements made over the last ten years. In Hanoi, for example, very few services and businesses actually pay the rate in effect. Conversely, despite a new law enacted in 2001 reducing the price to be paid by foreigners, some of them are still paying the old rate (6,500 dongs per cubic metre).

The issue of tariff structure is doubly crucial in Ho Chi Minh City, on the one hand because the demand is tremendous and on the other hand because the failure of different BOT projects is directly linked to the issue of the price of water.[14] The economic capital seems to be a reflection of crossover tension between a government that is holding on to its choice of water sector monopoly and the private sector that is hoping to get into the market. Management choices aside, the issue of the water tariff remains.

Water Company Management Models

The tariff structure for water depends in part on the status of the water companies. If they are made into commercial entities, but the People's Committees do not accept the tariff increases, the situation appears to be an impasse. If the rate is increased and if the water companies continue to work in the framework of subsidies without striving to make a profit and improve service, the system will not be sustainable in the long run. So the choice of what management model to adopt remains paramount. That is the basic issue raised by different water stakeholders, and no single, simple answer has been forthcoming. And obviously the question is as technical as it is political.

The first model, one of reforming the water company internally with foreign investments, such as in Hai Phong, enjoys strong backing. Decentralized management is possible because of the existence of several networks on the urban service area. The approach has shown good service performance and encourages the improvement of the public utility and consequently the revamping of public companies. But this model cannot be replicated uniformly throughout the country, especially not in the large cities.

Currently, urban growth in the two Vietnamese metropolises requires heavy investment that the government is unable to cover. However, the need is to meet an often-localized growing demand. Thus, mini-networks are being developed based on a variety of management formulae (BOT, private investor, Vietnamese urban projects, etc.) and are avenues that can be explored.

Despite attempts at privatizing water supply at the level of the big cities in the form of BOT projects, this new trend is not the preferred way to go, or seems to be still at the discussion stage. Forms of "public-public partnerships" (VINACONEX) appear to enjoy greater acceptance on the part of the government. What has to be determined is whether the public sector is in a position to meet the foreseeable needs financially and, more importantly, technically. Paradoxically, it is observed that the private sector, through the "socialization" of water, is strongly encouraged in rural communities, but there again under total management control (foreign NGOs or private Vietnamese firms). Eventually, these mini-networks, after entering into contracts with the provincial water companies, will come under them, in a one-off attempt to quickly cover domestic or other demands.

The "socialization" of water in urban contexts is now a hot issue and the government is learning from past experience; it is developing new approaches. It is leaving the door open to original mechanisms, attempting to adapt them to the plural realities of the country and to its strategic and ideological choices.

Concluding Thoughts

For Vietnam's large metropolises, the announced targets for network hook-up and consumption are as follows: 80 per cent in 2000 (150 l/p/d), 100 per cent in 2010 (160 l/p/d) and 100 per cent in 2020 (180 l/p/d). The number of urban CWS projects on the drawing board would cost 11,500 billion dongs, three quarters of which would be sourced abroad.

In its efforts to meet these targets, the CWS problem in Vietnam is driven by the supply. With the support of the World Bank and government of Finland, a two-phase strategy has been promoted. A first step (1990–2000) involved building the institutional and management capacity of water companies and servicing or overhauling urban delivery networks (in particular in the large cities of Hanoi, Ho Chi Minh City and Hai Phong).[15] The second step aims to control and increase the water available in order to meet the spiralling demand.

Furthermore, the problem of access to water for communities of poor working class people is acute in Hanoi as it is in most cities in less developed countries (LDC). But it is important to consider the macroeconomic dynamics that show a decline in poverty in Vietnam:[16] target of 10 per cent of the population below the poverty line in 2005 with a strong drop over the last twenty years (40 per cent were poor in 1985). In an initial phase (1993–98), "the main factor contributing to poverty reduction was economic growth relating to the assignment of land to small farmers, as well as agricultural liberalisation and diversification" (National Centre of Social Science and the Humanities 2002).

Meanwhile, an emerging industrial fabric resulting from polarized growth in Southeast Asia and led by China is contributing to renewed high growth (approaching two figures). A vast dynamics of urban inclusion is what is being looked for; this requires a proletarisation and structured segmentation of urban society. But at the same time, the phenomenon of socioeconomic marginality and urban exclusion does not have the lingering character observed in developing countries. Clearly, the degree of inclusion in the international division of labour will leave a deep mark on the physiognomy of urban sector policies and the like. It is clearly seen that the urgency of the CWS offer in Vietnam is due to the swing that it experienced in just a few years in terms of economic and urban growth (institutionally since 1986 with *Doi Moi*, then in practice since the early 1990s, then with a shakedown in 1997, followed by a sustained pace since 2000). In Vietnam, the offer has seemingly delayed in becoming aligned with the dynamics of the urban water demand for reasons of investment and funding.

The national budget deficit in Vietnam (negative balance of 3 per cent) and controlled inflation strongly limit the government's capacity to subsidise. And national savings, although on the rise, remain insufficient to cover public utility infrastructure needs. With the shortfall in national public financing, other resources will have to be mobilized. Vietnam is therefore not far from the debates that raged on everywhere during the 1990's on themes of subsidiarity, privatization and governance less directly dependent on political power. The public-private partnership formula used in many urban contexts (Casablanca, Rabat, Buenos Aires, etc.) seems also to be the way in which Vietnam will embark on, but with the immediate proviso that, in the strategic area of CWS, Vietnam will forge its own doctrine. Although since the inception of *Doi Moi,* Vietnam has not escaped the liberal wave and assault of international slogans, it has done so in a very specific mode: the central government is effectively turning to the market and opening up internationally, but keeping a firm grip on the reins. It is coming up with its own solutions on a "trial and error" basis. The "build operate-transfer" formula had its successful spell in the wake of the myth of transition that suggested in the 1990s that private operators would resolve the issue of financing the development of developing countries. Official development assistance was supposed to be superseded by flows of foreign direct investment.

But the 1997 Asian crisis made shareholders very jittery at the notation of "risk country", which was the agonizing re-evaluation that multinational firms made on the developing country portfolio,[17] and the swing from "BOT's commercially guaranteed by the State" to "BOT's not commercially guaranteed" (Jacquet and Charnoz 2003, p. 12)[18] was a strong impediment to the success of these mechanisms as the financial panacea of urban infrastructure. This situation has now caused the public-private partnership formula to resurface, but based on an innovative mode, because international operators cannot be depended upon.

In this regard, a detour to the great neighbour, China, may prove enlightening; it is interesting to read the following press clipping that comments bluntly on the direction taken by China in the field of mobile telephony:

> There is no way that the government, in its constant concern for national preference, will allow the great global players grab the cake. This nationalist option is clearly in favour of the operators;

> foreigners are undesirable except for holding shares (very minority) in the framework of World Trade Organisation agreements. Beijing is encouraging competition but exclusively among public entities. Two operators hold licences for mobile telephony, China Mobil and China Unicom. . . . As for components manufactures, the landscape is less rigid but the State remains a voluntaristic stakeholder in industrial policy, whether the corporations are public or private. The government has encouraged local electronics conglomerates to sign cooperation agreements with foreigners everywhere in order to quickly acquire technical savvy.[19]

The die is cast: there will be PPP in Southeast Asia, but based on a conspicuously different model from that which operators have been accustomed to up to the present, even at the international level.

In their realm of operation, water companies will seemingly be in charge of overhauling old networks, reducing leaks, getting rid of public water fountains (early 1990s) and getting away from lump-sum to individual meter-based billing.

Network extensions can take on different forms: ownership by the developer with the cost being passed on to new individual owners by charging for hook-up, with the intervention of private Vietnamese entities and intervention by large Vietnamese corporations.

Consequently, the following possible scenarios can be formulated regarding institutional changes in Vietnam's CWS sector:

- Public water companies and their staff will be maintained for historical reasons, but will not be developers in the field of urban extensions. This symbol of collectivist economy is spared. Also in view of the local electoral issues (provincial People's Committees) that are tied in with water, it would be difficult to speed up the pace of this reform.
- New investments in water delivery and treatment will be directly or indirectly paid for by the customer, more particularly, by those in the middle class.
- The choice of operator may give preference to Vietnamese investors, at least based on what seems to have been learned from experiments with private sector involvement. However, the most probable scenario is a run off among large Vietnamese technical and financial corporations established in the public interest coming under state capitalism and already active in such areas as construction (VINACONEX), along the lines of the Korean model (*chaebol*).

But the issue is less one of their financial foundation and managerial expertise than one of their ability to get a handle on the technology specific to the water sector. If this strategy of exclusivity, first Vietnamese and then very probably through state capitalism, was to be borne out in the area of new water production and delivery capacities, it would suggest a genuine appropriation of the technical expertise. However, foreign private operators in the sector (Ondéo, Veolia, SAUR) are perhaps no longer willing to wait any longer for an improbable deregulation of the sector. They may prefer to turn to countries that are safer — those of Central and Eastern Europe — or where the rules of the game are more predictable. They will perhaps tire of this game of being taken for a ride that resulted from the myth of transition, in which Vietnam was able to mobilize resources and expertise on an experimental basis for ten years.

Moreover, in the near future, water and sanitation companies will no longer be in a position to meet the substantial demand brought on by urban growth and the obvious environmental constraints in terms of wastewater treatment. But although this desire to build up the CWS sector into a genuinely Vietnamese-style public sector (although competitive) is being applied prematurely, it could be that the expertise and experience level of these state firms will still be inadequate. The services that would be provided by these new institutional and technical mechanisms would then be cryingly inadequate in relation to the escalating growth of the urban water and sanitation demand.

A strong sense of both independence and national pride is perceived to be behind this strategy. However, a real race against time is also seen, on the one hand between the urban water and sanitation demand, now gauged according to international standards — in volume if not in quality — and on the other, the corresponding acquisition of national institutional, financial and technological capacity in the field of CWS.

The haunting question to be answered is the specificity of the water sector, if any. Is this approach of national independence and development seen in all urban public utilities? Is it not an ideological legacy that is still hanging on, but only for a generation that will be retiring from business in another ten years? And if the odds in this race between the growth of the demand and construction of strictly national mechanisms turned out to be uneven, what alternative would become advisable or mandatory?

In the final analysis, it appears that the debate framed in terms of private or public is becoming stale in developing countries. After the widespread slide[20] of municipal water authorities, after the foretold triumph of the market, in recent years we have moved into a new step, because the direction is no longer just that of choosing between private or public but has now broadened to involve the private and public binomial. However, it would be hasty to consider these mechanisms as the panacea. Indeed, regardless of the partnership combination, the situation of operator exclusivity puts him in a monopoly situation on urban territory. The issue is not so much that of the mechanism and its private or public status, but rather that of regulating it in order to check or prevent monopoly situations.

Vietnam intends to take advantage of the competition between stakeholders with a regulation process that remains solidly in the hands of the State, but which does not rule out a compromise among the many variables found in the CWS sector. Vietnam provides an exciting example of creativity around the prospects opened up by public-private partnerships.

Notes

The distribution of clean water has been studied with a particular focus on the regional context of northern Vietnam. This study received the institutional and scientific support of Tran Hieu Nhue, Director of the Centre of Environmental Engineering of Towns and Industrial Areas (CEETIA), Hanoi University of Civil Engineering, and Dr Nguyen Van Tin, Deputy Director of the Faculty of Environment Technologies, Hanoi University of Civil Engineering.

We express our thanks to the Cooperation Centre for Urban Development [*Institut des Métiers de la Ville* (IMV)], the Embassy of France in Hanoi (SCAC), the Hanoi Economic Mission, the *Agence française de développement* (AFD), ADETEF, SAFEGE, CNEE as well as the NGO EAST for sharing with us various documents and information (press reviews, reports, contacts, etc.) that enabled us complete this analysis. We also thank the World Bank and the Urban Forum, along with the Vietnam Water and Sanitation Association.

1 Is this water "clean" in the sense of being drinkable? In Vietnam, water is more often called "clean" if it is clear, with no reference to potability.

2 From 403,000 to 674,000 m^3/d for high consumption days.

3 For purposes of comparison, the price of 1 cubic metre of water in 2001 in U.S. dollar was 1.60 in Chennai, 1.38 in Bangalore, 1.17 in Hyderabad and 0.61 in Colombo (India), and 0.53 in Kathmandu (Nepal) (Source: World Bank, *Water and Sanitation Program*).
In 1999, the price of water in Shanghai was US$1.15 (Source: *Le Quotidien du Peuple,* 4 December 2002).

4 Reducing losses to less than 10 per cent of production — even for a new network — is a challenging technical and economic objective and can be achieved with an incremental cost increase. It is felt that a 15-per cent loss rate is acceptable in a network in good condition. A water loss rate in excess of 20 per cent requires measures to reduce leaks or overhaul the network.

5 Decision No. 63/TTg and Directive No. 40/TTg from the prime minister.

6 In the context of European countries, annual average domestic consumption is generally estimated at 140 l/p/d.

7 But it would be wrong to see therein an expression straight out of the collectivist legacy. Indeed, in market economy contexts, the government is just as concerned with changes in prices of essential goods (such as the price of water per m^3). See the example of price management in the case of Casablanca, Morocco, with its public utility delegation to Ondéo (Suez-Lyonnaise des Eaux).

8 Faced with the national requirement — real or stated — to build a socialist-oriented market economy.

9 "We hope that models of partnership such as the Thu Duc project and those that have been successful elsewhere in the region can be examined closely in Vietnam and that such partnerships can be pursued more proactively to help relieve the burden on the Government in financing such infrastructure. The ADB stands ready to assist the Vietnamese Government in building the enabling institutional framework, regulatory capability and in providing access to the necessary technical expertise to support such partnerships." — Financing and Developing Environmental Infrastructure in Vietnam: The Case of Water Supply and Wastewater Treatment Practitioners' Workshop, by Mr John Samy, Resident Representative, Vietnam Resident Mission, Asian Development Bank. Hanoi, 22 March 2001.

10 SAUR pulled out in September 2003 when the Ha Long project went under. OTV-Vivendi is continuing to operate (projects funded by the ADB in smaller cities). SAFEGE is wondering if its presence in Vietnam is worth it, despite the good reputation it enjoys in the field. SADE in Da Nang is also getting out because the World Bank is no longer going to finance the project's continuation (the primary network has been installed, but the secondary network and construction of a new station remain unfinished). Lyonnaise des Eaux is also withdrawing due to the poor performance of the BOT project.

11 While being opposed to privatization, they say nothing about the necessary regulation of a public sector that they so desire.

12 At this point we will not delve into the extreme over-simplification conveyed by this slogan that totally dodges the equalization payments that prevail in the tariff-setting process or the strategies that govern inter-sectoral investments made in the areas of electricity, water, sanitation and mobile telephony.

13 Despite the effort put forth to improve network quality, there has not been a drop in losses; rather, they are tending to increase. It therefore seems that the problem of leaks is really linked to the problem of management on the part of the Hanoi Water Company. Two hypotheses are advanced: 1) either the level of financial loss is getting higher due to increasing embezzlement on the part of employees of the firm, 2) or arrangements among households and employees are increasing (lump sum) while consumption grows. Thus, the rate of loss is not

a consideration that the Water Company will give much attention to, knowing that the People's Committee will "make up the difference" in the form of subsidies.

14 Based on the proposal of the Ho Chi Minh City People's Committee, the average price of water for the 2004–13 period will be 4,200 dongs/m^3 instead of the current price of 2,500 dongs/m^3. The domestic price will increase from 1,700 dongs/m^3 to 2,800 dongs/m^3 <www.vnexpress.net>.

15 Fifty-three provincial capitals are affected by this target of a 70 per cent to 80 per cent urban hook-up rate. The estimated cost is US$750 million.

16 "Analysis of regional data for 1993–98 reveals for instance that the increase in income for the poorest fifth of the population was much greater than that for the richest two fifths (Basilacan, Pernia and Estrada 2003)", quoted by Jacquet and Charnoz (2003).

17 Showing preference for truly emerging countries or, better yet, eastern European countries.

18 The idea is a new sharing of risk to be established between the government and operators, such as on the price of inputs.

19 The government of China wants to promote the emergence of national champions, Frédéric Bobin, *Le Monde,* Tuesday 30 December 2003, p. 14.

20 Low productivity, opaque subsidization, overstaffing, high structural losses of water and revenue, mediocre service out of step with urban expansion.

References

ADETEF. "La réforme des entreprises publiques au Vietnam". 2003, 10 pp. (note).

Association de l'Eau et de l'Assainissement du Vietnam. "Water Supply and Sanitation in Provincial Towns in Vietnam". Hanoi, 30 November to 3 December 2000, 591 pp. (Technical Papers).

Basilacan, Arsenio M., Ernesto M. Pernia, and Gemma Esther B. Estrada. "Economic Growth and Poverty Reduction in Vietnam". ERD Working Paper no. 42. Bangkok: Asian Development Bank, 2003.

Centre National des Sciences Sociales et Humaines. *Rapport sur le développement humain du Vietnam 2001, Le Doi Moi et le développement humain au Vietnam.* Hanoi: Éditions Politiques Nationales, 2002, 149 pp.

Fukuyama, Francis. *La fin de l'histoire et le dernier homme*. Paris: Flammarion (Champs) 1994.

Jacquet, Pierre and Olivier Charnoz. "Infrastructures, croissance et réduction de la pauvreté". AFD, Article pour le Forum franco-vietnamien (6–13 Septembre 2003), 20 pp.

JICA. "The Study on Hanoi Water Supply Systems in 1997". Final Report, 1997, 29 pp.

Maison du Droit Vietnamo-Française. "Colloque franco-vietnamien sur les grands projects d'infrastructures". Actes juridiques et économiques et financiers, Hanoi 19–21 May 1997. Paris: Hachette, Lagardère SCA, 1997, 262 pp.

Ministère de la Construction. "Orientations de développement du système de l'approvisionnement en eau en milieu urbain jusqu'en 2020". Hanoi, 1998, 81 pp.

———. "Orientations d'aménagement global du développement urbain au Vietnam jusqu'en 2020" (selon la decision governmentale no. 10/1998/QD-TTg du 23/01/1998). Hanoi, 1999, 84 pp.

———. "Orientations d'aménagement global du développement urbain au Vietnam jusqu'en 2020". Hanoi, 1999, 110 pp.

———. "Hoi nghi cap nuoc do thi toan quoc lan thu IV" [IVe Séminaire sur l'approvisionnement en eau en ville]. Hanoi, 2001, 136 pp.

———. "Project d'approvisionnement en eau en milieu urbain au Viêt Nam (P073763). Étude de préfaisabilité". Hanoi: Black & Veatch International et VIWASE, 2003, 122 pp. + annexes.

Ministry of Agriculture and Rural Development. "National Workshop on Capacity Building for Water Resources Management in Vietnam, Water Resources Consulting Services". Asian Development Bank, 1999.

Ministry of Construction, Ministry of Agriculture and rural Development. "National Rural Clean Water Supply and Sanitation Strategy up to Year 2020". Hanoi, 2000, 83 pp.

Nguyên An Lich and Duong Duc Tin. "Public Health and Gender Impacts of Hanoi Water Supply System". Hanoi: Hanoi University Environmental and Sociological Study, 1994, 106 pp.

Pollard, Richard and Hoang Thi Hoa. "Global Small Towns Water and Sanitation Initiative. Comparative Study of Water Supply and Sanitation Services Management Models in Small Towns of Developing Countries, Vietnam Case Study". Preliminary findings. ADCOM Consulting Company with Hydroconseil, 2001, 18 pp.

SAGEP-SOGREA, WMI. "Project d'amélioration de la gestion technique et commerciale du service des eaux de la ville de Hadông, province de Ha Tay". Analyse technique, économique et financière du project. Étude de faisabilité. Protocole franco-vietnamien, 2000, 88 pp.

Van den Berg, Caroline. "Viet Nam Evolving Management Models for Small Towns Water Supply in a Transitional Economy". Water and Sanitation Program. ADCOM, 2002, 28 pp.

Viện, Quy hoạch Đô thị-Nông thôn (Chủ biên), Đặng Xuân Đường, dưới sự hướng dẫn của Tô Thị Minh Thông, hợp tác với Gubry Patrick, Huguet Jerrold W. *Dân số và môi trường đô thị thành phố Hà Nội. Hà Nội: Nhà xuất bản Chính trị quốc gia*, 1996, 110 tr. (Dự án VIE/92/P02).

New ref.: National Institute for Urban and Rural Planning (NIURP) (ed.), Dang Xuan Duong, under the dir. of To Thi Minh Thong, in coll. with Gubry Patrick, Huguet Jerrold W. "Population and urban living environment in Hanoi City".

Hanoi: The National Political Publishing House, 1996, 77 pp. (VIE/93/P02 project).

The World Bank, ADB, FAO, UNDP. *Viet Nam Water Resources Sector Review*. May 1996, 150 pp.

———. *Benchmarking, Urban Water Supply, Socialist Republic of Vietnam*. East Asia Urban Development Sector Unit, Vietnam, April 2002, 19 pp.

World Bank and Institute for Urban Studies. *Role of Community in Management and Operation for Water Supply and Sanitation Projects of Districts, Small Towns and Rural Residential Areas in Vietnam*. Hanoi 2002.

UNDP. Human Development Report 1999. New York: UNDP and Oxford University Press, 1999, 172 pp.

———. Human Development Report 2003. New York: UNDP and Oxford University Press, 2003, 292 pp.

Photo: Patrick Gubry, April 2005

Ho Chi Minh City: Phu My Hung New Town, District 7, modern blocks of flats

6

The Role of Civil Society in Urban Environmental Management

Rene Parenteau
Nguyen Quoc Thong

All international cooperation agencies promote public participation and assert the need to mobilize civil society in urban environmental management. The World Bank is one of the main promoters of this approach, which it describes as good urban governance (World Bank, 1999).

In fact, they all strictly adhere to the principles put forward by Agenda 21 (1992 Rio Conference). These principles advocate decentralizing environmental management responsibilities in favour of local government, as well as the need for local government to involve the population and to work in partnership with the private sector and with the associative and community sector. The majority of programmes privilege capacity-building and the transfer of real power to such stakeholders. However, such principles assume that civil society is an organized entity comprising stakeholders which are independent from the government and which can act as its potential partners.

The objective of our research has been to study the role of Vietnamese civil society in urban environmental management within the framework of actual environmental projects, so as to assess the connections or lack thereof between Vietnamese society's grassroots organizations (that is, People's Committee, patriotic associations and mass organizations) and what are commonly known as NGOs. Such projects should illustrate three types of civil society mobilization within the framework of urban environmental management practices: environmental planning and management, the provision of urban environmental services and the management of environmental conflicts.

Our overall theoretical construction operates under the concept of governance. Governance describes a general socio-political concept within which relations between governments and civil society take place, with the objective of reinforcing local capacities in order to decentralize administration. Civil society includes the private sector, but in current political strategies, it really mainly consists of grassroots community organizations (GCO).

The second stage consists in recognizing these organizations, developing their capacity and empowering them. The aim of developing capacities is to enable the construction of new, efficient and democratic local institutions in order to support the sustainable development of communities according to directions set out in the national objectives. GCOs are expected to turn around the approach to demand assessment, so that the supply of urban services is established using demand as the starting point. They are expected to help clarify and formulate demand; to mobilize the beneficiaries and parties involved through participative processes and public consultation; to take part in the management of urban services and infrastructures according to the beneficiaries' financial capacity; finally, they are expected to make technical decisions that privilege local knowledge, resources and materials, as well as soft technologies well-adapted to the local context, and to generate wealth and employment.

In the socialist regimes of Southeast Asia (Vietnam and Laos), public participation, as it is understood in the West, is limited. These countries have nevertheless established their own mechanisms for mobilizing the population within the framework of official institutions (for example, People's Committees, Fatherland Front, Association of Women, Youth Association and various unions). There is a dearth of knowledge regarding such mechanisms and institutions, as we generally do not understand exactly how they function in practice and as the spokespersons of such regimes show some reserve about expressing their role and functioning.

For all the above reasons, we have focused on observing and analysing the conditions and points of emergence of the components of Vietnamese civil society within the framework of urban environmental management practices, in the context of local and community development programmes and actual projects involving public participation and management of environmental conflict. In order to study these projects and programmes, we have set up a detailed evaluation grid based on the following assumptions:

- Participation of civil society in urban environmental management should take place using sustainability and good local governance as guidelines.
- There should be an actual and genuine participation of civil society stakeholders in the environmental management process.
- Intervention from civil society stakeholders should be autonomous and should promote further development of their autonomy.
- The participation of civil society stakeholders should not be without rewards. It should empower them to build capacity for their own development and for greater efficiency in their other interventions.
- Finally, sustainable participation of civil society stakeholders can only be guaranteed by their ability to acquire relative financial autonomy.

After having explained the concept of civil society, we will analyse the way in which it applies to Vietnam. We will then look at the way in which it functions in the context of two local and community development programmes.

Civil Society and Urban Environmental Management

The concept of civil society attempts to reflect a specific form of power within human communities: it describes the natural relationship between individuals within their shared environment (White et al. 1996, p. 146). It is now generally thought that civil organizations should present the following characteristics: they should be autonomous and independent from the public sector; participate in the strengthening of associative fabric; contribute to the integration of individuals; allow cross-section membership; operate according to their own internal democratic rules and structure; seek horizontal membership (Hadenius and Uggla 1998, pp. 49–50).

Post and Rosenblum (2002, p. 1) point out that civil society is not a structuring element in all traditions of thought, and indeed its Western definition may not correspond to the Oriental conception of the foundation of society. The concept has also been questioned by others as it may not be applicable to certain social systems. The components of civil society have nevertheless become one of the targets and partners of international development cooperation agencies. The United States is by far the country which most widely supports civil society organizations within the framework of aid programmes (Howell and Pearce 2001, p. 92).

Urban Civil Society

With regards to civil society, the issues that interest us tend to be connected to local development and good urban governance. During the 1960s and 1970s, such questions were initially related mainly to urbanization and issues linked to rehousing and infrastructure. In the 1980s, more emphasis was placed on the administration and management of cities in developing countries. Only recently has the research agenda come to include local government as a fundamental element for the direction of development (McCarney 1996, pp. 5–6). Governance research distinguishes itself from other types of research on government in its attempt to understand the connection between civil society and the state. Governance issues are now among the most crucial questions associated with the development of human populations. More generally, faced with the inability of governments to manage the city, urban civil societies have dealt with an increasingly wide range of issues and problems.

The Components of Civil Society

Besides associations, GCOs and NGOs, the components of civil society potentially include a range of social groups and movements, based on religion and ethnicity, as well as more fluctuating voluntary associations founded on ideology, profession, social activities or the pursuit of various interests. Various critics consider that the concept of civil society has become too fragmented and empirically diffuse to be of much theoretical use (Giddens 1985, pp. 21–22). This should remind us to stick to a clear and precise definition of the concept.

Civil Society and Societies in Transition

Transition towards a market economy and democratic politics is not a straightforward process. Transition also implies a strategy implemented by international agencies, Western financial institutions, foreign and humanitarian aid programmes and other non-governmental organizations. According to Steven Sampson (1996, p. 121), these forces are supported by pre-existing structures. Stakeholders originating from transition contexts are thus able to advocate idealistic visions of civil society and to use it as a political instrument or to defend purely private interests.

A Vietnamese Civil Society?

As we have already mentioned, Western theories generally tend to agree that civil society constitutes a sphere which excludes the family and state. This configuration has no equivalent in the major Oriental political philosophy of Confucianism. Firstly, Confucianism does not mention any social organizations other than of the family, within which the individual is deeply rooted. It outweighs the individual's connection to the state. Secondly, Confucianism does not prescribe a form of government according to shared democratic precepts (Nosco 2002, p. 345). The impact of this ideology can be observed in the fact that voluntary organizations are perceived as destabilizing for the paternal state. They occupy arenas conceded by the state. In short, according to tradition, civil society and its organizations do not occupy first rank in the theoretical panorama which Vietnamese society refers to.

These remarks should not be taken to mean that, in Vietnamese civil society, there are no organisations comparable to those found in the West. From our own angle, the configuration of the public sector and civil society within the Vietnamese context certainly implies specific partnership perspectives for the field of urban environmental management.

Civil Society and Urban Environmental Management

Our research has focused on various organizations which corresponded to an open-ended definition of the term "civil society", in order to identify the characteristics specific to each one. Organizations were selected based on actual urban environmental management projects, and we have assumed that all non-governmental individuals and organizations participating in the various stages of an urban environmental management project can be assimilated to the concept of civil society. This seems a justified and relevant approach as it explicitly directed our focus towards active groups with actual capacities who were involved in community projects.

Our Definition and Our Approach

We have used the following definitions of civil society within the framework of this research: a public arena between the state and its citizens where general interest projects are undertaken and in which persons and groups carry out autonomous, structured and collective activities. Thus Vietnamese civil society should be understood as comprising: people's mass organizations; local associations; professional and trade associations; non-governmental organizations; minority groups; religious groups and village groups; representatives of the local populations of neighbourhoods, streets and housing estates; ordinary citizens who intervene publicly. Stakeholders and groups studied were selected based on the development projects chosen.

Vietnamese Civil Society and Urban Environmental Management

Medieval and Colonial Periods

Under the Nguyen dynasty (1802–1945), urban management — for example in the city of Hanoi — was entrusted to a mandarin responsible for the entire province, as well as to district chiefs and traditional ward representatives, elders [*tien chi*] and village leaders [*ly truong*]. The urban world was not much different from the rural world: its communal social structures were in fact borrowed from the rural world. To this day, so-called "urban" villages are still found all over Hanoi.

Rural lifestyles transferred to an urban environment, combined with strong urban growth, provoked major environmental problems directly affecting individual and public health. These problems were mainly associated with water, waste and urban agricultural practices. Each urban village therefore developed urban codes of conduct very early on, in order to regulate individual behaviour. These codes were first transmitted orally and later transcribed in a formal code called *Huong Uoc* (that is, internal regulations of the village).

Generally speaking, the *Huong Uoc* dealt with land, agricultural, environmental, social and political matters, as well as issues of faith and culture. The *Huong Uoc* was a general code of living; its aim was to create awareness among inhabitants and connect the various issues it dealt with so as to formulate a sort of environmental culture: raising the edges of paths and fields, protecting the wells and drawing water, using fertilizer correctly, sweeping the streets, planting trees, etc. In order to enforce respect of the codes of communal life and achieve its programmes for the protection and promotion of the environment, it made use of a vast array of methods such as corporal punishment (for example, lashing), fines paid into a common fund and forced community labour. In general, the entire population was liable to forced labour for environmental actions. In the villages, environmental protection was shared and was entrusted to certain leaders. Responsibilities were shared between the village leader, the *Huong Li* notable and the

Khan Thu, who was elected by the village assembly. These elements made up an equitable and democratic system of conventions based on customs and habits. This system based on conventions prevailed until 1945.

Between 1945 and 1975

Between 1945 and 1975, the State progressively took over from village customs dealing with issues concerning the environment. During this period, the Vietnamese government took a number of measures to seize control of urban environmental management. There mostly were massive information and mobilisation campaigns, such as the national tree planting campaigns initiated by President Ho Chi Minh in 1958. Environmental management was undertaken following government initiatives at all levels of the city, and was supervised by local Party and government representatives. Large-scale public road and sewerage works were undertaken and shared between local authorities and public enterprises. Street blocks, wards and districts committees became the new intermediate institutions in charge of environmental management. Their leaders were appointed by the People's Committee and were joined by civil servants and representatives of mass organizations such as women's associations, youth associations, elderly people's associations, etc. These committees operated on an informal basis without additional earnings.

Between 1975 and 1986

Between 1975 and 1986, urban environmental management changed from a system of controlled self-reliance to a structured programme, which was centrally planned and entirely subsidized. Information, awareness-raising and mobilization activities aimed at inhabitants became more controlled; they took place in the workplace within the public sector and state enterprises, as well as in school. Mass organizations were assigned a specific and visible role. Mobilization of the population continued to be organized for cleaning up and fighting epidemics, while large-scale projects were also undertaken: dredging the waste channels, raising of the dykes, clearing of mines and land clearing. Vast efforts were made to improve living conditions in collective housing, schools and universities.

After 1986: The Stakeholders of Urban Environmental Management

Reforms undertaken after 1986 aimed to rationalize the system as a whole, even though they did not initiate decentralization as such. They brought about the definition of the role and responsibilities of the ministries, especially in the environmental field. Debate on local democracy and public participation was barely introduced; however, links between local authorities and ministerial instances became more direct, which opened up a new sphere of influence, at least for mass organizations. In this context, it became possible to define urban environmental management as its own sector, framed by laws, regulations, decrees and directives. Specific services were created within ministries and local representatives were put in place.

However, the overall system is quite ineffectual for several reasons: insufficient financing, lack of qualified human resources, absence of integrated management, dearth of information and initiatives from the grassroots to inform decisions taken at superior levels. Urban management in Vietnam is organized on three levels: city, district and ward. Resident groups are not recognized organisms, although their role in the implementation of programmes and urban environmental management actions is extremely important.

The People's Council is a political assembly present at all levels — national, provincial, city, district, ward and village — composed of representatives elected by the population. It makes decisions regarding laws, regulations, general affairs, public investment, and social and humanitarian actions. The same applies to the People's Committees and mass organizations. The People's Council has legislative powers affecting the preservation and improvement of the urban environment. The People's Committee has an executive role. Its members are appointed by the People's Council. It puts in practice and executes the decisions of the People's Council, and executes state programmes. The People's Committee has a strong presence at local level and assumes its roles with much dynamism. The People's Council and the People's Committee can have special committees at every level for certain areas and programmes (for example, committees for the environment). The People's Council, the People's Committee and the special committees are all managed and controlled by the Communist Party.

One of the particularities of Vietnam's socio-political system is the existence of an extensive and tightly woven network of socio-political organizations as well as social and humanitarian organizations. Organizations with a socio-political role comprise the General Confederation of Labour, the Fatherland Front, the Women's Association, the Youth Association, the Association of Veterans and the Farmer's Association. All these associations are headed by the Fatherland Front within the framework of programmes and actions implemented by the People's Committee. Organizations with a social and humanitarian role comprise the Elderly People's Association, the

Red Cross and a whole range of association with specific roles which often work under the management of the larger associations or in close partnership with them. Socio-political organizations are subsidized by the government through their long chain of command ranging from national to local level, and through the various levels of control of the People's Committee. Social and humanitarian organizations are not government-subsidized, except within the framework of specific programmes. In both cases, membership is voluntary; but actions carried out by the People's Committee are intended to benefit members of the associations.

Mass associations participate in the activities of the People's Council and the People's Committee through the Fatherland Front representative. Inhabitants can suggest initiatives through this representative and, occasionally, through association representatives. However, the People's Committee considers the Fatherland Front and the associations as tools whose function is to support the implementation of policies and programmes, participate in environmental protection, raise awareness and educate the public, and, occasionally, act as environmental police. Clean-up activities exemplify this: at 6.30 a.m. every Saturday, members of the Youth Association clean the streets and public spaces in collaboration with people's organizations and inhabitants. Yet the role of the associations has yet to be defined in a clear and consistent way.

Resident groups form the basic (that is, smallest) administrative unit and include thirty or more households from one street, street section or block within a ward. They play an important role in the wards as they support the actions of the People's Committee and take part in their implementation. They are mainly mobilized to deal with the cleanliness of the nearby environment.

In practice, international NGOs intending to carry out urban environmental management projects in Vietnam are generally directed towards research centres, which are considered as the local equivalent to NGOs. Beyond that, programmes and actions under the management of the local People's Committee mainly target the training of cadres. Participation in such training programmes is relatively low due to lack of interest and a heavy workload. The role of international aid in developing the capacity of civil society is thus rather slim. In the urban sector, the majority of programmes have dealt with the industrial sector and very few with urban infrastructure and services.

If we exclude the party, the People's Council and People's Committee (that is, local authorities) as well as research centres linked to governmental organizations, and which therefore do not represent the public, we are left with associations and resident groups as the only civil society participants in urban environmental management. Associations are ambivalent players as they are tightly controlled through a weighty chain of command and because they have a narrow margin for manoeuvre at local level. Resident groups are groups of families which play a very active role in community environmental management. For the time being, these groups are not being promoted and have not yet been reached by international aid through NGOs.

The Participation of Civil Society Stakeholders in Urban Projects

We will examine three urban projects in Hanoi. These projects were chosen among twenty for their value as examples in terms of participation to planning, execution and project management (Hanoi waste burial site in Nam Son); in terms of participation to the extension of water distribution services (Phuc Tan ward in Hanoi); and in terms of conflict management (reconstruction of the Nga Tu Vong intersection in Hanoi.

The same evaluation grid was used for all three case studies, based on the following groups of questions: has public and community participation taken place equitably? Has there been real participation covering the entire spectrum of NGO processes in the project's relevant field? Has participation taken place in an autonomous manner and did it support the development of autonomy for civil society stakeholders? Did the population reap any benefits from its participation? Finally, did their participation empower civil society stakeholders to acquire new resources, enabling them to achieve a degree of financial autonomy in order to develop their own activities and obtain credit?

The Projects

Nam Son was intended to become one of the major landfill sites — if not the major landfill — for the large conurbation of Hanoi. The project planned to bury waste in trenches after its initial treatment in water. It also planned to supervise sorting and salvaging activities by informal operators. The site is rapidly filling up and the pace at which trucks discharge waste, day and night, has almost doubled compared to initial projections. Major impacts have been caused by the discharge of waste washing water in the natural environment: health problems among residents of nearby villages, problems linked to agricultural and horticultural production (for example, dust, insects and vermin) and problems associated with sorting and salvaging activities (Figures 6.1 to 6.5).

FIGURE 6.1
Map of the Landfill in Nam Son, Hanoi

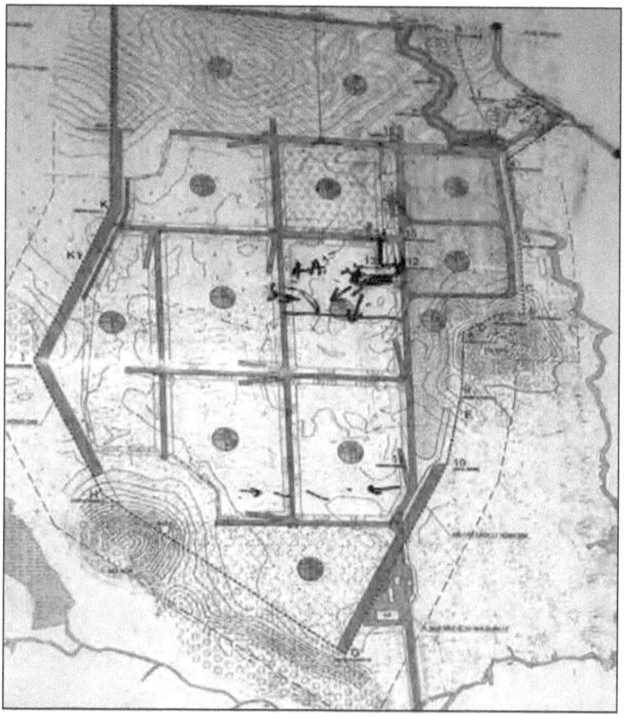

Source: Khanh Toan

FIGURE 6.2
Section View of the Landfill Bowl

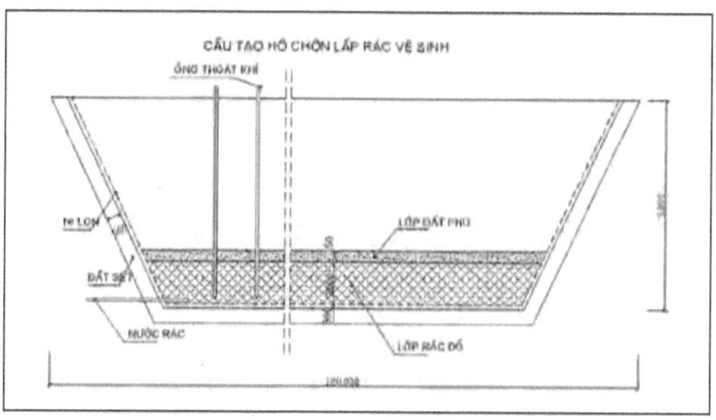

Source: Khanh Toan

FIGURE 6.3
Landfill Site

Photo: Khanh Toan

FIGURE 6.4
Washing of Waste in the Natural Environment

Photo: Khanh Toan

FIGURE 6.5
Sorting and Salvaging Waste

Photo: Khanh Toan

The objective of the water adduction project is to use the excess capacity of Gia Lam water treatment plant to supply Phuc Tan ward, where households are on low incomes and well water is unfit for human consumption. All previous attempts at tinkering with the old network have caused chronic health problems. Besides normal works carried out for the extension and penetration of the network in a densely populated area, this project aimed to connect all of the ward's households and to provide each with a water counter. The main problem encountered has been the difficulty for some households to pay the cost of connection (Figures 6.6 and 6.7).

The reconstruction and widening of the Nga Tu Vong urban intersection in the city of Hanoi aimed to solve traffic congestion problems and facilitate the circulation of different means of transport around the same axis. It involved the construction of a roundabout, asphalting, pavements, technical tunnels, pedestrian crossings and signalling. Besides the environmental impact of construction work (that is, noise, dust and traffic congestion), this project directly affects 146 households in the Phuong Liet ward who need to be rehoused. The majority of these households use their housefront as a shop. All or part of the inhabitants will be transferred to a new high density housing area. The major issue in this project has been the value of compensation for land (Figures 6.8 to 6.11).

FIGURE 6.6
Water Conduit from Gia Lam to Phuc Tan Ward under Chuong Duong Bridge

Photo: Khanh Toan

FIGURE 6.7
Water Counter Installed in a Household

Photo: Khanh Toan

FIGURE 6.8
Public Display for the Reconstruction Project of Nga Tu Vong Urban Intersection

Photo: Khanh Toan

FIGURE 6.9
Reconstruction Plan for the Nga Tu Vong Urban Intersection

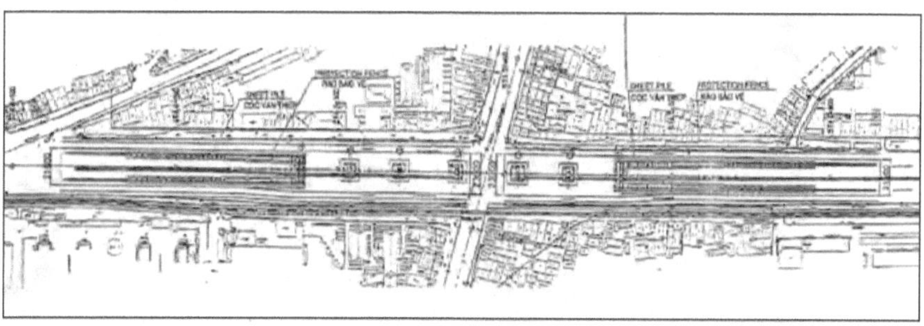

Photo: Khanh Toan

FIGURE 6.10
Nga Tu Vong Intersection after Reconstruction

Photo: Khanh Toan

FIGURE 6.11
Some of the Houses to be Destroyed for the Construction of Nga Tu Vong Intersection

Photo: Khanh Toan

Civil Society Stakeholders Involved in the Projects

Civil society stakeholders involved in these projects are all under the supervision of the People's Committee at ward, district or village level. They are also members of political organizations gathered under the aegis of the Fatherland Front and controlled by the Party. Only two groups were supervised by external agents. The main associations involved were the Fatherland Front, the Association of Veterans, the Women's Association and the Youth Association.

In the rehousing operation for the construction of the intersection, seventeen of the households involved included members of the Association of Veterans. They were called for individual meetings to be informed of the plans for relocation and rehousing. Representatives of the local People's Committee as well as Party representatives attended these meetings. Among the households concerned, thirty-six included a member of the ward's Women's Association. They were informed in the same fashion. Only local women's associations seem to have actively developed their relations with other local associations (that is, associations from the three villages involved in the Nam Son project). Vertical hierarchy also seems better organized and more personalized in the Women's Association. Local Communist Party cells are omnipresent in all three projects. The most active have been at resident group level. The communist youth associations were also mobilized in these projects, especially in the water adduction project.

Local associations did not have access to services and exchanges with external groups and associations in any of the three projects, except in two instances: in Nam Son, a cooperation project between the Netherlands and Vietnam enabled several of the villages' residents to attend lessons in the ecological use of chemicals in crops. The lessons took place under the management of Soc Son Medical Centre, and teachers originated from Vietnamese agencies. Foreign experts stuck to research and to publication of data sheets. Another project (Waste-Econ, CIDA, Canada) was carried out with the local youth association and aimed to encourage children to give up searching through waste in the landfill. We can gather from this that Vietnamese participants were left to their own devices, without any external supervision or support, except for the two activities mentioned, which are rather peripheral in relation to the main components of the project.

Issues Raised by the Inhabitants

The intersection project provoked a major conflict with the inhabitants. According to agencies responsible for evacuating the area, expropriation initially was meant to cost VND 5 million per square metre. They ended up having to offer up to VND 14 million per square metre in an attempt to take into account real commercial value. Inhabitants maintained that real market value was closer to VND 35 or 40 million. The average price per square metre of the new lodgings offered to households relocated to Den Lu was VND 4 million. The inhabitants considered rehousing in Den Lu as far less attractive, even though the financial compensation offered allowed them to resettle without incurring any additional costs. The average surface of a dwelling is 50 square metres and its real cost can reach VND 7 or 8 million per square metres. This price is considered very low compared to the sum received in compensation.

Inhabitants also consider themselves aggrieved not to have had access to public housing projects in the area. Expropriated households who lost an entire building, rather than a mere lodging, felt mistreated because they were compensated at the same rate, which failed to take into account the value of the businesses set up in the building. Inhabitants did not appreciate the tree planting programme carried out during the works, which was implemented without prior consultation. They were not consulted either about the construction of pedestrian tunnels, despite their being a major preoccupation as they risk being used for illegal and delinquent activities. Among other things, they wanted to suggest constituting a neutral commission in order to solve disputes regarding compensation for expropriation and relocation.

The most serious environmental problems caused by Nam Son landfill are associated with air, soil and water pollution. Serious health problems have been documented and their existence would be difficult to deny. Sorting and salvaging activities by informal workers, many of whom come from outside the commune, detract the village's quality of life and living environment. The stench of waste permeates the soil. Water used for the treatment of waste is discharged in the river and contaminates water sources. Cultures are infested with flies and mosquitoes; the growth of plants and fruit trees is impeded within a radius of 500 metres around the site.

The landfill attracts swarms of people come to sort and salvage waste. The sorting, salvaging, washing and drying of waste, as well as inconsiderate disposal of non salvageable materials, pollute the environment. Construction of the landfill and its sheer scale have forced out forty expropriated farmer households.

Inhabitants are frustrated at having to put up with these impacts without in any way being able to participate in the management of the site. Financial compensations for the impacts have not yet been paid in full and do not take into account primary and secondary impacts on health. Inhabitants also bemoan the lack of information regarding hygiene and environmental health. Recyclers do not have a separate site where they can sort and clean the waste. As a result, they bring waste into the village, which causes all kinds of nuisance. Displaced households received compensation for their lodging but not for farmland. Little is done to control the speed of trucks carrying waste and accidents are occurring with increasing frequency. Finally, inhabitants deplore the fact that the landfill has not created jobs for them.

In the case of the water adduction project in Phuc Tan, inhabitants were quite closely involved in the planning and execution. The stakes were mostly positive for them and their requests were precise and explicitly linked to the project. They requested that the network be fully completed, including in the alleyways. In places where streets were newly tarmaced, there was a risk that only one side of the street would be connected in order to avoid damaging the road. Inhabitants demanded that the network be duplicated on the other side of the street. Unforeseen problems with individual connections occurred: insufficient supply of concrete; uneven, only partially reimbursed or not at all not reimbursed cost of digging work; collection and storage of surplus materials or equipment; substitution of imported materials for local materials to save on costs. The cost of materials and works levied on inhabitants was sometimes higher than market prices. Some households were not refunded for expenses they were owed. Several households with financial difficulties or with insufficient income were not able to cover the cost of individual connection. However, in such cases, subsidies seem to have been generous and adequate.

Public Participation

Public participation is mostly limited to information, awareness-raising and mobilization. In the intersection project, households affected by relocation were called for a meeting; the development project was explained to them and they were told about the need for relocation. The process that followed was quite authoritarian: affected households had to be present for the survey and sign the plans drawn up following the survey, which amounted to recognizing their eviction status. Several refused to do so.

In all three projects, public participation was most often seen as instrumental for solving conflicts through persuasion and only targeted inhabitants involved in these conflicts. In the case of the intersection project, the Association of Veterans played an important part in getting the more intractable inhabitants to sign. The ward's Women's Association carried out very similar propaganda work among households to get them to sign the plans. Members of the association were also responsible for facilitating the work on the ground for surveyors and other professionals involved in the survey. In this instance, the population did not manage to organize, as it was strictly controlled by party cells and leaders. This is a case where individual and public interest are in conflict, where no foreign parties are involved, and where the administration refused to revise its plans and did not wish for public consultation to take place.

In Nam Son, local authorities were only informed about the project once everything had already been decided. Decisions were made by the City of Hanoi and the district People's Council. The public contributed to cleaning up, dredging canals and collecting waste through statute labour. Such activities were planned and organised by local associations under the aegis of the People's Committee. Participation to statute labour is voluntary in principle, but it is strongly encouraged. Information was conveyed to the population through radio programmes broadcast twice a day for thirty minutes. The Women's Association and the Youth Association participated, together with the company, in activities for fly and mosquito control, cleaning of mosquito nets, etc. Such activities were entirely subsidized by the company. Moreover, the Women's Association carried out its usual education and awareness raising activities regarding hygiene and sanitation. As for young people, they were mobilized, as elsewhere, for tree planting activities.

Site managers organised periodic meetings with commune leaders, association representatives and police officers in all three villages affected. The aim of these meetings was to discuss the most pressing issues. Managers attempted to maintain friendly relations with the population by organizing festivities. The waste treatment site company responded positively to local requests: it relocalized the recyclers' shelters; it enforced the directive banning under-sixteens from salvaging work on the site and it organized public meetings about the issues of odour and mosquitoes. The local Youth Association established contact with the association's national level to try and develop a research and follow-up programme on the site. Some of the village's recyclers expressed the wish to constitute a cooperative in order to reduce costs, maximize profits and manage their activities collectively.

In Nam Son, the public was regularly informed; associations participated in specific activities inherent to the project; new initiatives have appeared.

There was no significant active public participation as such in the management and follow-up plan for the site and its operations. New initiatives were introduced by foreign agencies (Dutch and Canadian). The company works primarily with local authorities and only addresses concerns expressed at that level. It could be said that the company negotiates its insertion in the environment through "good citizen" and "good neighbour" actions. It acknowledges civil society stakeholders on the ground and makes use of them according to their traditional methods of action.

In Phuc Tan, public participation was systematic and took place over a long period. The ward's People's Committee would first gather the representatives of resident groups, who would then pass on the information to inhabitants. Water supply plans and cost estimates were also presented to the inhabitants. Besides those means of communication, regular information was broadcast on the ward's loudspeakers three times a day, fifteen minutes in the morning, at midday and in the afternoon, and leaflets were distributed in the neighbourhood. The local People's Committee acted as the public's main representative dealing with project managers and other levels of authority. The ward's People's Committee created a special committee dealing with cases of households with insufficient income to ensure that they would be connected to the network.

Benefits Obtained from Civil Society Participation

Associations did not generally receive any additional funds for their participation in the projects. Their income is usually generated through membership fees, 50 per cent of which are transferred to their superior levels of authority, and through specific subsidies from the state or from their national levels. The associations' local cells do not have their own budget.

It is obvious that, in the case of the intersection project, there were no benefits whatsoever for the main parties concerned — that is, the evicted households.

In Nam Son, the community clearly benefits from salvaging. The site's management company allows over 800 inhabitants to search through waste. It also offers the community more than fifty days' work collecting scattered waste each month. However, the company's tolerance for recyclers set up on or near the site is wearing thin. Master recyclers share a part of the landfill, buy the collected waste, sort it, wash it and package it for resale. Without their expertise, profits from sorting and salvaging, if carried out by non-organized village inhabitants, will certainly drop. Finally, the number of local residents working for the waste treatment company can be estimated at around sixty. Despite new health problems caused by activities on the site, local health service subsidies have increased at the same rate as elsewhere.

The project in Phuc Tan resulted in actual benefits for the population. The government paid over VND 42 million in subsidies for part of the materials. Over 140 households received a grant for individual connection. Connection for households with insufficient income was subsidized for up to 30 per cent. In extreme cases, 100 per cent of the connection cost was subsidized.

Capacity Development

In Nam Son, despite very serious concerns regarding health and public hygiene issues linked to site activities, local populations received little information on the subject — other than the Dutch environmental health education programme. Only a few local party cell representatives attended some classes. Residents taking part in landfill search received no training, were not equipped for such work and had no insurance against injury or disease. Only the Youth Association organizes medical consultations for children working at the landfill. In Phuc Tan, the population was called upon for secondary work, which required no qualification. As a result, participants did not develop or acquire any new abilities. Results are much worse off for the intersection development project.

The Role of Civil Society in Local Development Programmes

Thanh Xuan Bac ward in Hanoi was the site of a major local development project financed by DANIDA (Danish International Development Agency). The programme aimed to improve the ward's environment and adopted a firmly participative approach.

The ward was built in the 1980s on the Soviet model known as *Khu Tap The* (KTT). It is divided into five large groups of residential buildings, comprises sixty-three large buildings and is organized around seventy-four blocks. Its density is relatively high, streets are damaged and poorly maintained and alleyways are clogged up by spontaneous markets. The ward numbers 4,800 households and 23,000 inhabitants. Each household includes on average four persons; two adults and two children. 10 per cent are single households; 18 per cent of families comprise three generations and 14 per cent of families one generation. There are 3,453 children under five years old, 2,486 from six to sixteen years old, 14,512 persons from seventeen to sixty years old and 3,046 over sixty. The ward's inhabitants are mostly government employees, many of whom are retired. The average income is VND 400,000 per person per month.

Blocks are composed of fifty to sixty households. Each block is represented by one of the group's members, usually a retired government employee. This representative is elected by the inhabitants and appointed by the ward's People's Committee. Each group is also represented by members of the various associations (that is, Elderly People's Association, Women's Association and Youth Association). Groups and associations both report to the superior levels of authority.

The Environment

Drinking water produced at Tu Liem plant is stored in four large reservoirs in Thanh Xuan Bac, then pumped into individual household tanks. Inhabitants consider the quality of the water to be poor. Sewage from Thanh Xuan Bac is discharged into Me Tri Lake through three sewers. The sewer system is poorly maintained and is regularly blocked by discarded waste. The electrical network is managed by Dong Da electricity sector. It comprises one transfer station, thirty-one low tension distribution stations and one technical maintenance station. The network is not secure as cables and wires are bare. Waste collection is provided by the urban environmental company URENCO, who supplied insufficient quantities of poor quality dustbins. Waste is scattered everywhere in public squares, markets, streets and alleyways.

The neighbourhood's courtyards and public spaces are taken over by lodging extensions at ground level and above. Furthermore, several lodgings have been divided in half to accommodate two households instead of one. This alters the original configuration of certain buildings and sharply increases density. The ward includes one community clinic and a few other facilities: a health centre for the Ministry of Construction, two primary schools, one secondary school, two nurseries and a few state higher education schools. There also is a supermarket, a cultural centre, a swimming pool, an athletics club, a tennis court and several public gardens.

The participative project is considered as a first in Hanoi and aims, amongst other things, to produce results that can be replicated in other neighbourhoods. It comprises a variety of activities: cleanup and repair of water tanks, sewer cleaning, improvement of the waste management system (including waste collection in public places and markets), tree planting and developing playgrounds and parks. Besides financing major urban services works, the project also created a funding account for smaller projects.

The project's executive committee is composed of representatives from the Ministry of Construction, Thanh Xuan Bac ward People's Committee, Hanoi Cadastral Survey, Hanoi Transport and Public Works Department, Hanoi Women's Association and Hanoi University of Architecture. The committee organizes periodic meetings to report and assess results. The project's management committee is composed of representatives from the ward's People's Committee and People's Council as well as from the Women's Association and the Youth Association. Its main tasks and duties consist in participating in activities put forward by the project director and in selecting, supervising and assessing projects financed by the DANIDA programme.

Public Participation

The Fatherland Front, which heads the various organizations, played a federative role in the project. It is composed of party and association representatives. Its duties have mainly consisted in supervising the activities

FIGURE 6.12
Routine Conference of Thanh Xuan Bac Fatherland Front on the Urban Environmental Management Project

Photo: University of Architecture of Hanoi, 2002

FIGURE 6.13
Fatherland Front Ward Meeting with the Project's External Experts

Photo: University of Architecture of Hanoi, 2002

FIGURE 6.14
The Fatherland Front Participates in Tree Planting in the Neighbourhood

Photo: University of Architecture of Hanoi, 2002

of the overall project and in managing petty cash in the small-scale projects. The budget of the front's local cell was VND 11 million, which did not increase to take into account its new responsibilities on the project.

Thanh Xuan Bac Women's Association counts 1,116 members. The Association's Executive Committee includes fifteen members including one president, one vice-president and three permanent members on a five-year mandate. The local association is supervised by the superior levels of authority (Figures 6.15 and 6.16). The president of the local association receives payment from the city of Hanoi (VND 350,000 per annum) and the vice-president from the association's national level, using membership fees levied from members at all levels. The running costs of the local association (VND 10 million per annum) are funded through a district subsidy. For additional expenses and special activities, women rely on membership fees (VND 6,000/annum per member), only 30 per cent of which they retain, while the remainder is passed on to the association's superior levels of authority. In addition, women collect special contributions (VND 2,000 per person) for charity activities; in this case, they are allowed to retain 50 per cent of sums collected for humanitarian purposes. Women in the ward are generally satisfied with the association: the cadres are competent and devoted;

FIGURE 6.15
Meeting of the Ward's Women's Association, 2003

Photo: University of Architecture of Hanoi, 2003

FIGURE 6.16
Seminar on the Role of Women in Environmental Protection, 2003

Photo: University of Architecture of Hanoi, 2003

they share their knowledge and experience; they maintain good relations with the other associations; they keep the association's running costs to a minimum; they organize regular activities. Women nevertheless bemoan the shortage of subsidies covering running costs. The association was one of the most active participants in the project for the improvement of the ward's environment. Its activities were mostly focused on waste management: raising awareness among the population, businesses and street vendors to stop them from discarding waste thoughtlessly; organizing distribution of rubbish bags among shopkeepers and households; initiating experimental sorting and salvaging programmes in the ward. They also organized or took part in awareness-raising events about public hygiene, mainly taking charge of posting civic messages. Finally, they organized statute work for cleaning public spaces in residential buildings (Figures 6.17 and 6.18).

The Youth Association counts 100 members out of 3,000 young people living in the ward. There are 24 sections of the association in the ward: 5 sections in schools (including one in secondary school, 2 in primary school and 2 in nursery school), 1 section of the ward's People's Committee and 18 youth sections in the resident groups. Each section has its own executive committee, usually composed of 3 people with the secretary playing the main

FIGURE 6.17
Interview of a Member of the Ward's Women's Association, November 2002

Photo: University of Architecture of Hanoi, 2002

role. The executive committee of the ward's Youth Association comprises 9 members including one secretary and one vice-secretary. The executive committee organizes meetings every week and cultural activities two nights a week. It has to report its activities to the local party committee every month. The association's secretary and vice-secretary take part in information and training sessions organized by the superior levels of the association. The role of the local association is primarily to educate young people (that is, politics and ideology), to mobilize them for national defence and to take care of young people in need. Young people's participation in the association's activities is low as it is limited to non-working hours and holidays. The subsidy provided for running costs is considered to be inadequate. Within the framework of the project, the activities of the Youth Association were generally carried out in the wake of initiatives undertaken by the Women's Association: public hygiene campaign; distribution of rubbish bags for waste collection. The association carried out its own embellishment activities, removing advertising boards, cleaning graffiti, collecting used needles strewn in public spaces, protecting trees by painting the bark with lime wash and installing public dustbins (Figure 6.18).

FIGURE 6.18
Tree Planting Activity Organized by the Ward's Women's Association

Photo: University of Architecture of Hanoi, 2002

The Association of Elderly People is an important organization which counts 1,452 members. It is organized in 51 groups and divided into 5 sections. It comprises 625 members of the Communist Party, 198 retired military officers, 2 Communist Party central commissioners, 2 members of the municipal Veteran's Association, 200 senior executives and over 300 university graduates. Currently, 27 per cent of members work in the central organizations, communes and districts. The association organizes regular quarterly meetings to review past activities and present the programme of activities for the following quarter. The association's running costs are paid by membership fees (VND 12,000 per annum per person). The People's Committee contributes an annual VND 5 million to 8 million in subsidies. The association's activities consist in helping elderly people in need and promoting elderly people's role in the community, mobilizing voters at

FIGURE 6.19
Artistic Activities Presented by Members of the Ward's Youth and Women's Association during the Seminar Titled "Urban Environmental Management"

Photo: University of Architecture of Hanoi, 2002

election time, taking part in combating social problems, organizing sports activities and helping to improve the living environment. These activities are seen as exemplary and were described as such by the superior levels of authority (Figures 6.20 and 6.21).

The local section of the Red Cross currently has about 300 members. Its main activities focus on public health through joint actions with the ward's Health Organization — essentially humanitarian and primary health care actions. The local section is run with membership fees (VND 6,000 per annum per person), only half of which it can keep. It receives a VND 5 million per year subsidy from the People's Committee to cover running costs. Monies collected through donations are devoted to humanitarian purposes. The local section of the Red Cross is experiencing financial difficulties.

The Association of Veterans counts 302 members split into 24 sections. Its major activities are in one way or another connected to defence and national security. As far as the environment is concerned, it acts as environmental police, recording and informing the authorities regarding cases of illegal construction, vandalism and illegal waste disposal.

Associations involved in the project benefited from relative autonomy, especially for the micro-projects they initiated. They were able to plan,

FIGURE 6.20
Meeting of the Ward's Elderly People's Association

Photo: University of Architecture of Hanoi, 2003

FIGURE 6.21
Elderly People Planting Trees in the Ward

Photo: University of Architecture of Hanoi, 2003

execute and supervise the implementation of the projects. They took the initiative of holding public meetings to keep the population informed. They were able to invite the project managers and technicians to these meetings. Women and young people participated in radio and television programmes about their micro-projects. The associations were able to manage autonomously the petty cash budgets devoted to their micro-projects. They acquired skills for organizing meetings and work groups. They had access to information from abroad concerning similar projects, as well as to a large part of the information concerning the project. Although access to sources of information and liaison officers from international NGOs had been planned, it was impeded by the language barrier and by insufficient ability to use and access information technology.

Participants in the project acquired new knowledge in the field of environmental management: sorting waste, managing waste collection, processing recyclable waste, installation of solar panels and use of solar energy to heat water. The presence in the ward of technical services and heavy equipment for major projects (for example, water, sanitation, electricity) enabled them to familiarize themselves with intervention techniques on networks, on the need for regular maintenance (for example, sewer cleaning,

cleaning up water tanks) and methods for doing so, and most of all on procedures for reporting breakage and malfunction. Professionals on the project had to sum up and simplify their expertise in order to publish short booklets which were then distributed to associations. Participants in the execution of small-scale projects acquired skills for the management of an entire environmental intervention project. They participated in the execution of the works and learnt to call on a specialized workforce and supervise the work. The project's professional team (Hanoi University of Architecture) was permanently on site in well located, open and accessible offices.

Associations involved in the project did not receive new financial resources as such. Budgets allocated to small-scale projects were modest and expenditure had been pre-approved. The project did not create new permanent employment locally. The required specialized workforce was recruited from district and city services as well as from large public enterprises.

On the whole, traditional associations were the ones who brought their participation to this project. However, their actions and know-how evolved throughout. The project led them beyond the traditional field of political supervision and humanitarian aid. They were confronted with concrete local issues of environmental management. They had to find and implement solutions, thus adding management of urban services and infrastructures to their traditional areas of intervention. Within this new field, they acted as an intermediary between the population, local authorities and specialised technical and administrative services.

Are the benefits from this experience sustainable? This can be put in question for several reasons. Firstly, associations did not change much; they remain strictly controlled by a tightly-woven and extensive chain of command; they depend on the People's Committee. Members who participated in the project nevertheless acquired new knowledge by taking part in training sessions; their management capacity was reinforced and participants were made aware of environmental issues. However, their participation in well-defined, small sectoral projects did not allow them to develop their knowledge and capacity in integrated and strategic environmental management and planning on the scale of a ward. Once the project professionals leave and funds from Denmark dry up, these associations will continue to be short of administrative, technical and financial support. Coordination between local associations, which was needed for the project, might not be pursued. Such coordination was encouraged within the framework of the project, especially between the Women's Association and the Youth Association, but results were uncertain due to the limited capacities of their leaders. These associations are part of a vertical structure under the party's guardianship and are headed at national level by the Fatherland Front. Horizontal ties are not encouraged.

Finally, the development of associations themselves can be questioned. As a consequence of the country's economic development and its improvement in living standards, households now have the means to obtain elsewhere the services which these associations provide. Not using their services also means avoiding their control.

There is a real possibility of a vacuum appearing in the organization of civil society, since resident groups [*To Dan Pho*] are the only entity standing between households and currently existing associations. Resident groups are also tightly controlled by the party and the People's Committee: their head is appointed and receives a salary from the People's Committee and his function is to act as an intermediary between the ward's administrative level and the resident groups. Resident groups were nevertheless very active in the project.

Trieu Khuc: A Rural Community Organization

Trieu Khuc is characteristic of a rural community within Hanoi and is incurring the impact of the extension of urban structure. The village has produced textiles for 500 years and has traded and recycled waste for the past 200 years. Trieu Khuc is part of Tan Trieu commune (Thang Tri District) and is located 12 kilometres southwest of Hanoi. The village counts over 8,800 inhabitants within 1,600 households, 1,050 of which work in textile production and recycling of plastic, copper, duck feathers and cardboard. Three hundred households practise agriculture.

The village does not benefit from the same environmental services as the city. There is no wastewater treatment system. Wastewater is discharged directly into the village ponds and canals. Until recently, the village did not benefit from any waste collection service from URENCO. Only one open dump was available for solid waste disposal. The village People's Committee now pays Thanh Tri District to transfer waste to the city's landfills. In order to control the impact of industrial activities, the People's Committee is also developing an industrial zone where companies and family activities can be moved (Figures 6.22 and 6.23).

The village is administered by the People's Committee, the Fatherland Front and the local Communist Party cell. Five local associations are covered in this system and four are relatively active: the Women's Association, the Farmer's Association, the Youth Association and the Association of Veterans. Each association's executive committee is elected by its members

FIGURE 6.22
Typical Landscape in the Village: The Dinh and Its Pond

Photo: Ngo Dao

FIGURE 6.23
Open Dump for Solid Waste Disposal

Photo: Ngo Dao

every five years. Executive committee members are often put forward by the People's Committee. An environmental Committee is formed composed of representatives from these four associations and from the People's Committee. The village leader and heads of the resident groups are paid a regular salary. The presidents and vice-presidents of the associations also receive a salary.

It is worth noting that, although Trieu Khuc has long been a traditional crafts village, there is no crafts association for family production activities. Once a year, the People's Committee calls a meeting for some of the village's biggest producers to exchange information. There are several well-established ancient temples in the village, which constitutes an exceptional heritage, but no religious association exists.

The Women's Association has been the most active in the village and for the longest. Participation in several of its activities is compulsory for members of the other associations. Amongst other activities, it carries out micro-credit programmes, which facilitate access to loans for some of its members trying to develop commercial or production activities.

The Environmental Services Community Group (ESCG) was created in August 1996 at the initiative of the Women's Association. This group brings together eleven women from two villages. They operate under the supervision of the association and of the People's Committee. The aim of the group is to take care of all environmental services in the commune such as waste collection, transport and disposal, as well as environmental cleanliness. Waste is generated by twelve residential wards, four primary and secondary schools and two small markets. As a large producer of recyclable materials, Trieu Khuc emits huge amounts of waste (Figure 6.24). The groups' running costs are partly funded by the local People's Committee and by collection fees from households. This income is used to pay the monthly contracts of people employed to collect and transport waste to the district's transfer sites, as well as to pay a salary to members of the association's Executive Committee. The latter also acts as environmental police and is empowered to impose fines and penalize behaviour that is harmful to the environment. Monies collected are paid into the People's Committee Fund.

The association also acts as political adviser in the field of environmental management: it suggests the composition of regulations on environmental protection to the People's Committee. If they are approved by the party and by the People's Committee, the People's Committee forwards them to the district's Justice Department to be promulgated. These legal documents are then printed and distributed to the village inhabitants. Besides, the association creates its own groups, which supervise these activities: family

FIGURE 6.24
Trieu Khuc's Environmental Services Community Group

Photo: Ngo Dao

planning group, family economic development group, etc. Such groups are usually created where a national or provincial group already covers the same area.

Every local association has to file a periodic report to the People's Committee and to the Communist Party regarding its plan of action and financial management assessment. They are not allowed to publish or circulate information without permission from the People's Committee. Moreover, they are supervised by the association's higher authorities (that is, municipal, provincial and national levels). They are not in contact with other neighbouring associations, NGOs or other kinds of foreign agencies.

The case of Trieu Khuc shows that the participation of local associations is vital to environmental management and solving local issues. They act as drive belts for government information and directives, but also as agents of change through their awareness-raising activities. However, their capacities are far from being used to the full for several reasons: they are largely dependent on local authorities; they have no overall vision or strategic plans regarding environmental management. Participation hinges on the concrete benefits it may provide and can only last as long as those benefits do. Associations are strictly controlled and isolated from neighbouring ones, NGOs and international agencies.

The question of granting these associations an independent legal status, which would allow them greater financial autonomy and, more importantly, enable them to engage in direct partnership with foreign NGOs, is being raised and discussed. This is not a simple issue. It would be more important to undertake a real decentralization and management process in partnership with civil society stakeholders. It would also be preferable, in the first stages, to allow actual, free and self-managed access to administrative, technical and financial resources by facilitating — amongst other things — international aid from NGOs and development aid agencies. Some local researchers are even wondering if the role of civil society stakeholders in urban environmental management should not simply be promoted by privatizing the main urban environmental infrastructure services and networks. After all, does not waste management by the women of Trieu Khuc function on a privatized model?

Conclusion

We initially defined civil society as "a public arena between the state and citizens where general interest projects are undertaken and in which persons and groups carry out autonomous, structured and collective activities".

We have come to the conclusion that, according to this definition, there is indeed, in Vietnam, a public arena between state and citizens in the field of urban environmental management. This public arena is mainly occupied by associations and resident groups at local level. Little is known about resident groups, except that they are quite similar to traditional village groups. Although they can be supervised by party representatives, participation in such groups is based on family units, as in traditional village groups. Associations and resident groups can carry out activities with relative autonomy; such activities are collective, and are programmed and structured by the superior levels of the associations and by the People's Committees. Both associations and groups participate in projects and programmes originating from the state and its organs, which consider them as representatives of the population; they can act as representative structures; they are considered as a legitimate form of organization of the population, including by foreign organizations.

We assumed that civil society participation in urban environmental management, using sustainability and good local governance as guidelines, implied equitable representation of the population. Associations and groups do not represent the entire population. Membership is voluntary and members of each association often represent less than 20 per cent of the target population. The Youth Association is particularly unrepresentative; the Women's Association and the Elderly People's Association are far more representative. In theory, resident groups include the entire population. Moreover, members' participation in groups and associations is largely motivated by interest and by benefits to be obtained from state projects and programmes. It is also quite obvious that in recruiting association members and active participants in groups, priority is given to party members. Elected group and association leaders are naturally very close to the Party and their election can be sanctioned by the People's Committee.

A large part of society remains non-organized. Among those are petty traders, producers and private craftsmen. For instance, in Trieu Khuc, craftsmen and small producers have no collective representation, despite the fact that they play a major part in the village's economic activities. The People's Committee is only interested in supervising bigger producers. However, the situation is evolving rapidly. Spontaneous, flexible and open groups of petty traders are appearing elsewhere. Religious groups are also appearing based on attendance at the same pagoda. These new groups appear to be rising forces.

Groups and associations have an active social life. Their actions target the entire population: information, awareness-raising and mobilization. They hold public assemblies, which in practice only mobilise their own members. They have the means to produce and distribute information on condition that permission is obtained from the People's Committee at their level. They are nevertheless confined to specific areas of intervention and to a limited turf. Associations have little mutual contact, except within certain projects, such as the Women Association's frequent supervision of the Youth Association. A single association or group cannot cover a wide range of social issues, including vulnerable and precarious populations. In Thanh Xuan, associations were able to extend their field of intervention in the environmental sector through small-scale, well-managed projects. However, we question the sustainability or replicability of this experience.

Participation in planning and environmental management of civil society stakeholders at local level is neither organized nor systematic. It must be said, however, that in the majority of major projects, local authorities themselves are only informed and mobilized when project execution is about to start. This makes it difficult for civil society stakeholder to intervene before local authorities are informed about the projects. In all the cases observed, civil society stakeholders were involved in order to facilitate the execution of projects: they were informed, nominally consulted and mobilized so as to act as drive belts for directives issued by central authorities. In Thanh Xuan, the associations mobilized carried out an actual exercise in beginning-to-end participation through small-scale projects — which included planning, decision-making, execution and follow-up. However, this was seen as merely experimental; the small-scale projects were relatively marginal compared to the interventions at the heart of the ward's environmental rehabilitation project. In Phuc Tan (water supply project), there was more concrete participation: information and participation in the overall project, influence on decisions regarding secondary networks, participation in kind as well as financial and material participation and follow-up.

We did not witness any participation from local civil society stakeholders in environmental assessments; with the exception of Thanh Xuan, we did not see them on working committees dealing with the planning, design, execution, operations and maintenance. The inhabitants of Nam Son did request to form and participate in such a committee. We did not come across any established conflict-management mechanisms (that is, mediation or arbitration); public assemblies in Nam Son are essentially aimed at local authorities. None of these projects and experiences in local development left any trace in terms of new institutions (that is, intermediary institutions) able to last and replicate these experiences, with the possible exception of the Special Committee established in Phuc Tan to distribute aid among households whose resources were insufficient to connect to the network. Post project activities could nevertheless lead to believe that capacity development in Thanh Xuan might support new initiatives: participants have recently organized information sessions regarding Agenda 21 and raised funds for the maintenance of parks and gardens.

The autonomy of civil society stakeholders is very relative. Firstly, their actions in traditional areas are supervised by superior levels of authority. Their actions at local level are controlled by local authorities (that is, People's Committees). They are required to contribute to major national programmes in a precise and limited way. The projects and programmes we have studied did not really enable stakeholders involved to develop their autonomy — though perhaps moderately so in the case of Thanh Xuan. They did not really have systematic and constant access to information on the projects and programmes.

Their access to experts and neutral liaison officers was restricted — the two foreign projects in Nam Son took place on the sidelines and have since been reclaimed or abandoned; contacts with foreign NGOs in Thanh Xuan were limited due to the language barrier and limitations in the access and use of communication technology. Stakeholders did not really produce any new information, except compared to what they usually produce. Finally, they did not receive access to new financial resources in return for their participation in these projects and programmes. In Thanh Xuan, new resources provided for the micro-projects came from external sources and will dry up when the project draws to an end; they are not sustainable.

These projects and programmes cannot be said to have initiated the development or the establishment of new ways of doing things. On the contrary, authorities did not try to do this. Stakeholders tried to adapt to new situations using their traditional approach. Foreign operators played a marginal role and withdrew without having ensured sure that the innovative practices timidly introduced would have some degree of sustainability.

Benefits obtained by participating civil society stakeholders during the project and programmes studied are either non-existent or minimal. There were few acquisitions in terms of technical knowledge, expertise, organizational and administrative capacity. None of the projects offered any technical training, except for the Dutch project in Nam Son, though in this instance training was only intended for cadres. In all other instances, stakeholders and other inhabitants witnessed the operations of heavy duty equipment, professional teams and specialized workers, but had no real contact with them, except in Thanh Xuan, where associations participating in micro-projects were able to recruit specialized workers themselves.

In all cases studied, stakeholders had to come in contact with representatives of the local authorities, public agencies and public enterprises carrying out the projects. They may have acquired a certain ability to come into contact with such agents in a less authoritarian and traditional manner, especially in Thanh Xuan and in Phuc Tan. None of the stakeholders were able to develop new organizational or administrative capacities, with the possible exception of Thanh Xuan Women's Association, which assumed leadership in organizing and implementing the micro-projects. Moreover, stakeholders did not have the opportunity to broaden their range of partners and form sustainable ties with foreign organizations through their participation. They remained confined in their traditional areas of expertise and were not able to form new alliances. Women's associations were able to strengthen their position in the ward by playing a leadership and federative role. Stakeholders did not develop new relations with the administration outside of traditional channels. Finally, there is no trace of any new administrative procedure, protocol, or of any new law or regulation, which these experiences could have generated.

In terms of financial resources, civil society stakeholders did not derive any benefit from their participation. The only resources at their disposal were the same subsidies they normally receive from the superior levels of authority. No additional funding — which they could have managed autonomously — was disbursed. Thanh Xuan is once again the exception, but one must keep in mind the fact that funds awarded to micro-projects were allocated for specific purposes and that their use was supervised. Funds mobilized on this occasion were distributed in the usual way among the levels of authority and shared with the People's Committee. Few new temporary jobs were created at local level and none of the projects enabled stakeholders to generate new and sustainable income. They did not gain any additional resources to be used for their own activities and, without any additional resources, are unable to obtain new secured loans on new self-managed resources.

General Considerations

Vietnamese society's administrative and supervisory network is tightly woven. One way or another, organizations are controlled by the Communist Party through the People's Committees. Group and association leaders are, for all practical purposes, civil servants working either for the local authorities or for the government and party. The most organized and active sections of society are women, the elderly and veterans. Entire sections of the population, including petty traders, craftsmen and the entire population without a permanent registration, fall outside of the net.

Civil society organizations, besides carrying out humanitarian work and supporting the implementation of government projects and programmes, are relegated to tasks within specifically designated areas. It is currently difficult to identify any organizations capable of working at different levels of urban management on the scale of the conurbation. The current situation supports a "top down" hierarchical system.

These civil society organizations nevertheless possess great capacities, which can be mobilized rapidly and efficiently. Foreign intervention can broaden their horizon. Foreign operators can take advantage of the structures of civil society but remain confined to partnerships with officially recognized organizations. The intervention of foreign NGOs is controlled and is relegated to parallel activities, far from the heart of real issues raised by the main projects. In the case of Thanh Xuan, foreign participants finally managed to create a relatively independent micro-project group. However, the sustainability of its outcome is quite uncertain.

Civil society stakeholders are few and far between. They can be summed up to two, three or four large organizations. The dynamics are relatively poor in terms of numbers, representativeness and capacity for initiative. Society is organized around associations and households, which come across as untapped forces endowed with strong capacities. A whole section of society, which large organizations would like to socialize, eludes this organizational system; they include informal operators and unregistered small private traders as a whole. Entire sections of society are as yet non-organized and therefore remain untapped.

Note

This research is the outcome of teamwork carried out by Rene Parenteau, Nguyen Quoc Thong, Trinh Duy Luan, Nguyen Huu Minh, Pascal Lavoie, Pham Khanh Toan, Vu An Khanh, Ngo Anh Dao, Nguyen Trong Phuong. The authors wish to thank all those involved for their ideas, which they have attempted to transcribe in this chapter.

References

Biekart, Kees. *The Politics of Civil Society Building: European Private Aid Agencies and Democratic Transition in Central America*. Amsterdam: Utrecht International Books, Transnational Institute, 1999.

Buchowski, Micheal. "The Shifting Meanings of Civil and Civic Society in Poland". In *Civil Society: Challenging Western Models*, edited by Chris Hann and Elizabeth Dunn. London, New York: Routledge, 1996, pp. 79–98.

Giddens, Anthony. *The Nation-State and Violence*. Cambridge: Policy Press, 1985.

Hadenius, Axel and Frederik Uggla. "Modeler la société civile". In *La société civile et le développement international*, edited by Bernard Amanda, Henny Helmich, and Percy B. Lehning. Paris: Centre Nord-Sud, OCDE, 1998, pp. 47–61.

Hann, Chris. "Introduction: Political Society and Civil Anthropology". In *Civil Society: Challenging Western Models*, edited by Chris Hann and Elizabeth Dunn. London, New York: Routledge, pp. 1–26.

Hann, Chris and Elizabeth Dunn. *Civil Society: Challenging Western Models*. London, New York: Routledge.

Howell, Jude and Jenny Pearce. *Civil Society and Development: A Critical Exploration*. Colorado: Lynne Rienner Publishers, 2001.

McCarney, Patricia. "Reviving Local Government: The Neglected Tier in Development". In *The Changing Nature of Local Government in Developing*

Countries, edited by Patricia McCarney. Toronto: University of Toronto Press, 1996, pp. 5–30.

Nosco, Peter. "Confucian Perspectives on Civil Society and Government". In *Civil Society and Government*, edited by Nancy L. Rosenblum, and Robert C. Post. Princeton, Oxford: Princeton University Press, 2002, pp. 334–59.

Post, Robert C. and Nancy L. Rosenblum. "Introduction". In *Civil Society and Government*. Princeton, Oxford: Princeton University Press, 2002, pp. 1–25.

Rosemont, Henry Jr. "Commentary and Addenda on Nosco's 'Confucian Perspectives on Civil Society and Government'". In *Civil Society and Government*, edited by Nancy L. Rosenblum, and Robert C. Post. Princeton, Oxford: Princeton University Press, 2002, pp. 360–69.

Sampson, Steven. "The Social Life of Projects: Importing Civil Society to Albania". In *Civil Society: Challenging Western Models*, edited by Chris Hann and Elizabeth Dunn. London, New York: Routledge, 1996, pp. 121–42.

Van Rooy, Alison. *Civil Society and the Aid Industry*. London: Earthscan, 1998.

Verba, Sidney, Norman Nie, and Kim Jae-On. *Participation and Political Equality*. Cambridge: Cambridge University Press, 1978.

White, Jenny B. "Civic Culture and Islam in Urban Turkey". In *Civil Society: Challenging Western Models*, edited by Chris Hann and Elizabeth Dunn. London, New York: Routledge, 1996, pp. 144–54.

White, Gordon, Jude Howell, and Shang Xiaoyuan. In *Search of Civil Society: Market Reform and Social Change in Contemporary China*. Oxford: Clarendon Press, 1996.

World Bank. *Strategic View of Urban and Local Government Issues: Implications for the Bank*. Washington, D.C.: The World Bank, 1999.

7

Assessment of Projects Supported by Official Development Assistance Based on Partnership Formats: From Ho Chi Minh City to Hanoi

Laurence Nguyen
Nguyen Duc Nhuan
Nguyen Trong Nam Tran

Projects implemented with the support of Official Development Assistance (ODA) are a powerful urban development driver in Vietnam's big cities. The facts show that since the Asian crisis, private investors are tending to back away from long-term investments such as urban infrastructure projects that do not guarantee a quick return. On the other hand, ODA-supported projects may be very large in scale, from urban highway to water supply and sanitation systems, and thus have a significant impact on spatial structures as well as on social and political strategies.

The projects studied involve a variety of stakeholders from international donors to bilateral cooperation arrangements and obviously include the national authorities, corporations, the concerned communities and their more or less formalized advocacy groups. Our goal was to get a clear picture of the design of these projects and their objectives and take stock of their performance. The key findings are presented herewith.

The researchers sought to find answers to questions about delegation of authority within these projects, more specifically decentralization, involvement of the communities and degree of independence of the Vietnamese stakeholders in relation to the funding agency. We also wanted to identify the forms of skills and technology transfer associated with these projects and their validity. Generally, questions were asked regarding the effectiveness of development assistance mechanisms, as well as identification and exposure of obstacles encountered during project implementation.

Our analytical framework and methodology comprised a review of public policies and an action research approach, along with qualitative surveys of the key stakeholders in the projects selected as case studies. We interviewed persons from the Project Management Units (PMUs), households affected by the project, economic sector officials and local authorities (districts and sub-divisions), as well as a number of associations. Over sixty qualitative interviews were conducted with project stakeholders.

A seminar to pool the findings of the research was held at the Institute for Economic Research in Ho Chi Minh City, which enabled the researchers and field men to compare their findings.[1] The insight gained on the relationship between the aid "suppliers" and aid "users" was then used as a basis to formulate a number of recommendations for ODA project stakeholders.

The interviews made it possible to assess the impact of the projects in terms of delegation of authority and transfers on the one hand and assess the effectiveness of the projects themselves on the other (Table 7.1). In other

TABLE 7.1
Summary of Interviews

Category of stakeholder	Interview themes
PMU members (Project Management Unit)	Methods Expert input system Degree of community involvement Transfers (technical skills)
City departments Local authorities (districts, sub-divisions) Corporations, associations Families affected by the projects	Degree of involvement in the project Project evaluation Community involvement Consultation method Project impacts Project evaluation

Source: PRUD Project

words, the general objectives of the research work were in part achieved when we got answers to our question about discrepancies in project objectives, transfers and delegation.

Weight of ODA in Urban Development in Vietnam

Urban growth is a challenge for Vietnam and a challenge that is only beginning. Vietnam's situation is exceptional with a yearly economic growth rate of 6 to 7 per cent, healthy industrial expansion and strong private company buoyancy. But with three quarters of its population still living in rural communities, an urban revolution is surely in the offing.

Based on official forecasts, Vietnam's total population will grow from 78 million in 2000 to 103 million in 2020 with the growth rate slowing to 1.2 per cent. But more than twice as many people will be living in cities, a jump from 18 million in 2000 to 46 million in 2020, with an average urban growth of 5 per cent. In this scenario, the metropolis of Ho Chi Minh City could reach 20 million and that of Hanoi, 9 to 10 million. It is estimated that the population of Ho Chi Minh City will increase by one million persons every three years. These projections are made in reference to countries that have experienced a development pattern similar to that of Vietnam. The development trend of big cities is irreversible and is resulting in substantial needs: the surface area of urbanized land is expected to be multiplied by 7.5 (from 60,000 hectares in 2000 to 450,000 hectares in 2020), the public road network will occupy 20 to 30 per cent of urbanised land compared to 10 per cent at the present time, all urban households will have a clean water supply as opposed to only 45 per cent today, wastewater and solid waste will be treated, 700 million square metres of housing will go up, schools and health facilities will be built, and so on.

In recent years ODA projects throughout Vietnam have helped put in basic equipment for major social and economic sectors of the country, including the transportation and communications sector (roads, ports, bridges, etc.); energy sector (thermal and hydroelectric generating plants, high voltage power lines, distribution networks); agriculture sector (dikes, pumping stations); coastal waters sector (fishing ports); environment sector (drainage, sanitation and water delivery systems); education and training (development of primary education for all, secondary school and university education and vocational training); and health (hospitals, etc.). Infrastructure building projects have become an increasing priority in the various forms of official assistance. Furthermore, the percentage of projects supported by

ODA in the form of commercial prime-rate loans is tending to increase in comparison to humanitarian ODA projects.

As of early 2002, the city of Hanoi had received 54 ODA projects with a total aid figure of US$624 million, including thirty-six projects in the form of grants in an amount of US$172 million or 23 per cent, and twelve projects in the form of loans with a value of US$452 million, or 73 per cent of the total. To be added to this are five technical assistance projects for the development of urban traffic, water delivery, sanitation, environmental protection and industrialization master plans.

ODA credits are concentrated primarily in infrastructure development with an amount of US$227 million, or 36.4 per cent of the total; sanitation and water supply projects with US$177 million, or 28.4 per cent of the total; environmental sector with US$41 million, or 6.6 per cent. The remainder is being funnelled into other sectors. Ninety per cent of the allocated funds come from bilateral aid packages and 10 per cent from multilateral donors. Japan is the largest provider of ODA in Hanoi with US$377 million, or 82 per cent of the total amount.

ODA funding has become a major source of capital and has accelerated social and economic development in Hanoi, particularly in the area of urban infrastructure. ODA projects have yielded decisive results in such sectors as sanitation and water supply, as well as in the provision of urban management and administration training. As for recent ODA projects in urban transportation infrastructure, we have to wait for their full start-up in order to evaluate their contribution to the improvement of traffic networks and urban landscapes.

With regard to ODA's in Ho Chi Minh City, in 2004, fifteen infrastructure projects with a total aggregate price tag in excess of US$2 billion were counted.

During the last five years, a diversification of ODA projects and objectives can be noted (Table 7.2). The majority of projects that started in 1993 relate to urban transportation, sanitation and water supply systems, such as the East-West highway, and to sanitation, as highlighted by the Nhieu Loc-Thi Nghe canal project:

1) *Urban transportation* gobbles up the largest share: about US$456 million or 44.7 per cent of the total. This sector is in the lead because of the extremely high cost of the East-West highway project funded by the Japan Bank for International Cooperation (JBIC). This puts urban transportation ahead of water supply system and environment projects. The technical assistance project for capacity building in

TABLE 7.2
Sectoral Breakdown of ODA Projects in Ho Chi Minh City (1991–2002)

Sector	Amount (millions of dollars US)	%
Urban transportation	455.70	44.7
Sanitation (wastewater disposal)	362.74	35.6
Environment	93.91	9.2
Water supply systems	87.25	8.6
Health and education	9.10	0.9
Management and training	5.24	0.5
Employment	4.90	0.5
Production	1.07	0.1
Total	1,019.91	100.0

Source: Statistics from Planning Department Plan VKT-2002.

urban transportation management is included in this sector, a project being financed by the World Bank with a capital of US$12 million, making it one of the most important projects implemented in recent years. In the urban transportation sector, the leading funding agencies are the JBIC and World Bank.

2) *Sanitation* comes in second place on the list with an amount of US$363 million and accounts for 35.6 per cent of total ODA inflow. In the field of sanitation, there is a project financed by the JBIC to the tune of US$188 million and another project to overhaul the city's wastewater disposal system for a total of US$166 million. These are the two largest projects over the last three years. These two projects financed by the JBIC and World Bank put the sanitation sector into position number two.
3) *Environment* is ranked third on the list with an amount in the neighbourhood of US$94 million, which accounts for 9.2 per cent of total ODA. The Asian Development Bank is financing one noteworthy environmental project with a price tag of US$71.8 million.
4) *Water supply systems* were the leading branch during the period from 1991 to 2000. However, this dropped to fourth position, with the Asian Development Bank as the main backer of a water supply project with a budget envelope of US$55 million.

Other branches such as health and education, urban management, employment and production account for 1 per cent of the overall capital.

The three largest funding agencies are Japan, the World Bank and the Asian Development Bank. Their projects focus essentially on:

- traffic improvement,
- interventions on the hydraulics system, and
- electrical power grid.

France, although far behind Japan, is a major aid source in the following areas:

- Hanoi: engineering study for a tramcar system and the Cooperation Centre for Urban Development [*Institut des Métiers de la Ville* (IMV)], and
- Ho Chi Minh City: development of a tramcar system project.

During the last twelve years, 4 million euros (US$6.18 million) have been committed. As for the *Agence française de développement,* Vietnam is the country where it has signed the most commitments for assistance projects in amounts that total several hundred million euros. As for use of development assistance, it is noteworthy that out of the 800 million euros that have been offered, only 450 million will be used. A stickler is the current problem with administrative performance.

Project Case Studies

The projects selected as case studies are now in the process of implementation. It was actually somewhat premature to assess them, but the important thing was that we were able to meet the key stakeholders in the projects, which is something very hard to do once projects are completed and the teams go home. The common denominator of the three projects selected for this assessment in Ho Chi Minh City is that they reflect the desire of the public authorities to improve the quality of life in the urban environment.

Thus, the two canal clean-up programmes — Tan Hoa-Lo Gom and Nhieu Loc-Thi Nghe — focus on the key objectives of re-absorbing migratory settlements and wastewater disposal. This latter project was selected for analysis because the first phase of work had been completed, which provided an appreciable basis for comparison in the assessment operations.

The 22-kilometre long East-West highway project being carried out with Japanese aid and financed through a loan from the Japan Bank for International Cooperation (JBIC) is designed to connect the urban community to the national and international highway network (Trans-Asia Highway now under construction), as well as to improve the city's internal motorways and pedestrian system. The extension and widening of the existing lanes for motor vehicles (up to six lanes) and construction of new stretches of road, bridges, a tunnel (Thu Thiem) under the Saigon River (total length 1.97 kilometres) are part of several urban transportation projects amounting to nearly half of the total amount of outside financial assistance (approximately US$460 million), outstripping sanitation (US$363 million) and environmental enhancement (US$94 million).

This huge programme will upset the stability of residential households, government buildings, marketplaces and infrastructure engineering companies alike. Thus, 6,985 households in several city districts (Districts 1, 2, 3, 5, 6, and 8) and 574 in Binh Chanh district are affected. Additionally, 278 government offices and two major markets (Ong Lanh Bridge and Ca Kho) have to be relocated.

In Hanoi, the two projects studied by the Institute of Socio-Economic Development Studies are tied in with Japanese aid.

Firstly, the Japanese aid programme (53 per cent of the total cost) is focusing on improving the traffic system of the city by putting in a cloverleaf intersection to free up traffic congestion at the Vong intersection (Nga Tu Vong). An initial phase is nearing completion with a traffic overpass (or "flyover"). Phase two calls for an underground tunnel to be put in for pedestrians. This requires the demolition of houses and businesses bordering the construction site (215 households affected), with the consequent socioeconomic problems to be resolved.

Secondly, the second project with Japanese funding is disposal of rainwater and sewage in Hanoi, with the JBIC handling 80 per cent of the investment (US$200 million). The preliminary studies started in June 1993 and the project got moving in 1996, with a projected completion date set for December 2003.

The key thrust is to resolve the problem of flooding encountered during the annual rainy season when as much as 170 millimetres can fall over a two-day period. The target area is a 77.5-square metre circle that covers seven city districts and part of the outlying districts of Tu Liem and Thanh Tri. Four rivers, the To Lich, Kim Nguu, Lu and Set, flow through this huge urban area and empty into the Red River. The programme also includes cleaning up the islands found in the course of the rivers, demolition of unsanitary habitat and widening thoroughfares along the edges.

Before outlining the findings and highlighting what has been learned from the assessment of these projects, we feel it would be good at this point to delineate difficulties encountered in Vietnam in using the capital released for ODA projects.

Limits and Difficulties in Using ODA Capital

Despite initial successful achievements, the process of obtaining and using ODA capital in Vietnam is still fraught with difficulties. We will summarize the main ones here on which there is a general consensus on the part of the partners.

Project Preparation and Approval Phases Continue to Move Slowly

Project review and approval procedures vary from donor to donor, which requires a great deal of experience and qualified staff to get projects to go full circle. This obviously limits the transferability of foreign expertise. Overall, there is a lack of initiative in collecting data needed for project design. When funding agencies find there is insufficient information on which to base the probability of approval, the applicants are unable to get funding for the preliminary surveys and feasibility studies needed for their projects and this puts them at risk of not meeting the requirements of audit experts, thus dragging out the project preparation stage.

Disparities in Donor Procedures and Formalities

Disparities are observed from the preparation phase to the assessment and approval phases. Government procurement contracting, expropriation, compensation and rehousing procedures are a source of blockages and delays in programme implementation.

Disparities in ODA Packages and Sluggish Disbursement of Funds

Many Vietnamese agencies have the idea that ODA is a form of financial and material assistance that should allow them the freedom to choose the relevant engineering approaches. On the other hand, funding agencies put a high value on the transfer of technology, information and expertise from the donor countries. In many projects such proposed transfers are considered by certain local partners to be exorbitant excess if not a total waste.

Remittances of ODA funds are slow. The volume of ODA fund remittances in a way reflects the absorptive capacity of the economy of the receiving country. Delays in loan remittances often mean that changes occur in the implementation objectives or the assessment criteria of the programmes, and this impedes performance, limits repayment capacities and increases delays in paying off the debt. ODA loans pile up from year to year, while project preparation time and donor authorisation procedures become more complex and disparate. Conditions for the release and use of ODA money in the country multiply the obstacles and difficulties, along with the application procedures and formalities, the financial mechanisms, provision of counterpart funds, compensation packages for persons whose property is expropriated and competitive bidding procedures. Based on observations from donors, the current procedures and formalities (ODA use and fund remittance procedures) could be streamlined.

Obstacles Linked to Expropriation and Compensation of Affected Communities

The greatest difficulty to be overcome at this time resides in the expropriation and compensation measures entailed by infrastructure projects; these must be carried out in close collaboration between project officials, the territorial authorities at the provincial, district and commune level and central and local engineering departments. In most cases, more is involved than simply relocating and compensating people, but more importantly providing new housing for them.

Shortfalls and delays in getting local counterpart funds together rolls back ODA fund remittance deadlines. Obviously, the capital contributions incumbent on the Vietnamese side appear in the feasibility study reports and are clearly spelled out in the contracts. But in many cases it is also stipulated that the donor will not release the corresponding loan until the Vietnamese party makes its financial counterpart payment in full as scheduled. The longer the delays, the greater are the costs of compensation and rehousing, given land and real estate speculation.

Inconsistency Between Legislation and Practices in Vietnam

Inconsistency is found in investments and cooperation. There are numerous conflicting points between Vietnam's legislation and practices and international agreements and the provisions contained in signed contracts. In such cases, investors have to make a special request for the central government's opinion and approval for each concrete project.

In many instances, the Vietnamese side does not give sufficient attention to studying and familiarizing themselves with the procedures to apply for

ODA loans and ways in which the projects under ODA financing can be carried out. They are often overwhelmed by the payment procedures due to a lack of accounting documents and necessary content.

After this look at general considerations, it is now appropriate to address the key issues of this research paper and outline the findings of the surveys conducted around the projects studied.

What Authority Delegation and What Transfers?

We can attempt to reply to these questions using the surveys conducted for the three case studies in Ho Chi Minh City: the Tan Hoa-Lo Gom canal clean-up project, the second phase of the Nhieu Loc-Thi Nghe project and the East-West highway.

Overview of the Three ODA Projects Studied in Ho Chi Minh City

Tan Hoa-Lo Gom (THLG) Canal Clean-up

This project is being funded through bilateral grants from the government of Belgium (65 per cent). In addition to the environmental objectives of cleaning up the canals and making them navigable, the project is also focusing on the migratory settlements that have gradually grown up along their banks by seeking to improve the living and working conditions of the inhabitants. Involvement of the communities is a noteworthy feature, and the municipal department describes it as exemplary. The three phases of the project — expropriation, construction and operation — make provision for the people to be consulted. Furthermore, donor involvement in the expropriation process is noted. However, the technology transfer sometimes appears to be out of sync with the Vietnamese context.

East-West Highway

This project financed to the tune of 70 per cent through JBIC prime-rate loans also includes a component for restoration and beautification of some of the city's canals. Based on the survey findings, there is little delegation of authority and the Vietnamese side is finding that disbursement of the budget is very difficult. In the area of economic spin-offs, the competitive bidding procedure is stacked in favour of Japanese companies in the area of design, contract supervision and expertise, with Vietnamese companies being left to care for labour subcontracting. And the donor gets to choose the new technology to be used in the tunnel construction.

Nhieu Loc-Thi Nghe (NLTN) Canal Clean-up Project

This project is getting 80 per cent of its funding by means of World Bank prime-rate loans. Unlike the previous project, there is considerable leeway as far as choice of technology is concerned. This made it possible for new techniques to be used for such things as sewer excavation. But some of the city's scientific staff feels that the project will not result in effective wastewater treatment. Despite the effort put into the expropriation, compensation and rehousing processes, difficulties and disputes continue.

Delegation of Authority and Its Risks

In the three projects studied, due to the scope of the expropriation and compensation measures contained in the projects, there was no choice but to involve the people. However, delegation of authority in project implementation and involvement of the communities cannot really be described as meaningful.

Indeed, organizationally speaking, the government often feels that City People's Committee is the main beneficiary of ODA loans. Downstream, the People's Committee appoints the members of the Project Management Unit. Some key positions (director, deputy director and comptroller) are filled by City People's Committee appointees. The city departments and district administrations are viewed on the same plane as this council. Their role is that of advisory members, but at the same time their input tends to slow down decision-making.

In Hanoi, for instance, according to observations provided in the report from its Institute of Socio-Economic Development Studies (HISEDS), discrepancies appear during the project implementation stage. Although the pecking order of the institutions involved is clearly shown in the original contracts, difficulties start when the members of these institutions take up their posts.

Indeed, the Vietnamese legal framework is often strict but (or because of that), in practice, the appointment of project officials, managers, representatives of ministries and other administrations appointed or imposed, as well as the relationship flowchart between the different project partners turn out to be quite baffling. Delegation of authority does not leave enough breathing room or it may allow members having officially only an advisory capacity, but who hold a key position to exercise a manipulatory role or at least to put the brakes on decision-making. Exacting and intricate legal regulations, red tape and overlapping of the many networks involved have thus hindered the smooth operation of authority delegation.

A few examples are given in the assessment reports on the Vong street intersection development program as well as on the rainwater and sewage disposal project in Hanoi.

The unit and sector departments involved in the project did not want to work or could not work in close coordination with the Project Management Unit (PMU). The PMU has to coordinate its work with the relevant departments who submit to it once a month the changes encountered and it is regularly faced with sorting out these difficulties.

Project managers are supposed to guarantee the quality of the construction and see that deadlines are met. They therefore need to have a team of specialists available that they can consult regarding procedures, and this is not always the case, given their lack of training. The result is that there is no way of getting a fast signature on contracts between the foreign investment entity and the Vietnamese government.

Thus, the difficulties encountered in ODA projects are related on the one hand to the dual control over Project Management Units: that of the City People's Committee and that of the city departments and, on the other hand, to the inadequate (excessively low) salaries paid to the staff on Project Management Units. The low level of professionalism of the persons staffing these units must also be mentioned.[2]

The financial self-sufficiency of PMU's is also very limited. It is very difficult to get approval for any budget change. And the Vietnamese side depends on the donor. For instance, in the case of the highway project, the Japan Bank for International Cooperation (JBIC) imposes its own closed way of awarding contracts and favours Japanese contract bidders. These problems raise the issue of transfers within ODA projects.

Expertise and Technology Transfers

The question of transfers comes up along with that of discrepancies in ODA design. Many Vietnamese agencies look at ODA in terms of getting in money or material support, while donors set a high value on the transfer of technology, information and expertise from firms in the donor countries. In many projects, technology transfer is imposed on the local partners who often feel it is useless or unsuitable.

Some PMUs do acknowledge that they have acquired new skills, notably in terms of project management, owing to the presence of foreign experts. Some of the transferred technology is effective and can be applied to other projects. But ODA project technology transfer often takes place in conditions that are far from ideal.

Technicians do not have enough leeway due to the procedures and often-stringent legal framework governing ODA. Red tape frustrates transfer operations. The Vietnamese consultants are also expected to be able to absorb the new technology and in turn pass it on. For instance, they need to be able to speak English and also be relatively young so that their newly acquired expertise can be used later. Continuing education is needed so that a link is established between theory and practice in order to avoid a situation where the training given is not in tune with the actual needs of the market.

In Hanoi, infrastructure development is playing an important role in two aid projects under JBIC funding. The guarantee of quality is a hallmark of project execution. The government has put forth much effort to resolve this problem. The contract system requiring signatures by both parties mentions positive innovations that have been particularly beneficial for the country that has a tremendous need for qualified workers and state-of-the-art technology.

In the case of the project to clean up rivers in the capital, certain methods are being used for the first time in Vietnam. They include equipment for mechanical drainage, heavy-duty pumping station equipment and machinery for urban waste treatment. The involvement of foreign experts is particularly necessary at all phases of the job run schedule, from measuring hydraulic power and doing hydrographical calculations to the technical procedures required to monitor the overall drainage layout. With their assistance, improvements were made to the flow capacity of the irrigation project, as well as to the quality of water in the retention reservoir and navigation on the river system.

In both medium-size and large-scale construction projects, there is a need to rent or purchase machinery from companies and pay foreign specialists, which is true of the projects in Hanoi. Therefore technology and expertise transfers are included in aid programmes in part to fill in these gaps. Although no one disputes the value of such transfers, the local partners sometimes challenge the way in which the choice of technology and skills supplied is made or most often imposed by the donor. The qualification of contractors and subcontractors hired by the projects also give rise to polemics.

Procedures for contract selection, review and approval, as well as supervising construction quality and maintenance require that programmes be set up to train Vietnamese experts. Their specialization in new technologies and foreign language ability are matters that require urgent attention, if only to take over from costly foreign experts, build national management capacity and bring it up to international standards. Along the same lines, encouragement is needed to promote the establishment of companies to supply rental equipment and hire out consultants to increase the capacity of the Vietnamese side as far as current construction and consultation standards are concerned, in other words to build their technical capacity and expertise.

In this regard, it would be advisable to increase the contribution made by the city and government in ODA-supported projects and set up training programmes to allow capitalization and a genuine skills and technological transfer.

Assessment of Project Performance and Exposure of Hindrances

An initial finding from the qualitative interviews conducted with the PMU's studied was the difficulty they have in managing large-scale foreign ODA contracts. This is something new. Approximately fifty ODA-supported projects have been implemented in Ho Chi Minh City over the last ten years. In the past few years, only about twenty of them involved large amounts of capital. The result is a certain lack of experience and familiarity with the mechanisms involved in handling this type of project. Also, rigid protocols must be fulfilled for international loan payments to be released. Institutions to which delegations of authority are to be made, such as PMUs, experience problems in finding qualified staff with the ability, for example, to produce the progress reports required on the anticipated achievements of the project contract and to fulfil the procedures for loan applications.

Additionally, our partners put much emphasis on the importance to be given to the actual sharing of investment expenditures between foreign aid and the Vietnamese contribution as an indicator of dependence. This is true of the East-West highway project for which, in principle, 85 per cent of the funds are disbursed by means of a JBIC loan and therefore 15 per cent by the Vietnamese authorities. In fact, the latter have had to make their investment first, before the foreign donor, and much more than the initial amounts, that is, 30 per cent overall instead of the 15 per cent planned. In other projects, the expropriation budget is relatively high, sometimes amounting to 50 per cent of the project envelope. Indeed, the increase in costs and the social and therefore political nature of operations upstream from project implementation, such as relocation procedures and compensation packages that are negotiated and renegotiated, have shot up considerably the principal of loans applied for by the Vietnamese side and, consequently, the debt load. That means that the public authorities now have to come up with domestic funds to pay back the foreign partner.

Major difficulties hinge around problems of financial management of the funds to be disbursed and repaid. The component involving the freeing up of land with its "eviction-compensation-rehousing" processes remains the stumbling block in all of the projects because of the time it takes to approve the expropriation measures, conduct the compensation negotiations and come up with an appropriate rehousing solution, which in turn stretches the timeframe for the remittance of foreign funds. These measures require close cooperation between the various stakeholders in the project: managers, territorial authorities, the communities involved, as well as central and local technical departments.

However, for some programmes, the Vietnamese government covers the total cost of these procedures from the national budget while keeping a grip on initiatives involving expropriation and compensation procedures. This is true of the rainwater and sewage drainage project in Hanoi being carried out with Japanese aid and in which the authorities determined these procedures and imposed them on the households concerned. Negotiations moved promptly and the programme was kept on schedule.

It is noted that the Vietnamese institutional stakeholders are very much in favour of foreign financial and technical aid, especially when these are state-of-the-art, which is the case in the projects we assessed. They provide needed support for infrastructure development and urban renewal that are beyond the means of the state budget alone. Nevertheless, they realise that foreign donors are thereby opening the way for their private capital. They must therefore take initiatives to keep a handle on how the loans are used and avoid waste. If not, they run the risk of leading the country into a situation of insolvency.

Example of the Tan Hoa-Lo Gom Project[3]

This project is different in that it is funded by means of non-repayable grants. Funding of this type requires different management procedures. It is a small-scale project with a dual objective:

- clean up the canal, and
- promote urban renewal for low-income communities.

Another project is being contemplated for the overall catchment area with other types of funding. The feasibility study has been completed. The project is moving into its second phase, which involves its expansion. The PMU was established in 1998 and the first phase ran until 2001. The second phase will be completed in 2004. The first phase cost US$5.5 million. It focused on identifying pilot projects and detailing the content of other projects. But there have been delays in implementation involving the amount of compensation, which has increased the amount of the city's contribution.

On the Positive Side

The project offers an innovative approach to wastewater treatment and is the first one that has had a real component to actively involve the communities. This has in fact facilitated both its acceptance and the compensation payment negotiations. The Vietnamese authorities formerly gave little heed to the role of the communities, but this project is showing that their involvement is important for things to run smoothly. There has been a high level of participation in the *Tan Hoa-Lo Gom* and *Nhieu Loc-Thi Nghe* projects. Simple objectives were stepped up to more complex ones. In the projects studied, the technical dimension is considered in tandem with the socioeconomic and environmental dimensions. Projects are becoming more complex and must include these new dimensions.

On the Negative Side

It would have been beneficial to arrange more awareness-raising campaigns on the choice of land for rehousing, the building types and structuring the future resettlement neighbourhood, the gainful employment of the persons involved in the habitat building and layout operations, in order to get the community involved in the project. Implementation was delayed because of a lack of support from the people. And since the funding was in the form of non-repayable grants, there was no motivation for the various stakeholders in the project to speed up execution. The problem posed is one of efficient use of the funding.

The Belgian side established its own procedures and regulatory system. There is no joint management procedure for this project. The requirements set by the donors must be met along with those of the Vietnamese authorities. The project has fallen very far behind schedule. And once the agreement was signed, the operating costs and service had to be paid off first.

Another point is that it is a pilot project. Other ODA projects of this type have been financed by the Asian Development Bank (ADB). This is the third one focussing on improving sanitation conditions in Ho Chi Minh City. But it is no longer in tune with the current situation in Vietnam because the speed of population growth has considerably altered the start-up situation. The Vietnamese side is responsible for the delay. The results are not those anticipated at the outset and additional expenditures are leading to an exorbitant overshooting of the budget, especially for operating costs. A lack of efficiency is noted, largely due to the foreign consultants and unforeseen expenses.

The canal project has been furthermore delayed by problems with the level of compensation approved for the evicted households, which was relatively high compared to that awarded in other projects in Ho Chi Minh City. This raises the question of product replication in other sectors of the city.

There is also a problem with the project dragging on. Households slated for relocation experience upset. They hesitate to do upkeep work in their homes, so their living conditions deteriorate. The interview with the PMU reveals that attaining the objectives will be very touch and go due to the complex system of stakeholder participation and the financial and political interests at play. Obviously, there is still little manoeuvrability between rigid planning and too much pragmatism. The downside of too much flexibility is the problem of widespread uncertainty affecting the people, the donors and contractors alike.

The survey reveals that there are two groups that might be called the "winners" and the "losers". The "losers" are the people who are threatened with eviction. The "winners" are the urban utility businesses, such as the Water and Electricity Company that is benefiting financially due to adjustments affecting the users; there are no illegal hook-ups in the rehabilitated neighbourhoods. However, civil servants appointed to head the PMU's are called upon to take on more work but without receiving a corresponding raise in salary, and this further deepens the gap between the foreign and Vietnamese experts who, although often equal in skills, receive an abysmally different salary, with the "losers" on the Vietnamese side.

This project experience can provide lessons for other ODA projects:

- ODA project design must take the overall picture into consideration.
- Expropriations must be worked out prior to concluding the agreements.
- More professionalism is needed in expropriation procedures.
- The Project Management Unit (PMU) has to play an intermediary role between the city and the community and is therefore subject to very strong pressure. The role of the PMU must be spelled out with regard to these technical aspects.
- The procedures followed by international donors are subject to stringent regulation, unlike those that come under the jurisdiction of Vietnam.
- Public structures have to be organised to improve project performance and notably the skills level of the management staff.

Example of the East-West Highway[4]

This project with an estimated price tag of US$1 billion is being financed by Japan. Difficulties came to light in receiving capital contributions at the stage of project preparation and design. Feasibility studies started in 1999, with environmental impact studies and mitigative procedures commissioned by the donor.

Work had not yet started at the time of this study. The delay was due to problems involving compensation and land release. The inhabitants did not agree to the compensation amounts. Expropriation is affecting 5,000 families. The relocation of utilities along the highway road allowance is also a cause of problems. The work site was to open in late January 2004.

Three forms of funding are involved: prime rate or low-interest loans, loans at regular rates and funding from the Vietnamese side.

Each type of loan is accompanied by its own adjudication procedures. Prime-rate loans are very demanding when it comes to such things as the competitive bidding process. The PMU director therefore feels very strongly about the tight grip the Japanese side is keeping on project execution and on the choice of prime contractor. Such conditions may take away from the value of this type of loan. Japanese contractors are many, European contractors few. Vietnamese contractors fall short on the skills necessary to share in the bidding process. The JBIC puts out few invitations to bid, which complicates project execution. The Vietnamese side would like six or seven open tendering procedures, while the JBIC authorizes only three.

Due to low interest rates, the balance of power is tilted strongly in favour of the donor. But the cost of Japanese consultants is exorbitant and companies from the creditor country are favoured. It was stressed that the Vietnamese side, due to a lack of skills at the bargaining table, could not hold its own when negotiating JBIC requirements.

Remark from the People's Committee, Ward 10, District 6

Expropriation gives rise to many difficulties. Indeed, the procedure started in 2000 and by late 2003, prices had changed. People wanted to improve their standard of living, but the rehousing process was upsetting their lives. The displaced persons demanded a price higher than the real price of their property. More must be done by way of awareness-raising campaigns so that the communities do not end up hindering the projects.

Remarks Concerning the Overall Performance of ODA Projects[5]

Performance problems are found in project management, implementation and evaluation on both the Vietnamese side and that of the donors. The Vietnamese side has its own agenda. A case in point is an ADB water supply project that was rejected in favour of another project which carried a much higher interest rate on the financial market but which allowed the Vietnamese authorities more freedom of movement.

It frequently happens that the municipality takes care of some overspending relating to ODA projects out of its own budget. The main difficulties spring from the calibre of project management by the PMUs and professional skills of the managers and supervisors.

Another difficulty is caused by the many objectives of ODA-supported projects. Such projects involve more than technical issues relating to infrastructure; they require multiple skills, notably in terms of management. In some cases, the skills level and knowledge of supervisors are deficient or askew, resulting in inappropriate decisions or, when decisions are made, there is inadequate follow through. In theory PMUs are supposed to spell out their programme in advance, but in actuality they take a piecemeal approach.

Donor representatives are subject to numerous formalities, notably with regard to deadlines. In the area of human resources, there is a continuous change in supervisory staff, with no continuity between the preparatory phase and implementation, which wastes a lot of time and slows down project progress.

There is a lack of clarity in the appointment of supervisors. The project coordinator cannot choose the people he will work with, but has to use those assigned to him.

Four major stakeholders are present in each project:

- project owner or beneficiary,
- project management unit,
- various levels of government and ministries, and
- donors.

These stakeholders play a pivotal role in project advancement. The main contractor and PMU come under the purview of the municipal departments. This role was only recently spelled out. When difficulties arose, it was necessary previously to go up the rungs of the authority ladder, which caused a loss of time. The line departments are supposed to allow project coordination with the PMUs, but the efficiency of such a management approach is questionable in view of the delays they entail. These procedures need to be streamlined.

As far as the levels of government and ministries are concerned, there is no clear connection between project implementation, land expropriation and release. When the communities are opposed and stand off, delays result and hence disagreements arise on the price of the land.

As for the donors, when a project is amended, they have to rework their project from start to finish. Donors are confronted with financial, technical, administrative and diplomatic issues.

Proposals

1. It would be advisable to have a delegation of authority in the area of human resources and choice of project associates. This would lead to more effective performance in project management and give greater freedom to the key persons in charge of projects in the choice of their assistants. The idea is to allow more flexibility to PMU officers.
2. In the area of expropriation, lessons must be learned from the past. The government should have the final word with regard to the amount of compensation.
3. The government must spell out the role to be played by each department.

These proposals were submitted to the Ho Chi Minh City People's Committee on the basis of a consultation session with the PMUs.

Social Costs of ODA Projects

This assessment of ODA-supported projects raises the matter of taking into consideration the costs generated by programme execution, costs that were not "counted" when the ODA projects were designed. Originally the research project did not include this essential aspect. We will consider here only the social costs generated by the projects. We will leave aside the economic costs that are easier to quantify because of being directly related to the costs of loans taken out from ODA funding agencies and the slowness of disbursement and obstacles to project implementation.

Problems Relating to Eviction

Eviction from one's residential zone and subsequent rehousing are a traumatic experience for communities affected by large urban projects. Indeed, people get accustomed to a place of residence and work, and eviction from and demolition of their homes entail difficulties in their daily life. Their living habits and/or vocational patterns are disrupted. They have to look for work in a new location that they are not necessarily familiar with, and perhaps where the work they did before cannot be done any more, such as small trades in proximity to middle-class neighbourhoods: housekeeping services, repairs, small food outlets, and so on. So in addition to the mental trauma, such evictions have repercussions on household income, for which reason compensation is in order.

Generally, the compensation package should be reckoned by considering a number of factors, such as the price of land where the family was previously housed (often in a downtown or inner city area, where there is a lot of traffic, near school, health and leisure facilities), what effect demolition of homes will have, the new circumstances that will be encountered in the resettlement area (most frequently in neighbourhoods far from the city centre, where land may be cheaper but travel more difficult) and temporary or long-term unemployment caused by the eviction.

The legal factors that should be considered in determining the rate of compensation are not clearly expressed or consistent in official documents that deal with eviction and rehousing in different geographical areas.

In particular, the compensation rate makes a distinction between people who have the full legal right to the land, as established by a real estate registration certificate (*sô do*) and those who are more or less "illegal" occupants ("squatters").

It is therefore quite understandable why it takes so long to get decisions on community resettlement. The compensation offered is not always readily accepted and sets the stage for protracted negotiations and talks.

Proposals to Reduce the Social and Economic Costs of Projects

Social support programmes applied to rehousing are something new in Vietnam, and most of them have no "social welfare" component. Indeed, current government regulations make no clear mention of provisions to improve the standard of living of displaced residents.

Therefore, the compensation policy requires amendment to contribute to poverty alleviation among such communities. The existing policy has not led to a properly established compensation and rehousing programme for these communities, particularly with regard to the amount that residents claim for land compensation, and this makes things difficult at a time they have to start their life over.

The relocation programme should be based on the principle of maintaining the income level of the people and, prior to having them move to another location, should make provisions available to them in the form of financial, job creation or training programmes. The following proposals are therefore in order:

- Prior to actual project execution, acquire public land banks, that is, lots that will subsequently be used for the resettlement of evicted residents;
- Set up specialized agencies to provide assistance for the future emigrants prior to their departure and again when they have to reorganise their daily lives and find employment once they do move to their new place of residence;
- Provide comprehensive information on rehousing programmes at meetings held with the communities involved. Calling on independent consultants, as was done in the water drainage project, is a good model to follow.

Proposals from Head-to-head Meetings with ODA Stakeholders

A great deal has been said about the drawbacks of ODA-supported projects. But ODA's also make an extremely significant contribution to a country's development, in particular the industrialization process; without them, it would be very difficult to carry out infrastructure renewal. The government of Vietnam's current policy of openness logically includes such projects. The growing number of commitments is a token of confidence in Vietnam. More such projects are needed in the education and health sector, which remains quite unappealing. Technical assistance projects will enable the country to better find its place in the international community. After discussion and improvement, it will also be necessary to accept the dictates of donors. Admittedly, ODA projects have disadvantages and come at a cost, but this cost must not be too exorbitant. Consultation among the stakeholders involved is crucial. It is therefore important to carry out in-depth sociological surveys. It would be good if these proposals could be passed on to the City People's Committee.

The Issue of Residents and Expropriation

ODA projects are supposed to improve the standard of living of the people. So, why minimize the price of land in expropriation procedures? Could one not, as some suggest, indemnify the inhabitants at market price and include in the compensation package both tangible and intangible considerations such as the loss of one's economic activity or difficulties in getting one's children to school? The problem is that no legal framework exists for this type of action. Project management units take the brunt of pressure from two fronts: the local authorities for whom they are managing the compensation budget as well as the donors who wait for the expropriation stage to be concluded before disbursing their funds and going to work on the site. Donors are demanding when it comes to compensation packages. Their principles are generous, but may be difficult to apply. Should we not have, as suggested by the Planning and Investment Department, a national ruling to resolve this problem and, in return, allow more management flexibility at the level of the PMUs? In fact, a national ruling would be difficult to make, because prices often change because of speculation and in any event are very specific to each geographical location. Land banks are needed for resettlement, but a budget is also needed to buy up the land. However, there are land speculation problems when information leaks out regarding future developments. The problem is that no law makes insider dealing an indictable offence. The matter of implementing an equitable land tax needs to be resolved. When it comes to rehousing, the economic aspects relating to employment have to be taken into consideration. In all such projects, there must be room for compromise regarding the place of work and place of dwelling, in other words take urban services into account in the rehousing process as well as the financial cost for each side.

Conditional Aid

As far as conditional aid is concerned, with Japan for instance, Japanese companies are able to arrive at a mutual understanding in offering the best prices. It is therefore necessary to strengthen bargaining positions by training Vietnamese experts and increase the balance of power in favour of the Vietnamese side by means of an appropriate legal framework. Vietnamese experts must also be trained to negotiate interest rates in harmony with current economic conditions.

Work must be done in consultation with the donors at the preparatory phase of projects. The principle of broadening out the competitive bidding process must also be negotiated, so as to avoid being hemmed in by too many constraints. Everything needs to be spelled out in the specifications and memorandum. A proposal must be made to the government for these aspects to be improved.

Skills and Project Management: Effectiveness Challenged

Delays experienced in project execution are detrimental to their performance. There must be a harmonisation between ODA-supported and Vietnamese funding. ODA's are loans, and efficient use of them is therefore of paramount concern, because future generations will be saddled with repaying the commitments taken out at prime rate. The issue of efficiency is related to another point, that being the professionalism of the PMUs. Project management is a professional skill. The Ho Chi Minh City People's Committee must be asked to provide a specific contingent for management of these projects. The problem of skills also comes up with reference to the line authorities of the PMUs, all the more so because they play an advisory role. Thus, much has been said about the inadequate skills of PMUs in the area of project management, but considerable deficiency is also seen on the part of the city departments. There is also a problem of motivation, because the salary of civil servants on a PMU remains unchanged despite an increased workload. The problem of inadequate training on the part of Vietnamese experts to carry out feasibility studies also needs to be addressed. Local experts require training. Perhaps the answer lies in bringing in foreign experts to train Vietnamese experts. The budget to be used to pay the salaries of the PMU staff must also be determined.

The UNDP worked with Vietnam to draft national guidelines for ODA projects. But the management of these projects continues to be weighed down with problems. As this research undertaking concludes, one of the proposals would be to draft a guidebook for ODAs that includes the training of national experts for future projects. A management model is needed to frame the relationship between the PMUs and other city departments. The source of the funds to produce such a guidebook must be determined. Agencies such as the AFD do not have cross-cutting funds for training programmes. Attention must be given to the frequent snags encountered in the socioeconomic aspects of projects, whereas donors typically see only the technical objectives at the beginning stage. Another area to be addressed is the major environmental problems that arise when a project will change the environment, for instance when certain networks are going to be exposed or pollution problems aggravated. Methodological approaches to these aspects are needed. In terms of cooperation prospects, it would be good to know just what each side is in a position to contribute. Can funding be looked for from French corporations such as the RATP (*Régie Autonome des Transports Parisiens*), Lyonnaise des Eaux or EDF/GDF (*Électricité de France/Gaz de France*)? Could consideration be given to establishing an institute to provide project management training? What the UNDP has done could be used as the basis to put together a guidebook for experts working on ODA projects.

Conclusion

It was anticipated that this research work would shed light on the specific partnership formats in ODA projects. The findings of the interviews and discussions reveal that the partnership arrangements are neither dictated nor totally negotiated, but in the majority of cases take shape according to the precise form of projects financing, in which the balance of power is clearly in favour of the donors.

Furthermore, ODA projects have not really revolutionized the relationship between the various Vietnamese stakeholders: the relationship mode remains extremely hierarchical, sectoral and compartmentalized. Things are far from one management mode per project; there is little delegation of authority in ODA projects; rather, it seems that the autonomy of the stakeholders is in part, limited by the donor who comes across as a regulatory agency. As for community involvement, it seems to be a matter of course because of the nature of the projects themselves that cause profound socio-spatial upsets due to the expropriation process. Consulting the people should be done in a framework that gives them the best possible bargaining position in the face of such upsets. An exception is the Tan Hoa-Lo Gom canal project, where community involvement has gone farther and given the people the opportunity to give input beyond the amount of compensation, including such things at the choice of rehousing plans. The issue of replicating such a project remains unanswered.

Notes

The team that carried out this research work included members of the Theory of Urban Mutations team (Laurence Nguyen, scientific co-supervisor) and the Society Development in Space and Time team (Nguyen Duc Nhuan, scientific co-supervisor, and Nguyen Trong Nam Traân). The partner teams are the Ho Chi Minh City Institute for Economic Research (IER) (Du Phuoc Tan and Le Van Thanh) and Official Development Assistance Partnership (ODAP) (Ton Nu Quynh Tran) and the Hanoi Institute of Socio-Economic Development Studies (HISEDS) (To Xuan Dan and Vu Quoc Binh).

1. Seminar held on 16 December 2003 as part of this research effort at the IER on the theme “The Role of ODA Projects in the Development of Two Big Cities in Vietnam: Realities and Prospects”.

[2] Contribution from Du Phuoc Tan, IER researcher.
[3] Contribution from the director of the PMU, Tan Hoa-Lo Gom canal project.
[4] Contribution from the PMU director, East-West highway project.
[5] Contribution from the Planning and Investment Department in liaison with the ODAP Office.

References

Context of Vietnamese Urban Policies

Bassand, Michel, Jean-Claude Bolay, and Antonio Cunha. *Développement durable, métropolisation et pollution des ressources naturelles à Ho Chi Minh Ville, Viêt-nam*. Lausanne, Hô Chi Minh Ville: EPFL (IREC/IGE/IATE), ENCO, 1996, 286 pp.

Le, Ba Thao. *Vietnam the Country and Its Geographical Regions*. Hanoi: The Gioi, 1997, 617 pp.

Nguyên, Duc Nhuân. "Le district rural vietnamien ou l'État en campagne". In *Habitations et habitat d'Asie du Sud-Est continentale*. Paris: L'Harmattan, 1992, pp. 343–74.

ODA Projects

Ho Chi Minh City People's Committee, UNDP. *Tan Hoa-Lo Gom Sanitation and Urban Upgrading Project*. Fifth Steering Committee Report/PMU, 2000, 74 pp. (National Project VIE/95/051).

Japan International Cooperation Agency (JICA), Hanoi People's Committee, Socialist Republic of Vietnam. *The Study on Urban Drainage and Waste Water Disposal System in Hanoi City*. Final report, vol. I, Master plan, 1994, 170 pp.

Ministry of Construction, The Finnish International Development Agency (FINNIDA). *Water Master Plan of Hanoi City for the Period of 1993–2010*. Final report, vol. I, 1993.

———. *National Urban Wastewater Collection and Sanitation Strategy*. 1995, 126 pp.

Minutes of Discussions on Saigon East-West Highway Construction Project Between Japan Bank For International Cooperation and The Government of the Socialist Republic of Vietnam, 28 October 1999.

Official Development Assistance Partnership (ODAP) for Ho Chi Minh City, *ODAP Newsletter*, December 1999, February 2000, May 2000, August 2000, October 2000, January 2001, March 2001, May 2001, August 2001.

———. *Resettlement in Ho Chi Minh City*. ODAP Workshop no. 1, 14–16 March 2000, 108 pp.

———. *Ho Chi Minh City District Planning and Relationships with ODA Projects*. ODA Workshop no. 4, 27 February 2001, 100 pp.

UNDP. *Overview of Official Development Assistance in Vietnam*. Hanoi, 1999, 18 pp.

———. *Overview of Official Development Assistance in Vietnam*. Hanoi, 2000, 33 pp.

———. *Environmental Management of Ho Chi Minh City*. Annual Project Report (August 1999–August 2000), 22 pp. (VIE 96/023).

NGO Initiatives and Community Involvement

Enda Vietnam. *Precup Research Action: Solid Waste Management in Ho Chi Minh City*. 1999, 24 pp.

———. *Environnement communautaire à Bing Hung Hoa, Hô Chi Minh Ville, Vietnam*. Programme Precup, 1999, 22 p. + annexes.

———. *Review of Enda's Urban Development Resettlement and Poverty Reduction in Ho Chi Minh City and Hanoi*, 2000.

Ministère des Affaires étrangères, Programme Prioritaire-Vietnam. Développement de quartier et relogement à Ho Chi Minh Ville. *Compte-rendu de l'année 1999*. Ho Chi Minh Ville: ENDA Vietnam, Villes en Transition, Sidi, Codev Viet Phap, 2000, 21 pp + annexes. (Projet C990040).

Renard, Nicolas. *Service d'eau à Hô Chi Minh Ville, l'apprentissage de la coopération entre opérateurs officiels et informels*. 2000, 24 pp.

Delegation of Authority and Public-Private Partnerships in Infrastructure Funding Packages

Association des Professionnels Développement Urbain et Coopération. *L'efficacité des services publics urbains*. Actes de la journée du 4 September 1998.

Cohen, Élie and Claude Henry. *Conseil d'analyse économique, Service public secteur public, Rapports*. Paris: La Documentation Française, 1997.

Institut de la Gestion Déléguée. *La régulation des services publics locaux*. Table ronde du 10 février 2000, Paris.

Institut Français des Sciences Administratives, Institut de la Gestion Déléguée. *La gestion déléguée du service public*. Actes du colloque des 14–15 November 1996.

Isted. *Services urbains et développement durable, l'analyse de six expériences de gestion déléguée dans le monde*, 1999.

———. *Retour d'expériences, six cas de gestion déléguée à l'étranger.* Actes de la journée débat à l'Agence Française de Développement, 23 March 2000.

Perrot, Jean-Yves and Gautier Chatelus. *Financement des infrastructures et des services collectifs*. Paris/Marne-la-Vallée: école Nationale des Ponts et Chaussées, 2000.

Pougnaud, Pierre, Institut de la Gestion Déléguée. *Service public «à la française», une exception en Europe?* 1999.

Photo: VeT Vietnam, October 2004

Hô Chi Minh City: Pilot Rehousing Project, Phuong 11, District 6, Tan Hoa-Lo Gom Canal, View of the Building Site

8

Relations between International Consultants and the Local Engineering Force in Urban Infrastructures

Eric Baye
Jean-Michel Cusset
in collaboration with Nguyen Thien Phu

Little research has been carried out on consultancy firms and consultants working in the field of infrastructure and urban technical services in Asia, with the notable exception of Rimmer and Dick's contribution on urban transport in South-East Asia and our own work on the subject (Baye and Cusset 1990; Baye and Lorrain 1997). In the past decade, the context of intervention has become increasingly complex for consultants, for several reasons: the diversification of options associated with a project, whether technological, financial (that is, urban transport infrastructure concession, BOT or "Build-Operate-Transfer", etc.) or institutional (project management strengthening, establishment of autonomous municipal enterprises, etc.); increased awareness of environmental impacts; the need for consultants to be able to work with representatives of the residents or users (participative and consultative methods, educating the public regarding public service pricing). In conjunction with this new configuration, the development of information technology in its widest sense has opened up new possibilities for the modelling, simulation and representation of phenomena (for example, satellite images, databases) by making new or previously unaffordable tools available to small professional engineering firms.

The increased complexity of applied methods might not always have resulted in increased efficiency. However, within a few decades, consultants' professional practice has been altered in such a way that they now occupy an important position within decision-making and innovation processes.

Two concepts are commonly used to describe the role of consultants in the development process. The first describes them as laying the groundwork for exporting equipment; the second concept is more insightful and portrays consultants as a driving force for the development of "models"[1] in countries receiving international aid. Rather than following either of these two concepts, our research — based on cases in Hanoi, Ho Chi Minh City and Phnom Penh — consisted in identifying which foreign consultancy firms were involved in urban infrastructure projects. Our aim was to observe their approach, their relation with project management and the way they were cooperating with the local engineering force, especially in terms of their influence on decision-making. The objective was simple: re-examine the issues surrounding the role of consultants in the urban development process. Our research was not actually restricted to the two Vietnamese metropolises.

Although they obviously do not represent international experts as a whole, our investigations have focused almost exclusively on consultancy firms and engineering firms. We restricted ourselves to planning, specific studies and the implementation of equipment associated with the following areas: transport and public roads, traffic regulation, urban water cycle and solid waste management cycle (mainly household waste). We nevertheless made use of opportunities to glimpse into other sectors, such as port and airport infrastructure, as they also contribute to the evolution of urban forms.

This chapter should be read as a synthesis of the main results rather than as an analysis. We will begin with an account of the presence of foreign and Vietnamese consultancy firms in the urban field, then attempts to outline the major elements surfacing from the confluence of international consultants' and local stakeholders' viewpoints. Since this book does not cover Cambodia, the specific situation in Phnom Penh will only be briefly mentioned for the sake of comparison. Finally, we will suggest some directions for further research.

Our method was based on the following four approaches:

- A survey of academic literature on the subject;
- General interviews with about thirty heads of cooperation agencies, donors and administration, conducted in France, Vietnam and Cambodia, as well as in Manila (Asian Development Bank);
- In-depth interviews: about thirty with international and Vietnamese consultants in Hanoi, Ho Chi Minh City and Phnom Penh, to improve our understanding of the organisations involved on the ground and learn from their experience; twenty-seven interviews with high ranking Vietnamese officials from central administration and People's Committees, aiming to record the experiences of "project management";
- Ongoing internet research in order to get a clearer picture of the profile of consultancy firms and of the projects they were involved in.

Finally, we set up an embryonic database containing international consultants' interventions in projects to flesh out our analyses with relatively precise information which, to our knowledge, had never so far been gathered.

Foreign Expertise in Vietnam

Foreign consultancy firms only really started to get involved in Vietnam at the beginning of the 1990s. Their interventions have largely been laid out by multilateral and bilateral aid initiatives, which traditionally allow for foreign consultants wages and — at least in theory — for a transfer of know-how.

Nationalities of the Consultancy Firms

We inventoried a total of ninety-three consultancy firms: their distribution per nationality is illustrated below (Figure 8.1). It corresponds quite closely to levels of bilateral aid to Vietnam, at least in the case of France, Finland, Denmark, Australia and, of course, Japan.

Large organisations clearly predominate among Westerners (groups of over one thousand people), either directly (for example, Systra, Jaakko Pöyry, Louis Berger, GHD, Maunsell, etc.) or through their subsidiaries, which themselves are often of considerable size (for example, MVA, Soil and Water, Elektrowatt, etc). As an emerging market, Vietnam is probably the target of gradual manoeuvres — the pace of which is determined at the initiative of financial backers — from major international engineering

FIGURE 8.1
International Consultants in Vietnam: Distribution by Nationality

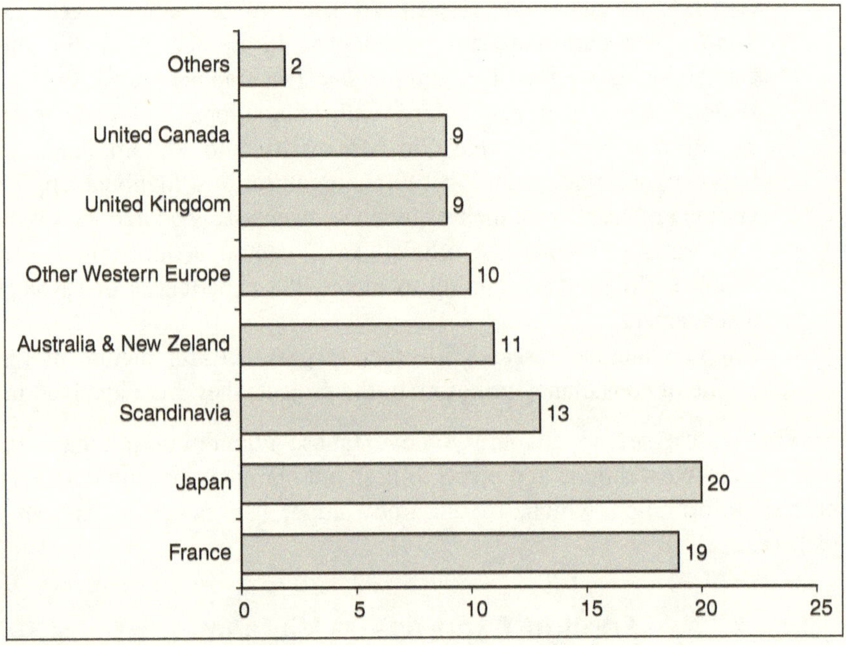

* Other Western Europe (France and United Kingdom excluded).
Source: Database of the authors.

firms interested not only in its cities, but who are also in staking out the country's overall infrastructure and energy projects. For these firms, the economic heart of the work lies in detailed studies and project supervision (or engineering project management) far more than in planning.

The local offices of these groups or their subsidiaries act as observation posts enabling them to keep track of the evolution of large-scale urban projects and interpret market signals.

Small Western consultancy firms (under fifty employees) are plentiful, but often intervene on a one-off basis, or else provide support for larger organisations with strong enough references and foundations to be working on international projects.

The Japanese are the most powerful as their market is sanction by JICA's and — to a lesser extent — JBIC's[2] cooperation system. Japanese engineering firms which have the strongest presence in the area of urban infrastructure are generally multisectoral (for example, Nippon Koei, Pacific Consultants

International, NJS Consultants Co. Ltd, Almec) and, on average, smaller than their large Western competitors (generally between 500 and 1,500 employees). However, there are few "small" Japanese consultancy firms.

In brief, having observed the consultancy market, we can distinguish four categories of engineering firms:

- Those with short-term views on Vietnam who have had access to a non-renewable opportunity such as bilateral funds.
- Companies not specifically established in the urban services market but otherwise committed to a polysectoral strategy of penetration of the Vietnamese market as a whole.
- Companies solidly and sustainably positioned in one or several sectors of the urban market, and which also often have a strong presence in other sectors. There is a strong Japanese presence in this category.
- More specialised, mid-sized companies, which make a name for themselves in Vietnam by getting involved in the preparation and planning of projects. Among others, we will mention Soil and Water, Burgeap, Safege and the international group MVA.

Sites and Sectors of Intervention

Foreign interventions in urban engineering have grown in parallel with related infrastructure projects and international aid. A total of 206 missions, either underway or completed, were inventoried in Vietnam, of which 96 were in Hanoi and Ho Chi Minh City, 80 in other cities, and 24 were interventions on a national scale which included urban aspects. Among provincial cities (excluding Ho Chi Minh City), Haiphong is clearly the main beneficiary with 15 projects, followed by Hue (8) and Danang (6).

The number of interventions by nationality emphasises the prominence of countries with the greatest number of consultancy firms. The French carried out 31 per cent of total interventions over a period of almost ten years and the Japanese 26 per cent (Figure 8.2). Australians only represent 7 per cent of the total, and Anglo-Saxons as a whole 22 per cent. However, the analysis of interventions since 2000 shows that the situation is not that favourable for French professional engineering firms, especially in their traditional areas of excellence, water and sanitation, partly due to the dynamism of FINIDA, DANIDA and AUSaid[3] programmes. The near absence of Asian countries can be explained by their low levels of bilateral aid to Vietnam as well as by the fact that their consultancy firms' lack the adequate references needed to be selected by multilateral institutions. However, some are involved in development operations (especially Koreans in Hanoi).

FIGURE 8.2
Distribution of Interventions in Vietnam by Nationality of Consultancy Firms

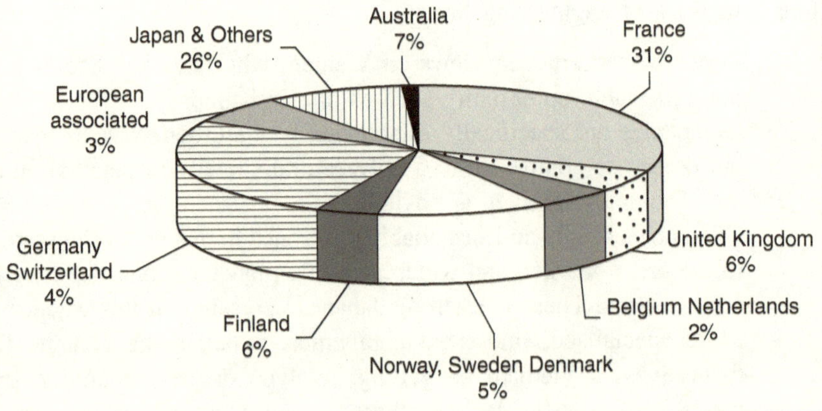

Source: Database of the authors.

Distribution by area of intervention by and large reflects the priorities defined by Vietnamese authorities in relation to the main donors (Figure 8.3).

Missions concerning the urban water cycle predominate with over 43 per cent of total foreign interventions, due mainly to the development of projects in provincial cities such as Nam Dinh, Hue, Haiphong and Dong Nai, with a high propensity for combining water, sanitation and sometimes waste. Although there is a far greater number of foreign interventions in Ho Chi Minh City, where Japanese intervention is privileged, the distribution of foreign intervention by sector in both Hanoi and Ho Chi Minh City is comparable to the rest of the country in the areas of transport, waste, sanitation and environment. At this stage of our investigation, it is still not clear whether this is a coincidence or the indirect result of Vietnamese authorities' determination to develop projects at a matching pace in both metropolises. Water is an exception to this rule: the number of foreign consultant missions in Hanoi (21.4 per cent) is almost double that in Ho Chi Minh City (11.1 per cent), which could be explained by the fact that the capital's network and equipment are in a more critical state.

The geographical distribution of interventions by sector shows a noticeable difference between Hanoi and Ho Chi Minh City, as well as between both metropolises and other cities. Water and sanitation constitute over 50 per

FIGURE 8.3
Distribution of Interventions by Sector over the Whole Country

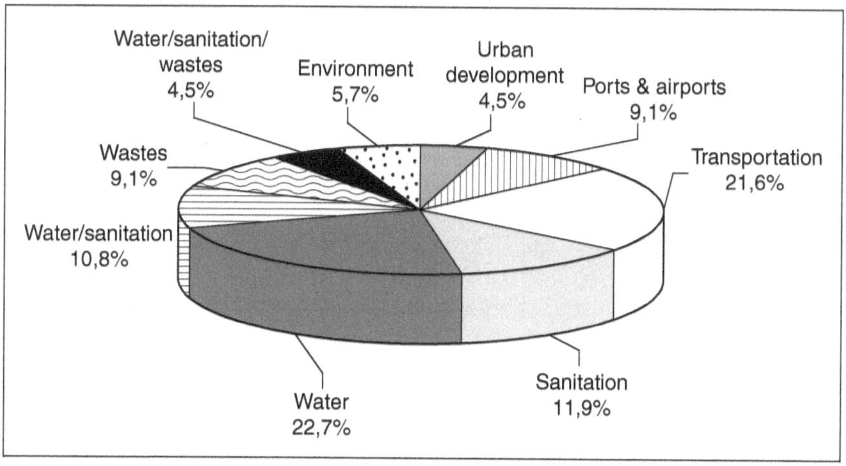

Source: Database of the authors.

cent of the total projects in provincial cities, whereas transport occupies a very low position (2.5 per cent). By contrast, urban transports are the first sector of intervention in Hanoi (40.5 per cent) and Ho Chi Minh City (35.2 per cent) (Figures 8.4 and 8.5).

FIGURE 8.4
Distribution of Interventions by Sector in Hanoi

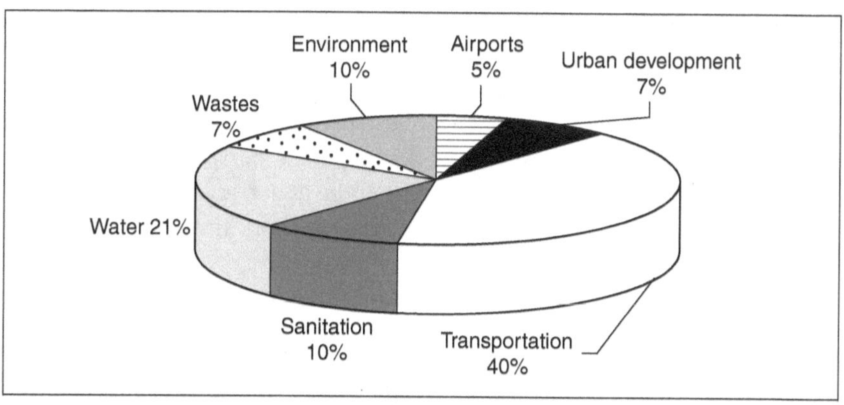

Source: Database of the authors.

FIGURE 8.5
Distribution of Interventions by Sector in Ho Chi Minh City

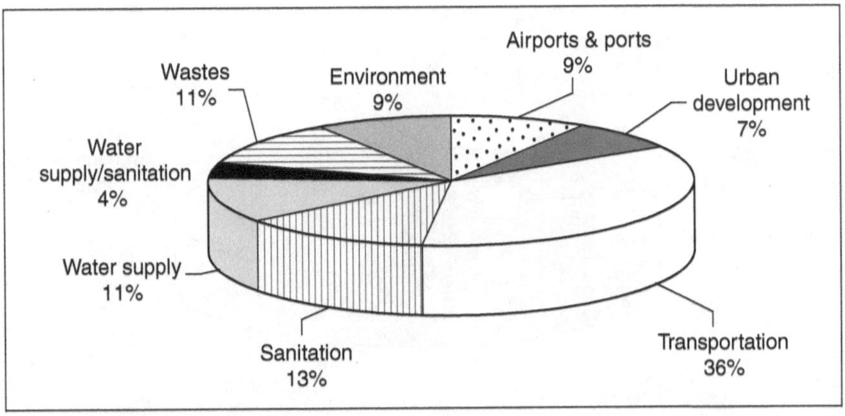

Source: Database of the authors.

Foreign Experts' Perception of the Vietnamese Market

Generally speaking, Vietnam today generates a lesser degree of enthusiasm than in the past, due to problems encountered by foreign investors and professionals, including consultants. The problems that development aid agencies have had to deal with in disbursing funds allocated for projects has had an impact on the evolution of mission opportunities offered to foreign consultants. Moreover, several engineering firms have found neighbouring countries, such as China and Thailand, to be more attractive in comparison.

Foreign consultancy firms do, however, perceive some positive points in their experience in Vietnam.

Beyond the dejection phase that often follows the initial — and perhaps excessive — enthusiasm, many foreign economic stakeholders tend to agree that the country has strong development perspectives, especially in the urban sector. Moreover, there is little doubt regarding Vietnamese people's aptitude for acquiring competences. In short, this is a country with a promising future.

In addition, many of the problems encountered are not specific to Vietnam, and are sometimes worse elsewhere, especially in countries where the administration is completely deficient.

Public project management generally pays a lot of attention to works carried out, even if it seems dubious that recommendations are actually being followed. Consultants are well aware that the country is currently going through a cultural gap between practices inherited from a planned economy and those associated with the current dominance of market economy. Despite this gap, Vietnamese project managers are assertive, pragmatic, and often know exactly what they do and do not want. If the gap can be bridged, this is an important condition for the implementation of profitable engineering practice.

Providing consulting services also implies having to face a strong demand for training young engineers. Vietnam has at its disposal a high quality skills pool with the capacity to take over from current senior executives eventually. Some consultancy firms such as Binnie Black and Veatch are firmly committed to partnerships with training institutions — in this case Ho Chi Minh City Polytechnic University.[4]

Interventions by foreign consultants are often carried out in close interaction with teams of Vietnamese experts. Almec and Sogreah, for instance, work with about thirty Vietnamese engineers (on the transport master plan for Ho Chi Minh City in the case of Almec and on ADB's water and sanitation project, also in Ho Chi Minh City, in the case of Sogreah). The American consultancy team Camp Dresser & MacKee had to collaborate with fifty or sixty local consultants from Viwase on the detailed design of two sanitation projects in Ho Chi Minh City. Such collaborations have advantages and disadvantages, but ultimately, they allow foreign engineering experts to suggest their own professional practices and to establish themselves more firmly in Vietnam. Incidentally, foreign consultants have no compunction about recruiting the best elements among those despatched to their offices by Vietnamese engineering firms, in order either to use them in Vietnam or to send them to other regions — such as the Middle East — at a reasonable cost.

Although this might seem beyond the remit of our research, we should mention the attachment that many expatriates feel for this country — especially as many men are married to Vietnamese women — and which is not limited to the *Viet Kieu.* Vietnamese stakeholders themselves are clearly aware of this bond and tend to make subtle use of it. This essential element can explain the combativeness with which some consultants persist in working in Vietnam.

Having said this, do foreign consultants feel that they are playing an immediate role in methodological or conceptual innovation within urban projects? When asked about their individual experience, the overall answer is negative. The general opinion that it is difficult to "convey messages" combines with the feeling that authorities ultimately act as they please, based on partially technical rationales. Foreign experts sometimes hold opposing views in their conceptions: an example of this was the choice between lagooning, recommended by consultants mandated by a Belgian cooperation, and activated sludge, advocated by the Japanese, for cleaning up Lo Gom Canal in Ho Chi Minh City. Such debates obviously help authorities to define their own positions. However, beyond this, even the Japanese find it very hard to measure the impact of their interventions on the ways of thinking and working of decision-makers and their subordinates, and this despite the wealth of means provided by JICA (for example, master plan elaboration methods, SCADA software for transport demand planning, scheme for training Vietnamese consultants in Japan, etc.). Other foreign consultants are highly dubious about the idea that they might be transferring a so-called model within the framework of their missions.

Nevertheless, the fact that consultancy firms only have a rather hazy notion of the overall activity of foreign engineers in Vietnam is somehow symptomatic. They are no better equipped than their Vietnamese partners in having a global and dynamic view of the exchange process and transfer of know-how over a long period. In fact, they communicate very little amongst themselves; the consultation processes recently put in place mainly affect cooperation agencies. Calls for tenders for engineering services do not require any prior understanding of the conditions of intervention; the only important elements — other than the price bid — are the references of the prospective bidder and the individual CVs submitted. They do not require the bidder to be interested in what becomes of his own recommendations. Is Semaly aware that the study it carried out in Ho Chi Minh City in 1997–98 still provides inspiration to decision-makers regarding the development of public transport services? Good research often leaves a deeper legacy than consultants might think. Vietnamese decision-makers and foreign consultants have different time frames. Without being specialists of the Vietnamese decision-making system, we can hazard a guess that decision-makers might have no other option but to "store" recommendations and deal with them progressively, through a sort of careful distillation process required by the complexity of choices and balance of power between individuals and administrations, not to mention objective constraints such as financial and social costs.

Vietnamese Consultancy Firms

There are currently over 620 Vietnamese consultancy firms, all sectors included. The engineering sector, which numbers a total of over 20,000 engineers, experts and technicians, has gradually become a numerically sizeable force as investment and construction projects have multiplied.

Vietnamese engineering and consultancy firms are currently proliferating. They can be divided into four categories: public engineering, university-based research centres and research institutes, private consultancies and joint ventures (that is, mixed capital companies) resulting from foreign intervention.

Public Engineering

Public engineering companies dominate the market. They originate from the technical ministries or public enterprises, mostly from the Ministry of Construction and the Ministry of Transport and Communications, and generally have public enterprise status. They benefit from largely captive markets: in international projects, their participation is often imposed by public project management, which is more or less well received by foreign consultants. Some consider that such an advantageous position hinders the improvement of their professional capacities. Public engineering firms have, to say the least, very patchy skills. They can be excessively influenced by civil engineering and by a monosectoral culture. Public engineering firms are slowly improving their know-how concerning master plans and methods used for carrying out studies (for example, modelling, use of digital mapping, research methods). Historically, the country's *de facto* polarisation has resulted in the market being relatively divided, with some companies predominantly involved in the South (for example, Wase, Nagecco, Transport Development and Strategy Institute South) and others in the North (for example, Viwase, CDC, Hanoi's Transport Development and Strategy Institute), which obviously also implies a sectoral division (for example, energy, transport, water, etc.).

Public engineering companies are currently undergoing a transition phase characterised by a tendency towards progressive emancipation from a rigid administrative modus operandi. International donors are also exerting pressure on the authorities to stop public engineering from holding an undisputed position in the public markets. There are curbs to this tendency, especially regarding the threat to employment from the progressive corporatization of public engineering. Some structures employ a surplus workforce in relation with the value added produced.

University-based Research Centres and Research Institutes

University-based research centres originate from research laboratories and position themselves as professional expertise — generally in the upstream phases of engineering (research and consultancy) in order to develop their own functioning and, in the case of "private" universities at least, to improve the way their experts are treated. There are many of them but they have limited human resources. Some are nevertheless making a name for themselves in certain sectors (waste, environment). Research institutes (for example, Ho Chi Minh City and Hanoi's Urban Planning Institutes, Ho Chi Minh City Economic Research Institute and Hanoi Economics Institute) or associative private institutes (for example, the Institute for Urban Studies for global urban planning) also position themselves in the expertise market.

Private Structures

There are still few truly private consulting firms in the areas covered by our research — indeed, the legal distinction between public and private remains unclear. There are few qualified independent consultants working full-time and making a living from this work. Most of the experts hired as freelancers on development programmes and international projects are, in fact, part-time consultants with a permanent position in either a research institute, a university, or an administration agency. There are also many former government employees pursuing an independent career after retirement age (fifty-five for women and sixty for men).

Private structures are usually created at the initiative of private individuals, or more often of networks of individuals. They position themselves freely in the market for private projects, but public engineering firms often hire those with the strongest reputation as subcontractors for specialized work. Some such consultancy firms are starting to become international (for example, Van Xuan, Hadecon), though this mostly remains limited to Laos. They are usually managed by experts with a high level of technical skills and a solid network of contacts — especially within the administration. Their value added is not merely technical but also cultural: they must be able to prevent or smooth out differences between foreign consultants and project management.

Joint Venture Companies

At one point, joint ventures with State enterprises were a legal necessity for foreign companies seeking to establish themselves in Vietnam in the long term. The number of joint ventures in the field of urban network engineering[5] remains limited, though not negligible. Firstly, few foreign consultants have reached a sufficient business volume in a single sector to consider a close partnership with a local company, as the latter is often mono-sectoral. As regulation became more flexible, they have tended to keep their margin for manoeuvre by favouring subcontracting or co-contracting contracts. As for Vietnamese consultancy firms, they hesitate to form partnerships with their foreign colleagues through fear that their best elements might get poached through the joint venture. The overall experience of joint ventures tends to show a distribution of roles whereby the subsidiary is confined to traditional civil engineering services, while the foreign shareholder takes charge of services requiring more elaborate know-how. Joint ventures have clearly not been truly innovative solutions. They even come across as a legacy from the past: their creation has led neither to the non-native partner being surpassed, nor to a real melting-pot of corporate cultures.

Vietnamese technical engineering remains fragmented and even splintered. Few connections exist beyond collaborations borne of technical or commercial necessity. Individualism predominates. One of the major stakes currently being played out is probably the ability of public organizations to keep an appropriate distance from project management. Most heads of Vietnamese consultancy firms are men of influence equipped with strong networks, and whose profile is ill-suited to the requirements of modern engineering. This leaves the young engineers, who are often discreet, yet key players in the successful implementation of international projects.

The Vietnamese Look at Foreign Engineering Activities

Foreign consultants are by and large seen by Vietnamese project management representatives as competent and professional, independently of problems encountered on the ground and of their national origin. From the Vietnamese perspective, there is a perfect convergence regarding the virtues expected from a high-level foreign consultant:

- ability to understand demand;
- ability to formulate clear-cut judgments and precise recommendations;
- knowledge of the practices and procedures of international organisations;
- experience acquired in other countries;
- specialisation, ability to address each issue in depth;
- development of tools for analysis (models) and rigorous approach, database construction and survey methodologies;
- knowledge of new technologies;
- fast and efficient work, rigorous adherence to the terms of reference, excellent communication abilities, very good document presentation.

The criteria are set very high, but international engineers can also be the object of biting criticism. While recognizing their professional superiority, some Vietnamese stakeholders talk about difficult and sometimes conflicting collaborations. The expert is not required to solve a problem — the choice remains in the hands of project management — but to express an unambiguous opinion. Nuanced analysis can thus be badly received and interpreted as incompetence. At the other extreme, the arrogant and even contemptuous attitude of some foreign consultants betrays a serious lack of consideration and a poor knowledge of the local context. In this respect, culture and communication are an essential aspect of the relation between foreign consultants and their local partners.

Many high-ranking officials in the administration nevertheless realize that not all problems on the ground can be blamed on foreign engineers: the unavailability of civil servants, the deficiency of several Vietnamese consultancy firms, the inadequate abilities and responsibilities of the PMUs,[6] who are meant to supervise consultants (for example, lack of understanding of the studies' terms of reference), or technical services' lack of independence from the political sphere.

Another fundamental problem is the lack of information regarding consultancy firms working in Vietnam and the skills they have to offer: besides the indications provided to project management by international organizations and experiences with various consultants, the community of engineering consultants and its operating practices are not well known. The Ministry of Construction would like some efforts to be made to fill these gaps.

In a context where urban issues are rapidly growing in complexity, Vietnam has high expectations from foreign consultancy firms in terms of transfer of know-how. The main task expected of them consists in guiding Vietnamese engineering firms in their appropriation of international professional practices: design and supervision of large-scale technical systems (for example, large purification units, high capacity landfills, underground railway and trams…), planning, management and maintenance planning, quality control, etc. Such transfers should be enacted through daily collaboration. In this respect, the Vietnamese feel that they are confronted with two major problems: the lack of enthusiasm shown by foreign consultancy firms for guiding the development of their local competitors, and the terms of the service contract as defined in the assistance contract. The Vietnamese sometimes express strong doubts regarding foreign engineering firms' actual intention of sharing their know-how.

Another endless source of conflict is the divergence in the conception of time between foreign consultants and their Vietnamese partners. Requirements imposed by financial institutions can be rigid and sometimes unrealistic in relation with the pace of decision-making in local administrations, which can put foreign consultancy firms in an untenable position.

Fair rates of payment for intellectual services and awareness of their financial value are still not part of dominant culture within Vietnamese administration. Wages paid to foreign consultants, which can be up to twenty times those of their Vietnamese counterparts, can often seem totally outlandish; moreover, the older generation of decision-makers are not always convinced of the interest of accumulating studies, considering that foreign experts come and go with the implicit aim of selling technology or projects (for example, underground railway, water refinery). From a Western point of view, one of the paradoxes of the Vietnamese context is the fact that technocrats obviously read studies with great interest, and probably make use of them in inter-administration rivalries.

Disagreements are considered normal. But it is the attitudes held on either side that can lead to deadlock. In this respect, project management seems to have more affinities with Asian experts, who are closer culturally, and with nationalities reputed for their flexible thinking (that is, Scandinavians).

Disagreements on recommendations often focus on two areas. Firstly, technological or technical aspects, where the options suggested can clash with regulations or existing administrative procedures (for example, drinking water), or be opposed by arguments regarding cultural issues (for example, public transport, public road works) or even political issues. Secondly, they focus on general planning decisions: foreign experts are more sensitive to issues such as preserving the ancient urban setting, space-saving and keeping expropriations to a minimum, whereas the Vietnamese aim first and foremost to address a clearly defined need, such as maintaining traffic flow by widening the roads. Foreign consultants are often accused of trying to impose at all costs an advanced technological solution (for example, waste treatment, water distribution) — which benefits corporations in their home countries — based on their previous experience in another country, regardless of whether they may be ill-adapted to the local context.

The Case of Urban Transport

International consultants in the field of transport in Vietnam are carrying out two types of intervention: one-off studies and strategic studies. The first deal with one specific infrastructure, such as urban road network, airport, bridge, renovation of intercity rail network, etc. They are essentially technical-economic studies. The link between infrastructure and urban transport is rather weak: even studies which take into account the transport system as a whole fail to have an overall perspective on what the objectives for this system should be at the date the infrastructure is put in operation, and on measures needed to put such a system in place.

The second type of interventions concern essentially strategic studies, which take into account the overall urban transport system and its future and recommend measures to be implemented in order to reach the given objectives.

It would be worth reviewing, at some stage, the recommendations suggested by consultants and looking into how they were taken in by political decision-makers. We will come back to this later.

The Interventions

More appropriate at this point is the presentation of the interventions according to their nature, the cities concerned and the nationality of consultants.

Hanoi and Ho Chi Minh City are the major recipients of the initiatives inventoried (thirty-eight) whereas medium-size cities only received three projects (in fact there were five: two more should be added, but which are not included in the current database).[7] Aid in the two metropolises has so far prioritized urban transport, whereas efforts deployed in provincial areas mostly targeted the road or motorway network and large-scale infrastructure such as tunnels and bridges, in order to improve communication with and between medium-size cities. Projects for the Hanoi-Haiphong and the Haiphong-Kunming corridors are two such examples.

Interventions can be grouped according to type in the two main cities (Table 8.1).

TABLE 8.1
Interventions of Transport Consultancy Firms, Hanoi and Ho Chi Minh City

Type of intervention	Hanoi	HCMC	Total
Public transport	11	6	17
Specific studies (pollution, etc.)	4	9	13
Master plan or equivalent	2	3	5
Studies/ infrastructure projects	0	1	1
Others	0	1	1
Total	17	20	37

Source: Database of the authors.

The dynamism of infrastructure projects wins the day in Ho Chi Minh City, with the biggest names in traditional Anglo-Saxon engineering, such as Arup, Maunsell, and Louis Berger International. In contrast, there are more studies on public transport in Hanoi, even if "projects for projects" add renewed vigour to Ho Chi Minh City — there is also talk of intervention by Russian consultants.

Hanoi and Ho Chi Minh City tally the same number of interventions by foreign consultants, that is, seventeen each (Table 8.2). French and Japanese missions predominate (twenty-one out of a total thirty-four), but the French figures are amplified by the presence of two agencies that are not consultancy firms, Transdev and RATP International, with one intervention each, not to mention the CETE/CERTU expertises mobilized in 2003 in Hanoi. Moreover, one of the French projects concerns lighting more than it does transport. These factors considerably reduce the actual proportion of French transport engineering, which can be summed up to two interventions by Systra and Semaly (public transport), the mission entrusted to the small Parisian consultancy firm Explicit[8] by ADEME, and a joint engineering intervention by Thales and Coyne and Bellier for the renovation of Hanoi's Long Bien Bridge.

Although not specifically urban, a study by BCEOM on transport in the central region of Vietnam could make up for this weak French presence, but, as is the case for the areas of water and waste, the assessment shows that French activity remains thin on the ground.

TABLE 8.2
Interventions in Transport Engineering per Consultants' Country of Origin, 2000–04

Country	Hanoi	HCMC	Total
Japan	5	6	11
France	5	5	10
United States	1	2	3
United Kingdom	1	2	3
Sweden	3	0	3
Germany	2	0	2
Australia	0	2	2
Total	17	17	34

Source: Database of the authors.

In contrast, Japanese interventions are characterized by the balance between general planning services, feasibility studies, detailed design and works supervision. They testify once again to the interest of the Japanese for urban transport in East Asia (Baye and Cusset 1990).

Japan has initiated three master plans out of the five large-scale general planning studies identified in the two cities over this period:

- master plan for transport in Ho Chi Minh City for 2010 (2002–04) — Almec Corporation;
- improvement of transport in Hanoi (1999–2002) — Arup Group (Hong Kong);
- master plan for Hanoi (1997) — Yachiyo Engineering Co and Katahira & Engineers International;
- study for the development of transport in Ho Chi Minh City for 2020 (1996–98) — MVA Consultancy, Maunsell and Transport Research Laboratory;
- general transport study in Hanoi based on the 1997 master plan (1998) — Pacific Consultants International.

The budgets at stake, as well as the social and economic implications (for example, cost of public transport, relocation of populations) are such that Vietnamese authorities are proceeding with caution in the area of transport. Some foreign consultants assume that relevant authorities are accumulating studies in this field in order better to compare their options.

Studies Conducted on Transport Systems

At least fifteen studies on urban transport — of which six were major studies — were carried out in the two Vietnamese metropolises from 1990 to 2002.[9] Other than the study conducted within the framework of the project "Vietnam Urban Transport Improvement",[10] no actual work was executed immediately after completion of any of these studies, due to a lack of funding. However, some of their major suggestions were in one way or another included in the urban transport policies implemented in Hanoi and Ho Chi Minh City. These studies are in fact enabling a long process of impregnation of Vietnamese attitudes.

Few of the strategic options and policies suggested by foreign consultants are new in themselves. They often consist in improving previous options, sometimes reinforcing them with technical analyses or by updating the collected data. The real issues seem to have been the inability to implement technically efficient urban transport policies and the lack of financial means.

Transfer of Know-how and Training Actions

The interventions of foreign consultants in the field of transport are generating an increasing transfer of know-how in different areas, whether it occurs during the course of in-depth studies or through the presence of a permanent team. We will mention a few significant examples.

In 1997, MVA in association with Maunsell carried out the first in-depth study of Ho Chi Minh City's transport system while conducting training and transfer of technology activities. Throughout the study, the Vietnamese team, which was composed of individuals from different departments (Transport and Public Works, Ho Chi Minh City Road Police, Ministry of Transport's Transport Development Strategy Institute), worked alongside teams of foreign consultants. In addition, a series of research trips to several Asian cities was organized. The Vietnamese team was able to observe the way in which other Asian cities deal with transport issues and to anticipate the consequences of decisions taken in Ho Chi Minh City.

MVA experts sent by the parent company organised seminars in association with the Vietnamese team. Some of the managers selected by TPWS were also trained by MVA and TRL (Transport Research Laboratory) in the United Kingdom. Two TPWS technicians attended a formal course at the University of Southampton. In addition, TDSI and TPWS staffs were trained to use the transport planning model. It would also be essential for TPWS staff to continue improving these skills and using these tools permanently. However, organisational inadequacy within Ho Chi Minh City administration has resulted in the inefficient use of the software and technical equipment provided by MVA.[11] The same problem occurred when foreign experts installed public transport networks management software which relied on data collection in real time.

More recently, the HOUTRANS[12] team in Ho Chi Minh City, coordinated by the Japanese consultant ALMEC, has brought together foreign experts of different nationalities to conduct training and transfer of technology actions.

The British Consultant ARUP (Hong Kong Office)

ARUP played a major role in improving the current traffic situation in Ho Chi Minh City and in Hanoi within the framework of the project "Vietnam Urban Transport Improvement" (2000–04). They set up quite efficient measures which did not necessarily require vast expenses. An example of this was the channelization of streets in the central districts, whereby several two-way streets were turned into one-way streets. This brought about an improvement in traffic circulation, especially at Bay Hien, one of the city's most important intersections. The success of these operations spurred the Transport and Public Works Service to extend the one-way system to other streets in the capital, such as Nguyen Kiem and part of Xo Viet Nghe Tinh.[13]

Before ARUP's intervention, there were only a few one-way streets in Ho Chi Minh City. The consultant initially encountered strong opposition from shop owners with frontage on the streets as well as private transport users concerned about the fact that a one-way system would make their route longer. Residents finally came to accept the one-way system as they realized that this was counterbalanced by a better flow of traffic and improved road safety.

Restructuring and Reinvigorating the Bus Network in Hanoi and Ho Chi Minh City

Since the beginning of the 1990s, international consultants have made several studies and proposals to revitalise the public transport system in Hanoi and Ho Chi Minh City, which had continued to collapse in the years following *Doi Moi*.

In Hanoi, the main measures concern the creation of pilot lines and segregated bus routes, the implementation of a better-adapted fare structure with attractive season tickets, and improvement of the service. A similar policy was later adopted in Ho Chi Minh City with similarly encouraging results.

SEMALY (France) and ALMEC (Japan)

SEMALY was the first foreign consultant to recommend segregated corridors in Vietnam: one corridor for the bus and for the tram on Tran Hung Dao Avenue. Urban transport policy makers in Ho Chi Minh City agreed to this proposal, but the amount of investment needed exceeded the city's means at the time, so the People's Committee did not follow up this recommendation. The idea was more recently suggested by ALMEC as part of its Policy Test Project from August to October 2003, which is an integral part of the transport master plan for Ho Chi Minh City (HOUTRANS) in 2004 and will be continued by Vietnamese authorities. The objectives of HOUTRANS are manifold. Firstly, their aim is to determine a long-term strategy to improve the mobility of inhabitants in this urban area with the development of a master plan for 2010 and 2020; secondly, to define a plan of action for 2005 based on the master plan and to carry out feasibility studies for priority projects.

During the trial period, a number of traffic management measures were implemented by Vietnamese authorities on Tran Hung Dao Avenue to

FIGURE 8.6
Bus Lanes in Ho Chi Minh City and in Hanoi

Photos: HOUTRANS Newsletter no. 3 and *Vietnam News.*

improve service efficiency on line 1: no parking on the road, cyclists to turn left in two stages, centre point marking and development of a priority bus lane.[14] ALMEC's survey of the avenue's frontage residents after the trial period showed a high level of public acceptance. In parallel with traffic management measures, new air conditioned, large capacity buses — 80 seats — were put in service to replace existing buses. Other performance indicators improved, especially with longer hours of service, from 4.30 a.m. to 9.30 p.m. Bus users noticed an improvement in the supply and quality of the bus transport service. Over 70 per cent of interviewed passengers approved of its new service period, as well as its punctuality, comfort on board and safety. Average daily patronage has noticeably increased, from 8,300 passengers in July 2003 — before the project was implemented — to 15,700 passengers in October 2003.[15]

In line with the recommendations of Dorsch Consult, we should mention the Hanoi Urban Transport Development Project initiated by Hanoi People's Committee. One of the important parts of this US$125 million project, which was mostly funded by the World Bank, is the establishment of bus routes with dedicated right-of-way.[16] The authorities of Hanoi have recently inaugurated a 4.2 kilometres designated bus lane from Nga Tu So to Ha Dong, used by ten bus lines either in part or throughout.

Restrictions on Private Motorized Transport

Several consultants, in their diagnosis of the transport system, estimate that the growing motorization of city-dwellers cannot continue at the current rate, that its social and private costs are increasing, and that it is making the shift to public transport more difficult, especially as public transport is still far from efficient.

The Japanese consultant Yachiyo Engineering who, from 1995 to 1997, was responsible for developing a master plan for urban transport in Hanoi, and for carrying out feasibility studies for priority projects, recommended restrictions on the use of private cars, even though there were only six cars for 1,000 inhabitants in 1995. A system such as the Area Licensing System — the Singaporean urban toll — was suggested for the Old Quarter and the French Quarter. According to Yachiyo Engineering, if authorities want to avoid congestion problems in the central districts, construction of car parks should also be restricted.

In 1996, MVA was the first foreign consultant in Ho Chi Minh City to raise the issue of restricting the use of motorised two-wheeled transport in some of the city's central areas. Although the People's Committee did not take the proposals into consideration at the time, it has started to impose restrictions on the circulation motorised of two-wheeled transport in October 2002.

These measures were not implemented immediately after the studies were completed. Consultants' recommendations sometimes undergo a long brewing period. Introducing measures for citizens who demand the right to circulate more easily to earn a living is no easy task. Despite an increase in congestion and the multiplication of traffic accidents, restrictive measures still encounter opposition among the population. The motorcycle was, until recently, a status symbol, but has become a convenient mode of transport to earn one's living. Authorities initially hesitated to take unpopular decisions. However, after the spectacular growth of the fleet of motorised vehicles, and in particular motorcycles in 2002, the Ministry of Transport, followed by the Transport and Public Works departments in both metropolises, announced restrictive measures through the press, although they actually only came into force in 2003.

Which Mass Public Transport System?

Consultants have different approaches in this area. Dorsch Consult (Germany, Egis Group), which was called upon for the development of urban rail transport in Hanoi, strongly recommended the development of BRT (Bus Rapid Transit) or public transport by bus in designated sites, whereas the Vietnamese, from inhabitants to authorities, will for the most part only consider heavy underground rail for Hanoi and Ho Chi Minh City. According to Dorsch Consult, rather than investing in a heavy rail line carrying 108,500 passengers a day for a cost of about US$298 million, the same amount can be invested in the development of seven or eight bus lines in designated sites distributed over the entire city.

Once the population has been encouraged to use the bus more frequently and the network sees an increase in patronage, it should be much easier to maintain the viability of a mass transport system based on rail with a solid level of certainty — which is vital considering the intensive capital investment required for such a system.

Should it be introduced directly, without first going through an intermediate stage, urban mass rail transport runs the risk of not attaining a sufficient rate of patronage and becoming a heavy financial burden for the Vietnamese authorities as well as potential investors. High financial debt could result from the costs of intensive line haul and maintenance of the rail systems, should these be inadequately covered by revenue from passenger fares.

The abovementioned consultant, Yachiyo, recommends the construction of a heavy underground rail on condition that the project be economically and financially viable. In this sense, its views are similar to Dorsch Consult, who carried out a study on urban rail for Hanoi. Systra, who was responsible for a feasibility study for a tram in Hanoi from the end of 2004, also thinks that heavy underground rail is an option to be considered in the long term, whereas light underground rail would constitute a first stage in the establishment of urban track-guided transport.

However, development programmes for mass public transport cannot in themselves change inhabitants' preference for private transport, especially as its cost is extremely low, considering that public road users do not pay the real social cost generate by their mobility.

In Hanoi, the main measures implemented concern the creation of pilot lines and of segregated corridors for buses, the implementation of better adapted fares with attractive season tickets and the improvement of the quality of service. Decentralized cooperation between the Île-de-France Region (IDF) and Hanoi People's Committee has largely contributed to the renewal of public transport in the city. The IDF Region has undertaken, together with Hanoi People's Committee and Brussels-Capital Region, to improve the functioning of the bus network by requesting co-funding from the European Commission on three pilot lines (Asiatrans project). Within this project, the IDF Region has mobilized the expertise of RATP professionals for renovating and providing equipment to one of the bus fleet's maintenance depot, and for training bus drivers and bus controllers. It also co-financed research and development for the first bus correspondence point from Hanoi to Cau Giay.

In anticipation of the need for more capacious modes of transport, the IDF Region played a driving role in the emergence of the East-West tram project. It commissioned a pre-feasibility study in 2001 at the People's Committee's request. Through the Urban Workshop Institute, its cooperation agency in Hanoi, the IDF Region undertook surveys of bus lines patronage and traffic, used as references for the feasibility study carried out by Systra in 2004 to estimate the tram patronage for 2010 and 2020.

The first bus pilot line, successfully launched at the initiative of a German consultant (see below), benefited from vast support from the Hanoi People's Committee, from the cooperation of the Tram Company's managing director, and assistance from several colleagues.

After the initial success of this pilot line, the consultant was called upon to improve the quality of service on line 22 operated by the 10/10 Bus Company. He is currently continuing his assistance and consulting work with MOCPT Hanoi within the framework of the Asiatrans project initiated by the IDF Region and Hanoi People's Committee (see below).

An Independent German Consultant in Hanoi

A German expert, sent in 1999 for a period of several years to work in an operational unit[17] of the TPWS (Transport and Public Works Service) in charge of public transport, had an essential and decisive role in the renovation of Hanoi's public transport network.

From the moment of his arrival, he suggested to three companies that they relaunch public transport. The Tram Company, with its young managing director, was the only one to take up the challenge. A pilot operation increasing the hours of service was conducted on line 32. The other companies considered that extending the service period until 9 p.m. was a waste, that the bus would be carrying wind rather than people, and that they could not assume the financial consequences.

"*I don't think there is any point in carrying out a radical reform. It is better to start out by making good use of the available rolling stock. Rather than making new investments, the bus frequency should be increased*," recommended this expert. He thus took the "spectacular" initiative of conducting a trial run on line 32 with only twelve old buses running every ten minutes, hours of service from 5 a.m. to 9 p.m. and attractive fares. On this pilot line, a stop in front of a university replaced a secondary stop. Students highly appreciated this change and bought 60 per cent of the 4,000 monthly passes. Previously, only 500 were sold.

A representative from MOCPT made the following significant statement in an interview carried out for this research: "... *He gave us the impetus to relaunch public transport. He is responsible for putting public transport by bus on the right track. He took it upon himself to mobilize support from NGOs and from the German government to organize a series of conferences on public transport aiming to raise awareness among transport specialists and city managers regarding the need to relaunch public transport by bus. He also played a very important role in securing the Asiatrans project. Such a tangible contribution can be translated into figures, but his brain power, his expertise and the enthusiasm he has brought to Hanoi are priceless. We have decided to invite him to continue working as a consultant for Hanoi until the end of this project.*"[18]

Recommendations by Foreign Experts in Urban Public Transport Policies

Interviews with Vietnamese policy makers in urban transport do not seem to indicate that the transport policy measures implemented in the two Vietnamese metropolises have any direct link with expert report recommendations. However, public speeches and press interviews given by authorities in charge of transport do point out that foreign expertise is indirectly or implicitly taken into account in urban transport policies. In fact, the straightening out of the bus network in Hanoi and Ho Chi Minh City, as well as actions carried out to control two-wheeled transport since the beginning of the 2000s, are striking illustrations of the change in attitude, triggered by several years of successive interventions by foreign consultants, of Vietnamese authorities at local as well as national level in relation to transport policies.

The case of public transport with dedicated right-of-way in Ho Chi Minh City is a good example of this change in attitude. Initially, financial constraints gave decision-makers no other choice but to "store" recommendations. Later on, with funding from JICA, they were able to approve the implementation of the consultant's idea.

Although policy makers themselves probably do not have time to read expert reports, officials from the Transport and Public Works Service (TPWS) in both cities, who advise policymakers on policy development, pay a lot of attention to what consultants have to say. This is the case of the current managing director of TPWS in Ho Chi Minh City. From August to November 2004, for instance, he was very firm regarding the implementation of restrictive measures. In order to convince the People's Council regarding the more revolutionary measures such as the urban toll, he quoted the conclusions of the Japanese experts: "*There will not be any space left to circulate in Ho Chi Minh City if the fleet of motorcycles exceeds*

2.5 million and if the number of cars does not cease to grow."[19] However, in order to mitigate the unpopularity of the measures, he recommended an opinion survey among 10,000 persons as an essential prerequisite.

In fact, the Ministry of Transport and the consultancy firms under its aegis, such as TDSI North and TDSI South, as well as most heads of technical services within both municipalities, all publicly agree on restrictions on motorcycles and private cars. They share the idea that it would not be fair to restrict motorized two-wheeled transport while letting private cars circulate freely. However, the People's Council in both municipalities, and especially in Ho Chi Minh City,[20] do not accept restrictive measures on motorcycles. According to them, motorcycles are an essential means of transport which enables the majority of the population to earn a living. As for restrictions on cars, the People's Council has to follow government directives. So what is the government opinion on the matter?

In his opening speech at the opening of a car factory in 2003, the vice-prime minister saw as unacceptable the fact that a country of nearly 100 million inhabitants did not have a car industry: "*The development of this industry will enable the development of the mechanical industry.*"[21] Paradoxically, towards the end of 2002, he spoke out in favour of a number of measures, including the restriction of motorized two-wheeled transport, to deal with the rapid increase in congestion and traffic accidents.

In short, foreign expertise has clearly been taken into account, at least in part, in urban transport policies. It is regrettable that there should not be a convergence in attitudes regarding what the urban transport system should be in the two big cities.

International and Vietnamese experts have always spoken of measures to be taken — including tax incentives — in order to discourage the excessive use of individual modes of transport. Vietnamese decision-makers have reacted to the critical situations of urban transport in the big Vietnamese cities; however, their reaction has not been translated into a favourable transformation of the system. Most urban transport officials are convinced that the use of individual modes of transport needs to be restricted. Yet the real decision-makers do not dare make unpopular decisions. They are often caught between the development of public transport and that of the motorcycle and car industries. An enlightened and proactive transport policy is essential to provoke a change of attitude among inhabitants, at least in favour of public modes of transport.

A sustainable urban transport system in Ho Chi Minh City, Hanoi and other big Vietnamese cities relies on clear orientations and firm commitments from both the government and municipal authorities.

Conclusion

One thing is certain: in Vietnam, the concept of the transfer of models through international consultants is not relevant.

The role of foreign consultants remains limited, despite the virtues attributed to them locally. Their presence is largely dependent on rules imposed by financial backers, and is sometimes tolerated rather than really called for by local stakeholders. From the Vietnamese perspective, their role consists more in suggesting clear and substantiated options than in providing an adequate solution. Considering the difficulty of obtaining data, and the difference in time frame between experts and public decision-making systems, consultants risk finding their experience deeply frustrating, especially if they set out with the idea that they will generate the implementation of a specific project.

The expectations of foreign consultants and of the Vietnamese do not always coincide — far from it. Solid foundations are needed to hold one's ground in a dynamic market, which demands high levels of skill, time and patience. International consultant's prior knowledge of Vietnam is obviously too patchy for them to avoid disappointment and wrong moves, whereas the Vietnamese lack sufficient understanding of the rationalities of the engineering sector, as well as a truly shared capitalization of the results of the numerous missions on the ground.

Considering the high stakes of urbanization in Vietnam, the need for expertise and the country's assets, engineering — as well as the deep cultural questioning it provokes — should be the subject of bolder initiatives from public stakeholders in the field of training cooperation. Aid to capitalize on experiences and institutional support for project management would also be welcome.

What teachings from the approach developed in Vietnam could be used in other countries?

Within the framework of PRUD (Urban Research Programme for Development), our team was also able to carry out research — albeit not as in-depth — about Cambodia. Vietnam and Cambodia are at different stages in their relationship with foreign engineering firms associated to urban projects. Vietnam formulates strong demands and truly seeks methods for the transfer of know-how and strengthening of its local engineering force. Progression is not easy but the route is laid out. Cambodia is still in a real state of dependency, due almost entirely to the volume and modalities of aid. NGOs played a considerable role in the international support for Cambodia's recovery at the beginning of the 1990s. Several of them are currently positioned in the field of urban expertise through social priority projects. For the past decade, consultancy firms have progressively imposed a significant presence. The numerical preponderance of Japanese and French consultants over the period from 1990 to 2004 corresponds to these countries' level of bilateral aid, which was vastly superior to that of other countries. Local Cambodian consultancy firms are embryonic and there is no structured local engineering sector as in Vietnam, Thailand or the Philippines, nor any consultant's associations. Mixed groupings of local and foreign consultants are created on very flexible terms, usually due to the requirement to be associated with a local partner. Such consortiums often bring together one or two Cambodian experts recognised for their skills and one or more juniors responsible for carrying out surveys, for instance. The role of the local partner can be limited to facilitating relations with public authorities and to lobbying.

The history of Cambodian urban expertise since 1993 is probably only just entering a second phase — one of resurgence — following the omnipresence of foreign consultants. The emergence of a third phase in five to ten years, with a fully formed local engineering sector, will probably remain marked by foreign professional influence more than elsewhere. Nevertheless, the same approach modalities of engineering seem to be operational in both cases, and open a field of observation and analysis for other countries and other sectors (for example, energy, port and airport infrastructure, development).

Basic investigations could be conducted in Cambodia as well as in Laos, and should be at least as comprehensive as those carried out by our team in Vietnam. From a regional perspective, an initiative including these three countries could be carried out, based on the PRUD's assets and experience and on the research network set up through this programme as well as on the active cooperation of development aid agencies. China, or at least its major metropolises, would also be a relevant subject for this type of study, even though its engineering force is at a different stage in its evolution — in fact, it would be appropriate to observe the difference in situation between the various provinces studied. Other countries currently neglected by French research programmes could also be studied: the Philippines, Indonesia, Thailand and Malaysia.

Urban dynamics at work in the Asia Pacific region show strong similarities, especially regarding infrastructure and environmental projects (Baye 1997). Beyond national idiosyncrasies, in order to be useful for cooperation strategies, analysis of engineering could be based on an approach capable of being replicated in different contexts. As for other regions, including South Asia, Africa, Latin America, the Middle East and Central Asia, it is important to remain cautious as to the relevance of our conclusions for regions that are very different culturally, and whose implementation mechanisms are not necessarily comparable. Nevertheless, it is likely that the issue of engineering will turn out to be just as relevant to urban research and cooperation there as in Southeast Asia.

Beyond national idiosyncrasies, in order to be useful for cooperation strategies, analysis of engineering could be based on an approach capable of being replicated in different contexts.

Notes

This chapter is based on the results of research conducted by Eric Baye, *Économie et Humanisme* (*Economics and Humanism*) as coordinator, Jean-Michel Cusset (Transport Economics Research Centre), Ton Nu Quynh Tran (CEFURD, Ho Chi Minh City), Nguyen Thien Phu (doctoral student at University Lyon 2) and Laurent Pandolfi, with the active participation of Nguyen Ngoc Hien (IMV — Cooperation Centre for Urban Development, Hanoi).

1 For example, to simplify matters: development of incineration rather than landfills, priority to overhead or underground urban transport and on-ground public transport with dedicated lanes over traditional on-ground public transport, centralised waste treatment systems rather than small decentralized treatment units, etc.

2 Respectively Japan International Cooperation Agency and Japan Bank for International Cooperation.

3 Finnish, Danish and Australian cooperation agencies.

4 Through funding of Ph.D.s in the United States and subcontracting work.

5 For example, Apeco (PCI, Japan), Vietconsult (Nippon Koei, Japan), Hyder Consulting Vietnam (Hyder Group, United Kingdom).

6 Project Management Units (PMU) are responsible for representing project management on international projects. They are the direct discussion partners of the foreign consultants mobilized on such projects.

7 Interventions by Finnroad (Finland) in Haiphong: feasability study for the construction of RAO II Bridge (since 2000, funding from the Finnish Foreign Affairs Ministry), detailed design and supervision of works for the construction of Binh Bridge (JBIC funding, mission carried out from 2000 to 2004 with the Japanese company Chodai Co Ltd and the Finnish company Kortes).

8 Supported by the Transport Economics Research Centre.

9 The Ho Chi Minh City Transport Study, by MVA, "Feasability Study for a Public Transport Line with Dedicated Right-of-Way from Benh Thanh to Binh Tay" by SEMALY, "The Master Plan of Urban Transport for Hanoi City in Vietnam", "Hanoi Urban Railway Feasibility Study" by Dorsch Consult and the most recent study, "HCMC Urban Transport Master Plan and Feasibility Study" (HOUTRANS).

10 With ARUP Hong Kong as consultant and funding from the World Bank.

11 Interview with Vu Kien Thiet, Deputy Director, PMU of the Investment in Urban Transport and Le Qua, First Permanent Deputy Director, PMU (Project Management Unit of East-West Highway) of Ho Chi Minh City.

12 "HCMC Urban Transport Master Plan and Feasibility Study" (HOUTRANS). The research team, led by JICA experts, is based with TDSI South (Transport Development Strategy Institute in the South). The Japanese consultant ALMEC, that has been active in Asia for several years, is responsible for the overall project.

13 Interview with Vu Kien Thiet, Deputy Director, PMU of the Investment in Urban Transport.

14 Interview with ALMEC Managing Director Shizuo Iwata broadcast on Ho Chi Minh City television on 12 September 2003.

15 *HOUTRANS Newsletter* no. 3.

16 Hanoi Urban Transport Project. Concept note for proposed GEF operation, 25 pp., <www.gefweb.org>.

17 MOCPT Hanoi (Management and Operation Centre for Public Transport).

18 Quoted by *Tuoi Tre* (Youth), Sunday, 8 December 2002.

19 Daily newspaper *Tuoi Tre* (Youth): "When Should Motorised Two-wheeled Vehicles be Restricted?", 5 August 2004.

20 During the 11th Session of the People's Council on 21 June 2004, the council rejected a proposal from the Transport and Public Works Service suggesting that Ho Chi Minh City restrict its motorcycle fleet to 2.6 million and its private cars to 145,000 in 2005.

21 According to *Vietnam Economic Times*, 20 June 2003.

References

Books and Articles on Experts, Consultants and Their Markets

Baye, Eric and Jean-Michel Cusset. *Stratégie et marché des consultants aux Philippines et en Indonésie: le cas des transports urbains*. Ministère de l'Équipement et des transports, 1990.

———. "Les consultants dans le secteur des transports urbains en Asie du Sud-Est: cas des Philippines et de l'Indonésie". In *Mobilité et transports dans les villes en développement. Transferts de modèles et échanges économiques Nord-Sud*. Paris: L'Harmattan, 1992.

Baye, Eric and Dominique Lorrain. *Le développement des infrastructures dans la zone Asie-Pacifique: mythes et réalités. 2001 plus...*, no. 39 [publication of Ministry of Equipment and Transportation (DRAST/CPVS), July 1996].

Baye, Eric and Gérard Debizet. *Des nouvelles problématiques urbaines à l'innovation de l'expertise transport: mise en parallèle et convergence avec trois pays européens: France, Allemagne, Royaume-Uni*. Recherche conduite dans le cadre du Predit, Ministère de l'équipement et des transports, 2001.

Dick, Howard W. and Peter Rimmer. "Urban Public Transport in Southeast Asia: A Case Study of Technological Imperialism?" *International Journal of Transport Economics* (June 1988): 177–96.

Godard, Xavier and Jean-Michel Cusset avec la collaboration de Matthias Schmitt. *Les termes d'une politique de transport urbain au Viêt-nam dans le contexte de la transition.* Colloque AUPELF/UREF sur Développement et transition vers l'économie de marché, Hanoi, 5–6 December 1996.

Molt, Walter. "The Transformation of Public Transport in Hanoi". In *IMV, Regards croisés sur Hanoi. Transition, spécificité urbaine et choix de développement.* Actes de séminaire, 2002, pp. 131–38.

Rimmer, Peter James. "The Internationalization of Engineering Consultancies: Problem of Breaking into the Club". *Environment and Planning*, A, vol. 20 (1988): 761–88.

Consultancy Reports

CONTRANS, MARITERM. *Urban Transport in Hanoi. Diagnostic Study 1993.* Hanoi: SIDA, Hanoi People's Committee, 1993, 122 pp.

CONTRANS. *Urban Transport in Hanoi. Diagnostic Study 1993.* Executive summary, 1994.

———. *Vietnam Urban Transport Assistance Project.* Hanoi: SIDA, 1995.

Ho Chi Minh City Transport Study. Draft final report. Viêt-nam DFID-MVA, 1998.

HOUTRANS, ALMEC Corporation. *Study on Urban Transport Master Plan and Feasibility Study in HCM Metropolitan Area.* Draft final report, 2004.

JBIC. *Urban Public Transportation in Vietnam. Improving Regulatory Framework.* Research Paper no. 4, 1999.

RATP International. "Le défi du transport collectif de Hô Chi Minh Ville". Le Projet "Saigon Métro", unpublished, 1999.

SEMALY, TDSI South. "Etude de faisabilité d'une ligne de TCSP de Ben Thanh à Binh Tay". Rapport économique, unpublished. 1998.

SYSTRA. *Etude de faisabilité d'une ligne-pilote de tramway à Hanoi*, 2004.

Technical University Dresden. "Pre-feasibility Study: Construction and Reinforcement of the Rail Transit Systems in HCMC by the year 2020". Summary, unpublished, 1997.

TEWETT-TDSI South. "Résumé de l'étude de faisabilité pour le projet de 2 lignes de métro prioritaires de Hô Chi Minh Ville", unpublished, 2003, 10 pp.

Thalès-SARECO. *Etude des transports intégrés et durables à Hanoi.* Étude initiée par la coopération entre la Région Île de France et le Comité populaire de Hanoi, financement du Fonds français pour l'environnement mondial, 2004.

World Bank. *Ho Chi Minh City Urban Transport Improvement Project.* Project Appraisal Document. Washington D.C., 1998.

YACHIYO-JICA. *The Master Plan of Urban Transport for Hanoi City in Vietnam.* Tokyo, 1997.

Conferences and Seminars (Conference Proceedings)

Actes de colloque (en vietnamien). *Les deux-roues à moteur: Responsable de la congestion et des accidents routiers* — État des lieux et Solutions. Organisé à Hô Chi Minh Ville le 14 November 2002 par le Journal *Le Travailleur*.

Actes du Colloque International. "Les transports du XXIe siècle". Hô Chi Minh Ville, 20–21 April 2000.

Colloque franco-vietnamien. "Transports urbains". Organisé par UBIFRANCE et la mission économique de l'ambassade de France. Hô Chi Minh Ville, 24 October 2003.

"Conference on Solutions for Public Transportation in Hanoi Capital". Organisée par Hanoi Foreign Affairs Department, Transport & Urban Public Works Service and Siemens AG. Hanoi, 13 December 2000.

"Les expériences du Japon de la création d'un fonds de développement du réseau routier et les mesures de la sécurité routière". TDSI South/JICA, 28 February 2003.

HCMC Department of Planning and Investment. Urban Public Transport in HCMC. Ho Chi Minh City, 14 September 2001.

"Seminar on Mass Transit Development Strategy in Ho Chi Minh City". Organisé par TDSI-JTCA. Ho Chi Minh City, 16 October 2000.

"The Seminar on Urban and Public Transport Development in Hanoi City". Organized by JTCA. Hanoi, 25 February 2003.

"Transports et environnement à Hô Chi Minh Ville: du diagnostic à l'action". TPWS-DOSTE. Hô Chi Minh Ville, 14–15 May 2002.

CONCLUSION

A Diverse Approach to Research on Urban Issues

Jean-Michel Cusset
Franck Castiglioni
Patrick Gubry
Nguyen Thi Thieng
Pham Thuy Huong

Vietnam has long been the subject of French urban research. However, it is difficult to get an overall perspective of the themes and issues of this research as it is fragmented between various organizations and institutions. The same problem applies to Vietnamese research, as institutions are highly compartmentalized, and suffer from a lack of international exposure. There is actually a wide variety of institutions producing urban research in France and Vietnam: research institutes attached to central administration or local government, universities, ministries, international institutions, NGOs, etc.

One of the PRUD's achievements has consisted in initiating specific studies which brought together French and Vietnamese teams from the north and south of the country and from diverse institutions. This publication reflects part of the results obtained.

The PRUD programme demonstrates that research can be conducted in parallel on very similar themes, yet according to very different problematics.

Now would be the opportunity to go over the outcome of this research using both a comparative and a synthetic approach, with an eye to joint publications.

It would be useful to improve the circulation of information on past, current and projected urban research in Vietnam — and, more generally, in Southeast Asia. This information is currently too scattered.[1] Consultation between research centres could lead to the publication of a periodic bulletin, which would make studies and research in this field more widely available. The Cooperation Centre for Urban Development (IMV) and the Ho Chi Minh City Urban Development Management Support Centre (PADDI) could coordinate such a project.

There is no point in attempting to formulate a synthesis of the presentations contained in the present publication given the diversity of the subjects. Our ambition here is, firstly, to recapitulate on some of the issues dealt with by the PRUD (Urban Research Programme for Development) projects, as well as to review some of the main characteristics of urban mutations in Vietnam during the current transition period as outlined in the work carried out by the research teams. Secondly, we will suggest orientations for future research: based on existing knowledge accumulated through research projects carried out within the scope of the PRUD, we will either further investigate current themes and issues or explore new ones.

The Research Carried Out and Cross-disciplinary Aspects

Miscellaneous Conclusions

Under the PRUD programme, teams of Vietnamese and French researchers investigated some of the most pressing issues linked to the urban environment and its current evolution: the role of international consultants in urban infrastructure, the role of civil society in the management of urban environmental issues, the development of intra-urban mobility, urban transition and its stakeholders, the evolution of public roads in the urban recomposition process, water management, public development aid, resettlement the population of precarious habitat zones, etc. This list is obviously not exhaustive.

This research is mostly focused on the two largest cities in Vietnam: Ho Chi Minh City and Hanoi. Some studies used comparative analysis, either between the two cities (for example, research on intra-urban mobility), or between Vietnam and its neighbours (for example, research on international consultants and their relations with the local engineering force in urban infrastructure) or with a more distant country (for example, research on the evolution of public water management), or with an analysis of different models of intervention (for example, research on resettlement). The overall methodology of the research was based on the analysis of existing data and on qualitative and quantitative surveys.

Moreover, we have used a historical approach to highlight the evolution of stakeholders in urban transformation and their strategies.

The development of public roads in Hanoi has been observed throughout different historical periods: this approach emphasizes the significance of the past and the current concern for preserving its heritage.

Intra-urban mobility in Ho Chi Minh City and Hanoi has greatly increased in the past few years. Migration flows are increasingly directed towards peripheral areas. Moving to the suburbs often results in better living conditions; however, due to the expansion of its overall living space, the population is also confronted by increasing problems of urban transport, which are magnified by the inadequacy of public transport — despite recent improvements — and by the lack of infrastructure in peripheral areas.

Resettlement the inhabitants of precarious zones raises specific issues. In order to resettle them in an efficient and sustainable manner, certain aspects such as habitability, accessibility, residential security and the financial capacity of the resettled population have to be taken into account. One of the conditions necessary for successful resettlement is the setting up of economic and social support for displaced households, not only prior to resettlement, but also during the post-resettlement transition period. Policies implemented raise the issue of the rights of the large part of the population without a permanent residence permit or land-use rights. The administrative and institutional conditions under which planned resettlement is carried out should be more flexible. In addition, this problem stumbles into land issues and, more specifically, the elevated cost of land within the context of social operations.

Under the theme of water management, we reached the major conclusion that, for underprivileged populations, access to water remains largely deficient in most of the country's cities, and even in Hanoi. An essential prerequisite for more efficient management would be for managers and technicians to have an adequate level of competence and experience.

Moreover, the participation of various existing associations — The Women's Union, the Elderly People's Association and the Youth Association — is vital in addressing environmental issues. Nevertheless, participating stakeholders were not provided with specific training. The prospects of developing more autonomous organisational and administrative abilities thus remain meagre. As for any financial benefits gained from participation, they are either very limited or non-existent.

The analysis of public development aid also sheds light on persistent red tape.

International consultants from different countries such as Japan and France are taking part in various urban projects relating to infrastructures. Transfer of know-how and the strengthening of the local engineering force are sought; although some such activity is indeed taking place, it remains limited.

Cross-disciplinary Aspects

Two important questions, which complete each other, have emerged throughout this research:

- The value of urban heritage is still rarely acknowledged in Vietnam: what are the reasons for this? To what extent will it be possible to avoid eradicating this past, considering the context of high growth and economic liberalization?
- Can one talk about a Vietnamese model of an Asian city? It seems that urban transition in Vietnam is not occurring in as radical and abrupt a manner as in China. Within the field of urban development and urban planning, possible reasons for this are Vietnam's capacity for absorbing external models, the quest for a third way between state intervention and economic liberalism, and the fact that architectural heritage is taken into account in urban planning.

Orientations for Research

Orientations for research in the urban field can be identified at both macro- and micro-level. Research on the following themes could be considered:

- Comparative analysis of the transition towards a market economy of socialist cities in Asia: China and Vietnam.
- Comparative studies of Hanoi and Ho Chi Minh City. Until now, comparative analysis could be carried out based on studies conducted in either city, but without a common investigation method. Systematic comparative analysis on urban transition in Hanoi and Ho Chi Minh City would probably make it possible to underline the specificities of each city in relation to its historical, cultural, economic and socio-political context.

- Transition towards market economy of medium-sized or secondary cities, such as Haiphong, Danang and Hue, which are still the subject of few studies. Are the modalities of transition and the issues at stake similar to those in Hanoi and Ho Chi Minh City? The same questions need to be asked about medium-sized cities.

Within the scope of urban policies, the fields of planning and programming, land rights, and the management of expropriations are closely linked and generate common interactions.

The implementation of urban management projects following their programming has direct consequences on land expropriations and their allocated use. However, the lack of legal clarity that characterizes poorly established or illegal land rights status, as well as the unpredictable nature of compensation procedures, imply long and arduous red tape and arbitrary decisions that often result in unequal or case by case treatment. The complexity of procedures often leads to loss of property for the poorest and those in precarious situations, or at least to land compensation that fails to match the real value of expropriated property. As a result, expropriations are often disputed, which extends the length of time needed to execute projects, as the negotiation period then needs to be taken into account. They can also result in judicial decisions that can jeopardize the urban operation itself (for example, contestation of the initial land use rights or of the value assigned to the property).

As well as exploring ways to curb the impact of planned urban development operations — for example, by preserving existing structures as far as possible — it would be necessary to undertake further analysis of the above-mentioned fields and their interactions so as to develop directions for proposals which would allow to rehabilitate — or at least level off and equalize — land management and the compensation system within the scope of urban planning. This would not only facilitate the work of decision-makers and urban planners, but also generate greater social equity:

- Social housing policies. This also warrants further investigation, considering the effects of economic transition, the liberalization of the housing market and the prospective demand for social housing, which can only increase in line with the country's current and future urbanization.
- Urban environment, migration and poverty.[2] There is an abundance of technical studies on the urban environment in Vietnam: analyses on air or soil pollution, studies on floods, issues raised by traffic

congestion and noise, etc. Precious few studies, however, have been conducted in the field of social science and even fewer have addressed the issue using a household survey. Examining environmental issues in parallel with migration status and poverty can lead to interesting results. Although not the poorest of the poor, migrants tend to settle in the suburbs of cities, where they are in direct contact with numerous sources of industrial pollution and where infrastructures are weak: if the poor cause some of the degradations of the urban environment, they are also their first victims; low income often leads people to settle on the cheapest land available, which is often the most affected by pollution.

- Changes in the residential control system.[3] Changes to the system of residential control are currently under examination in Vietnam, similar to the recent modifications undertaken in China. The system was initially set up for the distribution of ration cards and no longer serves any purpose. Surveys have shown that it does not prevent people from migrating to cities, though it remains a cause of social inequality, since only the wealthy can easily acquit themselves of its constraints. It represents a constant preoccupation for citizens, as permanent registration makes everyday life in the city much easier. It is worth considering the suppression of this system, whilst retaining the country's system of division into blocks for security purposes. With some technical improvements, it might be possible to maintain a permanent record of the population as has been done in several European countries.
- Urban transport and security.[4] The issue of road safety is particularly serious as helmets became compulsory for motorcyclists since 15 December 2007 only; enforcing helmet usage and seat belts are most likely to have the strongest impact. Controls could be extended to other aspects of road safety, such as vehicle overload, checking whether vehicles are roadworthy, issuing driving licenses, etc. This is a major issue for public health. The current situation almost amounts to criminal negligence, considering the countless road deaths, injuries and resulting disability, which cause untold suffering to individuals and families — not to mention the social cost from overloaded healthcare facilities and lost working days.
- Daily mobility and poverty in Vietnamese cities. To this day, copious amounts of research on urban poverty in Vietnam have been carried out. However, the everyday mobility of the most disadvantaged populations has not been addressed as such, whereas it has been the

subject of numerous studies elsewhere, especially in African countries.[5] Research on this issue could focus on several aspects. For instance, is the accessibility of the poor to essential goods and services hampered by low motorized mobility? Should poverty reduction strategies in Vietnam take the issue of transport into account?

Numerous other elements for reflection could be suggested. We will mention a few:

- The different ways in which consultancy report results as well as publications and reports used for research are being used, and, more generally, the issue of the use being made of research results. Foreign consultant reports mostly contain recommendations: for diverse reasons, these do not necessarily lead to immediate action, but, after several years, end up being applied, and, in a way, absorbed, as has been observed in the field of transport. On the other hand, very little is known about the actual impact of social science research on Vietnamese cities, even though they result — whether or not explicitly — in proposals for measures and policies.
- The use of census results: contrary to what is sometimes thought, population censuses are actually comprehensive and, allowing for a margin of error, include those without permanent registration (similar to China's "floating population"). However, foreigners in Vietnam had, until now, never been included in the general census.[6] This situation should be corrected, in a context where transborder movement is developing, especially with ASEAN countries. Furthermore, it would also be very useful in future if the census published a volume of specific data on cities, considering the growing importance of urban issues and the irreplaceable role of census data for apprehending urbanization. Finally, the situation in cities is rapidly changing, and a census should be carried out every five years, as was the case for the first time in Ho Chi Minh City in 2004.

Ultimately, the issues addressed in this publication, together with the aforementioned suggestions for further research, should collectively act as a catalyst for urban research in Vietnam. With this in mind, it would be useful to build a network including both French and Vietnamese research teams and institutions brought together by the PRUD programme, with the possibility of others joining later. The main mission of this streamlined organization would be to exchange information on past and present research, and to circulate bibliographies and reflections on urban issues and their future prospects. Those involved in this network could later join forces to set up research projects, with several teams working in cooperation, in response to national and international calls for tender. It would no doubt soon be called upon to help define some of these calls.

Notes

1 For example, *Lettre de l'IPRAUS* [Bulletin of the Parisian Research Institute: Architecture, Urbanism & Society] and *Lettre de l'AFRASE* [Bulletin of the French Association for Research in Southeast Asia] contain such information.

2 This theme is addressed in a research project funded by the Priority Solidarity Fund (FSP) of the French Embassy in Vietnam, on the subject of "Migration, Poverty and Urban Environment: Hanoi and Ho Chi Minh City". The project is conducted in cooperation with IRD in Paris, IDS in Ho Chi Minh City, and IPSS in Hanoi.

3 A research project has just been carried out on this topic. See: *Villes en Transition Vietnam* [Cities in Transition], Ho Chi Minh City Centre for Sociology and Development Studies, Hanoi Institute of Sociology, "Impacts of Existing Residence Registration Policy on Urban Poverty Alleviation. Two Case Studies in Hanoi and Ho Chi Minh City". Ho Chi Minh City, 2005, 278 pp.

4 A qualitative study has been conducted on this topic at the initiative of the French Red Cross, in association with the Vietnamese Red Cross.

5 See for instance: Diaz, Olvera L., D. Plat, P. Pochet and M. Sahabana. "Mobilité et pauvreté en Afrique sub-saharienne: Eclairages à partir de quelques enquêtes-ménages [Mobility and poverty in Sub-Saharan Africa: Evaluation Based on a few Household Surveys]. In *Mobilité et systèmes de transport en Afrique sub-saharienne : les défis de la pauvreté*. [Mobility and Transport Systems in Sub-Saharan Africa: The Challenges of Poverty]. SITRASS 8 proceedings, Saly, March 2004, MIET, IRD, LET, INRETS, 530 pp.

6 The "Mid-term Census" in Ho Chi Minh City from October 2004 was the first to take into account foreign nationals.

General Bibliography

Generalities, Southeast Asia, Socialist Cities, Transition to the Market, Urban Issues

Cusset, Jean-Michel. "Les transports urbains en Asie du sud-est: enjeux et perspectives". *Informations et Commentaires*, no. 112, juillet–septembre (2000): 51–59.

Dick Howard Want and Peter James Rimmer. "Urban Public Transport in Southeast Asia: A Case Study of Technological Imperialism?" *International Journal of Transport Economics*, June 1988, pp. 177–96.

———. "Beyond the Third World City: The New Urban Geography of South-east Asia". *Urban Studies* (Glasgow) 35, no. 12 (1998): 2303–21.

Douglass, Mike. "From Global Intercity Competition to Cooperation for Livable Cities and Economic and Economic Resilience in Pacific Asia". *Environment & Urbanization* (London) 14, no. 1 (2002): 53–68.

Evers, Hans-Dieter. "Urbanization and Urban Conflict in Southeast Asia". *Asian Survey* (Berkeley CA) 15, no. 9 (1975): 775–85.

Forbes, Dean Keith and Michael Lindfield. *Urbanisation in Asia: Lessons Learned and Innovative Responses*. Canberra: Australian Agency for International Development, 1997, 120 pp.

——— and Nigel J. Thrift. "International Impacts on the Urbanisation Process in the Asian Region: A Review". In Fuchs, R.J., Jones, Gavin W. and E.M. Pernia (eds.), *Urbanisation and Urban Policies in Pacific Asia*. Philadelphia (PA): Westview Press, 1987, pp. 67–87.

——— (eds.), *The Socialist Third World: Urban Development and Territorial Planning*. Oxford: Blackwell, 1987, 333 pp.

French, R. Antony and Ian F.E. Hamilton (eds.), *The Socialist City: Spatial Structure* and Urban Policy. John Wiley, 1979.

Fryer D.W. "The 'Million City' in Southeast Asia". *Geographical Review* 43, no. 4, (1953): 474–94.

Ginsburg, N., B. Koppel and Terrence Gary McGee (eds.). *The Extended Metropolis: Settlement Transition in Asia*. Honolulu: University of Hawaii Press, 1991.

Goldblum, Charles, Annik Osmont and Isabel Diaz (coord.). *Gouverner les villes du Sud. Défis pour la recherche et pour l'action*. Actes du colloque international du PRUD (Paris, UNESCO, 5–7 May 2004). Paris: Ministère des Affaires étrangères (Direction Générale de la Coopération Internationale et du Développement, DGCID), GEMDEV, ISTED, 2004, 296 pp. (Partenariats).

Jones, Gavin W. "Urbanization Issues in the Asian-Pacific Region". *Asian-Pacific Economic Literature* (Guildford, England) 5, no. 2 (1991): 5–33.

Kim, Won Bae (ed.). *Culture and the City in East Asia*. London: Clarendon Press, 1997, xvii–262 pp. (Oxford Geographical and Environmental Studies).

Lea, John P., and John M. Courtenay (eds.). *Cities in Conflict. Studies in the Management of Asian Cities*. Washington: The World Bank, 1985, 140 pp.

Mateo-Babiano, Iderlina and Ieda Hitoshi. "Street Space Renaissance: A Spatio-historical Survey of Two Asia Cities". *Journal of the Eastern Asia Society for Transportation Studies* (Tokyo) 6 (2005): 4317–32.

McGee, Terrence Gary. *The Southeast Asian City*. London, 1967.

———. "The Emergence of *Desakota* Regions in Asia: Expanding a Hypothesis". In Ginsburg, N., B. Koppel and Terrence Gary McGee (eds.). The Extended Metropolis: Settlement Transition in Asia. Honolulu: University of Hawaii Press, 1991, pp. 3–25.

——— and Ira Robinson (eds.). *The Mega-Urban Regions of Southeast Asia*. Vancouver: University of British Columbia Press, 1995.

Montgomery Mark R., Richard Stren, Barney Cohen and Holly E. Reed (eds.). *Cities Transformed: Demographic Change and Its Implications in the Developing World*. Washington (D.C.): The National Academies Press, 2003, 552 pp.

Murray, Pearse and Ivan Szelenyi (eds.). "The City in the Transition to Socialism". *International Journal of Urban and Regional Research* (London) 8, no. 1 (1984): 90–107.

———. "L'anti-urbanisme des États socialistes". *Les Annales de la Recherche Urbaine* (Paris), no. 38 (1988): 23–30.

Nosco, Peter. "Confucian Perspectives on Civil Society and Government". In Rosenblum, Nancy L. and Robert C. Post (eds.). *Civil Society and Government*. Princeton, Oxford: Princeton University Press, 2002, pp. 334–59.

Ott, T. "From Concentration to De-concentration: Migration Patterns in the Post-socialist City". *Cities* (London, Amsterdam, New York), 6 (2000): 403–12.

Scarpaci, Joseph L. "Introduction on the Transformation of Socialist Cities". *Urban Geography* (Columbia, MD) 21, no. 8 (2000): 659–69.

Sailer-Fliege, Ulrike. "Characteristics of Post-socialist Urban Transformation in East Central Europe". *GeoJournal* (Heidelberg, Berlin) 49, no. 1 (1999): 7–16.

Szelenyi, Ivan. *Urban Inequities, State Socialism*. Oxford: Oxford University Press, 1982.

———. Cities under Socialism and after. In Andruz, G., M. Harloe and Ivan Szelenyi (eds.). Cities after Socialism: Urban and Regional Change and Conflict in Post-socialist Societies. Oxford: Blackwell, 1996, pp. 286–317.

Timmerman, Peter and Rodney White. "Megahydropolis: Coastal Cities in the Context of Global Environmental Change". *Global Environmental Change* (London, Amsterdam, New York) 7, no. 3 (1997): 205–34.

The World Bank. "Urban Poverty in East Asia. A Review of Indonesia, the Philippines and Vietnam". Washington (D.C.), 2003, 132 pp. (East Asia Working Papers Series, no. 11).

Generalities about Vietnam

Banister, Judith. *Vietnam Population Dynamics and Prospects*. Berkeley (CA): University of California, Institute of East Asian Studies, 1993, xiv–105 pp. (Indochina Research Monograph, no. 6).

Basilacan, Arsenio M., Ernesto M. Pernia, and Gemma Esther B. Estrada. *Economic Growth and Poverty Reduction in Vietnam*. ERD Working Paper no. 42. Bangkok: Asian Development Bank, 2003.

Charbit, Yves (dir.) and Catherine Scornet (collab.). *Société et politiques de population au Viêt-nam*. Paris: L'Harmattan, 2002, IV–228 pp. (Collection Populations).

Coxhead, Ian, Phan Diep, and Erin Collins. *Income Growth and Internal Migration in Vietnam: Trends and Projections*. Madison WI: University of Wisconsin, 2008, 4 pp.

Đặng Nguyên Anh. *Di dân trong nước: Vận hội và thách thức đối với công cuộc đổi mới và phát triển ở Việt Nam* [Internal Migration: Opportunities and Challenges for the Renovations and Development in Viet Nam]. Hà Nội: Trung Tâm Kinh Tế Châu Á-Thái Bình Dương (VAPEC)/Vietnam Asia-Pacific Economic Center, Nhà Xuất Bản Thế Giới, 2005, 71 pp.

Dixon, Chris and Kilgour A. "State, Capital and Resistance to Globalisation in Vietnamese Transitional Economy. *Environment and Planning* (London) 34 (2002): 599–618.

Dovert, Stéphane and Benoît de Tréglodé (dir.). *Viêt Nam Contemporain*. Paris: IRASEC, 2004, XXXII–568 pp. (Les Indes Savantes).

Epprecht, Michael and Andreas Heinimann (eds.). *Tập bản đồ kinh tế-xã hội Việt Nam. Mô tả tổng điều tra dân số và nhà ở năm 1999* [Socioeconomic Atlas of Vietnam. A depiction of the 1999 Population and housing census]. Berne, Hanoi: Swiss National Centre of Competence in Research North-South, General Statistics Office Vietnam, Informatics Center for Agriculture and Rural Development (ICARD) Vietnam, Cartographic Publishing House, 2004, 168 pp. (CD-Rom available).

Gainsborough, M. "Beneath the Veneer Reform: The Politics of Economic Liberalisation in Vietnam". *Communist and Post-Communist Studies* (Amsterdam, New York) 35, no. 3 (2002): 353–68.

Gendreau, Francis, Vincent Fauveau and Dang Thu. *Démographie de la Péninsule Indochinoise*. Paris: Éditions ESTEM, 1997, 132 pp. (Universités francophones, Série Savoir Plus Universités).

Gironde, Christophe and Jean-Luc Maurer (dir.). *Le Vietnam à l'aube du XXIe siècle. Bilan et perspectives politiques, économiques et sociales. Mélanges pour commémorer le 100e anniversaire de la naissance de Pierre Gourou*. Paris: Karthala, IUED, CRAM, 2004, 353 pp. (Hommes et Sociétés).

Gubry, Patrick (dir.). *Population et développement au Viêt-nam*. Paris: Karthala, CEPED, 2000, 614 pp. + 16 pl. h.t. (Économie et Développement).
New ref.: Gubry Patrick, Nguyễn Hữu Dũng, Phạm Thúy Hương (chủ biên). *Dân số và phát triển ở Việt Nam*. Hà Nội: Thế Giới, IRD, ILSSA, IMV, 2004, 701 tr. + 16 phụ bản.

Hardy, Andrew, "Rules and Resources: Negotiating the Household Registration System in Vietnam under Reform". *SOJOURN: Journal of Social Issues in Southeast Asia* 16, no. 2 (2001): 187–212.

Hoang Xuan Thanh, Dang Nguyen Anh and Cecilia Tacoli. *Livelihood Diversification and Rural-urban Linkages in Vietnam's Red River Delta*. IIED, 2005, 29 pp. (Working Paper Series on rural-urban interactions and livelihood strategies, Working Paper no. 11).

Lê Bá Thảo. *Việt Nam. Lãnh thổ và các vùng địa lý*. Hà Nội: Thế Giới, 1997, 610 tr.
New ref.: Le Ba Thao. *Vietnam. The Country and Its Geographical Regions*. Hanoi: The Gioi, 1997, 617 pp.
New ref.: Lê Ba Thao. *Vietnam. Pays et régions géographiques*. Hanoi: Thê Gioi, 2000, 596 pp.

Logan, Malcolm I. "Progress in Planning — Has there been Any? The Case of the Cities of East Asia". *Progress in Planning* 57, no. 3–4 (2002): 239–60.

Nghi D.Q. and Hans Detlef Kammeier. "Balancing Data Integration Needs in Urban Planning. *Cities* (London, Amsterdam, New York) 18, no. 2 (2001): 61–75.

Nguyen Cao Duc. "Urbanization in Vietnam: Status and Solutions". *Vietnam's Socio-Economic Development* (Hanoi), no. 38 (Summer 2004): 55–80.

Nguyen Duc Nhuan, et al. "Viet Nam". In Kosta Mathey (ed.), *Housing Policies in the Third World*. Munich: Profil Verlag, 1991, 332 pp.

Nguyen Thi Thu Phuong, Tran Ngo Thi Minh Tam, Nguyen Thi Nguyet, and Remco Oostendorp. "Determinants and Impacts of Migration in Vietnam". In *Market, Policy and Poverty Reduction in Vietnam*. Hanoi: Vietnam Culture and Information Publishing House, 2008, pp. 59–92.

Papin, Philippe. *Viêt-nam. Parcours d'une Nation*. Paris: La Documentation Française, 1999, 179 pp. (Asie plurielle).

Programme de Recherche et de Liaison Universitaires pour le Développement (PRELUDE). *Co-développement urbain durable, enseignement supérieur, responsabilités de la recherche et de la gestion*. Symposium international

ISSHO-CSEAS-PRELUDE, Hô Chi Minh Ville, 9–12 March 1999. Namur, 2001, 553 pp. (*Prélude*, numéro spécial 41–43).

Tổng Cục Thống Kê, Chương Trình Phát Triển Liên Hợp Quốc. *Chuyên khảo về di cư nội địa và đô thị hóa ở Việt Nam*. Hà Nội: Nhà Xuất Bản Thống Kê, 2001, xiv–121 pp.
New ref.: General Statistical Office, United Nations Development Programme. *1999 Population and Housing Census. Census Monograph on Internal Migration and Urbanization in Viet Nam*. Hanoi: Statistical Publishing House, 2001, xiv–123 pp.

Tổng Cục Thống Kê, Quỹ Dân Số Liên Hợp Quốc. *Điều tra di cư Việt Nam năm 2004: Những kết quả chủ yếu*. Hà Nội: Nhà Xuất Bản Thống Kê, 2005, xvi–195 pp.
New ref.: General Statistics Office, United Nations Population Fund. *The 2004 Vietnam Migration Survey: Major Findings*. Hanoi: Statistical Publishing House, 2005, xvi–199 pp. (CD-ROM available).

Tổng Cục Thống Kê, Qũy Dân Số Liên Hợp Quốc (UNFPA), and Deshingkar Priya. *Điều tra di cư Việt Nam năm 2004: Chất lượng cuộc sống của người di cư ở Việt Nam*. Hà Nội, 2006, xii–149 tr.
New ref: General Statistics Office (GSO), United Nations Population Fund (UNFPA) and Deshingkar Priya. *The 2004 Vietnam Migration Survey: The Quality of Life of Migrants in Vietnam*. Hanoi, 2006, xii–145 pp.

Trung Tâm Khoa Học Xã hội và Nhân Văn Quốc Gia. *Báo cáo về phát triển con người ở Việt Nam 2001. Đổi mới và sự nghiệp phát triển con người*. Hà Nội: NXB Chính trị quốc gia, 2001, xx–155 tr.
New ref.: National Center for Social Sciences and Humanities. *National Human Development Report 2001. Doi Moi and Human Development in Viet Nam*. Hanoi: The Political Publishing House, 2001, xviii–115 pp.
New ref.: Centre National des Sciences Sociales et Humaines. *Rapport sur le développement humain au Vietnam 2001. Le Doi Moi et le développement humain*. Hanoi: Éditions Politiques Nationales, 2002, xviii–149 pp.

UNDP (ed.), Guest Philip. *The Dynamics of Internal Migration in Viet Nam*. Hanoi, 1998, 40 pp. (UNDP Discussion Paper 1).

Vũ Tự Lập and Christian Taillard. *Atlas du Viêt-nam/Atlat Việt Nam* [An Atlas of *Vietnam*]. Montpellier, Paris: Reclus, La Documentation Française, 1994, 421 pp. (Collection Dynamiques du territoire).

Winkels, Alexandra and Neil W. Adger. *Sustainable Livelihoods and Migration in Vietnam: The Importance of Social Capital as Access to Resources*. International symposium "Sustaining Food Security and Managing Natural Resources in Southeast Asia — Challenges for the 21st Century", 8–11 January 2002, Chiang Mai, 15 pp.

Xiaquan Zhang, Heather, Mick P. Kelly, Alexandra Winkels and Neil W. Adger. "Migration in a Transitional Economy: Beyond the Planned and Spontaneous Dichotomy in Vietnam". *Geoforum* (Oxford), no. 6 (2006): 1066–81.

Cities in Vietnam before Revolution

Fourniau, Charles. "Le phénomène urbain à l'époque coloniale". In Lafont Pierre-Bernard (dir.), *Péninsule Indochinoise. Études Urbaines*. Paris: L'Harmattan, 1991. 232 pp., pp. 167–83. (Recherches Asiatiques).

Langlet-Quach, Thanh Tâm. "Le phénomène urbain dans le Viêt-nam traditionnel". *Les Cahiers d'Outre-Mer* (Bordeaux-Talence), no. 184 (octobre-décembre 1993): 419–41.

Turley, William S. "Urban Transformation in South Vietnam". *Pacific Affairs* (Vancouver) 49, no. 4 (1977): 607–24.

Woodside, Alexander. "The Development of Social Organizations in Vietnamese Cities in the Late Colonial Period". *Pacific Affairs* (Vancouver) 44, no. 1 (1971): 39–64.

Wright, Gwendolyn. "Tradition in the Service of Modernity: Architecture and Urbanism in French Colonial Policy, 1900–1930". *The Journal of Modern History* (Chicago IL) 59, no. 2 (1987): 291–316.

Cities, Urban Planning in Socialist Vietnam before *Doi Moi*

Desbarats, Jacqueline. "Population Redistribution in the Socialist Republic of Vietnam". *Population and Development Review* (New York) 13, no. 1 (1987): 43–76.

Forbes, Dean Keith. *Urbanization and Urban Growth in Vietnam*. Canberra: The Australian National University, 1990, 10 pp. (International Population Dynamics Program, Research Note, no. 111).

———. "Recent Aspects of Urbanisation in Vietnam". In Hull, Terence H. and Dean Keith Forbes. *Demographic and Social Change in Vietnam*. Canberra: Australian National University, 1990. (Briefing Paper, no. 16).

——— and Nigel J. Thrift. "Territorial Organisation, Regional Development and the City in Vietnam". In Forbes Dean Keith and Nigel J. Thrift (eds.). *The Socialist Third World: Urban Development and Territorial Planning*. Oxford: Blackwell, 1987, 333 pp., pp. 98–128.

Institute for Economic Research. *Urbanisation and Socio-economic Development in Viet Nam from 1954 to Present*. Ho Chi Minh City, 1991, 57 pp. + 18 maps.

Langlet-Quach, Thanh Tâm. "Le phénomène urbain dans le Viêt-nam contemporain". *Bulletin de l'Association des Amis de l'Orient*, no. 37 (1993–94): 16–18.

La Robertie, Catherine de. "Le développement des villes moyennes au Viêt-Nam". *Péninsule* (Paris) 28, no. 1 (1994): 91–123.

Nguyên Duc Nhuân. *Industrialisation et restructuration de l'espace social au Viêt Nam*. Paris: CSU-DGRST, 1981, 63 pp.

———. *Dés-urbanisation et développement régional au Vietnam (1954–1977)*. Paris: CSU, 1978, 142 pp.

———. "Urban change in Viet Nam". *International Journal of Urban and Regional Research* (Brighton) 2, no. 2 (1978).

———. "Mandarins et révolutionnaires: leurs rapports à l'espace social au Vietnam". In Boudarel, Georges (ed.), *La bureaucratie au Vietnam.* Paris: L'Harmattan., 1983, 261 pp.

———. "Do the Urban and the Regional Policies of the Socialist Vietnam Reflect the Patterns of the Ancient Mandarin bureaucracy?" *International Journal of Urban and Regional Research* (Brighton) 8 (1984).

———. "The Price of Urbanization in Vietnam". *International Journal of Urban and Regional Research* (Brighton) 11 (1987).

———. "Vietnam in the Urban Turn: Metropolisation and Cosmopolisation". In *Modern Viet Nam: Transition Identities.* St Petersburg: St Petersburg State University Press, 2002, pp. 73–74.

———. "Viêt-nam, un demi siècle de chassé croisé urbain ou cinquante ans d'histoire urbaine (1946–1996)". *Cahiers d'études Vietnamiennes* (Paris), (2003): 80–96.

Nguyên Lê Mong. "Étude du rôle social, économique et politique des agglomérations au Vietnam". In Institut International des Civilisations Différentes/ International Institute of Differing Civilizations (INCIDI), Les agglomérations urbaines dans les pays du Tiers Monde. Leur rôle politique, social et économique [Urban Agglomerations in the States of the Third World. Their Political, Social and Economic Role]. Compte rendu de la 34e session d'étude de l'INCIDI tenue à Aix-en-Provence du 11 au 16 septembre 1967 [Report of the 34th INCIDI study session held in Aix-en-Provence from 11 to 16 September 1967]. Bruxelles: éditions de l'Institut de Sociologie, Université Libre de Bruxelles, 1971, 1085 pp., pp. 921–37. (Collection de l'Institut International des Civilisations Différentes).

Reuterswaerd, Lars, Maria Nystroem and Roslung Hans (eds). "Shelter Policies in Vietnam". *Trialog* (Frankfurt-am-Main), no. 6 (1985): 49–56.

Thrift, Nigel J. and Dean Keith Forbes. "Cities, Socialism and War: Hanoi, Saigon and the Vietnamese Experience of Urbanisation". *Environment and Planning* (London), no. 3 (1985): 279–308.

———. *The Price of War: Urbanisation in Vietnam 1954–1985.* London, Boston, Sydney: Allen and Unwin, 1986, 188 pp.

Cities, Urban Planning in Vietnam after *Doi Moi*

Ambassade de France en République Socialiste du Vietnam, Snrech Serge, Baudoin Nicolas, Montbas Alexandre de, Pandolfi Laurent, and David Margonstern. *Action de la France pour le développement urbain au Vietnam.* Hanoi, 2002, 34 pp. (Les Cahiers de la Coopération Française au Vietnam, no. 9 (2002).

Anh Nguyen Pham. *Public Spaces, State-society Relations, and Planning in Vietnam.* 8th International Conference of the Asian Planning Schools Association (APSA), "Cities for People", Penang, 11–14 September 2005, 15 pp.

Baye, Éric and Jean-Michel Cusset. "Expertises locales et étrangères dans les infrastructures urbaines au Vietnam et aperçu concernant le Cambodge". In

Goldblum Charles, Osmont Annik, Diaz Isabel (coord.), *Gouverner les villes du Sud. Défis pour la recherche et pour l'action*. Actes du colloque international du PRUD (Paris, UNESCO, 5–7 mai 2004). Paris: Ministère des Affaires étrangères (Direction Générale de la Coopération Internationale et du Développement, DGCID), GEMDEV, ISTED, 2004, 296 pp., pp. 55–57. (Partenariats).

Bộ Xây Dựng. *Quy hoạch xây dựng các đô thị Việt Nam. Tập I.* Hà Nội: Nhà Xuất Bản Xây Dựng, 323 tr.

[*Ministry of Construction. Urban Plan of the Cities in Vietnam. Vol. I. Hanoi: Construction Publishing House, 1999, 323 pp.*]

Chéron, Marie. *Les nouvelles formes d'exclusion urbaine au Vietnam: logiques et enjeux. Les mutations socio-économiques d'un pays en transition, au coeur de la trajectoire d'exclusion des sampaniers de la ville de Huê*, Centre Vietnam. Mémoire de maîtrise d'économie sociale, Université de Toulouse-Le Mirail, 2004, 126 pp.

Chi Y. et al. "Case Studies in Quantitative Urban Sustainability". *Technology in Society* 28, issues 1–2 (2006): 105–23.

Cour, Jean-Marie. *Migrations, urbanisation et transformation du monde rural au Vietnam*. Paris: Ministère des Affaires étrangères, ISTED, 2001, 43 pp.

New. ref.: Cour, Jean-Marie. *Di dân, đô thị hoá và phát triển nông thôn tại Việt Nam*. Paris: Bộ Ngoại Giao Pháp, ISTED, 2001, 45 tr.

———. *Urbanization and Sustainable Development: A Demo-economic Conceptual Framework and Its Application to Vietnam*. Hanoi: Vietnam Urban Forum, 2003, 53 pp.

Dang Huu Ngoc, et al. "Viet Nam". In Economic and Social Commission for Asia and the Pacific, *Urbanization and socio-economic development in Asia and the Pacific*. New York (NY): United Nations, 1993, vi–146 pp. (Asian Population Studies Series, no. 122).

Đang Nguyen Anh. *Urbanization in Vietnam: An Overview*. International Workshop on "Sustainable Urbanization, Women's Status and Religion in Vietnam", NIPSS, Tokyo, 2000, 9 pp.

———. "Population Distribution, Urbanization and Migration in Vietnam: What can be Learned from the 1999 Population and Housing Census?". *Vietnam's Socio-economic Development. A Social Science Review* (Hanoi), no. 27 (2001): 3–7.

Đang Nguyen Anh, Cecilia Tacoli and Hoang Xuan Thanh. *Migration in Vietnam. A Review of Information on Current Trends and Patterns, and Their Policy Implications*. Dahka: Refugee and Migratory Movements Research Unit (RMMRU), London: Department for International Development (DFID), 2003, ii–36 pp. (Migration, Development and Pro-poor Policy Choices in Asia).

Do Hau. *Urbanization in Vietnam. Features and Its Developing Trends in the Early 21st Century*. 8th International Conference of the Asian Planning Schools Association (APSA), "Cities for People", Penang, 11–14 September 2005, 16 pp.

Do Thi Kim Thanh. *Urban Environmental Management and Environmental Training Course at Hanoi Architectural University*. 8th International conference of the

Asian Planning Schools Association (APSA), "Cities for People", Penang, 11–14 September 2005, 4pp.

Douglass, Mike. *Pathways of Urbanisation and Socio-economic Development in East-Asia: Policy Research Agenda for Viet Nam's Urban Transition in a Global Era.* First meeting of the Viet Nam urban forum, Hanoi, 21 May 2001. Hanoi: UNDP, UN-Habitat, 33 pp.

———, et al. *The Urban Transition in Vietnam.* Honolulu: University of Hawai, Fukuoka: UN-Habitat, 2002, 289 pp.

Drakakis-Smith, David and Chris Dixon. "Sustainable urbanization in Vietnam". *Geoforum* (Oxford) 28, no. 1 (1997): 21–38.

Drummond, Lisa B.W. "Street Scenes: Practices of Public and Private Space in Urban Vietnam". *Urban Studies* (Glasgow) 37, no. 12 (2000): 2377–91.

——— and Mandy Thomas (Eds.). *Consuming Urban Culture in Contemporary Vietnam.* London, New York: RoutledgeCurzon, 2003, xii–248 pp.

Durand Frédéric. "Villes et urbanisation au Viêt-nam, une esquisse d'état des lieux bibliographique". *Péninsule* (Paris), no. 31 (1995): 141–62.

Durand Frédéric B. "The Stakes of Urban Planning and Management in Vietnam in the Context of *Doi Moi* reforms". In Institute of Social Sciences in Ho Chi Minh City, Center for Southeast Asian Studies, *Human Environment and Urbanization in Vietnam, Southeast Asia and Japan.* Ho Chi Minh City, 1997, 399 pp., pp. 159–97.

Godard, Xavier, Jean-Michel Cusset and Mathias Schmitt (collab.). "Des systèmes de transport urbain au Vietnam à la recherche de la modernité". *Cahiers des Sciences Humaines* (Paris) 32, no. 3 (1996): 555–75.

Grard Agathe. *Les réformes foncières au Vietnam: Étude des marchés fonciers périurbains de deux pôles secondaires du Nord Vietnam.* Mémoire de DESS d'Urbanisme et Aménagement, Institut Français d'Urbanisme, 2004, 128 pp.

Kengo Mizuno, Keitaro Ishigami. *Urban Development and Housing Sector in Vietnam.* JBIC Research Paper, no. 3. Tokyo: Japan Bank for International Cooperation (JBIC), 1999*a*, x–VI–157 pp.

Laquian, Aprodico A. "Viewpoint China and Vietnam: Urban Strategies in Societies Transition". *Third World Planning Review* (Liverpool) 18, no. 1 (1996): III–XII.

Leaf, Michael Leon. "A Tale of Two Villages. Globalization and Peri-urban Change in China and Vietnam". *Cities* (London, Amsterdam, New York) 19, no. 1 (2002): 23–31.

Lê Van Thanh. "L'urbanisation". In Gubry Patrick (dir.), *Population et développement au Viêt-nam.* Paris: Karthala, CEPED, 2000, 614 pp., pp. 219–42.

Le Bris, Émile and Christian Taillard. "Régionalisation et urbanisation du Viêt-nam central: Les dimensions scientifiques du débat sur l'aménagement du territoire". *Espace Géographique* (Montpellier), no. 1 (1998): 1–14.

Luu Duc Minh. *The Resettlement of Fishing-boat Dweller Community in Hue City, Vietnam: Solution for Environmental Problems.* 8th International Conference of the Asian Planning Schools Association (APSA), "Cities for People", Penang, 11–14 September 2005, 12 pp.

Mattner, Mark. "Power to the People? Local Governance and Politics in Vietnam". *Environment and Urbanization* (London) 16, no. 1 (April 2004): 121–27.

McGee, Terrence Gary. "The Urban Future of Viet Nam". *Third World Planning Review* (Liverpool) 17, no. 3 (1995): 104–28.

———. "The Urban Future of Vietnam Reconsidered". *Ritsumeikan Journal of Geography* 12 (2000): 1–22.

Miras, Claude de. "Transitions nationales, gouvernance urbaine et gestion de l'eau potable — Maroc et Vietnam". In Goldblum, Charles, Annik Osmont and Isabel Diaz (coord.), *Gouverner les villes du Sud. Défis pour la recherche et pour l'action.* Actes du colloque international du PRUD (Paris, UNESCO, 5–7 May 2004). Paris: Ministère des Affaires étrangères (Direction Générale de la Coopération Internationale et du Développement, DGCID), GEMDEV, ISTED, 2004, 296 pp., pp. 170–75. (Partenariats).

Nahiro Kitano, et al. *Urban Public Transportation in Vietnam — Improving Regulatory Framework.* JBIC Research Paper, no. 4. Tokyo: Japan Bank for International Cooperation (JBIC), 1999*b*, vi–V–39 pp.

Ngo Thi Bich Dao and René Parenteau. "Le rôle de la société civile dans la gestion environnementale urbaine (Vietnam)". In Goldblum, Osmont and Diaz, *Gouverner les villes du Sud. Défis pour la recherche et pour l'action.* Paris, 2004, pp. 58–61. (Partenariats).

Nguyên, Laurence and Nguyên Duc Nhuân. "L'évaluation des projets d'aide publique au développement urbain au Vietnam". In Goldblum, Osmont and Diaz, *Gouverner les villes du Sud. Défis pour la recherche et pour l'action.* Paris, 2004, pp. 152–57. (Partenariats).

Nguyễn Quang Vinh. Đô thị hóa ở đồng bằng sông Cửu long, xu thế tất yếu của phát triển. *Tạp Chí Xã Hội Học* (Hanoi), 49, số 1 (1995).

Nguyên Thiên Phu. "Un modèle vietnamien de transport urbain: Utopie ou réalités?" Thèse de doctorat de sciences économiques, Université Louis Lumière Lyon 2, 2005, 283 pp.

Nguyên Xuan Mai. "Urban Poverty in Vietnam and Subjects of the Poverty Reduction Process". In *Actors for Poverty Reduction in Vietnam*, edited by Vu Tuan Anh and Sakata Shozo. Chiba (Japan): Institute of Developing Economies, 2006, pp. 169–204.

Pham Hung. *Continuation of the Reforming Urban Planning in Vietnam.* 8th International Conference of the Asian Planning Schools Association (APSA), "Cities for People", Penang, 11–14 September 2005, 5 pp.

Pham Van Trinh and René Parenteau. Housing and Urban Development Policies in Vietnam. *Habitat International* (London, Amsterdam, New York) 15, no. 4 (1991): 153–69.

Pandolfi, Laurent. "Prix fonciers au Viêt-nam: Les Paradoxes du Socialisme de Marché". *Études Foncières* (Paris), no. 93 (September 2001): 38–41.

———. "Transition urbaine et formes émergentes de construction de la ville vietnamienne". In Dovert Stéphane, Tréglodé Benoît de (dir.), *Viêt Nam contemporain*. Paris: IRASEC, Les Indes Savantes, 2004, XXXII–568 pp., pp. 339–52.

Pédelahore de Loddis, Christian. "Les villes vietnamiennes aux risques du marché. Rapport ISTED". *Villes en développement* (Paris), 1996, 10 pp.

———. *Actualité de l'urbain au Vietnam: Mutations physiques et conceptuelles*. Rapport ARDU. Paris, 1997, 14 pp.

———. "Sự trở lại của kiến trúc đô thị của Việt nam giữa tính quốc tế và sự khủng hoảng về bản sắc". [Vietnamese Urban Planning in Globalization.] *Trong* Tạp chí Kiến trúc (chủ biên), Kiến trúc: tập hợp các bài viết. Hà nội, 2004, tr. 102–07.

Quertamp, Fanny. *La population urbaine au Viêt Nam: Définition, répartition et évolution entre 1979 et 1999. Traitement statistique et cartographique du recensement de 1999*. Hanoi: Institut des Métiers de la Ville, 2004, 65 pp.

Shannon, Kelly. *Vietnam's Hybrid Urban Landscapes: The Dream of Western Achitects/Urbanists?* ESF/N-AERUS annual workshop, Informality and Illegality in Human Settlements in Developing Countries, 23–26 May 2001, Louvain, Bruxelles, 2001, 7 pp.

———. Tabula Rasa Urbanism: City Extensions in Vietnam. *Trialog* (Frankfurt-am-Main), no. 4 (2002): 4–8.

Snrech, Serge. "Le Vietnam face au défi urbain". *Villes en Développement* (Paris), no. 55 (2002): 6–7.

Trân Cao Son. "Perspectives of Urbanisation in Vietnam". *Vietnam's Socio-Economic Development. A Social Science Review* (Hanoi), no. 27 (2001): 8–18.

Trân Dinh Gian. "Démographie et urbanisation au Viêt-nam, quelques aspects". *Historiens et Géographes* (Paris), no. 349 (1995): 113–18.

Trinh Duy Luan. *The Urban Housing Problem in Vietnam before and during "Renovation"*. Symposium international sur la gestion urbaine dans les villes en développement "De la métropole au micro-territoire: gérer la complexité, gérer la diversité", Montréal 13–15 June 1995, 21 pp. (Discussion Paper 16–5).

——— and Nguyen Quang Vinh. *Socio-economic Impacts of "Doi Moi" on Urban Housing in Vietnam*. Hanoi: Social Sciences Publishing House, 2001, 238 pp.

———, et al. "Urban Housing". In Boothroyd Peter, Pham Xuan Nam (Dir.), *Socioeconomic Renovation in Viet Nam. The Origin, Evolution, and Impact of Doi Moi*. Ottawa: CRDI, ISEAS, 2000.

Van de Walle, Dominique. *Infrastructure and Poverty in Vietnam*. Washington (D.C.): World Bank, 1996, XI–46 pp. (Living Standards Measurement Study Working Paper no. 121).

Vu Chi Dông. *Villes et organisation de l'espace du Viêt-nam: Essai d'analyse spatiale*. Thèse de doctorat de géographie, Université d'Avignon et des pays de Vaucluse, 1996.

Watson, Adam D. *An Examination of Vietnam's Urban Waste Management Capacity*. Master of Arts Degree, University of Toronto, 2004, VII–76 pp.

Hanoi

Amigues, Bernard. "Géographie du climat de Hanoi". *Hommes et Terres du Nord* (Lille), no. hors série USTL, 1993, pp. 68–77.

———. "Hanoi, une ville sous le Fleuve Rouge". *Géographie et Recherche* (Dijon), no. 93 (1995): 3–27.

Bernard-Hervé, Maréva, Aurélie Cevaer and Tifenn Gaudin. *L'eau et l'assainissement dans la ville de Hanoi, Vietnam*. Master ISUR. Rennes: IEP, ISTED, 2004, 92 pp.

Bo Binh Minh. "Upgrading the Living Quarters (KTT) in Hanoi". 8th International Conference of the Asian Planning Schools Association, Penang, 14–15 September 2005.

Bon, Hubert de and Tran Khac Tri. *The response of Peri-urban Agriculture to Urbanization in Vietnam*. Seminar FAO-CITYNET-AFMA "Feeding Asian Cities" (Bangkok, 27–30 November 2000), 2000, 5 pp.

Boudarel, Georges and Nguyen Van Ky. *Hanoi: City of the Rising Dragon*. Lanham (MD), Boulder (CO), New York (N.Y.): Rowman & Littlefield, 2002, XXVIII–189 pp.

Bouzaiene, Riadh and Xavier Choine. *L'électricité à Hanoi*. Master ISUR. Rennes: IEP, ISTED, 2004, 65 pp.

Bui Tam Trung. "La situation environnementale de Hanoi". *Ecodecision: Environment and Policy Magazine* (Montréal), no. 14 (Autumn 1994): 90–92.

Campbell, Tim (ed.). *A Tale of Two Cities in Vietnam. Towards a Strategy of Growth, Poverty and Environment in the Cities and Regions of Vietnam*. Washington (D.C.): The World Bank, 1999, 78 pp.

Center for Sustainable Urban Regeneration (CSUR). "Action Study 05, Hanoi, Socialist Republic of Vietnam". In *Sustainable Urban Regeneration. Volume 03. Feature: Action Studies in Asian Cities*. Tokyo: The University of Tokyo, 2006, pp. 66–75.

Cerise, Emmanuel. "Patrimoine de la ville «ordinaire», entre pratiques habitantes et urbanisme planifié à Hanoi". 2nd Congress of Asia Network, 28–30 September 2005 (EHESS, MSH), Paris, 2005, 7 pp.

——— and Sisoulath Bounleuam. "Projets de voirie et recompositions urbaines à Vientiane et Hanoi". In Goldblum, Osmont and Diaz, *Gouverner les villes du Sud. Défis pour la recherche et pour l'action*. Paris, 2004, pp. 104–09. (Partenariats).

Chabert, Olivier. *Les campagnes périurbaines de Ha Nôi: Espaces et société dans sa transition*. Thèse de doctorat de géographie, Université Michel de Montaigne-Bordeaux 3, 2004, 522 pp.

Chapalain, Anne and Aurélie Jehanno. *Hanoi, une ville en mouvement: les défis d'une gestion intégrée des déchets solides*. Master ISUR. Rennes: IEP, ISTED, 2 vol., 2004, 69 p., 17 pp.

———. "Hanoi, la ville à l'assaut des campagnes". *Informations et Commentaires* (Grenoble), no. 130 (January–March 2005): 8–13.

Charbonneau, François and Dô Hâu (éds.). *Hanoi. Enjeux modernes d'une ville millénaire*. Montréal: Éditions Trames, Université de Montréal-Faculté de l'aménagement, 2002, 270 pp.

Chateau, Bénédicte. *La densification du bâti dans la ville de Hanoi*. Mémoire de maîtrise de géographie, Université Louis Pasteur, Strasbourg, 2003, 122 pp.

Chéron, Marie. "Les franges urbaines de Hanoi. État des lieux et identification de projets alternatifs d'aménagement urbain". Hanoi: Institut des Métiers de la Ville, 2005, 81 pp.

Clément, Pierre and Nathalie Lancret (dir.) Cerise Emmanuel, Delaunay Dominique, Gaulis Inès, Ros Lisa (collab.) *Hanoi. Le cycle des métamorphoses. Formes architecturales et urbaines*. Paris: Éditions Recherches, IPRAUS, 2001, 351 pp. (Les Cahiers de l'IPRAUS, architecture, urbanistique, société).

New ref.: Clément, Pierre and Nathalie Lancret (chủ biên), với sự cộng tác của Cerise Emmanuel, Delaunay Dominique, Gaulis Inès, Ros Lisa, *Hà Nội. Chu kỳ của những đổi thay. Hình thái kiến trúc và đô thị*. Hà Nội: Dự Án Đào Tạo Chuyên Ngành Đô Thị Hà Nội (IMV), Nhà Xuất Bản Khoa Học và Kỹ Thuật, 2003, 345 tr. (Tập san nghiên cứu kiến trúc, đô thị và xã hội).

The Comprehensive Urban Development Programme in Hanoi Capital City (HAIDEP). *Hanoi Urban Environment Fact Book. Opinions of 20,000 Households*. Hanoi: HAIDEP Study Team, Hanoi People's Committee, JICA, 2005, 24 pp.

Cunliffe, Scott. "Shelter and Services for the Poor in Metropolitan Regions; Urban Services Provision in Vietnam: An Overview of Two Communities. *Habitat International* (London, Amsterdam, New York) 12, no. 3 (1988): 41–52.

Cusset, Jean-Michel and Luu Duc Hai. "Transport and Environment in Hanoi: Attitudes and Opinions towards Environmental Policy Measures". *Journal of the Eastern Asia Society for Transportation Studies* 4, no. 5 (2001): 71–88.

Cusset, Jean-Michel. "Mobilité urbaine et intégration des deux roues dans une politique intermodale: le cas de Hanoi". In Bussière Yves, Madre Jean-Loup, *Démographie et demande de transport: villes du nord et villes du sud*. Paris: L'Harmattan, 2002, 20 pp.

———. *Perception par la population des nuisances liées aux transports, et acceptabilité des mesures pour un transport durable. Analyse comparée de Hanoi et Ho Chi Minh Ville*. Séminaire "Transport et environnement à Ho Chi Minh Ville: du diagnostic à l'action", organisé par le Comité Populaire de HCMV (Département des Transports et des Travaux Publics, Département des Sciences et de l'Environnement) et l'ADEME, Hô Chi Minh Ville, 15–16 mai 2002.

———. "La bicyclette a-t-elle encore un avenir dans une ville asiatique en transition vers le marché? L'exemple de Hanoi". *Velo-City* (Paris) 23–26 septembre 2003.

———. "Transport-Environment Issues and Countermeasures in Various Metropolises: The Case of Hanoi". In Hayashi, Y., T. May and H. Nakamura (eds.), *Urban Transport and the Environment — An International Perspective*. Oxford: Elsevier, 2004, pp. 374–78.

Cusset, Jean-Michel and Nguyên Duc Nhuân (collab.). *Transports urbains et développement durable dans les villes asiatiques en transition vers le marché: Le cas de Hanoi*. Rapport de recherche dans le cadre du PICS 160 du CNRS. Lyon, Paris, Hanoi: LET, SEDET, CRURE, 2003, 75 pp.

Dang Nguyen Anh, et al. "Sustainable Urbanization, Migration and Living Environment in Vietnam: A Case Study of Hanoi and Ho Chi Minh City". In *National Institute of Population and Social Security Research, Sustainable Urbanization and Human and Environmental Security in Asia*: Final report. Tokyo, 2002, ii–452 pp., pp. 209–335. (Population Research Series, no. 304).

Dang Xuân Duong and Lê Hông Kê. "La population de Hanoi". In Gubry, Patrick (dir.), *Population et développement au Viêt-nam*. Paris: Karthala, CEPED, 2000, 614 pp., pp. 243–61. (Économie et Développement).
New ref.: Đặng Xuân Đường, Lê Hồng Kế, Hà Văn Quế. "Dân số Hà Nội". *Trong* Gubry, Patrick, Nguyễn Hữu Dũng, Phạm Thúy Hương (chủ biên), *Dân số và phát triển ở Việt Nam*. Hà Nội: Thế Giới, IRD, ILSSA, IMV, 2004, 701 tr. + 16 phụ bản, tr. 269–98.

Decoster, François, et al. *Hanoi, Fragments de Mutation*. Rapport de mission, 14 juillet–14 octobre 1994. Hanoi, Paris: Hanoi Planning Institute, Association Dynamiques Urbaines, 1994, 285 pp.

——— and Klouche Djamel. "Hanoi". Paris: IFA, Agence de la Francophonie ACCT. *Bulletin de l'IFA,* supplément au no. 206 (novembre 1997): 60 pp. (Collection portrait de ville).

Derderian, Richard L. "Urban Space in the French Imperial Past and the Postcolonial Present. Perspectives from France's Vietnamese and Algerian Communities". *Asia Europe Journal*, 1 (2003): 75–90.

DiGregorio, Michael R. *Peasants, Labor Systems and Management of the Urban Environment: An Analysis of Waste Recovery in Hanoi, Vietnam*. MS Thesis, University of Hawaii, 1993, xiv–226 pp.

———. *Urban Harvest: Recycling as a Peasant Industry in Northern Vietnam*. East-West Center Occasional Papers Environment Series no. 17. Honolulu: East-West Center, 1994, XX–212 pp.

DiGregorio, Michael R. et al. *Linking Community and Small Enterprise Activities with Urban Waste Management. Hanoi Case Study*. Gouda (NL): Waste, 1998, 72 pp.

Do Binh Minh. *Upgrading the Living Quarters (KTTs) in Hanoi*. 8th International Conference of the Asian Planning Schools Association (APSA), "Cities for People", Penang, 11–14 September 2005, 10 pp.

Đỗ Thị Thanh Hoa. *Di cư tự do trong quá trình đô thị hóa và tác động của nó tới môi trường thành phố Hà Nội*. Luận án Tiến sỹ Địa lý, Trường Đại học Sư phạm Hà Nội, 1999, 139 tr.
[Do Thi Thanh Hoa. "Spontaneous Migration in the Urbanization Process and Its Influence on Urban Environment in Hanoi". Ph.D. thesis in Geography, Teacher Training College, Hanoi, 1999, 139 pp.]

Drummond, Lisa B.W. "Peasants on the Move: Rural-urban Migration in the Hanoi Region". *Journal of Southeast Asian Studies* 31, no. 2 (2000): 454–55.

Duong, N.D., et al. "A Study of the Urban Growth of Hanoi Using Multitemporal and Multi-sensor Remote Sensing Data". *Asian Journal of Geoinformatics* (Pathumthani, Thailand) 3, no. 3 (2003).

Etteinger, Bernard. "Un nouveau schéma directeur pour Hanoi: Le dragon prépare son envol". *Cahiers de l'Institut d'Aménagement et d'Urbanisme de la Région Île-de-France* (Paris), no. 104–105, août (August 1993): 123–37.

Evertsz, Helen. *Popular Housing in Hanoi*. Hanoi: Cultural Publishing House, 2000, 171 pp. (Shelter and Living in Hanoi, 3).

Forbes, Dean Keith and Le Hong Ke. "A City in Transition. Socialist Reform and the Management of Hanoi". In Rüland Jürgen (ed.), *The Dynamics of Metropolitan Management in Southeast Asia*. Singapore: Institute of Southeast Asian Studies, 1996.

Forbes, Dean Keith. "Socio-Economic Change and the Planning of Hanoi". *Built Environment* 27, no. 2 (1996): 68–84.

Franchini, Philippe. "Hanoi, cité du dragon avec Confucius, Marianne et Marx". In Franchini, Philippe (dir.), *Tonkin 1873–1954. Colonie et Nation: le delta des mythes*. Paris: Autrement, 1994, 166 pp., pp. 122–30. (Série Mémoires, no. 32).

Gubry, Patrick, et al. "Les mobilités temporaires au sein des métropoles vietnamiennes: Hô Chi Minh Ville et Hanoi". In *Gouverner les villes du Sud. Défis pour la recherche et pour l'action*, edited by Goldblum, Osmont, and Diaz. Paris, 2004, pp. 92–97. (Partenariats).

Gubry, Patrick, Lê Thi Huong, Nguyên Thi Thiêng, Pham Thuy Huong, Trân Thi Thanh Thuy, and Vu Hoang Ngân (dir.)/Nguyễn Thị Thiềng, Lê Thị Hương, Phạm Thuý Hương, Vũ Hoàng Ngân, Trần Thị Thanh Thuỷ and Patrick Gubry (chủ biên). *Bouger pour vivre mieux. Les mobilités intra-urbaines à Hô Chi Minh Ville et Hanoi (Viêt-nam)/Di chuyển để sống tốt hơn. Di dân nội thị tại Thành Phố Hồ Chí Minh và Hà Nội (Việt Nam)*. Hanoi: Université nationale d'économie/Hà Nội: Nhà Xuất Bản Trường Đại Học Kinh Tế Quốc Dân, 2008, 293 pp. + 278 tr.

Halls-French, Lilian. "Organisation sociale des quartiers et de l'habitat à Hanoi: Une ville en transition". *Asie du Sud-Est et Monde Insulindien* (Paris) VIII, no. 2 (1977), "Espace social et analyse des sociétés en Asie du Sud-Est", pp. 163–75.

Hoang-Huu Phe. "Investment in Residential Property: Taxonomy of Home Improvers in Central Hanoi". *Habitat International* (London, Amsterdam, New York) 26, no. 4 (2002): 471–86.

Hoang-Huu Phe and Yukio Nishimura. "Housing in central Hanoi". *Habitat International* (London, Amsterdam, New York) 15, no. 1–2 (1991): 101–26.

Hoang Thi Lich. "Women's Access to Housing in Hanoi". In Tinker Irene, Summerfield Gale (eds.), *Women's Rights to House and Land: China, Laos, Vietnam*. Boulder, CO: Lynne Rienner Publishers, 1999, x–305 pp.

Huu Ngoc. *Esquisses pour un portrait de Hanoi*. Hanoi: Éditions Thê Gioi, 1997, 203 pp.

Institut Français d'Urbanisme (IFU). *Hanoi*. Paris: Agence de la Francophonie, 1997, 57 pp. (Portraits de villes).

Institut des Métiers de la Ville (IMV) and Rosier Charlotte. *État des lieux et perspectives du secteur des transports urbains à Hanoi*. Draft no. 2. Hanoi, 2003, 102 pp.

Jalabert, Guy (coord.), 2001, *Portraits de grandes villes. Société, pouvoirs, territoires*: Barcelone, Berlin, Buenos Aires, Hanoi, Hô Chi Minh Ville, Istanbul, Le Caire, Los Angeles, Mexico, Montréal, Moscou, Santiago du Chili, Shanghai, Toronto. Toulouse: Presses Universitaires du Mirail, 2001, 295 pp. (Villes & Territoires, 15).

Japan International Cooperation Agency (JICA), Hanoi People's Committee. *The Comprehensive Urban Development Programme in Hanoi Capital City of the Socialist Republic of Vietnam (HAIDEP)*. Tokyo: ALMEC Corporation, Nippon Koei Co., Yachiyo Engineering Co., 2007, 21 volumes.

Johnson, Craig-August. "Streetwise Sustainability: A Two Wheel Alternative to Balance Motorization and Street Life". *Trialog* (Frankfurt-am-Main), no. 82 (2004): 34–38.

Koh, David. "Illegal Construction in Hanoi and Hanoi's Wards". *European Journal of East Asian Studies* (Leiden, Boston, Tokyo) 3, no. 2 (2004): 337–69.

Leaf, Michael Leon. "Vietnam's Urban Edge. The Administration of Urban Development in Hanoi". *Third World Planning Review* (Liverpool) 21, no. 3 (1999): 297–315.

———. "Structure, Spontaneity and the Changing Landscape of Hanoi". In Chifos, C. and R. Yabes. (eds.), *Southeast Asian Urban Environments: Structured and Spontaneous*. Temp (AZ): Arizona State University Press, 2000, pp. 73–111.

Ledent, Jacques. *La population de Hanoi: Évolution passée et développement futur*. Montréal: INRS Urbanisation, Culture et Société, 2002, 33 pp.

Li, Tana. *Peasants on the Move: Rural-urban Migration in the Hanoi Region*. Singapore: Institute of Southeast Asian Studies, 1996, 80 pp. (Occasional Paper, no. 91).

Logan, William Stewart. "Russians on the Red River: The Soviet Impact on Hanoi's Townscape, 1955–90". *Europe-Asia Studies* (Glasgow) 47, no. 3 (1995): 443–68.

———. "Heritage Planning in Post-*Doi Moi* Hanoi". *Journal of the American Planning Association* (Chicago) 61, no. 3 (1995): 328–43.

———. *Hanoi — Biography of a City*. Seattle WA: University of Washington Press, 2000, xvi–304 pp.

McCoy, Alfred William. "A Tale of Three Cities: Hanoi, Saigon and Phnom Penh". *Australasia's Geographic Magazine* 5, no. 2 (1988): 18–39.

Margonstern, David. *Point sur l'urbanisme, l'aménagement et les transports à Hanoi*. Note à l'attention de l'Ambassadeur de France au Viêt-nam. Hanoi, 2001, 20 pp.

Masson, André, Jack A. Yaeger (tr.) and Daniel F. Doeppers (ed.), The Transformation of Hanoi, 1873–1888. Madison, WI: Center for Southeast Asian Studies, University of Wisconsin, 1983, vii–96 pp. (Wisconsin Papers on Southeast Asia, no. 8).

Miras, Claude de and Fanny Quertamp. *Expansion économique et urbanisation au Vietnam. La péri-urbanisation paradoxale de Hanoi: Une emprise spatiale circonscrite, une accumulation productive soutenue*. Bordeaux-Talence: UMR Regards, 1999, 20 pp. (Papiers, no. 15).

Moustier, Paule, Isabelle Vagneron and Bui Thi Hai. Organisation et efficience des marchés de légumes approvisionnant Hanoi. *Cahiers d'études et de recherches francophones/Agricultures* (Paris) 13 (2004): 142–47.

Nghi D.Q. and Hans Detlef Kammeier. "Balancing Data Integration Needs in Urban Planning. A Model for Ha Noi City, Viet Nam". *Cities* (London, Amsterdam, New York) 18, no. 2 (2001): 61–75.

Ngo Dao. "Waste and Informal Recycling Activities in Hanoi, Vietnam". *Third World Planning Review* (Liverpool) 23, no. 4 (2001): 405–29.

Ngo Viet Hung. *Conservation, Improvement and Sustainable Development: The "36 Old Streets" Quarter in Hanoi, Vietnam*. 8th International Conference of the Asian Planning Schools Association (APSA), "Cities for People", Penang, 11–14 September 2005, 8 pp.

Nguyễn Đình Hương. *Đô thị hoá và quản lý kinh tế đô thị ở Hà Nội* [Urbanization and Urban Economic Management in Hanoi]. Hà Nội: Nhà Xuất bản Chính trị Quốc gia, 2000, 145 tr.

Nguyen Hong Phuong. *Development of a Decision Support System for Earthquake Risk Assessment and Loss Mitigation: The Hanoi Case Study*. Hanoi: Institute of Oceanography (Technical Letter), 2005.

Nguyên, Laurence. "La question du patrimoine dans le renouveau vietnamien. La confrontation de Hanoi et d'Hô Chi Minh Ville". *Les Annales de la Recherche Urbaine* (Paris) (September 1996: 89–97.

———. *Esquisse d'une politique de modernisation et de développement urbain à Hanoi et à Hô Chi Minh Ville (1986–1996)*. Thèse de doctorat d'urbanisme, Université de Paris VIII, 2 vol., 1999, 563 pp.

———. "La production de la ville au Viêt-Nam". In La ville aujourd'hui entre public et privé. *Villes en Parallèle* (Paris-Nanterre), no. 32–33–34 (2001): 442–52.

Nguyen Quang and Hans Detlef Kammeier. "Changes in the Political Economy of Vietnam and Their Impacts on the Built Environment of Hanoi". *Cities* 19, no. 6 (2002): 373–88.

Nguyen Thi Binh and Nurul Amin A.T.M. "The Role of Foreign Direct Investment in Urban Environmental Management: Some Evidence from Hanoi, Vietnam". *Environment, Development and Sustainability*, 4 (2002): 279–97.

Nguyen To Lang. *Preservation of Characteristics of Residential Areas in Hanoi, Vietnam*. 8th International Conference of the Asian Planning Schools Association, Penang, 14–15 September 2005, 15 pp.

Nguyên Trac. *L'eau, la ville et l'urbanisme. Hanoi*. Nanterre: Académie de l'Eau, 1996, 32 pp.

Nguyen, Tung Lam. *Reform of Urban Housing Policy and Low-income Groups in Hanoi City, Vietnam*. 8th International Conference of the Asian Planning Schools Association (APSA), "Cities for People", Penang, 11–14 September 2005, 12 pp.

Palisse, J.P. "Un nouveau schéma directeur pour Hanoi: le dragon prépare son envol". *Cahiers de l'IAURIF* (Paris), no. 104/105 (1993): 123–37.

Palladino, Angela Lynn. *Industrial Waste Management in Hanoi, Vietnam: A Case Study of Thuong Dinh Industrial Zone*. Research paper for the degree of Master of Arts, University of Toronto, 2001, x–105 pp.

Pandolfi, Laurent. *Une terre sans prix. Réforme foncière et urbanisation au Viêt-nam. Hanoi, 1986–2000*. Thèse de doctorat en urbanisme et aménagement, Université de Paris VIII, 2001, 567 pp.

———. "Les projets d'aménagement à Hanoi: Les aléas de la conversion à l'urbanisme de marché". *Les Cahiers de l'IPRAUS* (Paris) no. 3, numéro spécial "Hanoi, le cycle des métamorphoses", (2001): 335–51.

Papin, Philippe. *Histoire de Hanoi*. Paris: Fayard, 2001, 404 pp. (Histoire des grandes villes du monde).

———. *La cité sino-vietnamienne: Quelques réflexions sur le statut et le rôle de Hanoi à l'époque classique*. Hanoi: Ambassade de France, 2002, 20 pp. (Les Cahiers de la Coopération Française au Vietnam, Cahier no. 6 (2002).

Parenteau, René (dir.). *Habitat et environnement urbain au Viêt-nam. Hanoi et Hô Chi Minh Ville*. Paris, Ottawa: Karthala, CRDI, 1997, 334 p. + 24 pl. h.t. (Hommes et Sociétés).

Parenteau, René and L. Champagne (éds.). *La conservation des quartiers historiques en Indochine*. Paris: Karthala, Agence de la Francophonie, 1997, 222 pp.

Parenteau, René, et al. "Impact of Restoration in Hanoi's French Colonial Quarter". *Cities* (London, Amsterdam, New York) 12, no. 3 (1995): 163–73.

Pédelahore de Loddis, Christian. *Les éléments constitutifs de Hanoi*. Paris: BRA/MULT, 1983, 150 pp.

———. "L'habitat collectif à Hanoi. Généalogies historiques et typologies de la transformation". *Les Cahiers de l'IPRAUS* (Paris), no. 3, numéro spécial «Hanoi, le cycle des métamorphoses», (2001): 297–334.

———. "Urbanités dialogiques. Le cas vietnamien. Logiques d'acteurs et production urbaine à Hanoi". In Goldblum, Osmont and Diaz, *Gouverner les villes du Sud. Défis pour la recherche et pour l'action*. Paris, 2004, 296 pp., pp. 117–20. (Partenariats).

Pham Bach Viet, Ho Dinh Duan, Venkatesh Raghavan, and Mamoru Shibayama. *Using Satelitte Imagery to Study Spatial Urban Expansion of Hanoi City*. International symposium on geoinformatics for spatial infrastructure development in earth and allied sciences, Ho Chi Minh City, 9–11 November 2006, 9 pp.

Pham Duc Uy and Nobukazu Nakagoshi. "Analyzing Urban Green Space Pattern and Eco-network in Hanoi, Vietnam". *Landscape and Ecological Engineering* (Hokkaido) 3 (2007): 143–57.

Pham Thi Thanh Hien and Dong-Chen He. *How Do People Perceive the City's Green Space? A View from Satellite Imagery (in Hanoi, Vietnam)*. Sherbrooke: Université de Sherbrooke, Département de géomatique appliquée, 2008, 2 pp.

PNUD. Strengthening the Capacity for Urban Management and Planning in Hanoi. Hanoi, 1995, 7 pp. (VIE/95/050/01/B/99).

Pouyllau, Michel. "Structures urbaines et modèle territorial de Hanoi". *Mappemonde* (Montpellier), no. 52 (1998–4): 30–34.

Quertamp, Fanny. *Hanoi, une périurbanisation paradoxale. Transition et métropolisation, analyse cartographique*. Thèse de doctorat de géographie, Université Michel de Montaigne Bordeaux 3-Talence, 2003, 2 tomes, 604 pp.

Quertamp, Fanny, Hubert de Bon, and Nicolas Baudoin (éds.). *Le développement périurbain à Hanoi. Nouveaux enjeux/ Phát triển vùng ven đô Hà Nội. Những thách thức mới*. Hanoi: Ambassade de France, 2002, 138 pp. (Les Cahiers de la Coopération Française au Vietnam, no. 5 (2002).

Saksena Sumeet, Pham Van Luong, Do Dang Quan, Pham Tien Nhat, Dao Truong Tho, Tran Ngoc Quang, Pham Ngoc Dang, Thang Nguyen, Le Ngoc Quynh, Du Hong Duc, and Peter Flachsbart. *Commuters' Exposure to Particulate Matter and Carbon Monoxide in Hanoi, Vietnam: A Pilot Study*. East-West Center Working Papers, Environmental Change, Vulnerability and Governance Series, no. 64. Honolulu Hi: East-West Center & University of Hawaii; Hanoi: Center for Environmental Engineering of Towns and Industrial Areas, 2007, 30 pp.

Schneider-Sliwa, Rita (Hg.). *Städte im Umbruch: Neustrukturierung von Berlin, Brussel, Hanoi, Ho Chi Minh Stadt, Hongkong, Jerusalem, Johannesburg, Moskau, St Petersburg, Sarajewo und Wien*. Berlin: Reimer, 2002, vii–361 S. [Schneider-Sliwa Rita (ed.). *Upside Down Cities: Restructuring Berlin, Brussels, Hanoi, Ho Chi Minh City, Hong Kong, Jerusalem, Johannesburg, Moscow, St Petersburg, Sarajevo and Vienna*. Berlin: Reimer, 2002, vii–361 pp.]

Seto, Karen C. "Landscapes in Transition: Examples from the Pearl River Delta, China, and the Red River Delta, Vietnam". In *Population, Land Use and Environment: Research directions*, edited by Entwisle Barbara and Stern Paul C. Washington (D.C.): National Research Council, 2005, 330 pp., pp. 193–216.

Shannon, Kelly. "A Tale of Two Cities: Hanoi and Ho Chi Minh City". *Archis* (Meppel, NL), no. 1 (2000): 36–53.

Sheehan, Neil. *Two Cities: Hanoi and Saigon*. London: Jonathan Cape, 1992, 131 pp.

Shimizu, T., A.T. Vu and Nguyen H.M. "A Study on Motorcycle-based Motorization and Traffic Flow in Hanoi City: Toward Urban Air Quality Management". In Brebbia C.A., *Air Pollution III*. Southampton: Wessex Institute of Technology Press (WIT Transactions on Ecology and the Environment, vol. 82).

Shubert, Clarence. *Hanoi: An Urban Profile*. United Nations Development Programme. Hanoi, 2000, iii–40 pp. (Project VIE/95/50).

Smith, David W. and Joseph L. Scarpaci. "Urbanization in Transitional Societies: An Overview of Vietnam and Hanoi". *Urban Geography* (Columbia, MD) 21, no. 8 (2000): 745–57.

Sun Sheng Han and Kim Trang Vu. "Lang Acquisition in Transitional Hanoi, Vietnam". *Urban Studies* 45, no. 5–6 (2008): 1097–1117.

Surborg, Björn. "Advanced Services, the New Economy and Built Environment in Hanoi". *Cities* (London, Amsterdam, New York), 2005, 11 pp.

Tâm Trung Bui. "La situation environnementale de Hanoi". *Écodécision* (Montréal) no. 14 (1994): 90–92.

To Lang Nguyen. *Preservation of Characteristics of Residential Areas in Hanoi, Vietnam*. 8th International Conference of the Asian Planning Schools Association (APSA), "Cities for People", Penang, 11–14 September 2005, 15 pp.

Tonnesson, Stein. "Hanoi's Long Century". In Young, Marilyn B. and Robert Buzzanco (eds.), *A Companion to the Vietnam War*. Malden (MA): Blackwell, 2002, 528 pp., pp. 1–16. (Blackwell Companions to American History).

Tran Mai Anh, Tetsuo Kidokoro and Do Hau. *A Study on the Role of Urban Planning Practices in Hanoi Urban Fringe Focusing on Management of Spontaneous Development. A Case Study in Phu Thuong Ward, Hanoi City*. 8th International Conference of the Asian Planning Schools Association (APSA), "Cities for People", Penang, 11–14 September 2005, 16 pp.

Trung Tâm Lưu Trữ Quốc Gia I. *Lịch sử Hà Nội qua tài liệu lưu trữ. Tập I: Địa giới hành chính Hà Nội từ 1873 đến 1954*. Hà Nội: Nhà Xuất Bản Văn Hóa-Thông Tin, xii-163 tr.

[Centre of National Archives. *History of Hanoi through the Archives. Vol. I: Administrative Limits of Hanoi from 1873 till 1954*. Hanoi: Culture-Information Publishers, 2000, xii-163 pp.]

Turley, William S. "Urbanization in War: Hanoi, 1946–1973". *Pacific Affairs* (Vancouver), no. 3 (1975): 370–97.

United States: Joint Publications Research Service. *Hanoi: The Capital of North Vietnam since 1954*. New York, 1961, 129 pp.

Ủy Ban Nhân Dân Thành Phố Hà Nội, Région Île-de-France, Pandolfi Laurent, Hà Văn Quế (éds.). *Regards croisés sur Hanoi. Transition, spécificité urbaine et choix de développement/Hà Nội. Thành phố đặc thù và những lựa chọn cho phát triển*. Actes du séminaire du PRUD/Kỷ yếu hội thảo của PRUD, Hanoi, 12–14 novembre 2002. Hanoi: Institut des Métiers de la Ville (IMV)/ Dự án đào tạo chuyên ngành đô thị, 2003, 287 pp.

Van den Berg, Leo M., Marteen Siebe Van Wijk and Pham Van Hoi. "The Transformation of Agriculture and Rural Life Downstream of Hanoi". *Environment and Urbanization* (London) 15, no. 1 (April 2003): 35–52.

Van Horen, Basil. "City Profile. Hanoi". *Cities* (London, Amsterdam, New York) 22, no. 2 (2005): 161–73.

Viện Quy Hoạch Đô Thị Nông Thôn. *Cẩm nang Dân số, đô thị hoá Hà Nội*. Hà Nội, 1992, 83 pp. (Dự án VIE/88/P02).

New ref.: National Institute for Urban and Rural Planning. *Hanoi Data Book*. Hanoi, 1994, 74 pp. (Project VIE/88/P02).

Viện Qui Hoạch Đô Thị-Nông Thôn (chủ biên), Đặng Xuân Đường, dưới sự hướng dẫn của Tô Thị Minh Thông, hợp tác với Gubry, Patrick, Jerrold W. Huguet. *Dân số và môi trường ở đo thị Thành phố Hà Nội*. Hà Nội: Nhà Xuất Bản Chính Trị Quốc Gia, 1996, 110 tr. (Dự án VIE/93/P02).

New ref.: National Institute for Urban and Rural Planning (NIURP) (ed.), Dang Xuan Duong, under the dir. of To Thi Minh Thong, in coll. with Gubry, Patrick and Jerrold W. Huguet. *Population and Urban Living Environment in Hanoi city*. Hanoi: The National Political Publishing House, 1996, 77 pp. (VIE/93/P02 project).

Villes en Transition Vietnam, Centre for Sociology and Development Studies Ho Chi Minh City, Institute of Sociology, Hanoi. *Impacts of Existing Residence Registration Policy on Urban Poverty Alleviation. Two Case Studies in Hanoi and Ho Chi Minh City*. Ho Chi Minh City, 2005, 278 pp.

VTGEO (CNST), UMR CNRS-IRD "REGARDS", Trường Đại Học Bordeaux III, Rossi Georges, Phạm Văn Cự (chủ biên), với sự tham gia của Quertamp, Fanny, Olivier Chabert. *Đô thi hóa Thành phố Hà Nội. Atlas thông tin địa lý Thành phố Hà Nội*. Hà Nội: Nhà Xuất Bản Bản Đồ, 2002, 379 tr.

New ref.: VTGEO (CNST), UMR CNRS-IRD "REGARDS", Université de Bordeaux III, Rossi Georges, Pham Van Cu (dir.), assistés de Quertamp, Fanny, Olivier Chabert. *Péri-urbanisation dans la province de Hanoi. Atlas infographique de la province de Hanoi*. Hanoi: Éditions de la cartographie, 2002, 379 pp.

Vũ Quốc Hương. *Di dân tự do từ nông thôn đến đô thị Hà Nội và ảnh hưởng kinh tế-xã hội của nó* [Rural-urban Migration to Hanoi and Its Socio-economic Influences] Luận án TS Địa lý, Trường Đại học Sư phạm Hà Nội, 2000, 168 tr.

Waibel, Michael. "The Ancient Quarter of Hanoi. A Reflection of Urban Transition Processes". *Asien*, no. 92 (July 2004): 30–48.

Weissberg, Daniel. "Hanoi et Hô Chi Minh Ville (Saigon), double métropolisation et développement". In Jalabert Guy (coord.), Portraits de grandes villes, Société-Pouvoirs-Territoires. Toulouse: Presses Universitaires du Mirail, 2001, 295 pp., pp. 263–80. (Villes et Territoires, no. 15).

[*See also: JBIC, 1999a; Thrift & Forbes, 1985*]

Ho Chi Minh City

Asia Urbs. *L'extension de Hô Chi Minh Ville et le développement durable des quartiers. Vers une planification pragmatique des quartiers d'extension de Hô Chi Minh Ville: Le cas du quartier de Binh Trung Dông*. Hô Chi Minh Ville: Institut de planification de la construction de Hô Chi Minh Ville, Agence d'urbanisme pour le développement de l'agglomération lyonnaise, Intercommunale namuroise de services publics, 2002, 53 pp. (Projet VNM 003).

Bampoki, Ludmila and Cécilie Dagmey. *Décentralisation, pouvoirs locaux et société civile au Vietnam. Approche des jeux et des enjeux d'acteurs dans la politique du logementt à Hô Chi Minh Ville*. Master ISUR. Rennes: IEP, ISTED, 2005, 26 pp.

Ban Chỉ Đạo Tổng Điều Tra Dân Số và Nhà ở Thành phố Hồ Chí Minh. *Dân số Thành phố Hồ_Chí Minh (Kết quả tổng điều tra ngày 01–04–1999)*. Thành phố Hồ Chí Minh, 2000, 218 pp.

[*Steering Committee of Population and Housing Census in Ho Chi Minh City. The Population of Ho Chi Minh City (Results of census of 1 April 1999)*. Ho Chi Minh City, 2000, 218 pp.]

Bassand, Michel, Thai Thi Ngoc Du, Tarradellas Joseph, Cunha Antonio, Bolay Jean-Claude (dir.). *Métropolisation, crise écologique et développement durable. L'eau et l'habitat précaire à Hô Chi Minh Ville, Vietnam*. Lausanne: Presses Polytechniques et Universitaires Romandes, 2000, XII–296 pp. (Science, Technique, Société).

Baudrit, André. *Guide historique des rues de Saigon*. Saigon: SILI, 1943, 532 pp.

Bolay, Jean-Claude. "Hô Chi Minh Ville: Chronique d'une métropolisation annoncée". *Urbanisme* (Paris), no. 303 (novembre–décembre 1998): 14–19.

Bolay, Jean-Claude, et al. "Sustainable Development and Urban Growth: Precarious Habitat and Water Management in Ho Chi Minh City". *Habitat International* (London, Amsterdam, New York) 21, no. 2 (1997): 185–97.

Bolay, Jean-Claude and Thai Thi Ngoc Du. "Sustainable Development, Urbanization and Environmental Risks: The Priority of Local Actions in Ho Chi Minh City, Vietnam". *Journal of Urban Technology* (New York) 6, no. 2 (1999): 65–85.

Bolay, Jean-Claude, Wust Sébastien, Castiglioni Franck, Dewaele Ludovic, Vuong Van Pho Danh, Vân Thi Ngoc Lan, Nguyên Quang Vinh, Trân Dan Tâm, Trân Thai Ngoc Thanh. *Les enjeux du relogement des zones d'habitat précaire à Hô Chi Minh Ville: Entre grands programmes et micro projets*. Hô Chi Minh Ville, 2004, 14 pp.

Bouchot, Jean. *Documents pour servir à l'histoire de Saigon, 1859 à 1865*. Saigon: Albert Portail, 1927, 527 pp.

Burlat, Anne. *Processus institutionnels et dynamiques urbaines dans l'urbanisation contemporaine de Hô Chi Minh Ville, 1988–1998. Planification, production, gestion des "secteurs d'habitat"*. Thèse de doctorat en urbanisme et aménagement, Université de Lyon II, 2001, 535 pp.

Cartoux, Sophie. *L'habitat spontané à Hô Chi Minh Ville: des quartiers en transition*. Mémoire de l'Institut d'Urbanisme de Lyon, Université Lumière Lyon 2, 1997.

Castiglioni, Franck. "Les enjeux du relogement des zones d'habitat précaire à Hô Chi Minh Ville: entre grands programmes et micro-projets". In Goldblum, Osmont and Diaz, *Gouverner les villes du Sud. Défis pour la recherche et pour l'action*. Paris, 2004, pp. 160–69.

Cauchetier, Raymond. *Saigon*. Paris: Albin Michel, 1995, 96 pp.

Chambon, Thibault, et al. *Hô Chi Minh Ville, Vietnam. Rapport intermédiaire*. Master ISUR. Rennes: IEP, ISTED, 2006, 108 pp.

Chartoire, Benjamin and Bénédicte Tardivo. *Rapport d'expertise des réseaux de transport-voirie à Hô Chi Minh Ville (Vietnam). La renaissance des transports collectifs comme solution aux problèmes des transports urbains à HCMV*. Master ISUR. Rennes: IEP, ISTED, 2006, 74 pp.

Chrétien, Kevin and Amandine Dukhan. *L'extension des services urbains en réseaux face à l'urbanisation rapide de Hô Chi Minh Ville. L'exemple du village de Vinh Lôc A dans le district rural de Binh Chanh. Rapport de stage*. Hô Chi Minh Ville: CEFURDS, IRD, Sciences Po Rennes, 2006, 133 pp. + annexes 50 pp.

Chrétien, Kevin and Fabian Hinojosa. *Le réseau électrique à Hô Chi Minh Ville, Vietnam*. Rapport d'expertise. Master ISUR. Rennes: IUP, ISTED, 2006, 47 pp.

Chu Thừa Châm. *Nghiên cứu các giải pháp nhằm sử dụng có hiệu quả của nguồn tài nguyên thiên nhiên trên địa bàn Thành phố Hồ Chí Minh trong quá trình công nghiệp hóa-hiện đại hóa nền kinh tế*. TP.HCM: Viện Kinh Tế Thành Phố Hồ Chí Minh, 1996, 106 tr.

[Chu Thua Cham. *Search for Solutions to Efficiently Use Natural Resources in the Industrialization-economic Modernization Process in Ho Chi Minh City*. HCMC: Institute for Economic Research of Ho Chi Minh City, 1996, 106 pp.]

Coit, Katharine. Housing Policy and Slum Upgrading in Ho Chi Minh City. *Habitat International* (London, Amsterdam, New York) 22, no. 3 (1998): 273–80.

Coulthart, Alan. "L'amélioration de l'habitat insalubre au Vietnam". *Villes en Développement* (Paris), no. 60–61, (June-September 2003): 17–18.

Cục Thống Kê Thành phố Hồ Chí Minh. *Điều tra dân số giữa kỳ năm 2004 Thành phố Hồ Chí Minh*. Thành phố Hồ Chí Minh, 2005, 457 tr.

[Statistical Office of Ho Chi Minh City. *Mid-term 2004 Population Census of Ho Chi Minh City*. Ho Chi Minh City, 2005, 457 pp.]

Cusset, Jean-Michel, Nguyên Thiên Phu, and Nguyên Quoc Tuân. *Mobilité quotidienne, image des modes et acceptabilité de politiques de transport. Vers une répartition modale plus équilibrée à Hô Chi Minh Ville? Résultats de l'enquête ménages de 2003*. Lyon, Hô Chi Minh Ville, Paris: LET, TEPC South-ENERTEAM, EXPLICIT, 2004, 40 pp.

Desbenois, H. *L'urbanisme à Hô Chi Minh Ville: Perspectives et projets des services municipaux*. Synthesis report in the framework of the partnership between Urban Community of Lyon and Ho Chi Minh City, 1995.

Dewaele, Ludovic and Laurent Pandolfi. *Le logement social à Hô Chi Minh Ville — Les standards actuels sont-ils appropriés à la production massive de logements sociaux?* Hanoi: Ambassade de France, 2003, 46 pp. (Les Cahiers de la Coopération Française au Vietnam, no. 10 (2003)).

New ref.: Dewaele, Ludovic and Laurent Pandolfi. *Nhà ở có chi phí thấp tại Thành phố Hồ Chí Minh — Qui định thiết kế nhà ở và tiêu chuẩn xây dựng hiện nay có phù hợp với mô hình sản xuất hàng loạt nhà ở với chi phí thấp không?* Hà Nội: Đại Sứ Quán Pháp, 2003, 45 tr. (Tài liệu gió thiệu về hoạt động hợp tác của Pháp ở Việt Nam, quyển số 10–2003).

New ref.: Dewaele, Ludovic and Laurent Pandolfi. *Low-cost Housing in Ho Chi Minh City — Are Current Official Housing Design and Construction Standards*

Appropriate to Massive Low-cost Housing Production? Hanoi: French Embassy, 2003, 45 pp. (Guidebooks to French cooperation in Vietnam, no. 10 (2003)).

Do Thi Loan. *Ho Chi Minh City: Spatial Structure and Characteristics*. Ph.D. thesis, Budapest, 1994, vi–299 pp.–XI pp.

Du Phuoc Tân, et al. *Kinh tế trên vỉa hè tại thành phố Hồ Chí Minh; hiện trạng và các giải pháp*. TP.HCM: Viện Kinh tế thành phố Hồ Chí Minh, 2004, 177 tr.

[*Du, Phuoc Tan, et al. The Pavement Economy in Ho Chi Minh City; Realities and Solutions. HCMC: Institute for Economic Research of Ho Chi Minh City, 2004, 177 pp.*]

Dukhan, Amandine, Pierre Lascabettes and Guillaume Tricot. *Les services urbains de l'eau et de l'assainissement à Hô Chi Minh Ville*. Master ISUR. Rennes: IEP, ISTED, 2006, 66 p. + annexes 30 pp.

ENDA Viêt-nam, Villes en Transition (VeT). *Projet pilote de Binh Trung Dong, District 2, Hô Chi Minh Ville, Viêt-nam*. Hô Chi Minh Ville, 2001, 12 pp.

Franchini, Philippe (dir.). *Saigon 1925–1945. De la 'Belle Colonie' à l'éclosion révolutionnaire ou la fin des dieux blancs*. Paris: Autrement, 1994, 261 pp. (Série Mémoires, no. 17).

Freeman, Donald B. "*Doi Moi* Policy and the Small-entrerprise Boom in Ho Chi Minh City, Vietnam". *Geographical Review* 86, no. 2 (1996): 178–97.

The French Embassy in Socialist Republic of Vietnam, The HCMC Chief Architect Office, World Bank PMU-Vietnam Urban Upgrading Programme, Nguyen Quang Vinh, Nguyen Tung Lam, Tran Thi Bach Lan, Dewaele Ludovic, Metzger Roger. *Analysis of Low-cost Housing Standards in Ho Chi Minh City. Review, Analysis and Recommendations for Specific Low-cost Housing Standards*. Ho Chi Minh City: VeT (Villes en Transition), 2002, pp. 202–76.

Gaillard, N.M. and J. Niebudek. *Hô Chi Minh Ville, le spontané et la ville planifiée*. Mémoire de fin d'études, École d'Architecture de Versailles, 1995.

Goodman, Allan E. and Lawrence M. Franks. *Between War and Peace: A Profile of Migrants to Saigon*. New York N.Y.: Southeast Asia Development Advisory Group of the Asia Society, 1974, 62 pp. (SEADAG papers on problems of development in Southeast Asia).

———. "The Dynamics of Migration to Saigon, 1964–1972". *Pacific Affairs* (Vancouver) 48, no. 2 (1975): 199–214.

Groslier, Bernard Philippe. "Une enquête démographique et sociale sur un quartier de Saigon-Cholon". *Bulletin de la Société des Études Indochinoises* (Saigon) 29, no. 1 (1954): 5–21.

Gubry, Patrick and Lê Thi Huong. "Présentation de Hô Chi Minh Ville". In Gubry Patrick, Vu Thi Hông and Lê Van Thanh (dir.). *Les chemins vers la ville. La migration vers Hô Chi Minh Ville à partir d'une zone du delta du Mékong*. Paris: Karthala, CEPED, 343 pp., pp. 113–27. (Hommes et Sociétés).

———. "Ho Chi Minh City: a future megacity in Vietnam". *Vietnam's Socio-Economic Development* (Hanoi), no. 40 (Winter 2004): 56–75.

Gubry, Patrick, Vu Thi Hông and Lê Van Thanh (dir.). *Les chemins vers la ville. La migration vers Hô Chi Minh Ville à partir d'une zone du delta du Mékong*. Paris: Karthala, CEPED, 2002, 343 pp. (Hommes et Sociétés).

New ref.: Vũ Thị Hồng, Patrick Gubry and Lê Văn Thành (Chủ biên). *Những con đường về Thành phố. Di dân đến Thành phố Hồ Chí Minh từ một vùng đồng bằng sông Cửu Long*. Thành phố Hồ Chí Minh: Viện Kinh Tế TP.HCM, Trung Tâm Dân Số và Phát Triển Pháp (CEPED), Nhà Xuất Bản TP.HCM, 2003, 389 tr.

Hiep Nguyen Duc. *Some Aspects of Air Quality in Ho Chi Minh City, Vietnam*. Seminar on environment and development in Vietnam, Australian National University, Canberra (6–7 December 1996), 15 pp.

Hoskins, Marilyn W. and Eleanor Shepherd. *Life in a Vietnamese Urban Quarter*. Carbondale: Southern Illinois University, 1965, x–356 pp.

Huong Ha and Wong Tai-Chee. *Economic Reforms and the New Master Plan of Ho Chi Minh City, Vietnam: Implementation Issues and Policy Recommendations*. *GeoJournal* (Heidelberg, Berlin) 49, no. 3 (1999): 309–11.

Huynh Tuyêt Trinh. *Saigon au XIXe siècle, avant l'arrivée des Français, après l'arrivée des Français*. Mémoire de maîtrise d'histoire, Université de Paris VII, 1992, 120 pp.

Kermadec, Jean-Michel de. *Cholon, ville chinoise*. Saigon: Société Asiatique d'Éditions, 1955.

———. *Aspects chinois de Cholon et Saigon*. Saigon: Imprimerie française d'Outre-Mer, 1956, 46 pp.

Lam Quang Huyen. "Sustainable Urbanization: Economic Development Getting along with Social Equality (Ho Chi Minh City Case)". In Programme de Recherche et de Liaison Universitaires pour le Développement (PRELUDE), *Co-développement urbain durable, enseignement supérieur, responsabilités de la recherche et de la gestion*. Symposium international ISSHO-CSEAS-PRELUDE, Hô Chi Minh Ville, 9–12 March 1999. 553 pp., pp. 45–50. (*Prélude*, numéro spécial 41–43).

Lang, Michael H. and Barry Kolb. "Locational Components of Urban and Regional Public Policy in Postwar Vietnam: The Case of Ho Chi Minh City (Saigon)". *GeoJournal* (Heidelberg, Berlin) 4, no. 1 (1982): 13–18.

Langlet-Quach, Thanh Tâm. "Saigon, capitale de la République du Sud Viêt-nam (1954–1975), ou une urbanisation sauvage". In Lafont Pierre-Bernard (dir.), *Péninsule indochinoise: études urbaines*. Paris: L'Harmattan, 1991, 232 pp., pp. 185–206. (Recherches asiatiques).

———. "Aperçu sur Hô Chi Minh Ville 1990". In Lafont Pierre-Bernard (dir.), *Péninsule indochinoise*. Paris, 1991, 232 pp., pp. 207–31. (Recherches asiatiques).

Lauras, Didier. *Saigon. Le chantier des utopies*. Paris: Autrement, 1997, 245 pp. (Collection Monde, HS no. 95).

Lê Thi Huong. "La population de Hô Chi Minh Ville". In Gubry, Patrick (dir.) *Population et développement au Viêt-nam*. Paris: Karthala, CEPED, 2000, 614 pp., pp. 263–84. (Économie et développement).

New ref.: Lê Thị Hương. "Dân số Thành phố Hồ Chi Minh". Trong Gubry Patrick, Nguyền Hữu Dũng, Phạm Thúy Hương (chủ biên), Dân số và Phát triển ở Việt Nam. Hà Nội: Nhà Xuất Bản Thế Giới, Viện Khoa Học Lao Động và Xã Hội (ILSSA), Viện Nghiên cứu vì sự Phát Triển (IRD), Viện Đào Tạo Chuyên Ngành Đô Thị (IMV), 701 tr., 2004, tr. 299–319.

Lê Van Thanh. "Development économique, urbanisation et changements de l'environnement à Hô Chi Minh Ville (Viêt-nam): Interrelations et politiques". In CICRED, *Population développement et environnement dans les espaces du Sud*. Actes du colloque international Pripode, 21–23 mars 2007. UNESCO, Paris. Paris, 2007, pp. 83–91.

Lu Hon Quang. *The Urban Political Ecology of Water Supply Planning and Management in Ho Chi Minh City, Vietnam*. MES, York University (Canada), 2002, 193 pp.

Metzger, roger. *Sustainable Slum Upgrading: Architectural Analysis of the Slum Housing in Ward 15, Ho Chi Minh City, Vietnam*. Lausanne: Département d'Architecture, École Polytechnique Fédérale de Lausanne (EPFL), 2000, 172 pp.

———. *Low-cost Housing in Vietnam: Core-housing in Binh Hung Hoa, District Binh Chanh, Ho Chi Minh City: A Resettlement Opinion for People Living on the Than Hoa-lo Gom River*. Lausanne: Département d'Architecture, École Polytechnique Fédérale de Lausanne (EPFL), 2002.

Nguyễn Đăng Sơn. *Strengthening the Capacity for Urban Management and Planning in Ho Chi Minh City* [Nâng cao năng lực quản lý và quy hoạch đô thị tại Thành phố Hồ Chí Minh]. Ho Chi Minh City: People Committee of HCMC, UNDP, 1997, 151 pp. (National project VIE/95/051).

Nguyên Dinh Dâu. *De Saigon à Hô Chi Minh Ville. 300 ans d'histoire*. Hô Chi Minh Ville: Service du cadastre, Édition Science et Technique, 1998, 188 pp.

Nguyen Khac Vien and Huu Ngoc. *From Saigon to Ho Chi Minh City. A Path of 300 years*. Hanoi: The Gioi Publishers, 1998, 357 pp.

Nguyên, Laurence. "Le renouveau des projets urbains au Vietnam: Exemples de réalisation à Hô Chi Minh Ville". In Gironde, Christophe, Jean-Luc Maurer (dir.), *Le Vietnam à l'aube du XXIe siècle. Bilan et perspectives politiques, économiques et sociales*. Mélanges pour commémorer le 100e anniversaire de la naissance de Pierre Gourou. Paris: Karthala, IUED, CRAM, 2004, 353 pp., pp. 257–76. (Hommes et Sociétés).

Nguyen Quang Vinh and Michael Leon Leaf. "City Life in the Village of Ghosts: A Case Study of Popular Housing in Ho Chi Minh City, Vietnam". *Habitat International* (London, Amsterdam, New York) 20, no. 2 (1996): 175–90.

Nguyễn Thế Nghĩa, Mạc Đường and Nguyễn Quang Vinh. *Vấn đề giảm nghèo trong quá trình đô thị hoá ở thành phố Hồ Chí Minh*. Hà Nội: Nhà Xuất Bản Khoa Học Xã Hội, 2001, 636 pp.

[Nguyen The Nghia, Mac Duong, and Nguyen Quang Vinh. *The Problem of Poverty Reduction and Urbanization in Ho Chi Minh City*. Hanoi: Social Sciences Publishing House, 2001, 636 pp.].

Nguyễn Thị Lan. *Sự hình thành các nguồn nước và một số giải pháp bảo vệ môi trường nước khu vực thành phố Hồ Chí Minh*. Luận án phó tiến sỹ khoa học địa lý-đia chất, Đại học khoa học tự nhiên, 1996, xiii–158 tr. + phụ lục.
[Nguyen, Thi Lan. *Inventory of Water Resources and Solutions for the Protection of the Aquatic Environnement in Ho Chi Minh City Area*. Ph.D. thesis in geography-geology, Hanoi National University, 1996, xiii–158 pp. + appendix.]

Nguyen Tuan Triet. "The Chinese in the Development Process of Saigon-Ho Chi Minh City". In Programme de Recherche et de Liaison Universitaires pour le Développement (PRELUDE), *Co-développement urbain durable, enseignement supérieur, responsabilités de la recherche et de la gestion*. Symposium international ISSHO-CSEAS-PRELUDE, Hô Chi Minh Ville, 9–12 mars 1999. 2001, 553 pp., pp. 317–21. (Prélude, numéro spécial 41–43).

Nguyên Van Linh. "Hô Chi Minh Ville: Problèmes économiques et perspectives". *Études Vietnamiennes* (Paris), no. 12 (82) (1986): 24–37.

Nguyễn Văn Tài. *Di dân tự do nông thôn-thành thị ở thành phố Hồ Chí Minh*. Nhà Xuất bản Nông nghiệp, 1998, 218 tr.
[Nguyen Van Tai. *Spontaneous Rural-urban Migration in Ho Chi Minh City*. Agriculture Publishing House, 1998, 218 pp.]

———, (Chủ biên). *Nghiên cứu hiện trạng, những tác nhân thúc đẩy và các vấn đề phát sinh từ hiện tượng di dân tự do đối với môi trường, sự phát triển kinh tế-xã hội ở Thành phố Hồ Chí Minh trong quá trình đổi mới nền kinh tế đất nước. Các giải pháp giải quyết*. TP.HCM: Đại Học Quốc Gia Thành phố Hồ Chí Minh, Đại Học Khoa Học Xã Hội và Nhân Văn, 1998, vi–130 tr. (Chương Trình Nghiên Cứu Việt Nam-Hà Lan).
[Nguyen Van Tai (ed.). *Study on Current Situation, Factors and Problems of Spontaneous Migration for the Environment, the Socioeconomic Development in Ho Chi Minh City in the Renovation Process of the Economy of the Country. Solutions and Resolutions*. HCMC: Ho Chi Minh City National University, University of Social Sciences and Humanities, 1998, vi–130 pp. (Vietnam-Netherlands Study Project.]

———. Vấn đề tổ chức, phát triển giao thông đô thị tại thành phố Hồ Chí Minh. TP.HCM: Nhà Xuất Bản Trẻ, 1999, 236 tr.
[*Nguyen Van Tai. Organization and Development of Urban Transportation in Ho Chi Minh City. HCMC: Youth Publishing House, 1999, 236 pp.*]

———. "Ho Chi Minh City and Sustainable Development Issues". In Programme de Recherche et de Liaison Universitaires pour le Développement (PRELUDE), *Co-développement urbain durable, enseignement supérieur, responsabilités de la recherche et de la gestion*. Symposium international ISSHO-CSEAS-PRELUDE, Hô Chi Minh Ville, 9–12 mars 1999. 2001, 553 pp., pp. 163–72. (*Prélude*, numéro spécial 41–43).

Nhóm Hành Động Chống Đói Nghèo, Trịnh Hồ Hạ Nghi, Huỳnh Thị Ngọc Tuyết, với phần bổ sung của Bill Tod. *Đánh giá nghèo có sự tham gia của cộng đồng tại Thành phố Hồ Chí Minh*. Thành phố Hồ Chí Minh, 2003, x–58 tr.

New ref.: Poverty Task Force, Trinh Ho Ha Nghi, Huynh Thi Ngoc Tuyet, with a supplement of Bill Tod. *Ho Chi Minh City: Participatory Poverty Assessment*. Ho Chi Minh City: Save The Children, 2003, ix–66 p.

People's Committee of Ho Chi Minh City. *Environmental Management Strategy for Ho Chi Minh City to 2010*. Ho Chi Minh City, 2002, multiple pagination.

Phạm, Phan Quốc Bảo. *Đánh giá hiện trạng quản lý môi trường và đề xuất chương trình nâng cao năng lực quản lý môi trường cho các khu chế xuất-công nghiệp Thành phố Hồ Chí Minh*. Thạc sĩ, Đại học Bách Khoa, TP.HCM, 2005, 90 tr.
[Pham Phan Quoc Bao. *Assessment of the Status of Environmental Management and Proposal of an Advanced Environmental Management Programme in the Industrial Production Free Zone of Ho Chi Minh City*. Master thesis, Polytechnical School, HCMC, 2005, 90 pp.]

Phạm Thị Xuân Thọ. *Di dân ở thành phố Hồ Chí Minh và tác động của nó đối với sự phát triển kinh tế-xã hội*. Luận án Tiến sỹ khoa học Địa lí, 2002, 198 tr.
[Pham Thi Xuan Tho. *The Migration in Ho Chi Minh City and Its Influence on Socioeconomic Development*. Ph.D. thesis in geography, 2002, 198 pp.]

Phan Văn Khiết. *Nghiên cứu cơ chế và chính sách phát triển giao thông nông thôn ở thành phố Hồ Chí Minh*. TP.HCM: Viện Kinh Tế Thành phố Hồ Chí Minh, 2000, ii–83 tr.
[Phan Van Khiet. *Research on the Mechanisms and Policies of Development of Rural Transports in Ho Chi Minh City*. HCMC: Institute for Economic Research of Ho Chi Minh City, 2000, ii–83 pp.]

Phan Xuân Biên, Hồ Bá Thâm and Phan Minh Tân (chủ Biên). *Nâng cao hiệu lực hiệu quả Quản lý đô thị. Thành phố Hồ Chí Minh*. Thành phố Hồ Chí Minh: Nhà Xuất Bản Tông Hợp. 2004, 441 [tr. Phan Xuan Bien, Ho Ba Tham and Phan Minh Tan, (eds). *Improving the Efficiency of Urban Management*. Ho Chi Minh City. Ho Chi Minh City: General Publishing House, 2004, 441 pp.]

Ranty, Amélie and Wang Jia. *La gestion des déchets solides à Hô Chi Minh Ville, Vietnam*. Master ISUR. Rennes: IEP, ISTED, 2006, 53 pp.

Scheibe, Florian. "The Informal Sector in Solid Waste Management in Developing Countries: Sustainability Effects of Formalisation Considering Ho Chi Minh City — Vietnam as an Example". Master's thesis, Vienna, 2006, x-102 pp.

Schmalz, Andreas. *Ho Chi Minh Stadt*. Dresden, 2005, 49s. (Aussereuropaische Stadtentwicklung — Metropolen im 21. Jahrhundert).

Schmitt, Mathias. *Situation et conditions de mutation du transport public par autobus à Hô Chi Minh Ville*. Mémoire de DEA en économie des transports, Université Lumière Lyon 2, 1995, 236 pp. + annexes.

———. "Transports urbains à Hô Chi Minh Ville: le coût d'une métamorphose mal maîtrisée". *Informations et Commentaires* (Lyon), no. 99 (1997): 27–32.

——— and Vu Thi Hông. "Singularité et adaptation des opérateurs de transports à Hô Chi Minh Ville". In Freeman Peter, Jamet Christian (eds.), *Urban Transport Policy: A Sustainable Development Tool*. Proceedings of the International

CODATU Conference, Cape Town, 21–25 September. Rotterdam: Balkema, 1998, pp. 995–1004.

Seabrook, Jeremy. "Ho Chi Minh City: Back to Saigon". In Seabrook Jeremy, *In the Cities of the South: Scenes from a Developing World*. London, New York: Verso, 1996, viii–303 pp.

Skidmore, Owings, Merril. *Saigon South Master Plan*. Ho Chi Minh City: Phu My Hung Corporation, 1994, 96 pp.

Sở Kế Hoạch và Đầu Tư TP.Hồ Chí Minh [Ho Chi Minh City Department of Planning and Investment]. "Giao thông công cộng đô thị tại TP.HCM [Urban Public Transport in HCMC]. Hội Thào ODAP, số 5, 14–9 September 2001 [ODAP workshop no. 5, 14–9 September 2001]. TP.HCM: Hợp Tác Hỗ Trợ Phát Triển Chính Thức (ODAP) cho Thành phố Hồ Chí Minh [Official Development Assistance Partnership for Ho Chi Minh City, 2001, không co số trang.]

Teulières, Roger and Nguyên Huy. "Une agglomération de sampans habités à Saigon". *Les Cahiers d'Outre-Mer* (Bordeaux-Talence), no. 58 (avril-juin 1962): 166–79.

Thạch Phương, Lê Trung Hoa (chủ biên). *Từ điển Thành phố Sài Gòn-Hồ Chí Minh*. TP.Hồ Chí Minh: Nhà Xuất Bản Trẻ, 2001, 1,139 tr.
[Thach Phuong and Le Trung Hoa (eds.), *Dictionary of Saigon-Ho Chi Minh City*. Ho Chi Minh City: Youth Publishing House, 2001, 1,139 pp.]

Thai Thi Ngoc Du. "L'évolution et la répartition de la population de Hô Chi Minh Ville (Viêt-nam)". *Les Cahiers d'Outre-Mer* (Bordeaux-Talence), no. 173 (janvier-mars 1991): 77–88.

———. "Métropolisation, gestion des villes et habitation à Hô Chi Minh Ville". *Les Cahiers d'Outre-Mer* (Bordeaux-Talence) 49, no. 196 (1996): 377–86.

———. "Women Influencing Housing in Ho Chi Minh City". In Tinker Irene, Summerfield Gale, (eds.), *Women's Rights to House and Land: China, Laos, Vietnam*. Boulder, CO: Lynne Rienner Publishers, 1999, x–305 pp.

Thai Thi Ngoc Du, et al. *Female Rural Migrant Workers in the Informal Sector in Ho Chi Minh City, Vietnam*. Canberra: The Australian National University, Gender Relations Centre, 2006, 18 pp. (Working Paper, no. 16).

Thai Thi Ngoc Du, Pham Gia Trân and Ngô Thanh Loan. "Dégradation du cadre de vie urbain et problèmes de santé de la population citadine à Hô Chi Minh Ville, Vietnam (1990). *Les Cahiers d'Outre-Mer* (Bordeaux-Talence) 46, no. 184 (octobre–décembre 1993): 349–98.

Ton Si Kinh, Dô Thi Loan and Thai Thi Ngoc Du (trad.). "De Saigon à la région-clé de développement. Nouvelle perspective d'un développement continu et dynamique de la grande métropole du Vietnam méridional". *Les Cahiers d'Outre-Mer* (Bordeaux-Talence) 49, no. 196 (1996): 415–22.

Trần Văn Giàu, Trần Bạch Đằng (chủ biên). *Địa chí văn hoá Thanh Phố Hồ Chí Minh. Tập I: Lịch sử. Tập II: Văn học — Báo chí — Giáo đốc. Tập III: Nghệ thuật. Tập IV: Tư tương và tín ngưỡng*. TP.HCM: Nhà Xuất Bản Thành phố Hồ Chí Minh, 1998, 676 tr., 870 tr., 640 tr., 576 tr.

[Tran, Van Giau and Tran Bach Dang (eds.). *Cultural Monograph on Ho Chi Minh City. Vol. I: History. Vol. II: Literature — Press — Education. Vol. III: Arts. Vol. IV: Ideology and Belief.* HCMC: Ho Chi Minh City Publishing House, 1998, 676 pp., 870 pp., 640 pp., 576 pp.]

Trân Xuân Phi Pasteur. *Perspectives à court et moyen termes du système de transport à Hô Chi Minh Ville; définition des enjeux et des stratégies de transport urbain.* Mémoire de maîtrise de géographie, Université de Paris Sorbonne, 2003, 172 pp.

Truong Si Anh. *Internal Migration into Ho Chi Minh City. Patterns, Consequences and Policy Issues.* Master of Science thesis, Asian Institute of Technology, Bangkok, 1994, viii–105 pp. + appendix.

Truong Si Anh, et al. *Hô Chi Minh Ville: de la migration à l'emploi.* Paris: Centre français sur la Population et le Développement, 1996, 52 pp. (Les Dossiers du CEPED, no. 40).

———. "Migration and Employment in Ho Chi Minh City". *Asia-Pacific Population Journal* (Bangkok) 11, no. 2 (1996): 3–22.

Turley, William S. *Urban Transformation in the Revolution: Saigon (Ho Chi Minh City) and Other Cities of South Vietnam since April, 1975.* Symposium on "Contemporary Southeast Asia — An Emerging Center of World Influence", Ohio University, Athens, 7 May 1976, 28 pp.

Turley, William S. and Womack Brantly. "Asian Socialism's Open Doors: Gwanzhou and Ho Chi Minh City". *The China Journal* (Canberra), no. 40, Special issue: Transforming Asian Socialism. China and Vietnam Compared, (1998): 95–119.

United Nations: Population Division. "Ho Chi Minh City (Viet Nam)". In *The Challenge of Urbanization: The World's Large Cities.* New York (N.Y.), 1995, x–290 pp., pp. 102–03. (ST/ESA/SER.A/151).

Ủy Ban Nhân Dân Thành phố Hồ Chí Minh. *Sơ đồ chung phát triển và phân bố lực lượng sản xuất thành phố Hồ Chí Minh thời kỳ 1986–2000* (Báo cáo tổng hợp), tập 1. TP.HCM, 1986, 108 tr.
[People's Committee of Ho Chi Minh City. *General Scheme of Development and Distribution of Productive Forces in Ho Chi Minh City for the Period 1986–2000* (Synthetic report), vol. 1. HCMC, 1986, 108 pp.]

Ủy Ban Nhân Dân Thành phố Hồ Chí Minh. *Báo cáo tổng hợp quy hoạch tổng thể phát triển kinh tế-Xã Hội thành phố Hồ Chí Minh đến năm 2010.* TP.HCM, 1996, xvi–723 tr.
[People's Committee of Ho Chi Minh City. *Synthetic Report on General Management of Socioeconomic Development of Ho Chi Minh City until year 2010.* HCMC, 1996, xvi–723 pp.]

Ủy Ban Nhân Dân Thành phố Hồ Chí Minh/Comité populaire de Hô Chi Minh Ville, Lyon và Céng Đồng Thành phố Lyon/Ville de Lyon et Communauté urbaine de Lyon, Tổng Lãnh Sự Pháp Tại Thành phố Hồ Chí Minh/Consulat Général de France à Hô Chi Minh Ville (eds.), Lê Quang Ninh, Dovert Stéphane (coord.). Saigon 1698–1998. Kiến trúc/Architectures, Quy hoạch/Urbanisme. Thành Phồ Hồ Chí Minh: Nhà Xuất Bản Thành phố Hồ Chí Minh, 1998, 242 tr.

VeT Viet Nam. *Développement urbain communautaire dans le District 7 — HCMV*. Hô Chi Minh Ville, 2003, 4 pp.

Viện Khoa Học Xã Hội Việt Nam (VNASS), Viện Khoa Học Xã Hội Vùng Nam Bộ (SISS). *Giảm nghèo, di dân-đô thị hóa: trường hợp TP.HCM trong tầm nhìn so sánh*. Hội thảo Quốc Tế, Thành Phố Hồ Chí Minh, 2/2004. Thành Phố Hồ Chí Minh, 2 tập, 2004, nhiều số trang.

New ref.: Viet Nam Academy of Social Sciences (VNASS), Southern Institute of Social Sciences (SISS). *Poverty Alleviation, Migration and Urbanization: Ho Chi Minh City in Comparative Perspectives*. International conference. Ho Chi Minh City, 2 vol., 2004, multiple pagination. (Project: Poverty alleviation in the process of urbanization in Ho Chi Minh City).

Viện Kinh Tế Thành phố Hồ Chí Minh. *Báo cáo kết quả điều tra di dân tự do vào Thành phố Hồ Chí Minh*. TP.HCM, 1997, 114–25 tr. (Dự án VIE/95/004).

New ref.: Institute for Economic Research of Ho Chi Minh City. *Survey of spontaneous migration to Ho Chi Minh City*. HCMC, 1997, 126 pp. (Project VIE/95/004).

Viện Kinh Tế Thành phố Hồ Chí Minh (Chủ biên), Vũ Thị Hồng, Lê Văn Thành, Trương Sĩ Anh, dưới sự hướng dẫn của Bạch Văn Bảy, hợp tác với Gubry, Patrick, Jerrold W. Huguet. *Di dân, nguồn nhân lực, việc làm và đô thị hóa ở Thành phố Hồ Chí Minh*. Hà Nội: Nhà Xuất Bản Chính Trị Quốc Gia, 1996, 114 tr. (Dự án VIE/93/P02).

New ref.: Institute for Economic Research of Ho Chi Minh City (IER) (ed.), Vu Thi Hong, Le Van Thanh, Truong Si Anh, under the dir. of Bach Van Bay, in coll. with Patrick Gubry and Jerrold W. Huguet. *Migration, Human Resources, Employment and Urbanization in Ho Chi Minh City*. Hanoi: The National Political Publishing House, 1996, 135 pp. (VIE/93/P02 project).

Viet Nam Academy of Social Sciences (VNASS) and Southern Institute of Social Sciences (SISS). "Poverty alleviation, migration and urbanization: Ho Chi Minh City in comparative perspectives". International conference. Ho Chi Minh City, 2004, 2 vol., multiple pagination. (Project: Poverty alleviation in the process of urbanization in Ho Chi Minh City).

Viện Quy Hoạch Đô Thị Nông Thôn. *Cẩm nang Dân số, đô thị hoá thành phố Hồ Chí Minh*. 1994, 127 tr. (Dự án VIE/88/P02).

New ref.: National Institute for Urban and Rural Planning. *Ho Chi Minh City data book*. Hanoi, 1994, 120 pp. (Project VIE/88/P02).

Villes en Transition (VeT). *Étude d'aménagement: projet pilote pour la réhabilitation du quartier Tan Dinh, Hô Chi Minh Ville*. Hô Chi Minh Ville: VeT, 1998, 77 pp.

Vo Thi Hiep. "Some Thoughts on the Orientation of the Sustainable Urban Development in Connection with the Rural Development in Binh Chanh, Ho Chi Minh City". In *Co-développement urbain durable, enseignement supérieur, responsabilités de la recherche et de la gestion*. 2001, pp. 37–43. (*Prélude*, numéro spécial 41–43).

Vũ Xuân Đề. *Quy hoạch khỏang xanh bảo vệ môi trường–cảnh quan phục vụ phát triển KT-XH Thành phố Hồ Chí Minh đến năm 2010*. TP.HCM: Viện Kinh Tế Thành phố Hồ Chí Minh, 1995, 28 tr.

[Vu, Xuan De. *Planning of Open Spaces for the Protection of Landscape Environment to Contribute to Socioeconomic Development of Ho Chi Minh City until Year 2010*. HCMC: Institute for Economic Research of Ho Chi Minh City, 1995, 28 pp.]

———. *Nghiên cứu xác định khỏang xanh đô thị cho Thành phố Hồ Chí Minh*. TP.HCM: Viện Kinh Tế Thành phố Hồ Chí Minh, 46 tr.

[Vu, Xuan De. *Research to Determine the Urban Open Space in Ho Chi Minh City*. HCMC: Institute for Economic Research of Ho Chi Minh City, 1998, 46 pp.]

Weissberg, Daniel and Thai Thi Ngoc Du. "De Saigon à Hô Chi Minh Ville, une métropole entre utopies et compromis". In Eveno Emmanuel (éd.), *Utopies urbaines*. Toulouse: Presses Universitaires du Mirail, 1998, 358 pp., pp. 41–56. (Villes et Territoires, no. 11).

Wust, Sébastien. *Métropolisation, habitat précaire et relogement forcé: entre phénomènes d'exclusion et tactiques populaires d'intégration. Le cas du canal Nhiêu Loc-Thi Nghe à Hô Chi Minh Ville, Vietnam*. Thèse de doctorat ès Sciences, École Polytechnique Fédérale (EPFL), Lausanne, 2001.

———. "Quartiers précaires, politique de l'habitat et relogement forcé à Hô Chi Minh Ville". In Gironde, Christophe, Jean-Luc Maurer (dir.), *Le Vietnam à l'aube du XXIe siècle. Bilan et perspectives politiques, économiques et sociales*. Mélanges pour commémorer le 100e anniversaire de la naissance de Pierre Gourou. Paris: Karthala, IUED, CRAM, 2004, 353 pp., pp. 229–56.

———. "Metropolization and the Ecological Crisis: Precarious Settlements in Ho Chi Minh City, Viet Nam". In Westendorff David (ed.), *From Unsustainable to Inclusive Cities*. Geneva: UNRISD, 2004, pp. 87–106.

Wust, Sébastien, Bolay Jean-Claude and Thai Thi Ngoc Du. "Community-led Upgrading. Metropolization and the Ecological Crisis: Precarious Settlements in Ho Chi Minh City, Viet Nam". *Environment and Urbanization* (London) 14, no. 2 (2002): 211–24.

[*See also: Campbell 1999; Cunliffe 1988; Dang Nguyen Anh, et al. 2002; Derderian 2003; Gubry, et al. 2004; Gubry et al. 2008; Jalabert 2001; JBIC 1999a; MCCOY 1983; Nguyên 1996, 1999 and 2001; Parenteau 1997; Schneider-Sliwa 2002; Shannon 2000; Sheehan 1992; Thrift and Forbes 1985; Turley 1977; Villes en Transition, et al. 2005; Weissberg 2001*].

Note

This bibliography sometimes resumes some of the references of the end of chapters, but extends widely beyond; it has vocation to constitute a reference document for researchers working on urbanization in Vietnam.

Index

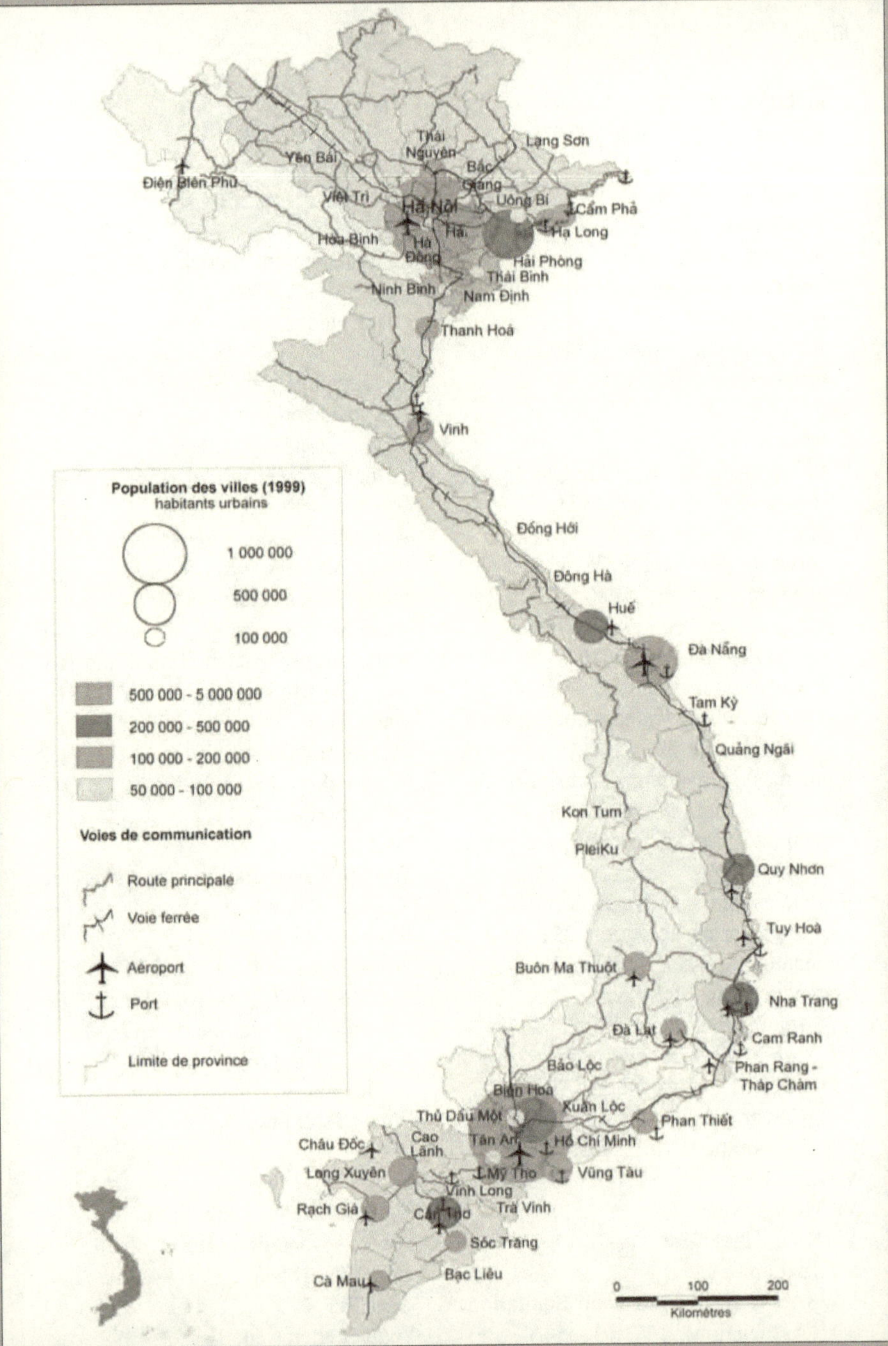

Map: Fanny Quertamp, 2004

Thoroughfares and Urban Hierarchy in Vietnam in 1999

[Extract from Quertamp, Fanny, "La population urbaine au Viêt Nam: Définition, répartition et évolution entre 1979 et 1999". Traitement statistique et cartographique du recensement de 1999. Hanoi: Institut des Métiers de la Ville, 2004, p. 65.]

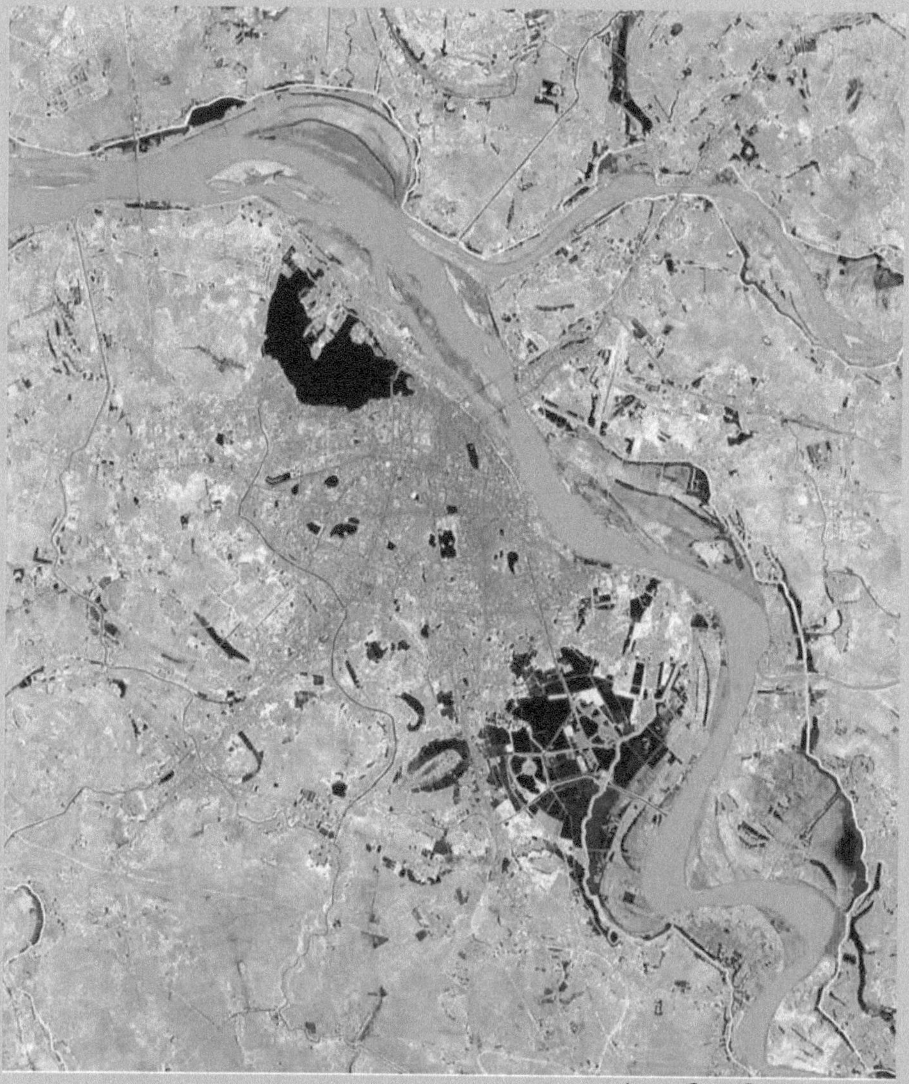

Image Spot, September 1999

Satellite Picture of Hanoi

In 1999, Hanoi counted 1.5 million inhabitants within its urban area (approximately 1.9 million in 2006). The following points are particularly noticeable: high density built environment in the city centre; peripheral rural housing in the form of hamlets typical of the Red River Delta; constructions extending along the road towards the southwest and Ha Tay Province; the left bank of the river, still rural but due to be built up rapidly; the dykes that contain the river highlight the existence of neighbourhoods built in the easily flooded area between dyke and river.

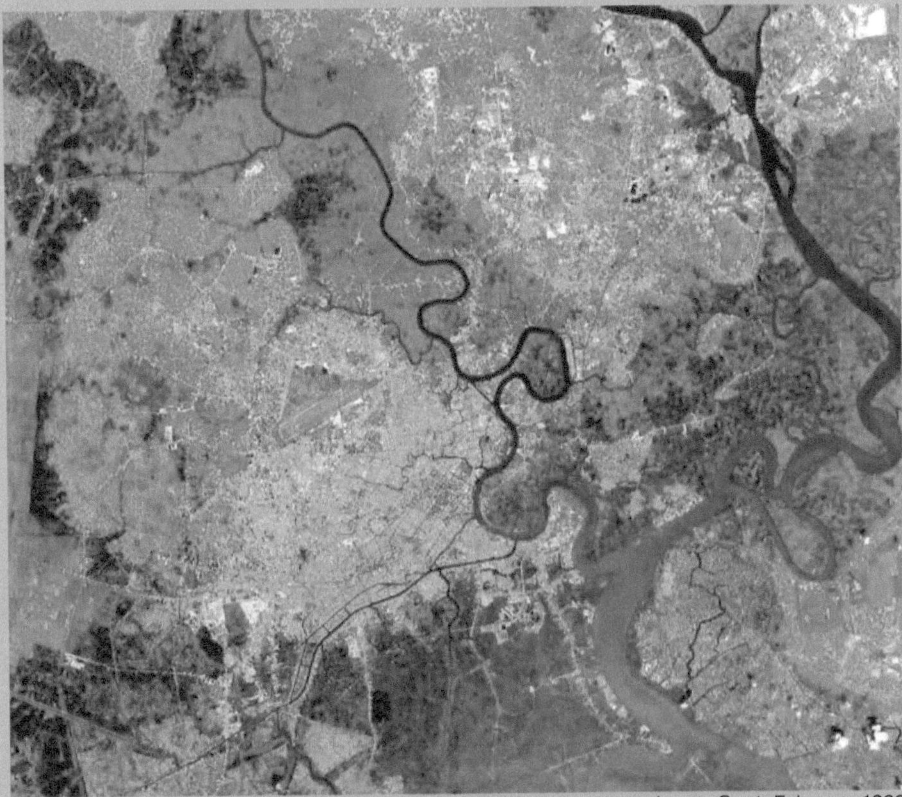

Image Spot, February 1999

Satellite Picture of Ho Chi Minh City

In 1999, Ho Chi Minh City numbered 4.2 inhabitants within its urban area (approximately 5.5 million in 2006). The following points are particularly noticeable: high density built environment in certain central areas, especially Cho Lon in the southwest part of the conurbation (especially District 5); scattered habitat in the outskirts; port infrastructure extending along the Saigon River; vast rural areas still remaining within the administrative limits of Ho Chi Minh City; constructions extending along the roads, especially towards Bien Hoa (Dong Nai Province, on the other side of the Dong Nai River), which indicates that built structures will soon form an uninterrupted line to the city centre, and that planning of the future megalopolis will need to take into account adjacent provinces.

Photo: Patrick Gubry, July 2003

The so-called "compartment" constructions, or penetrating contiguous houses, are typical of the city centre in Hanoi (above, in the area known as the "36 streets" in Hoan Kiem District, whose historical lake and newly built towers can be glimpsed) as well as in Ho Chi Minh City (below, in Ba Thang Hai Street, District 10).

Photo: Patrick Gubry, April 2003

Photo: Patrick Gubry, November 2002

Khu Tap The (KTT) are collective housing units built before Doi Moi (Renovation). The above estate is located in Hai Ba Trung District in Hanoi. Maximizing the available space by arranging balconies into a living area is common practice. The KTT below, located in Giang Vo, Ba Dinh District in Hanoi, was built in 1985. The community is responsible for the maintenance of external façades, which are often badly deteriorated, whereas the flats themselves can sometimes be unexpectedly luxurious, depending on the financial means of their inhabitants.

Photo: Emmanuel Cerise, June 2003

Photo: Patrick Gubry, October 2004

Water is an essential element in the Vietnamese landscape, including in the urban environment. The above photograph taken in My Tho shows both basic habitat on stilts on a small tributary of the Mekong and modern constructions in the background, and denotes an intense economic activity. Constructions on stilts enable their inhabitants to live in the vicinity of the city centre without land use rights. Even the sampans (below on the Perfume River in Hue) can be turned into temporary urban habitat when moored in the city.

Photo: Myriam de Loenzien, August 2005

Photo: VeT Viêt-nam, January 2005

Pilot resettlement programme, Phuong 11, District 6, Tan Hoa-Lo Gom Canal in Ho Chi Minh City (above). The photo was taken from the northern shore of the canal: from individual, illegal and unsanitary housing to collective, legal housing connected to urban services. Below: Thi Nghe area, Binh Thanh District in Ho Chi Minh City, view of the southern bank in District 1, after the inhabitants had cleared off and unsanitary housing had been destroyed.

Photo: Patrick Gubry, November 2004

Photo: Patrick Gubry, March 2003

The administrative limits of cities in Vietnam still include vast areas that are still objectively rural. This is the case in Hanoi as much as in Ho Chi Minh City. Above, a farm in the village of Le Phap, in the rural district (that is, *huyen*) of Dong Anh, on the left bank of the Red River. Below, a ferryboat on the Dong Nai River in District 9, which was recently classified as urban district (i.e., *quan*). These are fundamental factors to take into account when evaluating changes in the urban population.

Photo: Patrick Gubry, April 2003

Photo: Patrick Gubry, October 2005

Vietnam presents certain interesting urban particularities. Above, unbelievably intricate electrical connections in Bao Khanh Street, Hoan Kiem District in Hanoi; a loudspeaker used to broadcast municipal information is visible. Below, flooding in District 11 in Ho Chi Minh City: when high tide combines with strong rainfall, water drainage can become difficult and results in the city being flooded for several hours.

Photo: Patrick Gubry, October 2003

Photo: Myriam de Loenzien, August 2003

Waste collection and wastewater disposal are two major issues confronting the large metropolises. Above, Nguyen Trai Street in Hanoi. Below, Rach Ben Nghe (formerly known as the "Chinese Arroyo"), at the confluence of the Saigon River, which separates Ho Chi Minh City's District 1 from District 4 (opposite, with the Ho Chi Minh Museum, former seat of the *Compagnie des Messageries Maritimes*, an open sewer in all but name; wastewater drainage is hampered by the current flowing back upstream at high tide — which does not prevent some from bathing in it.

Photo: Myriam de Loenzien, April 2004

Photo: Patrick Gubry, October 2004

Photo: Patrick Gubry, July 2003

Occupation of public space for private use remains a characteristic of big cities, as can be seen here in Hanoi: whether for parking motorcycles on the pavement (above left, Cau Go Street, Hoan Kiem District), small informal businesses (above right, Hang Dao Street, Hoan Kiem District) or craft activities (below, Le Duan Avenue, Dong Da District, where a cabinet-maker makes furniture in the middle of the railway track leading from Hanoi to the south).

Photo: Myriam de Loenzien, March 2005

Photo: Yann Maublanc, IMV, October 2004

The vast majority of urban transport relies on motorcycles. "How will I ever cross the road?" (above, Hoang Hoa Tham Street, Ba Dinh District, Hanoi). Honda *xe om* drivers (moto-taxis; the term *om* refers to the fact that the passenger "hugs" the driver), under Long Bien Bridge (below, Hoan Kiem District, Hanoi).

Photo: Charlotte Rosier, IMV, 2003

Photo: Yann Maublanc, IMV, June 2005

Public transport, which existed until quite recently, but had almost disappeared, has been given a fresh start, in particular with a project in cooperation with the French, setting up bus lines running partially in dedicated site (above, Cau Giay District, Hanoi; below, Le Loi Avenue, District 1, Ho Chi Minh City). These lines are very popular due to very attractive fares.

Photo: Patrick Gubry, October 2001

Photo: Charlotte Rosier, IMV, 2003

Suburban areas nearer the city centre are experiencing the highest proliferation of building sites in response to recent urban population growth, which will continue for several decades. Above, Vinaconex 2 in Cau Giay District, Hanoi. Below, building site for the pilot rehousing project in Phuong 11, District 6, Tan Hoa-Lo Gom Canal, Ho Chi Minh City.

Photo: VeT Viêt-nam, October 2004

Three Modern Construction Programmes

Photo: Patrick Gubry, November 2002

Hanoi, Thanh Tri District: blocks of flats.

Hanoi, Thanh Xuan District: "compartment" houses.

Photo: Patrick Gubry, November 2002

Photo: Patrick Gubry, April 2005

Ho Chi Minh City, Phu My Hung New Town, "Saigon South" project, District 7: housing block and "compartment" houses at the onset of construction.

Photo: VeT Viêt-nam, February 2005

Ho Chi Minh City: Interior of the flats to be used for resettlement, pilot resettlement project, Phuong 11, District 6, Tan Hoa-Lo Gom Canal. Above, flat being completed; below, furnished and occupied flat. The bedroom is in the mezzanine, which is accessible with a ladder.

Photo: VeT Viêt-nam, February 2005

www.ingramcontent.com/pod-product-compliance
Lightning Source LLC
LaVergne TN
LVHW090306210926
848480LV00001B/146
* 9 7 8 9 8 1 2 3 0 8 2 5 2 *